Texas Ranger Captain William L. Wright

Richard B. McCaslin

University of North Texas Press
Denton, Texas

Printed in the United States of America.

10 9 8 7 6 5 4 3 2 1

Permissions:
University of North Texas Press
1155 Union Circle #311336
Denton, TX 76203-5017

The paper used in this book meets the minimum requirements of the American National Standard for Permanence of Paper for Printed Library Materials, z39.48.1984. Binding materials have been chosen for durability.

Library of Congress Cataloging-in-Publication Data

McCaslin, Richard B., author.
Texas Ranger Captain William L. Wright / Richard B. McCaslin.
pages cm
Includes bibliographical references and index.
ISBN-13 978-1-57441-845-3 (cloth)
ISBN-13 978-1-57441-855-2 (ebook)
1. LCSH: Wright, William L., 1868–1942. 2. Texas Rangers. Frontier Battalion. Company E—Biography. 3. Sheriffs—Texas—Biography. 4. Peace officers—Texas—Biography. 5. Frontier and pioneer life—Texas. 6. Texas—History—1846–1950. 7. LCGFT: Biographies.

F391.W945 M35 2021
976.4/05092 [B]–dc23

2021021846

The electronic edition of this book was made possible by the support of the Vick Family Foundation. Typeset by vPrompt eServices.

In Memory of Special Agent Jerry L. McCaslin,
Bureau of Alcohol, Tobacco, Firearms, and Explosives
The Most Important Lawman in My Life

Contents

Introduction and Acknowledgments

Marc Antony, in William Shakespeare's great drama entitled *Julius Caesar*, tells his fellow Romans, "The evil that men do lives after them; the good is oft interred with their bones." So it seems to be with the Texas Rangers among many modern scholars, activists, and public officials. A good example is the decision by the Dallas City Council in the summer of 2020 to remove a well-known statue of a Ranger from the main terminal at Love Field in response to a book on the Rangers that, at the time of the removal, had not yet been published or even officially reviewed in print. Just the mere threat of another work that criticized the Rangers, in this case *Cult of Glory* by Doug J. Swanson, was enough to stampede local leaders into another ill-considered decision to reduce the artistic wealth of their city by taking down *One Riot, One Ranger* by Waldine A. Tauch, the first native-born Texan to craft monuments in stone and bronze. Admittedly, Swanson had already published an article in a local magazine using an excerpt from his forthcoming work to urge the removal of the Love Field statue, and there was great public unrest concerning the death of a black man who had been accosted by white police officers in Minneapolis, but that hardly excuses the removal of a fine monument or the implied judgment on all Rangers.[1] But just as not every American soldier massacred Vietnamese civilians at My Lai, and not every Army officer is Lt. William L. Calley, it is also true that not every Ranger murdered Mexicans at Porvenir, and not every Ranger captain is J. Monroe Fox. The history of the Rangers, like the Army, is a tale of many people in various situations, with actors and outcomes both good and bad. In an effort to restore some analytical balance to the history of the Rangers, this book focuses on one of the good guys, William Leonidas Wright, who became an outstanding Ranger captain during the first half of the twentieth century.

Why study Wright? To start, he was an effective peace officer and dedicated public servant during a career as a lawman that spanned forty-five years, from 1894 to 1939. He served as a Ranger under eight Texas governors: Joseph D. Sayers, William P. Hobby, Pat M. Neff, Miriam A. "Ma" Ferguson, Daniel J. Moody, Ross S. Sterling, James V. Allred, and William L. O'Daniel. Regarding quality rather than quantity, Wright is one of four men regarded as outstanding captains during the early twentieth century by those who study the Rangers. The original "Great Captains," whose careers began in the nineteenth century, were James A. Brooks, John R. Hughes, William J. McDonald, and John H. Rogers. Wright first enlisted as a Ranger with Rogers, and he joined Francis A. "Frank" Hamer and Thomas R. "Tom" Hickman in the second generation of great captains, popularly known as the "Big Four." The fourth member of this group is usually said to be Manuel T. Gonzaullas, although Roy W. Aldrich does get a lot of support. Not all these captains have been inducted into the Texas Ranger Hall of Fame at Waco, but Wright was among the first class of twenty men accorded that honor. And Wright is important not only because he stands out in his length of service and achievements, but also for the fact that his career typifies that of many Rangers with whom he served during a period of rapidly changing demands on lawmen. As historian Harold J. Weiss Jr. has remarked, "different eras in Texas history produced different types of Rangers." Wright served during an important era of transition for the Rangers, so a study of him can provide great perspectives into the changing organization. Too, he worked closely with many local, state, and federal officers, and he was a sheriff for fifteen years, so further insights can be gained into those professions.[2] Biographies have been written of the first Great Captains, as well as Hamer and Gonzaullas.[3] It seems timely for Wright to have his turn in the limelight.

Wright, aware of his family's strong ties to the Rangers and having learned that his pay depended on his hard work, began establishing a high reputation early in his service as a lawman. Newspaper reporters repeatedly praised him, but he really came to the forefront in 1924, when J. William Falvella, a Laredo journalist, published a laudatory article about Wright in *Frontier Times*, a popular magazine. He concluded by boldly declaring, "When he gets orders from his commander in chief, the Governor, or the adjutant general to 'go and get him,' there is nothing on earth to prevent Capt. Wright carrying out the order if it is within man's power to do so." By 1927 Henry B. Yelvington, another Texas journalist, was campaigning for a revival of the Rangers by writing stories about Wright, whom he dubbed "*El Capitan Diablo*." Texas historian Walter P. Webb clearly read Yelvington's articles because he included some of the same incorrect statistics in a summary of Wright's November 1921 campaign against liquor smugglers on the Rio Grande during Prohibition, then concluded one of a series of articles for *The State Trooper*, a national publication for lawmen, by declaring: "With the restoration of Captain Wright to the service, the lawbreakers of the border say: '*El Capitan Diablo cabalga otra vez*.'" While the slightly built, diplomatic Wright probably did not deserve the devilish title bestowed upon him by Yelvington and Webb, he had become a well-known lawman in Texas by the late 1920s.[4]

In order to assess Wright's place within the historical literature, broadly defined, on the Texas Rangers, one has to understand how writers on the subject have divided into two camps. The ends of the continuum are defined by two men: Webb and Américo Paredes. Webb, a historian writing within the context of the impending centennial of Texas independence, sought to celebrate all that was good about the Rangers. He certainly did not ignore their transgressions, but he devoted more of his book to their positive contributions, which he tried to corroborate through research. Paredes, angry in general about a modern Texas he considered to be defined by racism and determined to refute specifically the generalizations of a fellow folklorist, J. Frank Dobie, eschewed any pretense at objectivity and did little research in denouncing the Rangers. The result was a book that was myopic or frequently inaccurate in its interpretations of Ranger history. Both men have academic progeny that follows their lead in writing about Rangers, and thus while Wright appears in books written by those who emulate Webb in trying to argue that the good outweighs the bad with the Rangers, he rarely is mentioned by those trying to prove that the "Rangers stirred up more trouble than they put down," as Paredes wrote.[5]

Among the historians who follow Webb's example, Ben H. Procter wrote that of the prominent Ranger captains during the interwar period in twentieth-century Texas, "In terms of deeds and previous reputation, Will Wright was by far the best known." He added that "No one was more knowledgeable of Southwest Texas or enforced the law more vigorously." Dan E. Kilgore, in a book published to honor the Rangers' sesquicentennial, declared that Wright was "one of the great modern Ranger captains" and "has not received the attention he deserves." More recently, Charles H. Harris III and Louis R. Sadler, in their landmark study of violence along the Rio Grande in the early twentieth century, described Wright as "an outstanding peace officer" who was "also a man of unswerving integrity." Addressing his status directly, they also wrote in the same book that Wright "was without question the most capable captain appointed during the entire decade and was of the caliber of the four captains of the original Ranger Force." When the same two historians in a second volume extended their study of the Rangers forward in time to about 1935, they stated that "Wright developed an enviable reputation not only as a fearless officer who, unlike some other captains, led from the front, but also one having a profound sense of duty." Of the post-Webb scholars who have tried to produce a comprehensive history of the Rangers, Robert M. Utley, a former chief historian for the National Park Service, declared that "Wright embodied probity, idealism and professionalism," adding that he served "long, successfully, and honorably, but without the dash and glamour of his fellow captains."[6] For these and other scholars, Wright provides a strong example of the positive contributions made by the Rangers.

Those who embrace Paredes' perspective either ignore Wright or present flawed accounts of his actions. Neither James A. Sandos nor Benjamin H. Johnson mentions Wright in their discussion of the murder of José M. Morín and Victoriano Ponce by Rangers in May 1916, even though Wright and others delivered both men safely to Kingsville before they were shot while in custody. Miguel A. Levario uses material from 1916 to 1919 to condemn the Rangers. Wright commanded Company K on the border during this time, but he is not mentioned despite the fact that he asked to be appointed in place of Fox, warning that his fellow captain would soon do something terrible. And in fact he did: four of Fox's Rangers participated in the Porvenir Massacre in January 1918, which Fox subsequently tried to deny. Julian Samora,

Joe Bernal, and Albert Peña devoted much attention to the 1919 legislative investigation initiated by José T. Canales and the state's injunction against the Rangers in 1925, both of which were important events in Wright's career, but he again does not appear in their text. Wright is mentioned only briefly within the context of the Canales investigation by Monica Muñoz Martínez, who omits that he was among the few lawmen praised by Canales. Nicholas Villanueva, in discussing Rangers as agents of state-sanctioned lynching, sadly never mentions Wright's investigation of the 1921 killing of Salvador Saucedo. Conversely, George T. Diaz, in his inquiry into Prohibition-era smuggling along the Rio Grande, portrays Wright as an angry killer who ambushed three Mexican smugglers in revenge for the killing of a federal agent. Diaz based his assertions upon *corridos* or folk songs, which simply are not corroborated by other substantial evidence available. Kelly Lytle Hernandez, like Diaz, borrows the phrase "revenge by proxy" from Webb, then employs it to condemn Wright and others for "arresting, brutalizing, and murdering an untold number of Mexicanos" during the 1901 manhunt for Gregorio Cortez Lira. Her point is that this culture shaped the excesses of the next generation of lawmen, especially those in the United States Customs Service, which included the Captain's son, Emanuel A. "Dogie" Wright. Again, there is no evidence that Wright killed anyone in the pursuit of Lira, and he and others worked hard to ensure that Lira reached the state penitentiary alive, which he did. Finally, when Roger M. and Diane D. Olien published a study of Texas oil-boom towns, they specifically disparaged Wright's campaign against crime in Wink as ineffective. But they never mentioned his name, nor did they indicate that they looked at Ranger records concerning his activities.[7]

No reasonable person would deny that law enforcement agencies, like all human institutions, periodically need reform. The Texas Rangers are no different, and in fact they have been the target of revision several times in their long history. Wright's story deserves to be told because he became a vital part of at least three efforts to upgrade the Rangers. He was first appointed as a Ranger captain in 1918 when it became obvious that, in the wake of what became known as the Bandit War, the Ranger Force badly needed an overhaul. That state officials made the right choice in appointing Wright became clear when he was one of a few Rangers leaders singled out for praise by legislative investigators in 1919. He returned to Ranger service as a captain again in 1927, when Governor Daniel J. "Dan" Moody focused on rebuilding the reputation of the Ranger Force after the scandals of the first administration of Governor Miriam A. "Ma" Ferguson. Finally, when the Rangers became part of the newly created Department of Public Safety in 1935, Wright remained in active service past his seventieth birthday, long after most of his contemporaries had retired. Those seeking to reform the modern-day Rangers, and by extension other law enforcement agencies, might benefit from taking a look at Wright, who was always mindful of his legacy and that of other family members who served as Rangers.

Wright may seem to many to be a rather unlikely subject upon which to base a bit of Ranger revisionism, but then again he might be perfect. Small with a bristly mustache, bespectacled rather than eagle-eyed, dressed as often in a coat and tie as he was in brush gear, he cut an interesting figure. Those who confronted him discovered that he would fight, he could see well enough to shoot straight, and he was much more comfortable in the saddle in South Texas chasing "horsebackers," as he called outlaws and smugglers, than behind any desk. While one newspaper reporter described his posture as "rigid," he had a great sense of humor and loved to tell stories and jokes, of which he had an "inexhaustible supply" in his "amazing memory." Rangers and civilians alike enjoyed listening to him, which of course he used to his advantage in many situations. Part of his demeanor were strange expressions, which he probably gathered during his upbringing in rural Texas. About a good lawman, he would say, "he'll do to ride the river with." Or if he was brave in a fight, "He is one of the old blue hen's chickens." He did not use profanity much; instead, if he thought you were making fun of him or trying to trick him, he would bark "*hueves*," which roughly translates as "you lay eggs." But he could enjoy a good funny story about himself; the most-often-told one, which may be apocryphal, is that late in his career, when asked to give the "disposition" of a suspect on yet another much-hated form, Wright allegedly wrote "Mean as Hell. Had to shoot him." It was about that same time that he gave a cap pistol to his cousin, Oscar N. Wright, who had worked with him in law enforcement several times in his career and had been asking him for a confiscated weapon. Finally, Wright loved to dance.[8] In sum, he was not the imposing, grim figure of popular lore. He was much more representative of the Rangers with whom he worked, which may well explain why no one has ever created a statue of him. He just does not fit the stereotypes that both sides have created of what a Ranger should be.

Like many human beings, Wright had his shortcomings. He smoked cigarettes, which he rolled himself. He also liked cigars and an occasional pipe. When possible, he kept fighting cocks, although no one recalls that he bet on them. Both of these traits were common among men of his generation raised in rural Texas, but he did not share another habit with most of them: he did not drink alcohol. A writer for the *Junction Eagle*, noting a Prohibition-era meeting for Wright with officials in Austin, joked at his expense: "It was at first thought that Capt. Wright brought samples with him, but newspapermen soon found this to be only a rumor." His abstinence may have been a product of his strong faith, which was reinforced by Rogers' early mentoring. Wright was a man who used violence, when necessary—he was always armed, and he never allowed a Ranger who worked for him to be unarmed at any time. He did have a strong temper, and another reporter remarked that in 1937, at the age of sixty-nine, he understood that Wright was still a "wildcat" in a fight. But he added, "Captain Wright was a very talkative man—and 99 times out of a hundred his subject was how to avoid bloodshed." To the great amusement of some of his colleagues, he would lecture his Rangers in camp at night about safety and avoiding conflict, and he found that defusing a situation was much preferable to a gunfight.[9] Concerning women, he considered his wife of almost fifty years, Mary Ann "Mollie" Brown Wright, to be indispensable in every stage of his career, while he found Governor Miriam A. "Ma" Ferguson to be infuriating. All the others in his life fell along the spectrum defined by those two points, and his relationships with them never strayed outside the bounds of early twentieth-century propriety.

When it comes to matters of race, Wright was a man of his time in his language, using words for African Americans especially that would be offensive to modern readers, and in his prejudices, referring to both African Americans and Hispanics in terms that indicate his belief that they were not his equals. But there is little evidence that his biases shaped his actions concerning the law. He always recalled that when he first became a sheriff, in 1902, Rogers advised him to be a "Ranger sheriff, acting impartially without regard to nationality, color, or wealth." More than three decades later, when he learned that his former sergeant, J. Warren Smith, had been elected sheriff in Frio County, Wright offered his advice in a badly typed note: "they are onley one thing to do and that is do your Duty, give everyone a fai[r] [d]eal, all alike, white yellow or black and you will always win, [t]hey cant say one word." Everyone was equal, as a victim or a perpetrator, and he tried to treat everyone fairly. He did not investigate more or less diligently because of the race of either his quarry or the victims. This was made abundantly clear in the Canales investigation, which would have been a perfect forum for discussing racist transgressions. Instead, Wright was praised for his work, and it became obvious why he had been asked to be a Ranger captain as part of the attempt to reform the organization. While he could laughingly recall using the threat of a lynching to convince a Hispanic prisoner to talk to him, Wright never lost a prisoner to a lynch mob as a deputy, sheriff, or Ranger. And several times, when Hispanics were victimized in South Texas, even by Rangers, Wright was sent to investigate. As for employing Hispanics or African Americans, he enlisted Hispanics as deputies when he was the sheriff of Wilson County and as Rangers in his company on the border in the 1920s because they knew the language, area, and culture, and he had at least two African Americans working for him in Wilson County, which had a substantial minority population. He never hired an African American Ranger, but there is also no record that one ever asked to join one of his companies, and there is certainly no evidence that his superiors in Austin would have approved such a request.[10]

There are some persistent problems with historical sources concerning Wright, some more serious than others. The first concerns his name. His mother, Ann Elizabeth Tumlinson Wright, noted the birth of "William Leonidas Wright" in her Bible in 1868, then recorded the marriage of "Willie Lee Wright" in 1892. Leonidas and Lee are used interchangeably in primary sources throughout his life. Other nicknames that surface among his associates include "Bud." It appears simple: Wright's mother caused a bit of confusion by using a childhood nickname when she added the happy news of her son's marriage in her Bible, and that has confused many people ever since. More serious, a story surfaces in several sources—including Maude T. Gilliland's *Horsebackers of the Brush Country: A Story of the Texas Rangers and Mexican Liquor Smugglers*, James R. Ward's "The Texas Rangers, 1919–1935: A Study in Law Enforcement," and Jim Coffey, "Will Wright: Rangers and Prohibition"—that Wright and other law officers killed four Mexican smugglers in September 1920. Contemporary newspaper reports indicate four smugglers were captured, while another four were seriously wounded. Similarly, Coffey recounts the death of nine smugglers in a January 1924 gunfight with Wright, his Rangers, and several federal agents. Again, no corroborating primary evidence has been located; according to an Austin newspaper there was a fierce clash in early January between Mexican rebels and eight federal officers with a deputy sheriff, but no Rangers were involved.[11] These stories represent the sort of tales that can surface about a lawman as active as Wright, and they had been omitted from this narrative of his life. Perhaps another scholar can find the truth behind them.

Sadly, a similar fate had to be bestowed upon the wonderful tales told about Wright by Carl G. Busch, who claimed that he served under Wright's command at Wink from 1927 to 1929. He described Wright as "an old-time Ranger that had a big old kind of a handlebar mustache, and he had boots that went way up to his knees. He was a tough old codger!" Busch colorfully recounts how the Rangers and other lawmen would arrest as many as 150 men at a time and lay them on mattresses under a shed, with their ankles tied together "like a trotline." The prisoners would simply pay their fines and return to their criminal activity, which led the sheriff to quit after about six months. It is a great story, and it may be that Busch met Wright somewhere or talked to someone who worked with him, but Busch was not a Ranger at Wink with Wright. Instead, his only such appointment was his enlistment as a Special Ranger for three months in January 1933 at the order of Ma Ferguson. Busch, a Galveston native, was a law officer in Groveton, 533 miles from Wink, at the time that he became a Ranger, which was several years after Wright's investigations. Once more, a great story fails to meet the good historian's requirement for corroboration.[12]

Wright was a man of high ideals and committed to the law, but he never recorded his own story. Friedrich H. "Frank" Burmeister, a former Texas legislator and district attorney, told the 1919 legislative committee that Wright was "an absolutely fearless officer and one of the finest executive officers that possibly has ever been in the Ranger service." Former Texas Adjutant General William W. Sterling, a longtime colleague of Wright, wrote in his memoirs, "He possessed all the requisites of a great captain: judgement, initiative, and high moral courage." He urged Wright to publish his story, but Wright never did, which Sterling described as a "distinct loss." The aging Ranger during his last years in service did explore some options. In 1937 he wrote to Roy W. Aldrich, a fellow Ranger with whom he had worked for many years, that while money would be welcome, "what I want to do is tell the truth from top to bottom." Aldrich offered to help him find the right writer, and Wright was working with Robert B. "Bob" McCracken of Corpus Christi when he died in 1942. McCracken never finished the project. Kilgore referred to a Ranger "tradition of silence" in explaining the failure of so many to tell their history, but Wright simply ran out of time.[13] As noted earlier, it is time to correct that for Wright because, after all, "he'll do to ride the river with."

This project began when Wright emerged as a strong character in my history of Sutherland Springs, Texas, which was published by the University of North Texas Press in 2017. I mentioned him to Dr. Jody E. Ginn, my former doctoral student and now my academic colleague, who surprised me by surrendering a box of materials on Wright given to him by Dr. Stephen L. Hardin, a mutual friend for many years. I owe a great deal of gratitude to both of them for enabling this latest manifestation of my scholarly habit. During this time of great turmoil, several archival staffs went far beyond the ordinary in helping me complete my research. Christina Stopka, the Director and Research Librarian of the Tobin and Anne Armstrong Texas Ranger Research Center, made the completion of this project possible with their patient support and voluminous knowledge about the Rangers. My work at the Research Center was also greatly facilitated by the assistance of Raymond E. "Rusty" Bloxom Jr., a Research Librarian who also has an amazing memory when it comes to Ranger matters. Byron A. Johnson, Director of the Texas Ranger

Hall of Fame and Museum, within which the Research Center is located, generously offered to let this work be included in the Center series honoring the bicentennial of the Texas Rangers. The staff of the Texas State Library and Archives coped with what probably seemed to be endless requests from me for materials, to which they responded with far more grace than I could muster on some days. I thank all these people—without them, there would be no long-overdue book on Wright.

The list of others to whom I owe a heartfelt thank-you is long, and I will unfortunately leave out many names. It includes the staffs at the Dolph Briscoe Center for American History at the University of Texas at Austin, the Texas History Research Room at the Emily Fowler Public Library in Denton, and the West Texas Collection of Angelo State University in San Angelo. Other archivists whom I never met did yeoman's work in developing websites that showcase their materials for my use, which I appreciate. At key junctures I have had some proofing and prodding from Ginn, who as Executive Director of the Texas Ranger Heritage Center in Fredericksburg has provided me with not only materials but also access to many helpful people. Likewise, I have gained much from conversations and correspondence with Darren L. Ivey, whose work on several fine volumes of Ranger biographies has made him a walking encyclopedia of Ranger lore. I rushed through several towns as the pandemic loomed in early 2020 and made several promises to return for research that I did not keep. Perhaps someday time, and policies, will allow me to return. I did gain much from my conversations with all these people, who were more than generous with their time.

As always, I am very blessed to have a supportive family, led by my wife of more than forty years, Jana. During the production of this book, we added a few to the circle (my oldest grandson Caleb, for example, married Rachel), but they all have continued to tolerate the odd writing habits of "Papa," even when we gather for the weekly family dinner. I am usually one of the last to join them, emerging slowly from my man cave where I write and staring pensively back at it while I struggle to remember the brilliant bit I want to record when I return to the keyboard. They keep me grounded, and I appreciate that.

Map 1. South Texas

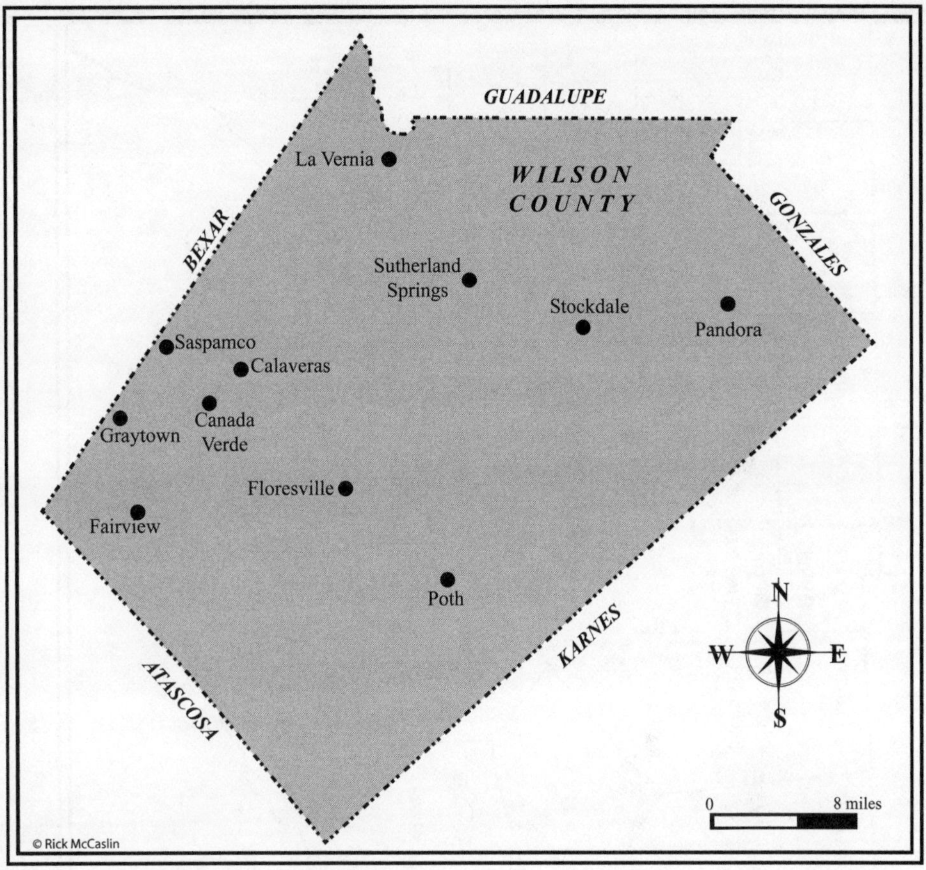

Map 2. Wilson County

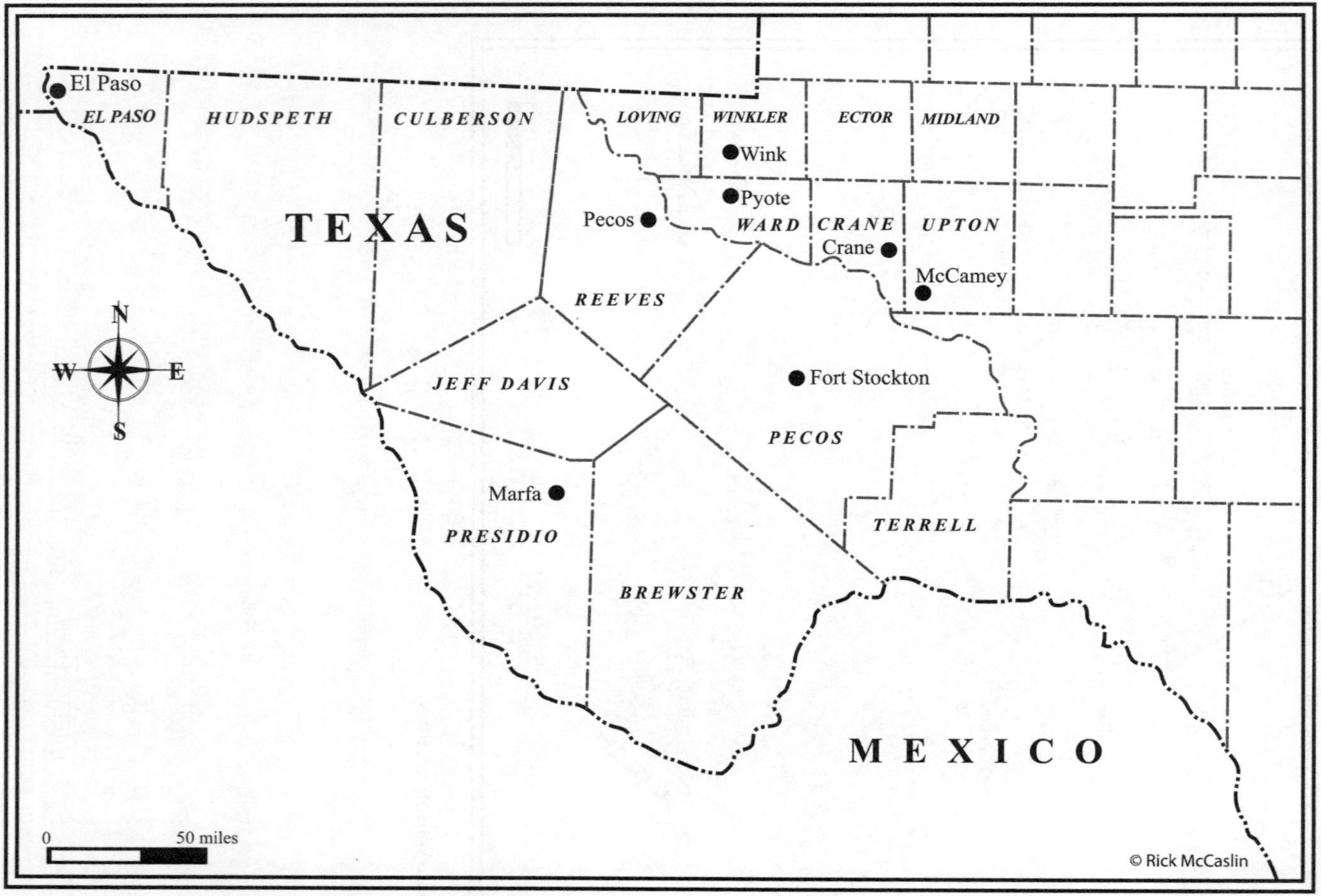

Map 3. West Texas

Chapter 1

Prelude, 1823–1899

William Leonidas Wright was born to be a Texas Ranger; hard work made him a great one. His mother, Ann Elizabeth Tumlinson Wright, was the proud daughter of a well-known antebellum Ranger, Joseph L. Tumlinson, whose two brothers, John J. Tumlinson Jr. and Peter F. Tumlinson, were Ranger captains. Wright's brother, Milam H. Wright, became a Ranger, and their sister Zora Lee Wright married erstwhile Ranger Charles P. Warren. Wright married Mary Ann "Mollie" Brown, whose father and two brothers—Sanford N., Charles B., and Gratz D. Brown—were Rangers, and they had five sons, three of whom—Charles H. ("Pat"), Emanuel A. ("Dogie"), and William B. ("Bill") Wright—served as Rangers. Wright tried working as a cowboy and farmer, like many men of his generation in rural Texas, but it did not suit him. Instead, he became a deputy sheriff and then a Ranger, as he seemed destined to do. His need for a better salary to support his growing family pushed him to leave the Rangers and become a sheriff, an office also held by his father Little Berry "L.B." Wright, brother Milam, son Dogie, and at least six cousins: Mike B. Wright, Thomas C. "Creed" Taylor, William A. "Alonzo" Taylor, William W. Taylor, Joseph Tumlinson, and Peter C. Tumlinson. Wright remained in that office longer than any of his predecessors in Wilson County, but when an opportunity came, he returned to the Rangers as a captain and served for most of two decades. Considering his lineage, it is hard to imagine what else he might have done. At least eight relatives were Rangers before the Civil War, while five served in the Frontier Battalion, and twenty-two were in the Ranger Force. That he outshone most of his contemporaries was due to his work ethic. After his father died when Wright was just fourteen years of age, he became a ranch hand to help take care of his widowed mother. Then came his attempt at farming, followed by his decision to be a deputy sheriff and Ranger, all prompted by the need to support his immediate family. At the same time, Texas experienced rapid population growth and economic development, with New South ideals challenging those of the Old West. Wright thus not only learned to rope and ride but also became well accustomed to enforcing the law in an era marked by change, all of which made him an effective Ranger as he worked hard to uphold his family legacy and earn his pay.[1]

Wright was born on February 10, 1868, in Caldwell County, Texas, the fourth of seven children for Little Berry and Ann Elizabeth Tumlinson Wright. Little Berry, or L.B. as he apparently preferred to be called, was a native of Perry County, Alabama, born on December 4, 1830. His parents, Robert W. and Matilda Watters Wright, were originally from Georgia, but they moved with him to Panola County, Mississippi, whence L.B. traveled to Texas in the late 1850s as a Baptist missionary. There he met his future wife, to whom he proposed by letter after returning home to Mississippi. They married at her home in Yorktown, in DeWitt County, on November 4, 1858, when she was twenty-six years of age and he was a month shy of his twenty-eighth birthday. Their marriage certificate identified him as a resident of Panola County in Mississippi, but by 1860 the couple lived in Karnes County, Texas, where L.B. served briefly as sheriff. By that time, L.B.'s parents had relocated to Caldwell County, where Robert W. Wright paid taxes in 1861 on 11 slaves, 4 horses, 26 cattle, and 400 acres. That same year, L.B.'s father-in-law, Joseph L. Tumlinson, paid his taxes in DeWitt County on 6 slaves, 400 horses, 50 sheep, and 1,799 acres. Family members claim that Tumlinson hired a substitute for L.B. during the Civil War so he could tend his father-in-law's cattle, which in 1861 numbered at least 8,700, while state records indicate that the younger man served as a corporal in the Helena Guards, a militia company, in 1861 and two years later as a lieutenant in his father-in-law's home guard company. L.B. apparently never owned slaves or much land, but in 1866 he paid taxes on a respectable herd of horses, cattle, and sheep. By the time William was born in 1868, L.B. had shifted to trading in horses, owned a store, and served as a justice of the peace and deputy inspector of hides in DeWitt County. He also served as the Grand Master of the Cameron Lodge at Yorktown, to which Tumlinson belonged, and he joined the International Order of Odd Fellows. After an extended illness, L.B. died on June 15, 1882, at the age of fifty-one, leaving his wife Ann with six surviving children, including their oldest son William, who was just fourteen years old.[2]

In April 1925, when William L. Wright was leaving the Texas Rangers for the second time after becoming disgusted with the efforts of Governor Miriam A. "Ma" Ferguson to weaken the organization, he was interviewed by several reporters, all of whom focused on his lineage in an effort to impress upon their readers how much the state was losing with the departure of veteran Rangers such as Wright. He recounted briefly, but fairly accurately, the story of his great-grandfather, John J. Tumlinson, who was an *alcalde* in Stephen F. Austin's colony when he was killed in 1823 near the site of present-day Seguin in Guadalupe County. Wright also talked about his great-uncle, John J. Tumlinson Jr., who became one of the first Ranger captains for the Republic of Texas and, as Wright recalled, fought at the Battle of Salado in 1842. Wright's maternal grandfather, Joseph L. Tumlinson, was John's younger brother; Wright said that he served in the Battle of San Jacinto, was wounded in the last battle with Indians near Kenedy in Karnes County, and died in late 1874, when young Wright was six years of age. While this published testimony indicated that Wright was very aware of his Ranger heritage, it also left much unsaid, perhaps simply because of the restrictions of the newspaper format.[3]

The story of the Tumlinsons in Texas began with the arrival of John J. Tumlinson and his brother, James S. Tumlinson, in 1821. Natives of North Carolina, they came to Texas from Arkansas, where John left an older son, Thomas C. Tumlinson, who had married and started a family. Texas was a province of Mexico at that time, and John was elected in November 1822 as the *alcalde*, or mayor, of the Colorado municipality, one of two districts in the colony that Austin was struggling to develop. The killing of local residents by Karankawas and white outlaws, including deserters from the vanquished Spanish army, led Tumlinson to ask Governor Jose Trespalacios to authorize a "paid military company" to provide more security for settlers. A skirmish between some Colorado volunteers and Karankawas underscored this request. A full-time military company organized in May 1823 under the command of Moses Morrison, and it proved to be effective in combatting Indians and outlaws. Tumlinson and Joseph A. Newman left their Colorado settlement for San Antonio in July 1823 to get gunpowder and lead for Morrison, but they never arrived. In a confrontation with unidentified Indians along the Guadalupe River on July 6, Tumlinson was killed, while Newman escaped after a long chase on horseback. Family members later remembered Tumlinson as the captain of the military company in the Colorado municipality, but in fact Morrison was its leader, and Austin later recruited more men for this command and led it, reinforcing its historic claims to be the first Texas Ranger unit. It is thus more accurate to write, as historian Dan E. Kilgore did, that Tumlinson was the "first man to die in the service of the Texas Rangers," since he helped found the company and was directly supporting its operations at the time of his death.[4]

Three sons of John J. Tumlinson later served as Rangers. The campaigns of his oldest, John J. Tumlinson Jr., began soon after the death of his father and, coincidentally, his oldest brother Thomas, who was also killed by Indians in Arkansas. A few months after the elder Tumlinson died, John Jr. led an attack on thirteen Waco Indians whom he thought were responsible for killing his father. His younger brother, Joseph L. Tumlinson, who was just twelve or thirteen years old, shot and killed the first Waco, and his comrades dispatched all but one of the others. John Jr. and his uncle James almost three years later were in a small militia detachment that attacked a Tawakoni camp near what is now La Grange in April 1826, killing half of the sixteen Indians. His brother Andrew, who was just two years younger than him, led several militia attacks on Indians until one killed him in 1830, stabbing Andrew repeatedly after being shot and mortally wounded by him. John Jr. by that time had, with his brother Joseph, obtained land in the DeWitt Colony, near Cuero in what became DeWitt County, and they settled there, so they were not present when Andrew became the third member of their family to be killed by Indians.[5]

John Jr. returned to the field during the eventful summer of 1835 in a Ranger company led by Michael R. Goheen, under the overall command of John H. Moore. When volunteers were called to fight Mexican troops that September, John Jr. became a lieutenant in a company commanded by Robert M. Coleman. According to Creed Taylor, they arrived at Gonzales in time to take part in the fight for the cannon on October 2, when John Jr. commanded his comrades in place of an ailing Coleman. Joseph apparently joined his older brother during the Siege of Bexar, when the company fought in the Grass Fight and at Concepcion in John A. York's division, but they went to intercept Mexican reinforcements and did not participate in the final assault in December that ended with the capture of the city that the Anglos officially renamed San Antonio. In the meantime, the provisional Texas government created a Ranger Corps of three companies during November 1835 and appointed John Jr. as one of the captains, while his cousin Littleton F. Tumlinson, the oldest son of James S. Tumlinson, became a lieutenant. Littleton had also served under York at San Antonio with his brothers, John H. and James S. Tumlinson Jr. Joseph was one of the thirty Rangers mustered by John Jr. during January 1836. They battled with Comanches, killing four and rescuing a captive white boy, and constructed a blockhouse on the Colorado River near present-day Leander, whence they patrolled the area. During the siege of the Alamo, where Littleton's brother George W. Tumlinson was killed, they were assigned to defend Bastrop; after the Alamo fell, they joined Sam Houston at Gonzales. The Rangers mustered by John Jr. then guarded refugees during the Runaway Scrape, but he took leave with Joseph to take care of their families. They rejoined Houston in time to serve as camp guards at Harrisburg during the Battle of San Jacinto, where David C. Tumlinson fought alongside his brothers James and John. As the captain of the first company of the Ranger Corps mustered under the act of November 1835, John Jr. earned the historic distinction of commanding the "first officially organized company of Rangers."[6]

John Jr. served several more times as a Ranger captain before his death in 1853, at the age of forty-nine. He commanded his Ranger Corps company until mid-August 1836, when he resigned. In the summer of 1838, while leading a survey party, he encountered the Comanches that had just kidnapped Matilda Lockhart and several other children, but he and a small band of volunteers failed to overtake the raiding party. In 1839 he joined another Ranger company, then became the captain of a "spy," or scout, company, for a month in the fall as part of a campaign against the Comanches by John C. Neill's Ranger battalion. After a diplomatic meeting with the Comanches degenerated into the Council House Fight at San Antonio in 1840, in part because of the terrible condition of Lockhart when she was presented as a Comanche captive, Tumlinson led another company of volunteers into the field from Cuero to combat the vengeful Comanches, who launched what became known as the Linville Raid. Tumlinson and his men united with two companies led by Adam Zumwalt and Benjamin McCulloch to create a battalion of about 160 riders, with Tumlinson as the overall commander. They skirmished with the Comanches at Garcitas Creek on August 9, then reinforced and pursued them for several days but did not arrive in time to fight in the final battle near Lockhart at Plum Creek, when a larger force of settlers routed the raiders. Tumlinson commanded a Ranger company again in the summer of 1841 for a little more than a month, and during October 1848 he and his brother Joseph once more served under York, this time in a skirmish against Lipan Apaches on Escondido Creek in what later became Karnes County. Three of the Rangers, including York, were killed when the Lipans ambushed them, and three others, including Joseph, were seriously wounded. It was the last fight with Indians in the south-central region of Texas where William L. Wright would be raised, and two of his Ranger ancestors fought in it.[7]

Peter F. Tumlinson became a Ranger captain after John Jr., his older brother, died in 1853. When their father and oldest brother Thomas were killed, Peter had returned to Arkansas to assist his widowed sister-in-law. He married there and had two sons before his first wife died. He subsequently moved back to Texas, where he remarried. He served as a private in William Scurlock's company of the army of the Republic of Texas for three months during the summer after San Jacinto. He then settled in Atascosa County, where he farmed and served briefly as a county commissioner. His first service as a Ranger came during 1855 when he joined a company organized by Levi English to fight Lipan Apaches. Kilgore wrote that Tumlinson in fact commanded in place of English and that his Rangers killed some Lipans and recovered stolen horses. Tumlinson officially led a Ranger company sent to the Rio Grande in late 1859 in response to the raids of Juan N. Cortina. While they were in the field, from November 1859 to February 1860, he commanded them in the successful engagement at Rio Grande City on December 27, as well as at Bolsa Bend on February 4. While John S. "Rip" Ford was not impressed with Tumlinson due to his lack of military discipline, including the summary execution of some Mexican prisoners by his Rangers, at least one man who served under Tumlinson recalled with pride the "terror" with which their foes regarded him and his comrades. Tumlinson also enjoyed chastising Ford for forgetting to bring his pistols as he entered the fight at Bolsa Bend, which "Uncle Pete" dismissed as "foolhardiness" in a "stern lecture" delivered while the Texans were under fire from Cortina's Mexican irregulars. One month after mustering out, as part of Governor Sam Houston's expansion of the mounted volunteers, Tumlinson led another Ranger company that included three of his sons—Absalom T., William O., and Joseph Tumlinson. They patrolled Atascosa County and adjacent areas from March until June 1860. Peter Tumlinson later followed English to Dimmitt County, where the latter founded the town of Carrizo Springs and Peter's son Joseph became the first sheriff. A Confederate veteran of the Thirty-Sixth Texas Cavalry, Joseph with "one hundred poorly armed men" repulsed an attack by four hundred Mexican raiders at Carrizo Springs in February 1885, three years after his father died, then led a retaliatory raid into Mexico a few months later. Wright years later enlisted many men in his Ranger companies from the Carrizo Springs area, including some of his cousins.[8]

Joseph L. Tumlinson, Wright's grandfather, served with his brother John Jr. in many units, but the wounds he suffered during their last Indian fight in 1848 apparently ended his career as a Ranger. In addition to his Ranger service with his brother, he joined Scurlock in July 1836 and was reportedly detailed to Byrd B. Lockhart's spy, or scout, company. In 1831 he acquired a headright near Cuero in what became DeWitt County, and during 1834 he married Johanna Taylor, whose brother, William R. Taylor, married Joseph's sister Elizabeth. Johanna died in 1838, and Joseph in March 1840 married Rebecca Elizabeth Newman, the daughter of Joseph Newman, the man who was with Joseph's father when he was attacked and killed by Indians in 1823. Wright's grandfather thus married into two very interesting families: among his first wife's brothers was Creed Taylor, one of the most enduring and colorful Rangers of nineteenth-century Texas, while one of his second wife's sisters was Sarah Jane Newman Scull, or Sally Skull, who reportedly could outfight any man and allegedly killed a few. Joseph and his second wife Elizabeth, as she preferred to be called, relocated to a larger ranch near Yorktown, where he raised cattle and horses. They also had six children, the first of whom was Ann Elizabeth Tumlinson, who married L.B. Wright and had seven children including William L. Wright, the second of her three sons and the oldest of the two boys who survived to adulthood.[9]

While Joseph was remembered for his Ranger service, he was also notorious for his role in the Sutton-Taylor Feud. Wright in 1936 wrote to Roy W. Aldrich, his longtime colleague as a Texas Ranger, about the conflict: "Most all of those you see on the Taylor side was killed with their boots on, I know them. All on the Tumlinson side lived and died a natural death. They were all good citizens." Wright attached a typescript of the peace agreement signed between the Suttons and Taylors in August 1873 as evidence for his assertions. But Creed Taylor claimed that the feud originated many years earlier when vigilantes led by Joseph organized in Karnes and DeWitt counties in 1857. Taylor commanded the men who opposed them and met with his foes in the Masonic Hall at Helena, where the Masons negotiated a first peace settlement. Modern historians say the killing of William P. "Buck" Taylor, son of William R. and Elizabeth Tumlinson Taylor, reignited the feud. William E. "Bill" Sutton with his friends shot Buck and Richard T. "Dick" Chisholm on Christmas Eve in 1868. After several Taylors shot and killed Sheriff John T. Littleton, who had warrants to arrest them, Joseph L. Tumlinson joined Jack Helm in his heavy-handed legal efforts, thus becoming a Sutton ally against the Taylors, among whom were his sister and brother-in-law. Helm became a State Police captain when that organization was created in July 1870, and Tumlinson enlisted as his sergeant. Violence escalated with the addition of gunmen such as John Wesley Hardin to the Taylor ranks; Tumlinson survived two attempts by Hardin to kill him, including a siege at his home when he was surrounded by a larger force led by Hardin, who killed Helm. The 1873 agreement ended the siege and brought peace, but the killing of Sutton in March 1874 led Tumlinson, as the surviving leader of the Sutton faction, to lead another violent campaign. It ended only after the arrival in August of Captain Leander H. McNelly, a former Confederate and State Police captain, and his company of the new Frontier Battalion, which had ironically inherited the title of Texas Rangers. At one point a gunfight erupted between McNelly's men, who were escorting a witness to a murder trial for Tumlinson, and gunmen led by Tumlinson, who claimed he mistook the Rangers for Taylors. Tumlinson died in November 1874 during his trial, but another outburst brought McNelly's Rangers back to DeWitt County in the fall of 1876 under the command of Lieutenant Jesse Leigh "Lee" Hall. Interestingly, Joseph's son, Peter C. Tumlinson, who signed the peace agreement but was indicted for murder, later served in the Frontier Battalion and twice as the sheriff of Dimmitt County.[10]

Wright was six and eight years old when Rangers under the command of McNelly, and then Hall, came to DeWitt County to assist in bringing his grandfather and other vigilantes to justice. Ironically, he later claimed that he was greatly impressed with the men of the Frontier Battalion and, after visiting with them, decided he wanted to join them. Wright also told a newspaper reporter many years hence that as a boy he met William A. A. "Bigfoot" Wallace, the legendary Ranger captain from the antebellum period. Wallace lived until 1899, and occasionally visited San Antonio from his home in Frio County, so it is possible that their paths crossed. Of more immediate importance for young Wright was the schooling he had in the DeWitt County communities of Cuero and Yorktown, named for the man with whom his grandfather and great-uncle had served twice, as well as his early work as a cowboy for local ranches. Among the well-known cattlemen for whom Wright worked as a teenager were Herman P. Eckhardt, John L. Rutledge, and John R. Blocker, who in 1915 became the first president of the Old Time Trail

Drivers Association. At the age of 21, in 1889, Wright helped drive cattle from the vicinity of San Angelo, two hundred miles northwest of San Antonio, to Cheyenne, Wyoming, but decided the latter was much too cold to repeat the experience. His decision may also have been prompted by the fact that the Great Die-Up of the 1880s and the expansion of the railroads in Texas were prompting ranchers to abandon the long cattle drives and reorganize their operations by the start of the last decade of the nineteenth century.[11]

Two weeks after his twenty-second birthday, in February 1890, Wright wrote to his mother that he was earning forty dollars every month as a ranch hand and would send her some money soon, but if she insisted, he would quit, come to Sutherland Springs, and try farming. By the next year he was living in Sutherland Springs with her and his surviving brother, Milam H. Wright, who was ten years younger than him. The Wrights probably settled in Sutherland Springs because Ann Elizabeth Tumlinson Wright's second daughter, Zora Lee Wright, lived there with her husband, Charles P. Warren, after they married in 1885, just two years after he served in the Frontier Battalion for three months in the same company as Peter C. Tumlinson. L.B. Wright, Ann's husband and Zora's father, died in 1882, so Ann must have relocated after her husband passed and while her oldest son was working for several local ranches. The community was slowly growing when Wright joined her due to the popularity of its medicinal springs; among the residents was Sanford N. Brown, a Tennessee native who came to Texas with his parents in 1837, when he was not yet seven years of age, and in December 1854 served in Company C of the Texas Mounted Volunteers, led by William R. Henry. This was one of three Ranger companies sent by Major General Persifor F. Smith, under the command of Maj. John S. Simonson, to Fort Davis, a new Army post, to campaign against Apaches alongside a company of the Eighth United States Infantry. Brown also served in Company K of the Eighth Texas Infantry during the Civil War. He married Mary Reynolds in February 1856 in Guadalupe County, and they had thirteen children, of whom eleven, five sons and six daughters, survived to adulthood. One of the latter was Mary Ann, nicknamed Mollie, who became a person of great interest to William L. Wright. His mother carefully recorded in her Bible that "Willie Lee Wright and Mollie Brown were married December 22, 1892 in Sutherland Springs."[12]

Strangely, few sources mention that Wright's uncle, John Jackson "Pegleg" Tumlinson, also settled in Wilson County about this time, near Stockdale. He was the younger brother of Wright's mother. Although he had lost his right leg above the knee as a youth after he accidentally shot himself, he raised cattle and was indicted for murder during the Sutton-Taylor Feud, when he joined his father Joseph L. Tumlinson in signing the peace treaty in 1873 but apparently later lapsed. Sometime after his wife, the former Isabella Garland "Belle" Cresap, died in 1885, Tumlinson relocated to Stockdale, where he was listed in the census as a bartender boarding with a family near the home of his married son, John Jackson Tumlinson Jr., who was a farmer. The elder Tumlinson was immortalized by J. Frank Dobie for his involvement in the search for the infamous lost Spanish silver mine in Texas. He died at Sutherland Springs in 1920 and was buried at Stockdale, but his grandson, Travis E. Tumlinson, after serving several terms in the Texas penitentiary system in the early 1930s, spent much of his life continuing to look for treasure.[13] Given that Wright spent most of his life in law enforcement, it is entirely possible that he had little to do with this branch of his family.

Wright initially tried to support himself at Sutherland Springs by ranching, and he did acquire a small herd of cattle by early 1891, but he had told his mother that he would become a farmer, and he also had a disapproving father-in-law to satisfy. According to family lore, Brown did not like the idea of his daughter Mollie marrying Wright because "he knew of the fighting blood in the Tumlinson side." But he helped the newlyweds acquire some land on Cibolo Creek, and he sent his son Gratz to help cultivate it. Wright like his father had primarily focused on ranching, and his efforts to become a farmer did not result in any significant success. Asked about this later in life, Wright quipped, "I didn't like it. It didn't rain enough." Other family members remembered that he and Gratz spent a lot of time hunting rather than tending crops. The birth of his first son, Charles H. "Pat" Wright, in February 1894 may well have prompted Wright to rethink his commitment to farming, and perhaps to consider following many of his relatives into law enforcement. During the fall of 1894, at the age of twenty-six, he became a deputy for newly elected Sheriff John S. Craighead of Wilson County.[14]

Craighead served as sheriff of Wilson County for two terms, from 1894 to 1898, and Wright apparently was a deputy for all those years. Born in 1847 and a Confederate veteran of Col. T. Scott Anderson's cavalry regiment, Craighead had good local political connections as the grandson of the founder of Sutherland Springs, John Sutherland. This reinforced Wright's ties to the original settlers of Wilson County, as his wife's sister, Frances M. Brown, had married Abner H. "Hub" Polley, son of Joseph H. Polley, another prominent early developer of Sutherland Springs. Hub's brother, Joseph B. Polley, was a well-known attorney in Floresville, the seat of Wilson County, and during Wright's service as a deputy he served as both the president of Hood's Texas Brigade Association, which held a reunion at Floresville in 1896, and commander of the Texas Division of the United Confederate Veterans. In sum, Wright had not only a good mentor in Craighead, but he also became known in the political and social circles who could help him with his future career in the former Confederate state of Texas, especially Wilson County.[15]

Wright told a newspaper reporter in 1925 that he made the most important arrest of his entire career during his third year as a deputy sheriff in Wilson County. The crime was certainly spectacular, and it resulted in the first legal execution in the county. Maximo Martinez, a thirty-six-year-old Tejano ranch hand, was separated from his wife and working at a place near Floresville. He became infatuated with a young female neighbor, eighteen-year-old Juanita Acosta, and tried to convince her to run away with him. Three times they agreed to meet, but each time she failed to appear. Enraged, Maximo on the night of June 5, 1897, attacked Juanita in her bedroom at her grandparents' home. Stabbed in the back, she tried to climb out of a window but was stabbed again in the chest. When her grandparents, Plutarco and Dolores Carillo, attempted to intervene, Martinez killed each of them in turn by smashing their heads with an axe. He then "ravished" Juanita, stabbed her at least two more times, and carried her body, wrapped in a quilt, out to the yard, where he left it and rode for Mexico. Juanita's uncle, who was attending a dance, came home to find her dead in the yard, nude from the waist down. He also found his mother dead, and his father died soon afterward, never regaining consciousness.[16]

Sheriff Craighead must have been out of town or otherwise unavailable, because the first law enforcement officials who arrived at the scene were County Judge Henry B. Gouger, County Physician Jefferson M. "Mack" Mason, and four deputy sheriffs, including Wright. Gouger questioned the uncle and several neighbors, all of whom told him to find Martinez. Sheriff W. T. "Brack" Morris, of adjacent Karnes County, led the pursuit south to the Rio Grande, believing Martinez had fled directly to Mexico. The posse included Wright and fellow Wilson County deputy Juan Garza, along with Morris and two of his deputies. Well-known trackers Emanuel M. and Charles T. Tom joined the group in Atascosa County. On June 10, they found the killer, "afoot and shoeless," hiding in some cactus on the Osborn Ranch near the boundary of Webb and McMullen counties, 150 miles from Floresville. He surrendered without a fight to Garza and readily confessed because he feared that he would be lynched if the lawmen did not take him into custody. Among the alarming details he told his captors was that he had intended to kill his estranged wife and their two children as well as those he murdered, but daylight came too soon, and so he fled without completing his scheme.[17]

Martinez did avoid being lynched, but he was legally hanged after a series of events that Wright would vividly remember. Detailed to accompany Morris in escorting Martinez back to the county jail in Floresville, where he would remain during his trial, Wright with the sheriff and their prisoner exited the train a short distance away from their destination. Riders waited there to transport them into town. When the train pulled into the Floresville depot, hundreds of people greeted it, apparently intending to lynch Martinez. They were not pleased to discover that their intended victim had been safely placed in the local jail while they waited for him at the station. Some attempted to storm the jail later, but local officers stood their ground and the would-be lynch mob departed. Martinez was convicted on June 23, 1897 and hanged on July 30 from a gallows built next to the jail. As the first legal execution in Wilson County, the event attracted a lot of attention, and Martinez made the most of it. Permitted to speak to curious newsmen, he told them that he had killed the older couple so there would be no witnesses. He wanted a brass band to play at his hanging, but that request was denied.

A crowd of several thousand watched the execution, which was done under the direction of Sheriff Craighead. Before the hanging, salesmen circulated, plying their trade. A gramophone dealer made records and played them, while a fire extinguisher vendor caused a stampede by setting a model house afire for a demonstration. Wright recalled that it was the "wildest crowd" he ever saw at an execution. At the appointed time, Martinez, who had been given a tin cup of whiskey, stepped through a second-story window from the jail onto the gallows. There he gave a speech and sang several songs, including a *corrido* about himself and a love song to his victim, which was recorded on the gramophone with the understanding that a portion of the profits from the recordings would be given to his wife. Wright put a black hood on him, put a noose around his neck, and almost forgot to step off the trap door before it fell open, dropping Martinez and breaking his neck.[18]

Wright's remaining time as a deputy sheriff in Wilson County was comparatively quiet; at least, he had little to say about it in later interviews. Meanwhile, his family obligations continued to multiply. He and Mollie had a second son, Maurice H. "Jack" Wright, in March 1895, before the Martinez case, and then a daughter in September 1898. She was named Zora Belle Wright, in honor of Wright's sister, Zora Lee Wright Warren, who had died in January 1898 and left her husband, Charles, with three young children to support, which was difficult for him because he was partly paralyzed from a work accident. The widower also had his mother-in-law, Ann Elizabeth Tumlinson Wright, living with him, as well as his brother Eugene H. Warren and brother-in-law Milam H. Wright. Ann helped with the children, and both Eugene and Milam worked as salesmen in Charles' dry goods store in Sutherland Springs, but at the age of thirty Wright and his wife Mollie probably had to help as well, if not financially then at least with the physical labor of tending such an extended family. Interestingly, there is no evidence that at this time Wright considered buying livestock like his grandfather and father, thus embracing the Old West ethos in which he was raised. Although the cattle drives were over, ranching remained viable for many men in Texas, but Wright was not one of them. At the same time, he did not return to farming, as his father-in-law had advised, nor did he join his brother-in-law in business, both of which were common options as

Texas increasingly became part of the New South as the nineteenth century came to an end. Instead, he remained a lawman.[19]

By the fall of 1898, Wright had worked four years as a deputy sheriff in Wilson County, and he perhaps entertained thoughts of becoming a sheriff himself. But the realities of Texas politics intruded when Manuel J. Ximenes won the election in November and succeeded Craighead as sheriff of Wilson County. There is no evidence of animosity between Wright and Ximenes, who had established a good reputation in a previous term as sheriff from 1892 to 1894, but by February 1899 Wright wrote to the Adjutant General of Texas, Thomas Scurry, asking for a commission as a Special Ranger. He explained that he had begun working as a deputy for Sheriff John P. Campbell of Bexar County, but he had since been offered a better job as a security guard by stockmen in Atascosa County. Having a commission as a Special Ranger did not provide him with any more pay, but it did allow him to carry a sidearm, which was otherwise not allowed in Texas. William W. Sterling, a future Texas Adjutant General who would become friends with Wright in the 1920s when they were both Rangers in South Texas, wrote in his memoirs that Craighead at this time recommended Wright to Captain John H. Rogers, who apparently had a vacancy in his Frontier Battalion company. While no such letter has been found, Rogers did ask Wright to join him, and by the end of February 1899, Wright joined Rogers' Rangers at Cotulla in La Salle County. Wright's wife Mollie came with him, along with their two infant sons, Charley and Jack, and their daughter Zora Belle, who was not yet six months old.[20]

Whether he was aware of it or not, a chapter in Wright's life thus closed and the next began as he became a Texas Ranger, as so many others in his family had done. He was certainly qualified for the job. He had been raised within a tradition of paramilitary and military service to Texas, as well as law enforcement. He was familiar with livestock, could rope and ride, and his devotion to his extended family reflected both a good work ethic and a deep sense of personal responsibility. He was older than the other members of his new company except for Rogers, who may have regarded Wright's age, and thus his experience, as an advantage. He was also one of the few in Rogers' company who had worked as a lawman before joining the Frontier

Battalion, and even fewer had been involved in a capital case. All these characteristics would serve him well during his first enlistment as a Ranger during a time when they no longer battled Indians, as had his grandfather and great uncles. Instead, the organization had become a state law enforcement reserve force, where both Old West skills and New South sensibilities were useful. As Wright would write to one of his superiors many years later, he had become a man who could, and would, earn his pay while adding to his family's legacy as a Ranger.

Chapter 2

Ranger, 1899–1902

Four captains dominate the literature concerning the Texas Rangers in their transition period from the nineteenth to the twentieth century: James A. Brooks, John R. Hughes, William J. McDonald, and John H. Rogers. These men were the four "Great Captains" of the Frontier Battalion, the organization which in 1901 officially became the Ranger Force but was already popularly known as the Texas Rangers. Wright was fortunate enough to serve from 1899 to 1902 under Rogers, who proved to be a fine mentor for the relatively young lawman with a long career ahead of him. Rogers taught his Rangers to draw fast and shoot straight, but he also stressed ethics and professionalism. These traits served Wright well as he, along with many other Rangers, endured frustrating changes under Adjutant General Thomas Scurry, a Dallas businessman who briefly served as a major during the Spanish–American War. Most important, Wright worked hard to earn his pay as a member of the Frontier Battalion during its last years and the Ranger Force in its first, continuing to develop as a law enforcement officer while upholding his family's legacy of service as a Ranger.[1]

Wright officially joined Company E of the Frontier Battalion, commanded by Rogers, at Cotulla in La Salle County on February 20, 1899. At that time, each company had been reduced to a captain, one sergeant, and no more than six privates. His sergeant was Henry G. "Harry" DuBose, who was elected in September 1898, three months after the company relocated to Cotulla. Born in Nueces County in 1873, DuBose had originally joined Rogers in January 1897. In addition to Wright, the privates were Frank D. McMahan, Jim Moore, Augustus Y. "Augie" Old, William A. "Billy" Old, and Thomas C. "Creed" Taylor. McMahan, a native of McLennan County, joined Company E at the age of twenty-six in May 1897, when he was a commissioner for La Salle County. Moore was a farmer from Kerr County who enlisted with Rogers at the age of twenty-two in September 1898. The Old brothers were born in Morris County. Augie had served in Company E since the fall of 1896, when he enlisted at the age of twenty-two. His older brother, Billy, joined in February 1898 at the age of twenty-seven, after working as a ranch hand. Taylor had enlisted with Rogers two days before Wright. A nineteen-year-old cowboy and former deputy sheriff from Bee County, he was the youngest man when Wright arrived, a great-nephew of the original Creed Taylor, and a distant cousin to Wright.[2]

Wright was an interesting addition to Company E. At thirty-one years of age, he was the second oldest man in the unit; only Rogers, who was thirty-five, was older than him. Wright was also apparently the only one who had law enforcement experience prior to joining the Rangers. Moore did have a family connection to the law: his uncle, Francis M. "Frank" Moore, was the sheriff of Kerr County from 1882 to 1892, and his cousin, James H. Moore, had served in the Frontier Battalion until 1887, when he died in an ambush in which Rogers was gravely wounded. Taylor's father, James O. Taylor, was the sheriff of Bee County, and the younger Taylor became the sheriff of Kimble County and worked for the United States Customs Service after he left the Rangers. But Taylor was not the only one of Wright's comrades who served in other law enforcement agencies after leaving the Rangers. DuBose was shot and killed in a mysterious case in August 1914 while serving as the chief of the United States Bureau of Immigration at Brownsville. Moore became the sheriff of Crockett County. Billy Old after leaving the Rangers moved west, where he became an Arizona Ranger. He later was a security officer for the Southern Pacific Railroad and a deputy sheriff in Cochise

County, Arizona. In 1899, however, almost all of Wright's companions in Company E had been Rangers for less time than he had been a deputy sheriff in Wilson County. Only Rogers, who joined the Rangers in 1882, had been a law enforcement officer longer than Wright. After Rogers, the senior member of the company, in terms of time in service, was Augie Old, who had served as a Ranger less than three years before Wright came.[3]

Wright soon learned that the roster of a Ranger company was constantly changing. In the summer of 1899, Company E expanded to include eight privates. While McMahan left the Frontier Battalion during June, and Adjutant General Scurry ordered Billy Old transferred to Company B in July, four men took their place. The first was Henry W. Locke, a native of Chicago who claimed that he had worked for several private detective agencies. He had been a Special Ranger, or unpaid volunteer, with McDonald in 1895 and served as a sergeant in two Texas regiments during the Spanish–American War, so Rogers took a chance with the slow moving but obviously educated recruit. Locke did not stay long with Company E, departing on Halloween five months after he enlisted to resume work as a private detective and later a railroad security officer. Edwin M. DuBose, a brother of Sergeant DuBose, joined in June. Rogers found the 29-year-old rancher to be a "good man for rough scouting in stock country." He also stayed with Rogers only briefly, leaving in January 1900 after allegedly using a judge's hat for target practice while drinking. Billy Old was replaced with his brother Levi, who was just twenty-one years of age. He remained with Rogers for the longest tenure of the four newcomers, but he departed after less than a year. The fourth recruit was Sidney S. "Sid" Hutchison, a twenty-eight-year-old ranch hand from Karnes County. He served just four months with Rogers, then re-enlisted in December 1917 and served for three years under Wright after he became a captain. In sum, Rogers had these recruits for only a short time, which made someone like Wright, who stayed with him for more than three years, a valued commodity. Too, Wright, unlike Locke, could ride a horse and pack a mule, and he knew something about livestock. All of these were reasons Rogers gave for dismissing Locke, who apparently did not care to learn such things.[4]

Rogers enjoyed another expansion of his company in the fall of 1899, to ten privates. He had to replace Locke and Hutchison, who left in October and November, respectively, but he recruited four new men, including, in order of enlistment, his own brother, Wright's brother-in-law, and Wright's brother. The first was Curren Lee "Kid" Rogers, who had already served in the Frontier Battalion "off and on, for 13 years," as he wrote on his application. He had joined Brooks' company, in which his older brother was sergeant, in 1886, then transferred to Company E when Rogers became its captain and stayed until 1898. Gratz D. Brown, who had helped Wright with his failed attempt at farming, joined Company E in mid-December. He left by the end of February 1900 in a "reduction of the company." Milam H. Wright had been trying to secure an appointment in the Frontier Battalion since August 1899, when his older brother wrote to him that Billy Old had told him there would soon be a vacancy in Company B. Ranger Wright even penned a letter for his younger brother to sign and submit, but McDonald responded that there was, in fact, no opening in his company. Milam persisted, and in December he joined Company E, marking the beginning of a long career in state and federal law enforcement for the twenty-one-year-old recruit. The fourth newcomer was Charles H. Sandherr, a thirty-five-year-old "stockman" from Arkansas who re-enlisted three times with Rogers before his final departure from the Rangers.[5]

A reshuffling and conflict that led to several more departures reduced Company E to six privates again by the summer of 1900. Edwin DuBose departed during the first week of January 1900, but Billy Old returned that same month. The dismissal of Brown at the end of February dropped the number of privates to nine by the end of the first quarter of 1900. In another state-mandated reduction of Rogers' command in May, Milam Wright and Levi Old were discharged. Eight days later, Levi's brother Billy was dropped for "for making unbecoming talks about his superior officer," perhaps angry comments about the dismissal of his younger sibling. Augie Old, who had previously expressed his unhappiness about the promotion of Henry DuBose to sergeant rather than him, was dismissed "by reasons of his own request" on May 31. These changes left Rogers with only five privates, but after Billy Old departed, Milam Wright was reinstated. If William Wright had any strong opinions about the turmoil in Company E, he did not record them. Given his departure a little more than two years later, he may have resented the callous management of the state officials at this time. At the same time, he certainly must have been pleased that his brother Milam returned to service just nine days after being dismissed. None of the three Old brothers ever served again as a Texas Ranger. In fact, Billy later denounced Rogers as incompetent and demanded his removal in a letter-writing campaign that ended only when Rogers won general acclaim by arresting Gregorio Cortez Lira.[6]

Even more changes came during June 1900 as a result of a longstanding conflict between local officials and the Frontier Battalion. As the organization transitioned from defending border settlers to serving as a statewide law enforcement reserve force in the late nineteenth century, the legislature had authorized its members to arrest suspected lawbreakers. Protests from several corners of the state led opponents to challenge their authority to arrest anyone. They argued that, since the Frontier Battalion had been created to defend settlers, it was no longer needed, and its members should not be serving as law enforcement officers. When a Texas judge decreed that only a Battalion officer, not privates, could arrest anyone, Governor Joseph D. Sayers asked Attorney General Thomas S. Smith for an opinion. To the dismay of the Texas Rangers, as the members of the Frontier Battalion were popularly known, Smith declared that they had been making illegal arrests for decades. Adjutant General Scurry responded by quickly promoting many Ranger sergeants and privates to lieutenants, but this was just a temporary fix until the legislature could approve a permanent remedy. In Company E, Henry DuBose and William Wright both became first lieutenants on June 1, while Kid Rogers became a second lieutenant. DuBose and Kid Rogers were then assigned to Company A, taking privates Moore and Sandherr with them. To reinforce Company E, Captain Rogers got Joe C. Hudson, a newly minted lieutenant, and Enoch Cook from Hughes' Company D. Hudson, a twenty-six-year-old Texas-born "cowboy" who first became a Ranger in September 1898, had been evaluated as a good horseman, marksman, and trailer by Hughes, while Cook was a former "night watchman" who was about the same age and joined at the same time as Hudson. Neither stayed long with Rogers—Hudson left the Rangers in October 1900, while Cook returned to Company D in 1901 and became a sergeant for Hughes. Meanwhile Wright, who stayed with Rogers, thanked Scurry for his appointment, adding, "I will always try to do my duty as I understand it."[7]

After the legal crisis and subsequent changes in the summer of 1900, Rogers submitted a muster roll for Company E at the end of August that included only six names. In addition to the captain, William Wright remained as first lieutenant, Hudson as second lieutenant, and Cook, Taylor and Milam Wright as privates. When Hudson left in October, he was replaced with Tolbert F. "Tol" McKinney. A forty-three-year-old cowboy from Uvalde, McKinney had enlisted in Hughes' Company D in December 1899. Cook's transfer at the end of February 1901 was followed by the arrival of four new recruits. Joseph W. Petty, a thirty-year-old former constable at Cotulla, enrolled in March. William M. Burwell, Rogers' brother-in-law who had served as the sheriff at Cotulla, rejoined Company E in April; he had previously served with Rogers in Brooks' company, then in Company E under Rogers from 1893 to 1896, when he fell ill and resigned. He became a sergeant for Rogers, then left the Rangers again in 1903 and served as the sheriff of Potter County. Alex Ormand, a thirty-four-year-old stockman from Goliad County, joined Company E during May 1901. Wright knew him and told Rogers that he was an "extra good man;" Ormand's sister was in fact married to Judge Henry B. Gouger of Wilson County, and Ormand later became the city marshal at Floresville. William H. Steele enlisted during July, raising the number in Company E to nine, including Rogers. A twenty-four-year-old rancher from McMullen County, Steele as an infant survived a raid by Indians and Mexicans, who killed his two older brothers and sixteen other settlers. His mother escaped by wading the Nueces River with three young children, including him. The family subsequently settled in Cotulla, where Rogers recruited Steele.[8]

Scurry made it clear to the legislators that a more effective solution to the legal problems of the Rangers was needed, and they agreed. The Texas legislature on March 29, 1901, abolished the Frontier Battalion and replaced it with a Ranger Force of four mounted companies, each with a captain, sergeant, and up to twenty privates. All Rangers, regardless of rank, became law enforcement officers. Their monthly pay increased to $100 for captains,

$50 for sergeants, and $40 for privates, although recruits continued to provide their own guns and horses. While this was a substantial pay raise—privates had been paid $30 per month—it did not actually lead immediately to a significant increase in the size of companies. In practice, legislative appropriations still only allowed the hiring of about eight privates in each company. Rogers' company, relabeled as "C," experienced some reshuffling during the summer of 1901. McKinney was discharged on July 8. Monthly returns indicate that Petty transferred to Company D, but service records indicate that he left the Rangers. The latter is probably correct because he had a finger amputated after being shot through the hand in March 1901 by a colleague of a Mexican whom he attempted to arrest for "disturbing the peace." In their place, Henry DuBose, Moore, and Sandherr returned from Company A. DuBose and Moore had been lieutenants in Company A; under Rogers, DuBose again became a sergeant, and Moore succeeded him at that rank after he departed in 1902. At the same time, William Wright lost his rank of lieutenant and became a private again. Presumably, this was only because the expanded legal authority of all Rangers and the return of the more senior DuBose meant that Wright's temporary elevated status was no longer necessary. Rogers thus had one sergeant and eight privates in his company by the fall of 1901.[9]

Budget restraints led to several changes in personnel for Company C during the year prior to Wright's departure on September 1, 1902. Oscar L. Latta, a former deputy sheriff from Kimble County who first became a Ranger in 1898 after a fellow deputy was killed, joined Rogers in October 1901. A thirty-three-year-old native of Kansas, Latta impressed Rogers, who wrote in January 1902 that he was a "very active, industrious, courageous, and desirable young man." The occasion for Rogers to write such an opinion of Latta was his re-enlistment in January 1902 because, on the last day of December 1901, both Latta and Milam Wright were discharged in a mandatory reduction of Company C, less than nine months after the creation of the Ranger Force. Rogers must have been even more frustrated in March 1902 when Latta was once more discharged, along with Ormand, in another layoff, followed by Steele and Taylor in May 1902. William Wright's departure in the late summer of 1902 left Rogers with just one sergeant, DuBose, and three privates—Burwell, Moore, and Sandherr—although Steele returned to Company C a few weeks later.[10]

Wright thus served with a total of twenty-three men, including Rogers, in a little more than three years with the Rangers. His place within this larger group of colleagues was similar to that among the seven he originally joined in 1899. Only nine, including Rogers, were senior to Wright in their years of service in the Frontier Battalion, while Wright was one of only four who had served previously as a law officer. He was also older than all but five, which again included Rogers. While many who served with Wright during his first Ranger enlistment would, like him, continue for years in law enforcement, they were, for the moment, mostly young men under the command of Rogers, whom they were quite fortunate to have as their captain. Rogers led this company, as E and then C, until he resigned in 1911. After serving as a federal marshal, he rejoined the Rangers in 1927 as a captain, as did Wright that same year, and stayed with them until his death in 1930. Rogers thus served as a mentor for many of these men, including Wright, for decades, with a leadership style that mixed morality with pragmatism. He set an example by being dedicated, tireless, brave, quiet, and modest. A Presbyterian elder, he required his Rangers to attend services and believed that "any officer who drinks … is almost sure to do wrong." At the same time, Wright and the others practiced fast draws under his direction. Rogers would have them face each other, with unloaded pistols in their holsters, then at his signal draw their weapons and pull the triggers. Wright proved to be a quick study and a "star pupil" in the fast draw training. He also acquired a better saddle, which he used for decades, and the four-inch-wide gun belt preferred by Rangers. Both allegedly came from a train robber that Company E arrested at about the time that Wright enlisted.[11]

Rogers had to submit written official comments on his men in late 1899. While not all these reports survive, those that remain in the state archives reveal much about the men and their captain. About Wright, Rogers reported that he was "talkative" and "good humored." He believed that the new recruit would become a "good detective," but he added that because he had only known him about six months, it was hard to tell much about him yet. Rogers had stronger opinions about Moore, who had served under him for a little more than one year. He wrote that Moore was "Talkative, industrious, humorous," but he was "not particularly bright." Rogers then clearly wanted to say something positive about Moore, so he added that he followed orders well, and "He always makes more fun than the other men and soon gets well known wherever he may be." In a particularly insightful report, Rogers noted that Augie Old was brave, intelligent, and well-educated, but he was inflexible in enforcing the law and had "rather a bad disposition." About Billy Old, Rogers wrote that he was a "man of strong prejudices" and inclined to develop a "personal dislike" for those with whom he had conflicts. Since Augie and Billy both left Company E after a dispute, Rogers proved accurate in his assessments. Furthermore, Augie subsequently became a Methodist minister, but his career stalled after his stubborn refusal to endorse prohibition at a time when the nation was trending in that direction, culminating with an amendment to the United States Constitution. Billy became an Arizona Ranger as well as a deputy sheriff, but he also tried to get Rogers removed from command and was shot and killed by his own wife in 1914. In sum, while Rogers tried to be supportive, he was also perceptive and honest in assessing his men, traits that again made him a good mentor for those who served under him, including Wright.[12]

By the time Rogers submitted his report on Wright, he had already observed him in action on the border. Scurry's first dilemma as adjutant general, and Wright's first gunfight as a Ranger, came in March 1899 at Laredo, when locals rebelled against a vaccination and quarantine program intended to combat an outbreak of smallpox. Scurry ordered Rogers to investigate the report of State Health Officer Walter F. Blunt that protestors had stockpiled guns and ammunition in preparation for armed resistance to his efforts to move smallpox patients into the local hospital, quarantine camps, and an "abandoned mill and tannery" that served as a makeshift pesthouse. Both Mexicans and Tejanos, not understanding what Blunt was doing, refused to let sick relatives and friends be taken from their homes. Blunt had served in the Confederate army before earning a medical degree at Texas Medical College in Galveston, so he was not easily rattled. Nevertheless, Rogers initially took only one Ranger, Augie Old, with him to Laredo. The two Rangers—with Blunt, Laredo Marshal A. Joseph Barthelow, and others—helped move smallpox patients to a large tent that served as a temporary hospital on March 19 until noon without trouble. While eating lunch, Rogers was told that gunshots had been heard in another part of town. Upon investigating with Old, he found that Barthelow and his assistant marshal, Nicasio Idar, had been trying to disperse protestors when the shooting erupted. Neither lawman had been shot, but Idar, a popular labor organizer and newspaper editor, had been struck on the head with a rock, while one of the crowd, Pablo Aguilar, had been shot in the leg. Rogers and Old rescued Idar and Barthelow, then escorted the marshal safely to his office. Prudently, any efforts to move patients were suspended, and Rogers sent a telegram to Cotulla calling for help.[13]

Sergeant DuBose arrived in Laredo the next day with four privates from Company E—Moore, Billy Old, Taylor, and William Wright. Taylor recalled that Rogers had told him and Wright, when they enlisted, not to buy a rifle until after the legislature approved the annual appropriation for the Frontier Battalion because there was a chance the new recruits might not ever get paid. Even then it might be some time before they acquired a full complement of gear because privates made just thirty dollars per month at that time and had to provide their own equipment. Taylor remembered that he spent eighty dollars on his horse, saddle, bedroll, and weapons. Wright had to borrow a rifle for the trip to Laredo, while Taylor borrowed a twelve-gauge shotgun and six buckshot rounds. They were joined at Laredo by two Special Rangers: Thomas Ragland, a thirty-three-year-old cattle inspector from Alice, and Oscar N. "Newt" Wright, a distant cousin of William Wright who later served in several public offices in Nueces and San Patricio counties, including as deputy sheriff.[14]

Rogers sent his reinforcements to the Hamilton Hotel, where he and Augie Old had established a headquarters. Sheriff Luis R. Ortiz meanwhile obtained a search warrant to look for weapons. Believing that being accompanied by fewer law officers would be best, Ortiz did not take any Rangers with him to search other than Rogers. He did have three of his Tejano deputies escort him, and he assured Rogers that if problems arose, they would call for assistance. The first search of a house allegedly went well, but for some reason Augie Old and Ragland joined the little group for the next one, which belonged to Agapito Herrera, a former deputy. When Ortiz presented his warrant, Herrera asked to speak with him alone. Rogers remained nearby; he could not hear what was said, but he assumed Herrera was refusing to let them go inside. As the two men turned back toward the house, Ortiz put his hand on Herrera's shoulder and called to one of his deputies in Spanish. Chaos erupted. A Mexican at the corner of the house shot at Rogers, then scrambled to find cover as Rogers returned fire. Ortiz and all his deputies disappeared when Herrera and two other Hispanic men charged with Winchester rifles in their hands. Rogers shot Herrera in the chest with his pistol but not before Herrera shattered his upper right arm with a rifle round. Augie Old then killed Herrera by shooting him in the head and neck as he lay on the ground. In the flurry of gunfire that followed, Santiago Grimaldo and Refugia Herrera, the dead man's sister, were also badly wounded, in the stomach and arm, respectively.[15]

Augie Old and Ragland protected Rogers while he commandeered a buggy, then, pistols empty, followed him through a shower of stones thrown by angry women to the Hamilton Hotel. Leaving their captain with a doctor, the two at Blunt's direction returned to the fight with DuBose, Billy Old, Taylor, and the Wrights. Moore remained at the hotel with Rogers. Taylor later recalled that he stayed close to William Wright as they ran down the road because he seemed to know what he was doing. They met a crowd of Mexicans and Tejanos, about twenty-five of whom were armed and opened fire. The Rangers, of course, retaliated; Taylor recalled: "We were shooting at everything that moved." Wright pointed to a Mexican and told Taylor to watch him; Taylor emptied his shotgun and years later told a reporter that the Mexican was found dead the following day with several buckshot wounds. Whether his comrade hit anyone or not, Wright recalled that Taylor "saved the day" with his shotgun blasts. After the battle had raged for thirty minutes, African American troopers from the Tenth United States Cavalry arrived from Fort McIntosh, and the crowd dispersed in response to the frantic pleading of Marshal Barthelow. The Rangers had wounded thirteen combatants, five of whom they named in an after-action report: Antonio Pacheco, Marguerita Herrera (another of Agapito's sisters, who allegedly fired at the Rangers from the window of a house), Candido Garcia, Anastacio Garcia, and Juan Gonzales. Other wounded combatants avoided being identified by crossing the Rio Grande. Herrera had the distinction of being the only one known to have been killed, but the Rangers reported that one man who fled into Mexico may have died there, and of course, Taylor years later said that he killed another. Among the Rangers, Rogers proved to be the most seriously injured; he had several inches of bone removed from his upper right arm and had to have a rifle custom-made so he could fire it with his shortened limb. Newt Wright was badly bruised when a spent round struck him in the groin, while William Wright was hit in the oversized buckle of his gun belt, which probably saved his life.[16]

Captain Hughes arrived with three of his men to reinforce the remaining members of Rogers' company. Until the Rangers left Laredo on March 27, African American troopers patrolled the streets under the direction of Captain Charles G. Ayers, who the previous year had led them in combat in Cuba. The soldiers moved a Gatling gun from point-to-point to threaten any crowd that assembled, and one of them knocked at least one protestor down with his carbine. According to the *San Antonio Express*, the injured man later died. In response to a request from Mayor Louis J. Christen, Mexican cavalry patrolled the far side of the Rio Grande to keep anyone from crossing. In the wake of what would become known as the "Laredo Smallpox Riot," Blunt and the Rangers completed the task of moving smallpox patients to pest houses and makeshift hospitals, often in wagons escorted by African American troopers, and Blunt inoculated all those who were not yet sick. Rangers and other local law enforcement officers—as many as two dozen—were also assigned to guard quarantine sites and help with many other duties, and they arrested twenty-one protestors. With state health regulations enforced, the epidemic came to an end, and Blunt ended the quarantine on May 1, 1899.[17]

After a few quiet months, DuBose took William Wright, Taylor, and Billy Old to Columbus, the seat of Colorado County, which was embroiled in a feud that had reignited during the 1898 election. Incumbent sheriff Samuel H. Reese had run for reelection against his deputy, Larkin S. Hope, who was shot and killed in August, probably by Jim Coleman, a friend of Reese's sons. Reese subsequently lost the election to another candidate, William T.

"Will" Burford, then was killed in a gunfight with Deputy Sheriff William D. Clements in March 1899. Behind the violence was ex-legislator Marcus H. "Mark" Townsend, whose machine dominated local politics. DuBose and the others arrived in May 1899 in response to a plea from Colorado County Judge Joseph J. Mansfield after Burrell G. W. "Dick" Reese, the deceased ex-sheriff's brother, and his African American employee, Dick Gant, were shot and killed by two other deputy sheriffs, James G. "Jim" Townsend and Stephen "Step" Yates. The killing continued for years between the factions, most of whom were Townsend or Reese relatives by marriage or blood, but Wright initially stayed only two months. He first worked for Captain Lamartine P. Sieker, a Confederate veteran and longtime Ranger who had recently resumed his duties as quartermaster for the Frontier Battalion after a brief retirement. As tensions mounted, Wright and his colleagues were joined by Scurry, Captain McDonald (who had already spent a week in Columbus during March 1899), and Private Dudley S. "Dud" Barker. Barker, one of McDonald's company who had survived several shootouts at San Saba in 1898, was known as a man who "would shoot you at the drop of a hat," while Wright, who had battled a mob in Laredo, gained a better reputation as a Ranger who would think before he fired. But Wright did make his first two arrests as a Ranger in May 1899: Albert Bushy and Fritz Hasty for "assault to murder." Neither man was indicted, which was a common problem for the Rangers. Nevertheless, Wright did well, and by early June all the Rangers except him and Taylor had departed, Barker to leave the Rangers and get married.[18]

Wright and Taylor stayed close to Sheriff Burford in June 1899, sleeping each night in the jail at Columbus. Wright mostly arrested people for petty crimes or cattle theft, but Taylor almost became a casualty of the feud. On June 5, the day before Captain McDonald departed, Wright arrested J. Walter Reese, the late ex-sheriff's son, for "using abusive language," which apparently infuriated that faction again. Wright went with Burford out of town to retrieve a prisoner two days later, and that afternoon two Townsend "boys" were walking near a saloon where Reeses "held out." A shot rang out from inside the saloon, and Taylor, with Deputy Robert W. Westmoreland, joined the two Townsends in the street. Entering the dark saloon, Taylor discovered that "a blind had been set up at the end of the bar," and Walter Reese with his brother Herbert sat behind it with shotguns. When questioned, one claimed the other had accidentally fired "while fooling with the gun." Taylor decided they intended to kill the two Townsends, so he took their weapons as well as the shotguns of six more men he found hiding in a back storeroom. Stacking all the guns on the bar, Taylor returned to the storeroom to tell the men there that they could go home or to jail, but then he heard someone enter the front of the saloon. It proved to be fifteen Townsends, intent on confronting the Reeses. They ordered Taylor to step aside, and he refused. The Ranger finally convinced the Townsends to leave, and then he and Westmoreland escorted all the Reeses to their homes at their request.[19]

Wright became more involved in the still-simmering feud when he returned to Columbus with Sheriff Burford. A Townsend brought Taylor a "code telegram" and told him that it said six armed men had left Hallettsville for Columbus. Taylor assumed that they would be coming to join the Reeses, and he told Wright that. He and Wright subsequently "took all the guns out" of the saloon, then went to the house of the late ex-sheriff, where his widow Keron Townsend "Keetie" Reese still lived, and waited in the shadow of a large oak tree. As they expected, at one in the morning a buckboard arrived carrying six armed men. They all went in the house, and the two Rangers, estimating there were now as many as fourteen armed men inside the place, returned to the jail and went to bed. Wright and Taylor then tried to keep order by declaring that no more than two men could walk together in Columbus, and on June 10 Wright arrested six men—Yates, Jim, and Mark Townsend, J. T. Reese, James A. Clements, and Marion Hope—for carrying pistols. All but Reese were suspects in the killing of the ex-sheriff and his brother. The next day, with Taylor incapacitated by illness and at least fourteen men still gathered at the Reese home, Wright telegraphed for help. Scurry returned on June 12 with Sergeant DuBose and Augie Old, as Wright recommended. Taylor recalled that Scurry brought two more Rangers with him, but he did not identify them, so they may have been Special Rangers whom he did not know. The Adjutant General took a report from Taylor, then went to the Reese house accompanied by him and Wright. There Scurry told the intruders to go home by midnight; Taylor later wrote that Scurry declared that if they did not, "then he would ask the Governor for Marshall law [*sic*] and buck and gag every one of them." Scurry added that he had a half dozen Rangers with him, "and if this isn't enough there is 32 in the State and he would have them all there by morning."[20]

Scurry's intervention did not end Wright's work in Columbus. Subsequent discussions with members of the Reese family revealed that the source of the ongoing conflict might well be Keetie Reese, who was a vengeful widow. When Wright interviewed her at her home, she escorted him into her bedroom and showed him the bloodstained clothes worn by her husband and his brother when they were killed, which she kept draped over chairs near her bed. She told Wright that only having the heart of Marcus Townsend would satisfy her. To underscore her point, she always carried a pistol, and her son Walter, when he was arrested, had two shells in his shotgun marked with the initials of Townsend and his brother-in-law, Sheriff Burford. Wright must have been quite relieved when Keetie left for Orange on June 18. He told Scurry that she had agreed that perhaps it would be best for her and everyone involved if she sold her land and left Columbus forever. While Wright reported a lot more talk by both sides about doing something, Columbus remained relatively quiet. He made four more arrests for theft before the end of June, and another three on minor charges before he and Taylor departed in early July. The two Rangers returned briefly in mid-July for what Wright reported as a "false alarm," but left again after Wright assured Scurry that Rangers were not needed until the state district court met in September. Wright's eleven arrests in June were almost two-thirds of the eighteen made by Company E that month. Taylor also arrested five men in July, but neither he nor Wright got many indictments—of the dozen they detained during their last four weeks in Columbus, only two were indicted, Duff Hines for stealing cattle and William Stallion for "assault with intent to rape." Hines was convicted and sentenced to two years in the state penitentiary, while no further record concerning Stallion has been found. His case may be the one about which Wright wrote on July 14: "The case we was [*sic*] witnesses in today was tried and acquitted. I never saw the like in my life. With plain evidence and then turn them a loose." Wright was probably glad to leave Columbus, but the feud was not over, nor were the two Rangers done with it.[21]

From Columbus, Wright went to Richmond, in Fort Bend County, to assist Sieker in providing food and other supplies to flood victims. Nine inches of rain had fallen in eleven days during June 1899, pushing the Brazos River out of its banks. The floodwaters covered 12,000 square miles and claimed 284 lives. With thousands stranded or homeless, assistance was badly needed. But Wright's humanitarian work was interrupted on July 19 when he witnessed a "desperate street fight" between Walter M. Burton and his daughter Hattie on one side and A. S. Stephenson on the other. Burton was a former slave who had become a Republican sheriff and legislator, as well as a minister, while Hattie was a schoolteacher. Stephenson was a black physician. In an exchange of about a dozen gunshots, Burton had his leg broken by a bullet, Hattie was shot in the face and suffered a broken jaw, and Stephenson was hit three times and quickly died of his wounds. The Burtons were both arrested and then released on $5,000 bonds, and Hattie succumbed several weeks later. Since no further record of this case has been found, and Burton died at home in Richmond in 1913, presumably he did not go to prison for killing Stephenson.[22]

Wright remained busy through the fall of 1899. When Rogers went to Orange on the Louisiana line in August to investigate the killing of Fred Holsten and the wounding of two other African American men by a mob of twenty whites, Wright, Taylor, and Augie Old accompanied him. They learned that on August 12, "without cause or provocation," whites had fired into a house, killing Holsten. It was part of a pattern of violence against African Americans by whites known as "Whitecappers" that had erupted that summer, primarily focused on getting African Americans to quit their jobs in local lumber mills and leave. Rogers reported: "I found it an 'up hill' business in getting evidence against them, as such a large per cent of the people there are in sympathy with them and want the negroes scared and run out of the country." He interviewed several African Americans who had fled to other towns, but they told him nothing. Rogers even paid an informant to join the Whitecappers but again acquired no information. Old arrested William Diggs and Frank Weatherford in late August for Holsten's murder, but they had to be released because of a lack of evidence. In September, Rogers had Wright and Taylor return to Columbus, where trials had begun for some of those implicated in the feud. Wright had made no arrests in Orange, but at Columbus he arrested seven men, four for murder. Only one man, Arthur M. McDow, whom Wright had previously arrested in July 1899 for "assault with intent to murder," was indicted. But there is no record of his conviction and McDow still lived in Colorado County in 1930, so apparently little came of either incident. Overall, Columbus proved to be relatively quiet for Wright, perhaps because the district judge decided to move the feud trials to Bastrop for the January 1900 session. Wright took a well-deserved leave during the first week of October and visited relatives in Wilson County. But work always intruded: asked to assist with an arson case, he arrested three men. Two of them were African Americans: William Douglas and Jesse Wilson. The matter must have ended in a manner favorable to them, however, because a few years later Wilson became the principal of a new school for African Americans in Sutherland Springs. Returning to Cotulla, Wright took charge several times when Rogers had to go out of town on business.[23]

Wright went to Hempstead in Waller County with Kid Rogers in December 1899. He recalled in a newspaper interview in 1925 that the local sheriff, James C. Lipscomb, made it very clear to them that he opposed their presence, even though Lipscomb admitted there was widespread violence in his town. Conflict had begun in November, centering on a dispute between two communities over a schoolhouse. When one group threatened to occupy the building, which had been nailed shut in response to an order from the state district judge, and the sheriff could not be located, a local justice of the peace asked for the Hempstead Light Infantry, a militia unit, to "quell" the "riot." Sent to investigate the incident, Sieker reported that the problem seemed to be the Hempstead Light Infantry, many of whom drank heavily and practiced their marksmanship on random targets in town. He recommended disbanding the unit, as did others who wrote to Governor Sayers. Scurry asked Rogers to send two men to investigate further, and so he sent his brother and Wright, who reported on December 20 that Lipscomb "met me at the depot and seemed to be very angry over us being sent here over his protest." Wright diagnosed the real source of trouble as a clash between the sheriff and county judge, each of whom had many supporters, and he underscored the gravity of the situation by asking Sieker to ship him two boxes of

Winchester rounds. Lipscomb decided to side with the Rangers, who worked hard to make friends on both sides, although one fellow who promised to help had to be jailed for using his gun too liberally to intimidate locals. Wright made two additional arrests for similarly minor infractions, and he and Rogers enjoyed a quiet Christmas and New Year's Eve, unlike the previous year when shots were fired into several local stores. Hempstead merchants in gratitude gave each Ranger a twenty-dollar gold piece. In February 1900, Scurry disbanded the Hempstead Light Infantry.[24]

As scheduled, the district court considered the Columbus cases at Bastrop during January 1900. In an effort to keep order, Wright boarded the train at Columbus with about 150 people from the Reese and Townsend factions. Captain Rogers joined him at La Grange, halfway to Bastrop, with six additional Rangers, including Taylor, Augie Old and Kid Rogers. As their trip continued, Rogers had his men search the travelers and luggage, but they found few firearms. Upon arriving at Bastrop, Rangers escorted the visitors to their hotels and guarded them constantly. Captains Brooks and McDonald were also present. Step Yates had died of tuberculosis before he could be tried for killing Dick Reese, but his accomplice Jim Townsend was brought to trial. The town was filled with Townsends and Reeses and their supporters, and when the judge agreed to a continuance on January 15, violence once more erupted. Arrangements were made to transport the two groups separately out of Bastrop, and the Reese clan was waiting in a bar for a train. When three men walked by, those in the bar started shooting. They wounded the man they probably intended to kill, William Clements, who had continued to brag about shooting Samuel Reese. Howard Townsend, another deputy sheriff, escaped unscathed, but young Arthur L. Burford, the son of Sheriff Burford, was hit in the head and died instantly. A recent law graduate from the University of Texas, he had come to Bastrop as a spectator. In accordance with Rogers' orders, he and the other two shooting victims were not armed. The Rangers arrested seventeen suspects, of whom four were indicted: Walter Reese, Jim Coleman, who was also the prime suspect in the killing of Larkin Hope; Thomas B. Daniels; and Leslie W. Reese, a nephew of the late ex-sheriff. All four were scheduled to be tried at Bastrop in February 1900, when Wright and his comrades again rode the trains with Townsends and Reeses and their allies, and once more searched diligently for weapons. While the four shooters were indicted, eventually all had their cases dismissed by the state district court at San Antonio.[25]

When Brooks, Rogers, and most of Company E traveled to Richmond in March 1900 to provide security for more trials concerning the Columbus feud, Wright did not go with them. Instead, he had returned to Orange, where matters had taken a deadly turn for the Rangers. Captain McDonald's men made dozens of arrests in Orange by late December 1899 for crimes that included the killing of Holsten, and many indictments were returned, five for murder and as many as twenty for conspiracy to commit murder. But when Ranger T. Lawrence Fuller arrested yet another troublemaker on December 21, he was attacked by Oscar Poole with a knife, and Fuller shot and killed him. Poole, the son of County Judge George F. Poole, had clashed with Augie Old three months earlier. When Fuller was released on bond in January, and a grand jury declined to indict him for the shooting, Judge Poole, arguing that members of the Frontier Battalion had no authority to arrest anyone, convinced the jurors to indict both Fuller and his partner, Andrew L. Saxon, for falsely arresting five men in November 1899. To make matters worse, local police killed an African American man in a gunfight in February 1900, prompting a flurry of hate mail and official requests for Rangers to provide security, despite protests from Judge Poole. Augie Old, Kid Rogers, Wright, and Wright's brother-in-law Gratz Brown replaced McDonald's Rangers, who were no longer welcome. Old and Rogers left at the end of February, then Wright's brother Milam succeeded Brown after he was discharged. Together the Wright brothers made seven arrests in Orange in March 1900, half of the total for Company E that month, and they arrested the same number in April. Asked to establish a permanent Ranger post at Orange, Governor Sayers declined, saying that he preferred to use the Rangers as a law enforcement reserve. William Wright assured Scurry that Sheriff P. Frank Eastin, who had supported intervention by the Rangers, could keep order, and so the two Wright brothers left Orange when McDonald returned with Fuller and Saxon for their initial trials in April 1900.[26]

The situation at Orange ended badly for the Rangers. Despite the angry protests of McDonald, Fuller and Saxon traveled again to Orange to be tried for false arrest in mid-October 1900. During a break, the two men went to a barbershop. Saxon was in the chair and Fuller was washing his face in a basin when he was murdered with a single shot from a Winchester. The shooter was Thomas F. Poole, Oscar's brother, who was acquitted at his trial in May 1901. City Marshal James A. Jett of Orange shot and killed Thomas Poole ten months later, only to die in May 1902 in a gun battle with George H. Poole, brother of Oscar and Thomas, and two other Poole relatives. Ironically, Fuller, who was the last member of the Frontier Battalion to be killed in service and the only man Captain McDonald ever lost, died as a lieutenant. He had been promoted in the reorganization that followed the assertions of judges such as George F. Poole that Ranger privates did not have the authority to arrest criminals. Saxon had been told that as well by Texas District Judge William M. Pardue, who then fined him and sentenced him to jail for false arrest in Hall County. That ruling led to the temporary appointment of lieutenants such as Wright, and Governor Sayers pardoned Saxon. Meanwhile, during the trial of Thomas Poole, William and Milam Wright returned once more to Orange to provide security, despite the dire warnings of local leaders like Charles A. Hotchkiss of Dallas, a Confederate veteran and alleged organizer of the original Ku Klux Klan at Jefferson who perhaps knew more than he revealed in his letter to Scurry. More important, Judge Poole requested all of William Wright's arrest records from his time in Orange during the spring of 1900, and he probably watched him closely during the spring of 1901.[27]

During October 1900, when Fuller was killed, Wright survived his own armed challenge, which also had a complicated backstory. When Company E was assigned in June 1898 to Cotulla in La Salle County, where it had served earlier and Rogers married, it confronted yet another feud in a town noted for violence. Wright had grim family ties to Cotulla: his mother, Anne Elizabeth Tumlinson Wright, was a first cousin of Joseph Tumlinson, the ex-sheriff of Dimmitt County who in January 1893 killed his wife and then himself while serving as the sheriff of La Salle County. Five years later, Rogers investigated the murder of attorney William J. Bowen, who had been shot twice in the back as he walked home in May 1898. Bowen had links to two other murders in Cotulla. His brother, Walter C. Bowen, was shot and killed by former deputy sheriff Alfred Y. Allee and an accomplice during a scuffle on a train in June 1891, during which William was wounded in the arm. The offense that sparked the attack was Walter Bowen's criticism of Allee in his newspaper, the *Cotulla Ledger*. Allee was acquitted for this killing, his fourth, only to be stabbed to death at Laredo by marshal A. Joseph Barthelow in 1896. William Bowen survived being shot only to become embroiled in a second conflict when he agreed to defend another newsman, J. Guy Reed, who published a weekly, *La Salle's Isonomy*, at Cotulla under the *nom de plume* of J. Guy Smith. Reed had already earned notoriety when he tried to stop James R. Davenport and Henry May from attacking Mexicans at a saloon in April 1898. Shot by May in the back and side, Reed managed to shoot and kill his assailant and survive. Bowen became Reed's defense counsel for a libel case filed when he, in his newspaper, ridiculed Joseph Cotulla, the Polish-born Union veteran who founded the town that bore his name. Reed was acquitted for killing May, which was self-defense, but he was convicted of libel and, four days after the death of his attorney, failed in his efforts to appeal the conviction.[28]

Wright of course had no direct involvement in the deaths of Sheriff Tumlinson or Walter Bowen, which occurred before he arrived in Cotulla, and he played only a minor role in investigating the violent demise of William Bowen. Before Wright enlisted in Rogers' company, A. J. Poteet was arrested and indicted in December 1898 for killing the attorney. His motive was simply that he had lost his claim for some of the school lands in La Salle County, for which he blamed Bowen, who was the counsel for the opposing side in the dispute. Rogers worked closely with his brother-in-law, Sheriff William M. Burwell, in the investigation of Bowen's murder, and he assigned Wright to gather evidence after he joined his company, which may have led to his comments about Wright being a good detective in his later report. Poteet was confined safely in the jail at San Antonio, where he secured several changes of venue for his murder trial. Historian Paul N. Spellman, finding no evidence to the contrary, has surmised that he was never convicted for killing Bowen.[29]

The problem for Wright was that men remained in Cotulla who resented the Rangers. George W. Reed, a saloon keeper, had too much to drink during the first week of July 1898 and punctuated his denouncements of the Rangers with shotgun blasts. After Rogers peacefully confronted him, disarmed him, and took him to jail, his outbursts apparently ceased. Others were not so easily quieted. Among the most troublesome was Davenport, who had accompanied May during his fatal foray to a Cotulla saloon. Davenport was arrested by Augie Old during February 1899 for "unlawfully carrying a pistol," and again in November 1899 on the same charge by Wright. A native of Arkansas, Davenport ostensibly was just a thirty-six-year-old cowboy working for A. Armstrong Jr., May's uncle. But the Rangers knew that he had a violent history, including killing his boss fourteen years earlier. E. M. Hereford, manager of the M. Haeff and Brothers ranch near Marathon, dismissed Davenport and several others during August 1886. Davenport went to Hereford's home the next night and shot him five times. Rangers Baz Outlaw and Joseph M. Mize tracked Davenport and engaged him in a gunfight. The lawmen suffered minor wounds, mostly from the shrapnel of Winchester bullets, while Davenport, who was also slightly wounded by Outlaw, fled to Mexico. Arrested by Mexican officials and extradited to the United States, Davenport was tried in El Paso, where he claimed that he shot Hereford because he "made insulting proposals" to his wife, not because he had been fired. Sentenced to only five years, Davenport served his time in jail and then, rather than work with his father at his barbecue restaurant in El Paso or his brother in a Mexican mining operation, resumed being a cowboy and troublemaker.[30]

Somehow Wright became a preferred target for Davenport and one of his new friends, Reed, whom he had apparently forgiven for killing his employer's nephew. The pair would fire their pistols "accidentally" to rattle the Ranger lieutenant. Davenport then began boasting that he was "going to get" Wright. Presumably left in charge, as he often was, during Rogers' absence—the captain went to Nacogdoches to make sure that a murderer whose sentence had been commuted from hanging to life in prison reached the Texas penitentiary—and perhaps concerned that he was one of only four Rangers in Cotulla, Wright staged a preemptive strike. He declared there had been reports of impending violence and began searching locals for concealed weapons on October 24, 1900. About three in the afternoon he encountered Davenport, who had been drinking, and they exchanged words.

Davenport then retired to Reed's office, where he and the editor lingered for several hours. Meanwhile, Wright prepared for another confrontation by placing his Winchester just inside the door of a local saloon and settling into a chair outside to wait with Joseph W. Petty, the Cotulla constable. About six in the evening Davenport reappeared with Reed. Davenport called to Wright, said he wanted to talk, and told him that he had a pistol in his hip pocket. Reed went into the saloon while Wright told Davenport he was under arrest for "unlawfully carrying a pistol," as he had done at least once before. Davenport responded with angry profanity. When Wright reached for the gun, Davenport "jumped back and jerked his pistol and fired" a shot through Wright's coat. The Ranger swiftly knocked his assailant's revolver aside and emptied his, with all five rounds hitting Davenport in the chest (the hammer usually rested on an empty chamber for safety). Davenport fired a wild shot as he fell, then died fifteen minutes later without saying another word.[31]

Reed heard the fusillade of pistol shots but remained in the saloon, with his back to the door, drinking steadily. Wright reloaded, went into the bar, retrieved his Winchester, and poked Reed in the back with his rifle barrel. Turning around, Reed in response to an inquiry from Wright admitted that he had a gun and surrendered a revolver. Wright repeated the question twice more, and each time Reed gave him an "automatic" pistol. After having Petty search Reed one last time, which produced "a dirk and a set of brass knucks," Wright, satisfied the editor was entirely unarmed, placed him under arrest. Reed posted a low bail, having only been charged with unlawfully carrying a weapon, then published his account of Davenport's death in his newspaper. Of course, it contained details that, if true, would have ended Wright's career as a Ranger. Reed claimed that he and Davenport were only going to the saloon when Wright accosted them. Since he did not see what ensued, Reed relied on testimony from alleged eyewitnesses, who said the Ranger drew his gun before reaching for Davenport's pocket, that Wright fired first and shot Davenport as he drew his weapon, and that Wright stood over the fallen man and shot him three more times. Reed declared his friend had no chance to defend himself. Clearly many locals did not agree, because Wright had to post a $5,000 bond but was "exonerated" in an "examining trial" before a grand jury, who heard the testimony of several "citizens."

As another eyewitness wrote to the *Brownville Daily Herald*, "I don't know what Davenport and Smith [Reed] came up town together for but it looked as if they had planned to do up somebody." By 1902 Reed relocated to San Antonio, where he published *Reed's Isonomy: A Journal of Justice*, presumably for a more receptive audience.[32]

Wright had left his wife Mary Ann, or "Mollie," and mother, Ann Elizabeth Tumlinson Wright, who was visiting, at his home when he went to confront Davenport. They heard the shots and were relieved to be told the outcome of the fight, but the confrontation complicated matters for Rogers. He decided it was prudent to move his headquarters in November 1900 to Laredo, where apparently public attitudes were less toxic toward the Rangers. But Wright now had a statewide reputation as a gunman, thanks to accounts of his clash with Davenport that appeared in newspapers all over Texas, so Rogers sent him with his brother Milam to a more remote county, Atascosa, where ranchers had asked for Rangers to "scout for cattle thieves." The Wright brothers worked mostly with Sheriff A. Mathis Avant, with the lieutenant getting credit for six arrests thanks to that year's changes negating the authority of Ranger privates, such as his younger brother Milam, to detain suspects. Most of the arrests were for cattle theft or forgery, but William Wright did accost Fodau Garcia for murder in a case for which no other records have been found. Then, after a few quiet weeks, Joseph E. Newman shot and killed Jim Walker in December. Traveling to Floresville, Wright spoke with Newman's father, Andrew R. Newman, and convinced him to talk to his son, who was hiding in DeWitt County. The fugitive surrendered to a deputy sheriff in Karnes County, where he had been born and presumably had family, and then was brought to Floresville, whence Wright escorted him to Pleasanton and gave him to Avant. Newman pled self-defense, and census records indicate that he did not spend much time in jail, if any.[33]

Wright in January 1901 returned to Laredo, where he arrested Charles Hardy for smuggling and delivered him to U.S. Deputy Marshal William W. Hanson. It was otherwise a rather dull time, so he may have welcomed the change of scenery in February when he was sent to Galveston with ten other Rangers and Captain Rogers to enforce the controversial state law against prizefighting. Galveston was the home of a rising star, John A.

"Jack" Johnson, a talented African American fighter who would become famous as the "Galveston Giant." Johnson had already fought several professional bouts, most recently in January 1901 under the auspices of the Galveston Athletic Association. He was scheduled to fight Joseph B. Choynski, the "Chrysanthemum Kid," on February 25, again under the sponsorship of the Association. To avoid having the Rangers arrest the boxers, the event was advertised as an "exhibition," but when Choynski knocked Johnson out in the third round, it became immediately apparent that this was indeed a prizefight. Wright and the others, who were dressed as "sports" and scattered among the crowd, swarmed into the ring and arrested the fighters, who were jailed with bonds of $5,000 apiece, which neither man could pay. They remained under arrest, but Sheriff Henry Thomas allowed them to leave the jail each night to sleep. During the day they sparred and trained, often in front of audiences, and Choynski, an experienced fighter, tutored the younger Johnson. A Galveston grand jury on March 8 declined to indict either man, but Governor Sayers had them rearrested on new charges. The case was brought before a grand jury at least two more times, the third in May 1901, after Choynski and Johnson had left Texas.[34]

Wright left Galveston long before Johnson and Choynski. In March 1901 he attended a stock raisers' convention with Rogers, then reported at Austin to be briefed and assigned, at the request of former state district judge Thomas H. Spooner, to investigate the killing of ex-sheriff William E. Jones in Bandera County. Jones during the Civil War had been a captain in the Eighth Texas Cavalry, popularly known as Terry's Texas Rangers. He had been killed near Medina on March 1, 1900, by the Rev. W. D. Robinson, a Methodist minister who had served as the chaplain of the Fourth Texas Volunteer Infantry in the Spanish–American War. Jones had been critical of Robinson, sparking a dispute, and Robinson decided to end it. He ambushed Jones as he was traveling home alone in a buggy from Medina to his ranch, seven miles from town. Robinson then surrendered to Sheriff Isaac W. "Ike" Stevens, himself a Civil War veteran of the Fifth Texas Infantry, and told him where to find Jones, riddled with buckshot and still in his buggy. Robinson posted a $4,000 bond and remained free while the inquiry continued for more than a year. Wright interviewed people in San Antonio and Kerrville, as well as elsewhere in Bandera County, before a trial commenced in April 1901. Witnesses were afraid to testify until Wright assured them that he could protect them, and he and another Ranger attended the court sessions to provide security. Robinson was convicted of second-degree murder and sent to the state penitentiary for ten years in July 1901, but Governor Samuel W. T. Lanham pardoned him in August 1904.[35]

District attorney J. W. Baker wrote to Governor Sayers from Bandera County thanking him for Wright's work during the Robinson investigation, declaring that his services were "invaluable." At the same time, Baker insisted that Robinson had accomplices and asked for Wright to remain in the area, where he could also investigate a livestock theft ring. U.S. Deputy Marshal Hanson, who had joined Wright in Bandera County for Robinson's trial, agreed with Baker that the Ranger "did good and efficient work and the good people of Bandera and Kerr Counties are loud in their praises of him both as an officer and a gentleman," and that he needed to continue to pursue Robinson's accomplices and the many local livestock rustlers. Wright had already returned to Laredo and then rejoined Sheriff Avant in Atascosa County, arresting two men at Pleasanton in the latter half of April 1901, one for perjury and one for cattle theft. But he and his brother Milam by May 1901 were back in Bandera County, whence the lieutenant wrote to Rogers, "I have got my hands full." He made three arrests for trespassing, cattle theft, and stealing goats. Minor as these were, they comprised half of the total for Company E in May. Captain Rogers and Taylor even joined the Wright brothers, establishing a headquarters at a local ranch to press the investigation while Lieutenant Wright made several scouts in tandem with Constable Tom M. York of Bandera County.[36]

From Medina, Wright joined in one of the most famous manhunts in Texas history: the pursuit of Gregorio Cortez Lira. It began when, at the request of Sheriff Avant of Atascosa County, William T. "Brack" Morris, the sheriff of Karnes County, questioned Gregorio and his brother Romaldo about a stolen horse at the latter's house on June 12, 1901. Morris's deputy, Daniel Boone Choate, translated because neither brother spoke English well, nor could Morris understand Spanish. Choate's garbled translations led to a fight in which Morris shot a knife-wielding Romaldo and in turn was shot by Gregorio.

Both wounded men soon died. Fleeing to a friend's home in Gonzales County, Cortez and his supporters shot and killed Sheriff Richard M. "Dick" Glover Jr. and Constable Henry J. Schnabel when they arrived with a posse to arrest him. Most of the others who were in the house and involved in the gunfight were arrested, but Cortez escaped again. The ten-day manhunt ended when a Mexican herder approached Captain Rogers in the field near Laredo and told him that Cortez was sleeping in a lean-to in his goat camp. He led Rogers there, and the Ranger captain quietly arrested the exhausted and unarmed fugitive. Cortez was convicted for his role in all three deaths, but those convictions were overturned by the Texas Court of Criminal Appeals. He was ultimately sent to the state penitentiary for life after a second trial for the killing of Glover ended with his conviction, but he was pardoned by Governor Oscar B. Colquitt in 1913.[37]

Wright joined the pursuit after Cortez killed Glover and Schnabel. Emanuel M. Tom, the expert tracker who had assisted in the capture of Maximo Martinez in 1897, was hired, and Wright, who as a deputy sheriff had worked with him and Sheriff Morris in the earlier chase, again rode with him. Wright was the only member of the posse who stayed with Tom for the entire manhunt. The others in their small group, which included Sheriff Avant, Wilson County Sheriff James J. Heathcock, and former Wilson County sheriff Manuel J. Ximenes, dropped out. Tom and Wright communicated with Rogers as often as they could by telegraph, and they were close behind Cortez when Rogers arrested him. Since Cortez was captured near Laredo, a weary Wright probably welcomed the opportunity to return home and see his growing family, which included three sons and a daughter by this time. The youngest of the four children, one-year-old Emanuel Avant "Dogie" Wright, was named in honor of two other participants in the pursuit of Cortez, tracker Tom and Sheriff Avant.[38]

Many songs and stories made Cortez into a folk hero, while the Rangers became the villains of the story in spite of the fact that they defended him from lynch mobs and ensured that he lived long enough to reach the penitentiary at Huntsville. During his trial at Karnes City in September 1901, Rogers and others were assigned to protect him from "mob violence." Rogers had the two Wright brothers and Taylor from his company at Floresville, along with

Anderson Y. Baker, Alonzo W. "Lon" Livingston, and Charles Sandherr from Company A. Leaving Milam Wright and Livingston at Floresville, because "they were not witnesses in the case," Rogers traveled to Karnes City with William Wright, Taylor, Baker, and Sandherr. A large crowd had gathered for the trial, so Rogers prudently had the Rangers he left behind join the guard detail on October 1. All the Rangers slept in the jail during the trial. At the request of the prosecutor, Rogers sent William Wright to Houston in search of "Dagmon," a witness whose testimony the defense team declared they had to have. Wright returned with Dagmon "in plenty of time," then left Karnes City on October 10 to testify in another murder trial in Atascosa County. Rogers departed the next day for Laredo with Milam Wright and Taylor, leaving Baker, who was a sergeant, with Sandherr and Livingston to help Sheriff William C. Hunter, a deputy who had succeeded Glover after he was killed, escort Cortez to Houston, where the state district court judge had ordered that he be held pending a review by the Texas Court of Criminal Appeals.[39]

Except for matters concerning Cortez, Wright spent most of the last six months of 1901 in Atascosa and Bandera counties, working with sheriffs Avant and York, the former constable who had succeeded Stevens. He arrested Beecher Beaver, who was wanted for murder in the Indian Territory and horse theft in Uvalde County, during July in Bandera County and delivered him to York. The only arrests by Rogers' company in September were five men detained by Wright in Bandera County—two for hog theft, one for burglary, and two for murder. The latter two, Webster C. "Pomp" Freeman, age forty-five, and his nineteen-year-old son George W. Freeman, were arrested by Wright on September 5 and 12, respectively, after an investigation that lasted about a month. Pomp, who lived near Medina, had lost his farm in a flood in August 1900 that almost claimed the lives of his family. A year later, he and his son, who were African Americans, confronted a white neighbor, Charles Sexton, and an unidentified colleague in a dispute over land boundaries. Angry words led to gunfire, and Sexton was shot with a Winchester. He died two hours later, and the elder Freeman surrendered to Sheriff York. George was "acquitted" the day after Wright arrested him as an accessory to the death of Sexton, while his father, who apparently had shot Sexton, was released on a $4,000 bond. Since no further disposition has been found, perhaps the matter ended favorably for both of the Freemans. On Halloween, Wright arrested Jose Martinez for murder in Atascosa County, giving him to Avant for disposition. Wright did return briefly to Laredo, where Rogers reported that Wright in mid- November had "returned from Austin and other points," where Governor Sayers "had been using him in the secret service." Nothing more has been found about this mysterious assignment.[40]

Wright during December 1901 did some scouting in Starr County and attended the district court in Floresville, then he spent the first two months of 1902 chasing fence cutters in East Texas. He and Burwell established their headquarters in Huntsville and scoured the region. Wright tried everything, working undercover with the assumed name of "Will Lee." He built a wire pen, put cattle in it, and waited for cutters to steal them. Nothing worked, despite repeated assertions from the local ranchers that they had a real problem and needed the two Rangers to solve it. To make matters worse, Wright by late January was sick in bed at Huntsville. He and Burwell returned to Laredo empty-handed during the first week of March, then went back to East Texas that same month for another busy week with no better luck.[41]

A routine task took a bizarre twist for Wright in late March 1902, when he went with Sandherr and Oscar Latta to Junction City in Kimble County to provide security for a murder trial at the request of Sheriff William W. Taylor, a cousin to Wright and a future Ranger captain. During his first days there, Wright noticed armed men hovering close to the courthouse, but he assumed they were guards as well. What he did not know was that school lands in Kimble County were being made available for purchase, and Leslie Beasley, a prominent rancher who had been using the property for pasture, had hired men to remain near the county clerk's office, two at a time in twelve-hour shifts, to ensure that his bid was filed first. The clerk, anticipating trouble, locked his door and announced that bids would be accepted after midnight on a certain date through either the mail slot or a hole cut for that purpose. One night, Wright got a report that something had occurred at the courthouse. He asked Latta, who had previously served as a deputy sheriff in Kimble County, and Sandherr to investigate, and they soon called him to join them.

Arriving at the scene, he found a crowd in the hall outside of the clerk's office. A man lay in front of the door with a bloody wound in his forehead; another man, battered and splattered with blood, sat in a chair against the door itself. Assuming the fellow on the floor was dead, Wright arrested the man in the chair, which prompted protests from the crowd and a hurried, and only partially intelligible, explanation from the prisoner, who had a thick foreign accent and said his name was "Battice." He explained that he arrived at the door late that night to file a claim for the school land, found two of Beasley's men asleep, climbed over them, and settled in the chair in front of the door to await the proper time to submit a bid. The sleeping sentries awoke and protested, and one of them decided to fight for the honor of being first in line. He and Battice beat on each other with revolvers until the latter landed a blow on his attacker's forehead that felled him and produced the bloody wound that Wright saw.[42]

Observing that the man on the hall floor was in fact not dead, and learning that the clerk had rescheduled the filing time to seven on the following Monday morning, Wright delivered his prisoner, Battice, to Sheriff Taylor. Wright supervised as everyone was escorted out of the courthouse, watched as two of Beasley's men took their posts outside, and wearily returned to bed. Apparently Battice's felled opponent had to be hospitalized, but Battice rejoined the throng awaiting the land rush. That Monday, Sheriff Taylor positioned Wright by the county clerk's door and other men along the hallway, then opened the courthouse. A scramble ensued, with Battice in the lead, and Wright stopped a fight between him and another man while more scuffles were handled by other guards. Meanwhile, a "little drunk fellow by the name of Fairchild" crawled underneath the brawling mob and cleverly pushed his bid through the opening in the clerk's door, thus winning the opportunity to buy land first. This was probably William J. L. Fairchild, who had moved with his wife Mattie in 1901 to Kimble County, where they raised six daughters. Wright and his colleagues later reported that they arrested three men, Jim McAtee and George Clemmens for "assault to murder," and Alvin Copp for aggravated assault. No further record of their disposition has been found but, faced with similar situations in other counties, the Texas legislature amended the procedures for selling school lands.[43]

Wright and his fellow Rangers had been asked to come to Kimble County by Sheriff Taylor, who anticipated trouble during a murder trial. They did not expect the violence of the land rush, and when it ended Wright took a long leave to visit Sutherland Springs, where his mother, Ann Elizabeth Tumlinson Wright, lived with his late sister's husband, Charles P. Warren, and his two daughters, Florence and Inez. Warren's son, Charles Jr., had died in 1901 at the age of seven. At about this time, Rebecca Elizabeth Newman Tumlinson, Ann's mother and the widow of Joseph L. Tumlinson, joined the Warren household. This family situation may have led to some soul-searching by Wright. According to his wife Mollie, he began thinking about returning to Wilson County, possibly as sheriff, in the fall of 1901. He certainly must have been concerned about supporting his growing nuclear family—Mollie had their fourth child at Laredo in April 1901—as well as the others, and the instability and low pay of Ranger service did not offer much promise. Five members of Company C were discharged in 1902 alone, including his brother Milam. For Wright, the creation of the Ranger Force led to his demotion to private, while Henry DuBose resumed his post as sergeant under Rogers. The salary of a private had risen to fifty dollars a month, which Wright and many others received even when they temporarily served as lieutenants, indicating it would probably not increase again anytime soon. Wright also realized that his chances of becoming a captain and securing better pay were also minimal, while sheriffs in Texas could make more money from the fees and fines that they collected. Too, Wilson County was home, and people there were urging him to run for sheriff.[44]

The timing of Wright's decision to leave the Rangers indicates that he perhaps had a specific grievance. Hearing there were to be more mandatory reductions in March 1902, he wrote to Sieker, with whom he had previously worked, to tell him that the man who should be cut from Company C was Rogers' brother-in-law, Burwell. Wright repeatedly declared that it was "unpleasant" to write on such a topic, but he had to do so because of Burwell's "faults," about which Captain Brooks and several sheriffs could testify. Furthermore, "He run and left me the time I had my truble with Devenport [*sic*]." Wright added that he had not previously said anything out of respect for Rogers, whom he described as a "fine man and good officer." He closed by writing that he knew he was not among the impending discharges, but if he was ever cut, he had been offered other positions, adding "But I want to remain awhile yet any way." Sieker forwarded Wright's letter to Scurry, who wrote to Brooks and Avant. Brooks declined to answer, explaining that it had been many years since Burwell had served in his company, and then just briefly. Avant was only a little more forthcoming, writing that he had "never seen him tried" but heard from "reliable" sources that his "efficiency as an officer" was questionable. In the meantime, Rogers dropped Latta, who had done very well with Wright in Kimble County, and Ormand, whom Wright had personally endorsed. Rogers explained that DuBose, who again had been restored as the sergeant of his company while Wright was demoted from lieutenant to private, said Ormand was "not the man he was recommended to be." In sum, Rogers' dismissal of Wright's brother Milam in December 1901, followed by two men Wright liked in March 1902, and then Wright's cousin and erstwhile partner Taylor during May 1902, while Burwell was retained, must have had an effect on Wright.[45]

Wright in late April 1902 returned to Laredo, where he told Rogers that he might enter the race for sheriff in Wilson County. Rogers said that was fine but reminded him that as a Ranger he could not campaign actively. To do that, he would have to resign. Wright decided to stay in the service until the first day of September, when he would go home and "Enter the campaign propper [*sic*]." Scurry agreed with Rogers, instructing Wright not to announce his candidacy while he was a Ranger. While there is no evidence that Wright violated these instructions, he did accompany Rogers to the annual meeting of the Sheriffs' Association of Texas for the first time in July 1902. And in August, Scurry got an angry letter from Texas Democratic legislator John Nance Garner, who was making his first bid for a seat in Congress. The politico complained that Wright and DuBose were campaigning in favor of his opponent, John C. Scott, a Republican. Too, he had heard that Wright was running for sheriff in Wilson County as an "independent candidate" against the Democratic incumbent, James J. Heathcock. Garner exploded, "I do object most strenuously to men getting out and making an active fight against the Democratic nominees, when they are drawing their salaries and their daily subsistence by reason of

Democratic appointments." Wright's colleague Jim Moore then got a threatening note from the president of the "Garner Democratic Club," Billy Old, who declared that if Moore did not cease his opposition to the election of Levi Old as district attorney in Garner's home county of Uvalde, he would see that Moore was fired. But Garner had earlier urged the abolition of the Rangers, and Old had made his distaste for Rogers well known, so their words had little impact. Rogers wrote to Scurry after an investigation that DuBose definitely was not involved in politics, while Old with his threats against Moore was engaged in "child's play." As for Wright, who in fact favored Garner in the race for Congress, he had made no formal announcement, and he would not until September 1902.[46]

Company C had just six men in the summer of 1902—Captain Rogers, Sergeant DuBose, Burwell, Moore, Wright, and Sandherr—so they shuttled from task to task. Rogers sent Wright in May to join United States Customs Service officers in patrolling the border in Starr, Zapata, and McMullen counties, looking for rustlers and smugglers. Wright spent part of June with Sheriff Avant in Atascosa County, again looking for rustlers. In July he went to Guadalupe County at the request of Sheriff William Duke to investigate "several burglary cases" and a murder. Duke wrote to Scurry that Wright "can do more good here now than any man in Texas," adding, "He was raised here, and his knowledge of Mexicans will be of great service if we can get him." Wright apparently did well; Guadalupe County Judge Ferdinand C. Weinert thanked Scurry for sending him, explaining that local "depredations," which included fence cutting at the Judge's place, had declined despite divisions among local law enforcement officers that reduced their "usefulness." Wright on his own behalf reported that there was "much to do," especially since "The officers are against each other and the sheriff is drunk all the time." Regarding the Mexicans in Guadalupe County, they had "stood the officers off the day before I arrived." They remained "very dangerous as these officers have let them run over them so much, but up to date I haven't had any trouble myself." Despite the indications of impending violence, the only arrests Wright made were for burglary.[47]

Wright resigned effective September 1, 1902, to try to become the sheriff of Wilson County.[48] But instead of campaigning as just a former deputy, he now had a reputation as a respected Texas Ranger known not only for his ability with a gun, but also his skills in investigation and independent leadership. He had been in gunfights, but he had also shown that he could defuse situations and avoid violence. He had learned some hard lessons in Texas politics as well, to which he would add during his next fifteen years as a sheriff. He submitted no grand letter of resignation with ringing statements concerning the law and such; after all, captains might write letters when they left the Rangers, but privates rarely did, and even fewer ever read them. Instead, he could take some reassurance that as he moved into the next chapter of his life, he had certainly earned his pay as a Ranger, and the experience had prepared him to be a better sheriff.

Chapter 3

Sheriff, 1902–1910

William L. Wright left the Texas Rangers in 1902 to become the sheriff of Wilson County, where he had previously served as a deputy sheriff and his mother and other relatives still lived. Rangers had a lot of autonomy and status, but so did Texas sheriffs, and the latter could make more money. Wright did well as sheriff, serving longer than any previous lawman in the history of Wilson County. He investigated a variety of crimes, some of which he could not have anticipated, and earned a reputation as a persistent, diligent, and fair-minded peace officer, just as his former Ranger commander, John H. Rogers, advised him to be. He did not solve every case in his jurisdiction, nor did he apprehend every lawbreaker, and this certainly may have worried him by 1910, when he approached the end of his fourth term as sheriff. But the Ranger Force remained understaffed and underpaid, and he was bypassed in the appointment of a new captain, so he continued to serve as a sheriff, adding to his credentials and his reputation as a lawman who earned his pay as he watched for a good opportunity to rejoin the Rangers, like so many others in his family.

Wright became the sheriff of Wilson County by defeating the incumbent, James J. Heathcock, in the November 1902 election. A native of Sutherland

Springs, Heathcock had served as a deputy under two previous sheriffs, John S. Craighead and Manuel J. Ximenes, and he rode with Wright, Ximenes, and others in the pursuit of Gregorio Cortez Lira during June 1901. According to Wright's son, Emanuel A. "Dogie" Wright, angry Wilson County residents asked his father to run after local Democrats nominated Heathcock for reelection after a "heated" contest. Wright had begun seriously considering the position in the fall of 1901 according to a letter about the difficulties he was facing written by his wife, Mary Ann "Mollie" Brown Wright, to his mother, Ann Elizabeth Tumlinson Wright. But as a Ranger he could not campaign for an elected office, so he had to settle for entering the race late as an independent against Heathcock, who worked hard to keep his badge. When Democratic legislator John Nance Garner came to Floresville in mid-September 1902 to debate his Republican opponent in the race for Congress, John C. Scott, Heathcock served as the marshal for a local parade organized to honor Garner, while Ximenes carried the Democratic banner in the long procession. That same month, Wright resigned from Rogers' company to return to Wilson County and focus on the election, which he won handily. In her 1901 note to her mother-in-law expressing concern about her husband campaigning for sheriff, Mollie had also declared, "If Will could ever get the office I think he could hold it and it would be a good thing for us." Apparently, many others agreed; it was the first of eight electoral victories for Wright in Wilson County, where he served a total of fifteen years as sheriff.[1]

Wright recalled that when he became sheriff, Rogers telegraphed him, instructing him to be a "Ranger sheriff, acting impartially without regard to nationality, color, or wealth." Wright did not issue a manifesto about his intentions, and Wilson County did not harbor any prominent criminal activities. His shift in careers was perhaps prompted by unhappiness over who was dismissed from Ranger service and who remained, but it was also motivated by his financial and family circumstances. He well knew the difficulties of living on a Ranger's salary—he and Mollie, probably to help support themselves and their three children, let Thomas C. "Creed" Taylor and Wright's brother Milam board with them in Laredo. The Wrights certainly anticipated having more children, and while he was sheriff, they added two more sons to their family. Wright's mother also came to live with them after the death of her own mother, Rebecca Elizabeth Newman Tumlinson, in 1906 at Sutherland Springs, where both lived with Wright's brother-in-law, Charles P. Warren, a widower with two children to raise since the death of his wife, Zora Lee Wright Warren, in 1898. Wright could see that, because of legislative parsimony and the longevity of senior Rangers, he had little opportunity to become a captain anytime soon, so he would probably be making fifty dollars a month as a private for a long time. Sheriffs, on the other hand, earned a mixture of both salary and fees, including per diems for prisoners, fees for serving papers and making arrests, and mileage. A hard-working sheriff could make about three hundred dollars a month, depending on the number of people in his county and how they behaved. The popular support for Wright throughout his tenure as sheriff indicates that he did not take undue advantage of the system, nor was he accused of being corrupt, but he certainly made more money as a "Ranger sheriff," as Rogers called him, than he did as a Ranger private.[2]

One benefit, such as it was, of being sheriff was that Wright and his family lived in the Floresville jail. Built in the 1880s, the white brick two-story building had quarters for them in the front, two rooms upstairs and two downstairs, with cells for prisoners in the back. The living quarters were quite small—as Wright and his wife Mollie had more children, some of them slept on pallets because there were not enough beds. And since his mother later lived with them, there was even less space for everyone. For prisoners, the upper two floors had three cells each in the center of a large room, with a walkway all around. These cells were inside a cage, with a hallway along one side to provide access to each interior division. There were additional small cells flanking the stairs that led to each upper level. During the day, inmates could roam the area, but at night the jailer would lock them in the cells. Prisoners were brought into the jail on the lower floor, down a hallway between the two rooms used by the family. The hall led through a "steel door" into an area known as the "runaround," from which several small cells could be accessed. Sometimes troublesome inmates would be chained to a large pillar that stood in the runaround, at least until they quit being a problem. King George Wiley, a resident of Nockenut whose grandfather fought at San Jacinto and whose father was a Confederate veteran, had to be shackled like this. Later, when Wright was helping John V. Blake, the county doctor, tend to an injured Mexican prisoner in a cell off the runaround, Wiley slipped up behind the sheriff and asked when he would be unchained. When Wright did not answer, Wiley attacked him, and a battle ensued. It took both Wright and Blake to subdue him. Despite this incident, Wright's son Dogie recalled that life was usually quiet in the jail, and even Wiley eventually had his chains removed and lived to be a very old, and free, man.[3]

Wright as sheriff had a long roster of deputies, both paid and unpaid, especially in towns distant from Floresville, the county seat. Because he often could not pay them much [and apparently not all of the eight districts in Wilson County always had a constable], he recruited what were known as "pistol deputies:" volunteers that could provide information and intervene if needed. Such officers were not unusual in this period; like the unpaid Special Rangers in state service, they volunteered for prestige, adventure, the right to carry a sidearm, or as part of their business if what they did required security. In the early twentieth century, Texas deputies, like sheriffs, had no formal training, but Wright remained in the field much of the time to provide support. There was usually an official jailer for county jails, and Wright apparently had several, while bailiffs worked when the state district court was in session. If the number of witnesses to be summoned was more than bailiffs or constables could handle, Wright drafted his sons to deliver subpoenas. During his first four terms as sheriff, Wright's known deputies included his brother Milam H. Wright; Andres F. Trevino, whose father Lorenzo had served as the Wilson County sheriff in 1868; Nemencio R. de la Zerda, the only deputy identified as such in the federal census; James P. N. "Pat" Craighead, the son of former sheriff John S. Craighead; George A. Monkhouse, a Floresville banker and rancher; William B. "Will" Clements, a farmer and constable in Stockdale; Thad J. Rees, a rancher who like Wright had trailed cattle north during the era of the long drives; and Alfred B. "Burt" Carnes, who served several terms as a constable at Floresville. Both Trevino and de la Zerda apparently worked only a few years for Wright, and Milam Wright and Craighead became Rangers in 1904 and 1910 respectively, but Monkhouse, Rees, Clements, and Carnes stayed with

Wright through most of his time as sheriff, and Carnes succeeded him in that office.[4]

Because Wright traveled a lot, and again had little money to pay staff, his wife Mollie often served as his chief deputy. She tended the jail and fielded communications while also raising her large family that eventually included five children. Sometimes she would put one of their boys on a horse and send him to find a deputy or his father to "handle a situation." She always had a large pot of hot water on the woodstove on Saturday nights, because it was not unusual for a wounded prisoner, sometimes "cut up or shot up," to be brought in, and Blake would want lots of hot water to tend them. There were even times when her sons had to help the doctor with his work. As each boy became old enough, which Dogie recalled as being ten years of age, they also took turns helping her feed the inmates. An article in the *Floresville Chronicle Journal* heaped praise on Mollie at the time of Wright's departure from Wilson County in early 1918. The writer declared that "She was the best sheriff Wilson County ever had, and we regret to see her retire to other fields. For fifteen years she sat at headquarters with her steady nerve and never-failing judgment directing the machinery of that office." He explained that Mollie produced accurate records, made sure that tasks were done, fed the prisoners (for whom she cooked, like many wives of sheriffs at that time), safeguarded evidence and property, dispatched deputies when Wright was absent, and kept her husband's personal affairs in order. And she patiently did all that without complaining.[5]

Sometimes Mollie surprised her husband with how pragmatic, or even callous, she could be. Luke Davis was an African American who occasionally helped with tasks around the jail, like cleaning the yard. He was a "real landmark guy and a great character" who "hung around the saloons" and helped clean them as well, according to Dogie. Once Wright went to a German dance at Poth in a buggy and came home with a bottle of whiskey in the back. When questioned by his wife, he claimed it was not his, and that he did not know who had put it there. She told him not to drink it because it might be poisoned, but she did not throw it away. Sometime later, Davis was tending the jail yard, and she asked him if he wanted a drink. He did, and she gave him one from that bottle. When it appeared to do no harm, she gave him several more, all with no toxic result. When she informed her husband later that she had decided that it would be alright for him to drink from the bottle, and he asked why she had changed her mind, he was astounded at her explanation of what she had done to Davis. Dogie added in recounting the story, "But that's the way my mother was, I don't know."[6]

Serving as the sheriff of Wilson County proved to be good training for Wright as a future Ranger captain. While it certainly had less crime than more urban areas, Wright coped with a lot of criminals. There were of course many petty incidents that resulted in a small fine or a few days in the local jail, or both, but he also confronted some serious culprits. During his fifteen years as sheriff, Wright arrested fifty-three men who were sent to the state penitentiary at Huntsville. Of these, eighteen committed violent crimes: murder (first and second degree), manslaughter, attempted murder, and assault with intent to murder, as well as rape and assault with intent to rape. Nonviolent criminals sentenced to the state prison included a bail jumper, burglars, forgers, and men who had stolen everything from personal goods to hogs and cattle. Keeping in mind the advice of Rogers to enforce the law without regard to race, it is interesting to note that sixteen of the men Wright sent to Huntsville were white, thirteen were African American, twelve were Mexican, and eleven were Tejano (Mexican descent but born in Texas). These figures do not match the profile of the growing population of Wilson County, which grew by 24% from 1900 to 1920 (the two decades during which Wright served as sheriff). For example, the African American portion declined, from 8% to 4.4% of the total, while the Mexican-born proportion increased to 9.6%. But in assessing bias in Wright's law enforcement efforts, it has to be noted that about a third of the men he sent to the state prison committed violent crimes, and fifteen of those eighteen were African Americans, Mexicans, or Tejanos. Too, stealing items such as livestock was much more likely in the lower economic strata of rural Texas, where most African Americans and Hispanics, regardless of nativity, were trapped during the Jim Crow era. This becomes clear when one considers the jobs of the men who went to Huntsville. Twenty-three of them were laborers, or almost half. Of the rest, fifteen were farmers, two were "cowboys," two had no employment, one was a soldier, and ten had a trade (four carpenters, two barbers, a boilermaker, a cook, a tailor, and a teacher). The most significant change in crime during Wright's tenure as sheriff was a slight increase in violence during his last three years, which may have contributed to his decision to return to Ranger service. In sum, as sheriff he coped with a growing population that contained a variety of criminals, and there is little evidence that he failed to follow Rogers' advice.[7]

If Wright thought that serving as sheriff of Wilson County would be less harrowing than the life of a Ranger on the Rio Grande border, he proved to be only partly correct. There were long periods of time when he dealt with nonviolent matters, but violent crimes always interrupted these interludes. He had only been in office for five months when Marguerito Reyna, a twenty-eight-year-old native of Mexico who moved to Wilson County in 1902, raped Monica Arredondo, the seven-year-old daughter of a woman with whom he was living near Stockdale. Reyna threatened to kill them if anyone notified the authorities, but the mother did just that. Wright captured Reyna within a few days, then took him to Hallettsville, where the state criminal court for his district was in session. By the end of the month, a jury convicted Reyna and, after deliberating just ten minutes, sentenced him to death. After his appeal was denied by the Texas Court of Criminal Appeals, Reyna caused a public sensation in June 1903 when he escaped from the jail in Hallettsville, but he was recaptured. His attorney took petitions for clemency to Governor Samuel W. T. Lanham from three Texas counties where Reyna had lived—Wilson, Live Oak, and Duval—as well as one from Lavaca County, where he had been convicted, but Lanham declined to commute Reyna's sentence to life in prison. He was hanged at the Hallettsville jail in December 1903 by Sheriff A. B. "Ted" Noble, after once more declaring that he was innocent. Wright did not attend the execution.[8]

Rape cases periodically resurfaced throughout Wright's time as sheriff. In late May 1905, the sixteen-year-old daughter of Jesus Cadena reported that she had been sexually assaulted by an African American man while working in a field near her parents' home at Labatt, a railroad town, six miles north of Floresville. Wright assembled a team of four other men to pursue the suspect: constables Carnes of Floresville and J. B. "Jake" Tolleson of Sutherland Springs, Green Glass, and Perry A. Sammons, a farmer. The culprit fled the area, and they chased him through the night; the following day, when he appeared to be going in the direction of Bexar County, Sheriff John W. Tobin joined the pursuit. Tobin was the grandson of Alamo courier John W. Smith and the son of William G. Tobin, a well-known Ranger captain during the nineteenth century, so it would have been a perfect ending to the story if he had caught the fugitive, but instead it was Wright and his men who captured him ten miles north of Sutherland Springs. He proved to be Tom Bradley, of Karnes County, and he admitted his guilt. Convicted on June 22, 1905, he was sentenced to ninety-nine years in the state penitentiary.[9]

Wright played only a peripheral role in a more violent rape case that came to a grim conclusion at Cuero, near where he was raised in DeWitt County. Henry "Monk" Gibson, a sixteen-year-old black field hand working for Joseph F. Conditt at his farm in Jackson County, committed a particularly heinous crime in September 1905. He and Felix Powell, a thirty-year-old black field hand, used a crowbar and knife to kill Conditt's wife, daughter, and three of his four sons after raping the women. Conditt was absent and survived, as did his youngest son, whom the killers spared because he was only ten months old and thus could not be a witness. Lawmen, worried that they could not stop a lynch mob, arranged for Gibson's transfer to the jail in Halletsville, but he escaped and remained at large for nine days. After an intense manhunt by Rangers, local law enforcement officers, and several companies of militia, Gibson was found by a civilian and returned to custody. His attorney secured a change of venue for him to San Antonio, where Wright and his brother Milam were among the law officers assigned to provide security for him. After the San Antonio jury failed to reach a verdict, the trial was moved to Cuero, where Gibson was convicted. He was executed on June 28, 1908, with the same rope that had been used to dispatch Powell. The latter, who insisted on being tried separately from Gibson, had been convicted at Victoria and hanged on April 2, 1907.[10]

Wright had to investigate two rape cases in 1906. In April, he arrested Melchior Ximenes, a twenty-six-year-old Tejano laborer, at Labatt, six miles north of Floresville, for attempting to assault a sixteen-year-old Mexican girl. When she screamed, her younger brother ran to defend her. Ximenes chased the boy away with a knife and then fled. He was convicted in mid-May 1906 and sentenced to five years in the state penitentiary system. He served for a little more than fifty-one months and was discharged, and he may have been arrested again in Wilson County by Wright or one of his deputies. During December 1911 one Melchior Ximenes, described as a thirty-three-year-old Tejano farmer, was convicted of burglary and sent to the state penitentiary for two years. Meanwhile, during the fall of 1906, Elojio Estrada, a twenty-eight-year-old Mexican barber, was convicted of rape and served almost eight years of a ten-year sentence in the Texas prison system.[11]

Wright in the summer of 1909 hanged the only prisoner executed in Wilson County while he was sheriff, and he almost died in the process. Refugio Jaureque, a twenty-five-year-old Brownsville native, raped, beat, and stabbed fifteen-year-old Albina Olenick on July 2, 1908. She was walking home alone from Sutherland Springs when Jaureque dragged her through a wire fence into the brush, assaulted her, stabbed her three times, and then kicked several of her teeth loose before leaving her for dead. After nightfall, she crawled home with the knife protruding from her chest. The crime was even more horrific because she had met Jaureque several times, knew him well enough to use his nickname, "Coo-Coo," and that day had helped him buy medicine in Sutherland Springs because he did not speak English well. He attacked her as she approached his campsite alongside the road to her home. When she arrived at her house, apparently dying, and told her parents that Coo-Coo had done this, her father walked to Sutherland Springs and telephoned Wright, who arrived at one in the morning and made an arrest just three hours later. The next afternoon Wright went to the Olenick house with three deputies, County Attorney Claude A. Cone, and Jaureque, whom Albina identified as her attacker. Meanwhile, a mob gathered at Sutherland Springs. When the sheriff came into town with his prisoner and commandeered a wagon for the trip to Floresville, a large angry crowd, allegedly led by one of Wright's pistol deputies, blocked his exit and demanded the surrender of Jaureque. Standing in the back of the wagon, Wright had to knock his pistol deputy unconscious with the barrel of his rifle as a fight erupted. Suddenly his brother-in-law, Gratz D. Brown, who had served as a Ranger in Rogers' company with Wright, climbed into the wagon with his Winchester. Together, they delivered Jaureque to the jail in Floresville.[12]

Jaureque was quickly indicted, and a district court jury convicted him and sentenced him to hang. An appeal to the Texas Criminal Court of Appeals resulted in an affirmation of his verdict and sentence, while pleas for clemency to the Board of Pardon Advisors and Governor Thomas M. Campbell were also denied. Wright did not want to hang Jaureque, "and the matter bothered him more and more as the day for the event approached." Facing the inevitable, he did everything he could to ensure that the execution went as smoothly as possible. The trap door for the gallows area at the top of the stairs inside the Floresville jail did not work well. Wright modified it by installing a new trap door and cutting a second hole in the floor below, making the fatal drop much longer. The rope for hanging Jaureque was provided by Sheriff Jesse B. Farris of DeWitt County, who told a reporter later that it was the same rope used to execute Monk Gibson. It in fact had been used for several hangings, but Wright stretched it again by tying a sandbag to it and dropping it repeatedly through the new trap door in his improved gallows inside the jail. His young sons ghoulishly enjoyed this part of their father's careful preparations, pulling the lever over and over.[13]

When the day finally came to hang Jaureque, June 11, 1909, Wright sent his wife Mollie and their children to Sutherland Springs, to keep them away from the event and the crowd. He may well have remembered the chaos surrounding the execution of the only other prisoner hanged in Wilson County, Maximo Martinez, who committed an even more heinous crime when Wright was a deputy. Wright took his place on the gallows platform with his brother Milam, sheriffs Farris of DeWitt County and Eli C. Seale of Karnes County, and Constable John E. Trainer of San Antonio. Executing a man was a difficult matter, and lawmen worked together on such days to support each other. Wright had assisted Farris in several hangings, and Farris returned the favor by joining him at Floresville in June 1909. When Wright attempted to put a black hood over Jaureque's head, as was customary, the prisoner protested and asked for his brother to be allowed to shake his hand. After this was done, Wright stepped forward with the hood raised only to be stabbed in the chest by Jaureque with a sharpened spoon. Fortunately for the sheriff, he suffered only a "slight cut" because the weapon was so flimsy that it was deflected by one of his ribs. With blood staining his shirtfront, Wright helped subdue Jaureque, who abandoned his previously cheerful manner and fought furiously, kicking, biting, and scratching his executioners. After the prisoner had finally been secured and hooded, Wright left the gallows area with Blake, the county doctor. Rather than accept his fate, Jaureque refused to stand upright, then flung himself across the opening when Milam Wright pulled the lever, thus stopping his descent. Retrieved and held erect on the center of the trap door, he dropped straight down when it opened but strangled for a long time. Blake pronounced him dead after he hung for thirty minutes.[14]

Wright as sheriff also investigated a series of murders in Wilson County. His first came during the late spring of 1903, when he arrested Joseph Clark, a forty-three-year-old Anglo farmer born in Texas, for second-degree murder. Convicted on June 26 by the state district court and sentenced to fifteen years in the Texas penitentiary system, which was affirmed in October 1903, Clark served less than two years before he was pardoned on May 27, 1905. After M. Hernandez was stabbed at a dance near Stockdale in late October 1906, Wright with Deputy Andres Trevino arrested Francis Hernandez for the assault, which may have been fatal. Nothing more has been found about a disposition in the Hernandez case, and the same is true about Stephen Pantola, who bashed Refugio Reifefo in the head with a "cordwood standard" at a ranch near Stockdale in December 1906, killing him. Pantola immediately telephoned Wright and confessed, asking the sheriff to come get him. Justice of the Peace William H. King set his bail at $500 after he pled self-defense. During January 1907, two convicts arrived at the state prison in Huntsville from Wilson County, but they were not Hernandez and Pantola. One was Tomas Reyes, a twenty-five-year-old Tejano farmer who had been sentenced to two years in the prison system for manslaughter. He served almost twenty-three months. The other man was Clemente Garcia, a thirty-six-year-old Mexican laborer who had been convicted of murder and received a life sentence. He was pardoned by Governor James E. "Pa" Ferguson in June 1917.[15]

Murder cases often proved to be among the most difficult for Wright to solve. Nasario Palacios in May 1905 stabbed another Mexican and fled to Mexico, settling in Guerrero. Almost six years later, in February 1911,

Constable Serapio Gonzalez of San Ygnacio, a town south of Laredo on the Rio Grande in Zapata County, contacted Wright and said he had seen Palacios at a ranch near Aguilares, about thirty-five miles east of Laredo. Gonzalez sent his brother to watch Palacios while Wright caught a train to Laredo, where he convinced two U.S. Customs Service officers, Samuel V. "Pete" Edwards Jr. and Robert S. "Bob" Rumsey Jr., to accompany him to Aguilares. Edwards was a former Ranger who had joined the federal service in 1898 after serving as the sheriff of La Salle County; about Rumsey, another ex-Ranger who was shot dead by Mexican smugglers in the summer of 1922, Wright later declared, "There will never be another border officer as efficient in his territory as Bob Rumsey. They do not make but one like him in each world." The three Anglos were not the heroes that day, however. When Palacios attempted to run as they approached the ranch house in February 1911, Gonzalez's brother grabbed the fugitive and held him until the three lawmen could handcuff their prisoner and take him into custody. Nothing more about Palacios has been found.[16]

Wright got a chance to work with several Rangers, including his brother Milam, in the summer of 1905, but ironically it became one of the most frustrating murder cases of his tenure as the sheriff of Wilson County. In late August, Placido Garza was shot to death by a man known only as Juan Garcia at a dance ten miles from Floresville. Wright, with Alfred Carnes, tracked the killer through the brush for twenty-five miles before losing him. Almost two weeks later a man who claimed to be Garcia's nephew came to Wilson County and departed with Garcia's wife. Wright contacted Constable Charles F. Stevens of San Antonio, who discovered that the pair had boarded a train in San Antonio that was traveling to Laredo. Wright also hurried by rail to Laredo, where he was joined by Sheriff William T. Hill of La Salle County and four Texas Rangers—his brother Milam and Sgt. Tom M. Ross of Captain John R. Hughes' company, and Manoah G. "Blaze" Delling and Louis E. Flach of Captain William J. McDonald's company. There Wright learned that his fugitive was in fact Dionicio Martinez, a well-known Mexican bandit with several murder indictments in Texas. More important, Martinez had been spotted at a local ranch, so Wright was close to his quarry.[17]

Rangers Delling and Flach were the first to arrive in Laredo. Approaching the ranch on Tordillo Creek where they understood Martinez was hiding, they were peppered with rifle fire from two men hiding inside a *jacal*. Returning fire, Delling killed one shooter but the other escaped across the Rio Grande after Flach either missed him entirely or only slightly wounded him. Inquiries revealed the dead man was Jose Martinez, who had recently escaped from prison in Mexico, while the escapee was his uncle Dionicio. The Texans could not pursue the fugitive into Mexico without official permission, and Mexican authorities would do nothing despite their promises of assistance. Reinforced by Milam and Sergeant Ross, Wright secured an agreement with Mexican *rurales* to flush Martinez from a hiding place in another nearby *jacal* and chase him toward the river. There the Texans would be waiting for him on a muddy island in midstream and could easily grab him, or so Wright thought. The plan unraveled when one of the small boats being paddled by the Texans flipped, dumping Milam and Flach into the chilly water and causing them to lose their hats and rifles. Then the *rurales* arrived empty-handed, explaining that their intended target could not be found. Angry, puzzled, and disappointed, Wright canceled the pursuit after a month in the field and went home. His comrades scattered to their assigned posts.[18]

Wright refused to quit chasing Martinez. Soon after arriving home he left again, going to Austin to ask Governor Lanham for a "requisition" to extradite the fugitive from Mexico. With this document in hand, Wright returned to the border in October 1905 with "several deputies," expecting a gun battle. He did not get in a fight, but he also did not capture Martinez. In February 1909, he told a newspaper reporter that the fugitive, who remained at large, was the "only living real bad Texas outlaw." He added that Martinez was wanted for nine murders in Mexico and at least seven in Texas after twenty-five years of crimes that also included cattle rustling. Furthermore, according to Wright, Martinez had been in gun battles with Texas law officers no less than seven times, had six of his comrades shot and two horses killed, and had been wounded but never captured. Perhaps recounting what happened when he got a requisition from Lanham, Wright talked about a time when he thought he had Martinez trapped on an island in the Rio Grande near Palafox, Texas, upstream from Laredo. He had seven *rurales* positioned on their side of the river with Wright and Sheriff Hill of La Salle County and a deputy from Webb County on the Texas riverbank. Growing impatient, Wright and his comrades decided to cross on horseback to the island. They became trapped in the mud and were considering their plight when Wright noticed six men with rifles advancing under the cover of rocks at the base of a cliff on the Texas side. Not wanting to abandon their horses, the Texans remained in their saddles, hoping the men, who were clearly stalking them, would make a mistake by leaving their cover to attack. The tension broke when the six gunmen revealed themselves to be Rangers. Having heard Martinez was nearby, they were convinced that the riders trapped in the riverbed were their quarry. To the great relief of both sides, they had realized the horsemen were Americans, so there was a happy ending. Together the Texan lawmen found a way onto the island, only to discover no trace of Martinez.[19]

Wright believed he had Martinez in 1911. He discovered that his man was staying at a ranch in Mexico near Nuevo Laredo owned by Amador Sánchez, the longtime political boss and mayor of Laredo who had been appointed sheriff of Webb County in 1910. Mexican authorities arrested the fugitive on the last day of January 1911, and his extradition was ordered in June. Wright hurried south again with a deputy and crossed into Mexico with District Attorney John A. Valls of Webb County, only to be told by Mexican officials that Martinez had filed a writ of habeas corpus and would not be released, despite his indictment for the murder of Garza in Wilson County. Governor Oscar B. Colquitt, who had instructed Wright to retrieve Martinez, contacted authorities on both sides of the border, and Ambassador Henry Lane Wilson made a "thorough investigation," but to no avail. Apparently, Governor Espiridión Lara of Tamaulipas ordered the officials in Nuevo Laredo to transfer Martinez to Wright, but they refused to comply, creating a legal conflict that could only be resolved by the Supreme Court of Mexico. Matters became even more complicated when Sánchez was arrested by U.S. authorities for violating neutrality laws by supporting the insurgency of Gen. Bernardo Reyes. Once again, Wright returned home empty-handed. Martinez brought his history with Wright to a close in January 1914, when he escaped from the Nuevo Laredo jail, as he allegedly had done from several other places where he was incarcerated.[20]

Reports of Martinez's death in late 1927 sparked reflections on his long career along the border. He had first appeared in Texas newspapers in the late 1890s when he killed a rancher in north Mexico and eluded *rurales* by hiding in a network of old mine shafts, whence he ambushed Mexican lawmen at least once before escaping. *Rurales* later surrounded him in a shack on a ranch near Colombio, on the Mexican side of the Rio Grande, but again he escaped. He later shot a Mexican in Texas, wounding him badly, which brought him to the attention of the Rangers. Wright's story about chasing him gained an amendment: Martinez killed his wife after getting her out of Wilson County, believing she knew who he really was and would betray him. Wright's pursuit to the border, along with the fight with Delling and Flach at the ranch on Tordillo Creek, was also amended to add that the nephew killed there was also guilty of several murders. Martinez had later become a captain in a military organization allied with Venustiano Carranza and earned a pardon for his service, but old habits resurfaced, and he had to flee after charges were issued for robberies. He continued to raid in northern Mexico and often traveled to Nuevo Laredo, whence he would send messages to Delling, who had become a federal officer, that he would get him for killing his nephew. The report of his death explained that Mexican soldiers caught and killed him and others in the mountains.[21]

While chasing the elusive Martinez occupied a lot of Wright's time, it was certainly not his last murder case. Louis Gibson, an African American resident of La Vernia, killed his mother-in-law and sister-in-law, Bettie and Cora Taylor, in November 1907 and fled, pursued by Wright. Gibson had a strange history with his victims. Bettie may well have arranged her daughter Stella's marriage without the full consent of the groom; allegedly on his wedding day Gibson suddenly pulled a pistol, fired in the air several times, and tried to run away, "shouting that someone was trying to kill him." Brought back, he was forced to complete the ceremony. Gibson ran away from Stella several times since but always returned. He also had a "shooting affray" with a male relative, Allie Taylor, several years earlier, and Taylor spent almost two years in the state penitentiary after being arrested by Wright and convicted of "assault to murder." Gibson did not go to jail for that altercation or for another in which he stabbed another man. He killed Bettie with an axe, nearly decapitating her, while he slashed 15-year-old Cora's throat with a pocket knife and smashed her head with a rock. Joe Morgan, who was also an African American, helped Wright track Gibson. They almost captured him after discovering that he was sleeping in a corn crib at a local farm, but an "unfortunate and unlooked for accident" thwarted their efforts. On December 2, the day after the two victims were buried in the cemetery at Cruse Colony, where they had lived, Morgan led an African American posse to La Vernia. There they found Gibson hiding in the brush, just as Wright, who was not with them, suspected he would be. When Gibson ran, the posse began shooting. Hit in the "bowels," the fugitive tried to swim across a creek but was shot once more in the leg. His pursuers saved him from drowning, but he was mortally wounded. Placed on a makeshift litter by his captors, who intended to take him to the jail in La Vernia, he died before they arrived at their destination.[22]

Wright almost had to execute another man in Wilson County when Dr. J. D. Becton shot his son-in-law, Albert Toombs, to death in a field near La Vernia during the first week of September 1908. The two men had argued previously, but this time a shotgun blast in the stomach killed Toombs. The killer fled, but Wright retrieved him within a few days and brought him back to Wilson County. Indicted, but with apparently no money to post a bond and left on his own by a wife who had filed for divorce, Becton was awaiting trial in the Floresville jail when he became seriously ill. Transported to the Physicians and Surgeons Hospital in San Antonio by Wright, Becton died during surgery in the first week of December 1908. Wright, who had brought Becton to San Antonio as a prisoner, had to care for the body because no relative stepped forward during the next few weeks to claim it. The sheriff spent that Christmas at his usual place to stay in San Antonio, the Southern Hotel, before Becton was finally interred.[23]

Sometimes the best of intentions led to a violent end. Moses Brooks, a black man in La Vernia, began hosting "festivals" at his home, charging a nominal admission fee. In September 1910, a fight erupted between three people at one of his events—Annie Simmons, her mother Mollie Mitchell, and William Haywood. When Brooks tried to intervene, one of them stabbed him to death. Wright arrested the trio with the assistance of two of his deputies, Will Clements and Thad Rees. Both Simmons and Haywood were held without bond, while Mitchell failed to raise her assigned bail of $1,000. All three were taken to the jail in Floresville, whence at least Simmons was apparently released because she was arrested again at San Antonio in May 1911 by Wright and Bexar County Deputy Sheriff Alfonso Newton Jr. on an indictment for murdering Brooks. She was once more taken to the Floresville jail, but nothing more about this case has been found.[24]

Wright was meticulous in his investigations, and he tried to correct mistakes. In November 1906 an elderly former slave in Wilson County was beaten and robbed by two African American employees of the itinerant Van Amburg circus, which had performed in Floresville. Wright learned that the two had approached David Powell at his home, told him that they were leaving the circus, and asked if they could stay with him for the night. He agreed, and then fell asleep when they went outside. He awoke covered in blood from head wounds, alone in his bed, and robbed of six dollars, all the money he had. Two men were taken off the circus train at Kerrville, Taylor Reese and Dennis Richards, and Powell declared they were the ones who robbed him, which was corroborated by two other witnesses. They were convicted of robbery and sentenced to five years, despite their declarations of innocence and Wright's belief that they were telling the truth. In January 1907 Houston detectives Bob McFarlane and Frank Smith were assigned to investigate reports that two African Americans employed by the Van Amburg circus, then in town, had been involved in a bloody robbery. They arrested Oscar Smith and John Taylor, then invited Wright to Houston. After hearing Wright's description of the earlier crime, the Houston lawmen knew they had the right culprits for both robberies, and they arranged for the men to confess with a notary public and stenographer present. Wright was pleased and told a newspaper reporter that every effort would be made to secure the release of Reese and Richards. To his dismay, the two prisoners appealed their convictions in April 1907, but the Texas Court of Criminal Appeals affirmed their sentences. Wright carried a request for pardons for both men, endorsed by the Wilson County district attorney and district judge as well as other local officials, to Governor Campbell in May 1907. There is no record of executive action, but there is also no indication that Reese and Richards arrived at the state penitentiary. In the meantime, Smith and Taylor, each sentenced to two years, did go to Huntsville, where the former died of injuries suffered in a railroad accident and the latter was discharged in March 1909.[25]

Not every major case for Wright as a sheriff was violent. In March 1906 he had an odd one at Floresville in which he arrested a stranger, W. X. Carter, for trapping and shipping thousands of live wild quail. Texas law, in response to concerns about overhunting, prohibited the gathering of quail except in limited numbers for breeding or scientific study. Constable Stevens in Bexar County had earlier in 1906 arrested Will W. Carter and his son Freeman Carter for the same crime as W. X. Carter. Freeman Carter, who had more than 400 quail with him, had a permit from the Fish and Game Commission of New Jersey to collect quail for breeding, but documents confiscated at the time of the arrests indicated that he and his father had shipped hundreds of quail to a New York merchant, and they also had a contract to send thousands more to companies in Denver and Chicago. Stevens was investigating the New Jersey permits when Wright arrested W. X. Carter and thereby acquired records showing that his prisoner had shipped 2,000 quail. Game law reformers, who had been pressing for effective enforcement for years, sent their attorneys to Floresville to press for a vigorous prosecution, and indeed W. X. Carter, who had no permit from anyone to collect quail, was charged with 400 counts of violating Texas game laws and had to post a $40,000 bail. While the final resolution of his case is not clear, Will and Freeman Carter spent months in jail before being ordered to pay court costs, and then they were released for time served amid a great flurry of indignation among Texas sportsmen and hunters.[26]

One criminal highlight for Wright in the summer of 1907 came when he discovered a cattle-rustling operation at Graytown, a ranching community located about eleven miles northwest from his office in Floresville. Two dozen men, mostly Mexicans, lived there in a compound on the San Antonio River, stealing cattle from Austin to the Rio Grande. They would round up the animals, quickly drive them to their place, butcher them, burn all heads, hides, and offal, and sell the meat, which certainly could not be easily traced to a specific source without a brand. One of the rustlers attracted Wright's attention when he became too reckless, or bold, and sold a hide with a brand rather than destroying it. Wright discovered through his investigation that this criminal ring was well organized and had been operating for at least two years, if not longer. When he and several of his deputies raided the riverside compound, they arrested five men, but Wright told newspaper reporters that he expected to capture those still at large, who numbered about twenty. He tracked these thieves to San Antonio, where he joined Constable Charles F. Stevens in reviewing the inventory of local brokers, many of whom had hides with no legal record of how they were acquired. There is no indication that they made any more arrests, but there also is no evidence that the cattle rustling operation continued at Graytown.[27]

During March 1908 someone blew up two safes in La Vernia with nitroglycerine, wrecking the buildings in each case and stealing about $300. Having blown the doors off each safe, the robber, or robbers, escaped in a buggy, according to the tracks left at each site. The first target was a store that also served as a post office owned by Postmaster Hugo Kott, mail carrier E. C. Reich, and Henry A. Linne. The second was the Wells Fargo Express Building. Since the stolen money included federal funds, the crimes attracted more attention than usual. Wright was at a hospital in San Antonio with relatives but hurried to La Vernia the day after the robberies, joining Ranger Oscar L. Latta in the investigation. Latta had worked with Wright at Junction City in early 1902, when they were both in Rogers' company, and had just rejoined Rogers in January. Also with them was Captain Henry S. Sisk of the Southern Pacific Railroad Company Police Department, a Confederate veteran who had served as the sheriff of Parker County, a U.S. deputy marshal, and an agent for the penitentiary at Huntsville. In May 1908, Constable Stevens of San Antonio arrested two men thought to be partners in blowing safes in the area, including those in La Vernia. The main culprit said his name was Frank Ivanhoe, but he was apparently also known as Jerry Sullivan and "the shadow." He said nothing more, but his partner told others that he assisted him in robbing safes. Wright and others interviewed Ivanhoe, but no one could say with certainty that he was the person seen in La Vernia shortly before the robberies. Joe Allen, a notorious "safeblower," surfaced in San Antonio in December 1908. He eluded sheriffs Wright, Seale, and B. D. Lindsey of Bexar County, who pursued him together, but after he jumped aboard a northbound train, he was captured at Hillsboro by Sheriff Euclid M. Cox, who had gotten a telegram from Lindsey. Whether Wright arrested the right man or not, the blowing of safes in Sutherland Springs at the post office in the fall of 1915 and at a drugstore in the spring of 1917 indicated that he had not solved the problem.[28]

Wright as sheriff also occasionally encountered imaginative, and possibly criminal, frauds. A "fake doctor" came through Wilson County in the fall of 1908, claiming to have a "matchless machine" that would cure a variety of maladies. He rode in an impressive coach drawn by four horses and spoke well. Having swindled people in both Wilson and Karnes counties, he became a person of interest for both sheriffs, Wright and Seale, but they agreed to have him tried first in Wilson County. No record has been found concerning the outcome of his case, but there are no further reports of him in local papers. In the summer of 1909, an interesting character appeared in San Antonio. Calling himself "Two Braids," he said he was Tommy Stringfield, who as a boy in 1870 had seen his parents killed by Indians on the Nueces River and had subsequently been raised as a captive. He claimed that he had been among the Indians led by Geronimo, and his wife was Geronimo's niece. He also said that he had visited President William H. Taft to ask for a pardon. Two Braids and his young daughter, whom he called "Nuck-eye Two Braids," enjoyed more than three months of hospitality in Wilson, Bandera, and McMullen counties from Stringfield relatives and other well-wishers eager to believe he was in fact the lost boy. His story even appeared in the *Brooklyn Daily Eagle*, in New York. For some reason, Wright became suspicious. He wrote to U.S. Representative John Nance Garner, who confirmed that Two Braids had not talked to Taft. Wright also learned that the imposter's real name was O. A. Woodman and that he was a woodcutter from Lawton, Oklahoma whose wife was also white, not Indian. Sheriff Samuel A. Elrod of Lawton, contacted by Wright, traveled to San Antonio and confirmed Two Braids was in fact Woodman, for whom a fraud warrant had been issued in Oklahoma. Elrod may have taken him back to Oklahoma, but by the summer of 1910 Two Braids was performing in a self-produced Wild West show throughout Texas, and the following year he published his story as a slim tract with the Herald Print Company of Hamilton, Texas.[29]

Wright always watched for an opportunity to return to the Texas Rangers as a captain. Two vacancies suddenly appeared in early 1907, when James A. Brooks resigned and William J. McDonald was appointed by Governor Campbell to serve as the state revenue agent. Tax Collector Thomas M. Stell of DeWitt County, who had previously served as sheriff of that county for fourteen years, went to Austin to lobby for Wright, who told everyone that he wanted to be a Ranger captain. Ranchers in South Texas added their support to a grassroots campaign on his behalf. Unfortunately for him, many people apparently also wrote to Campbell asking him not to appoint Wright as a captain because they wanted him to continue as their sheriff. Tom M. Ross, who had joined Wright two years earlier to chase Dionicio Martinez at Laredo, was appointed by Campbell to replace McDonald in January 1907, while the Brooks appointment went to Sheriff Francis N. "Frank" Johnson of Mitchell County. Ross was a grandson of José Antonio Navarro, who signed the first two constitutions of Texas, and had overcome the loss of a leg to remain active in law enforcement, but Johnson was "pretty much a nonentity," according to historians Charles H. Harris III and Louis R. Sadler. Being listed alongside Ross as a top contender for the positions, then losing to someone no one expected, must have been hard on Wright. A writer for the *San Antonio Express* declared that he was just "too popular at home." It may have provided a bit of consolation that when Wright visited three Rangers from Hughes's company—Ross, James C. White, and Desiderio "Jesse" Perez—at the Southern Hotel in early April 1907, the *San Antonio Express* remarked, "This body of men is composed of individuals who are among the best-known fighters in Texas and every one of them has a record of envious deeds of bravery. Every one of them can shoot so quick and so straight that they are respected by every outlaw in Texas."[30]

Wright occasionally got a jarring reminder of the risks of being a Ranger, as did many others in and out of the organization. Ranger Quirl B. Carnes, Cameron County Deputy Sheriff Henry B. "Benny" Lawrence, and John Zoll, who worked for the San Benito Land & Water Company, were three of ten men who attempted to ambush a large raiding party of Mexicans on the night of July 30, 1910, at San Benito, twenty miles northwest of Brownsville. When they challenged some intruders in the brush, a hail of bullets killed Carnes and Lawrence. Zoll emptied his pistol and ran until he found Ranger James P. N. "Pat" Craighead and Cameron County Constable Larkin Earl West, who hurried to confront the raiders who had attacked their comrades. In another furious exchange of gunfire, West was seriously but not mortally wounded when a bullet tore through his right shoulder, while Craighead suffered a wound from friendly fire that required the amputation of his left leg below the knee. It provided scant comfort to the Rangers that at least one of the Mexican raiders, who had been working as an informant for them but whose actual role in the fight was unclear, was also found dead at the scene.[31]

The ambush of the Rangers at San Benito struck close to home for Sheriff Wright. Carnes, just twenty-six years old, had joined Company B, commanded by Ross, in 1908. More important to Wright, he was the younger brother of Alfred B. "Burt" Carnes, one of his most trusted deputies and the lawman who would succeed him as the sheriff of Wilson County. Their brother, Herff A. Carnes, was a sergeant in Captain John R. Hughes' Ranger company, in which Wright's brother Milam served, while the Carnes brothers had a grandfather and brother-in-law, David F. Webb and John E. Gilliland of Wilson County, who had been or would become Rangers. Moreover, at least four of their cousins from Wilson County later served under Wright when he became a Ranger captain: Grenade Donaldson "Don" Gilliland, David Cornelius "Jack" Webb, Grover Cleveland Webb, and Lake Thomas Webb. West's brother was Milton H. West, a young man in Floresville who would later become a Ranger and U.S. congressman. Craighead was the son of former Wilson County sheriff John S. Craighead, for whom Wright worked as a deputy, and he had been a deputy for Wright. Both he and his younger brother Charles A. Craighead had enlisted as Rangers under Hughes, the latter in 1908 and the former a little more than four months before he lost his left leg. Wright hurried with former sheriff Craighead, deputy Carnes, Milton West, Grover Webb and three other men to retrieve the body of Quirl Carnes, comfort Pat Craighead and Earl West, and participate in the ensuing investigation. Adjutant General James O. Newton mobilized the Brownsville Rifles for a manhunt; they were joined by Wright with his Wilson County comrades as well as Herff Carnes, Charles Craighead, and other Rangers. Texas Representative José T. Canales convinced Governor Campbell to offer rewards of $500 apiece for the men who had killed Carnes and Lawrence, but no one was ever arrested for the two murders. Carnes was buried at Floresville and Lawrence at Alice, in Jim Wells County, while Pat Craighead and West remained in law enforcement.[32]

After failing to find the men who ambushed the Rangers on the border, Wright in August 1910 stopped in San Antonio to conduct some business on his way home. About dinner time one night he saw Oscar J. Rountree, a former Ranger who like Wright had served in Rogers' company, and Dennis B. Chapin, a former judge for Hidalgo County, together at the Southern Hotel, where Wright often stayed. Later Wright heard gunshots at Dan Breen's saloon. Hurrying there with policeman W. A. Harvey, he found Chapin standing behind the cigar case. Wright asked him what was happening, and Chapin said he was under arrest for shooting Rountree, but that he had shot the former Ranger only in self-defense. When Wright questioned if this claim was true, Chapin again declared it was and asked Albert Sammons, standing nearby, to corroborate what he said. He also begged Wright to stay because he thought he might need protection, as he had been disarmed when arrested. Wright learned that Rountree, after he resigned from the Rangers, had taken the place of Henry L. Ransom as a bodyguard for Ed Roos, a San Antonio real estate developer who had clashed with Chapin, his former business associate who was developing a town in South Texas that had been named for him. Rountree and Chapin had argued at Breen's place, and a short scuffle ensued that ended with Chapin shooting Rountree in the forehead at close range with a .44 caliber revolver. Rountree was still conscious when he arrived at the hospital, but he expired when the medical staff sedated him for treatment.[33]

Since he had spoken with Chapin at the crime scene, Wright became a witness for the trial that followed. The state district court venue was moved to Victoria to secure a more impartial jury, while Chapin retained Carlos Bee as his counsel. Bee, the son of former Confederate general Hamilton P. Bee and a rising star in Texas political circles, had already served as a district attorney and chair of the state Democratic convention. Wright did not initially attend the trial because he had to tend to some legal matters, nor did Chapin make an appearance. Instead, the latter claimed that he was bedridden with an illness and thus could not testify in his own behalf. Judge John M. Green in May 1911 became angry at the absence of several witnesses, so he fined several of them, including Wright, fifty dollars for failing to appear. He refused to accept Wright's explanation that his own district court, in Floresville, was also in session and a heavy criminal docket kept him away from the Chapin trial. After several more days of delay, arrangements were made for Wright to testify on a Sunday, when the court in Floresville would be adjourned, and Judge Green dismissed the fine against him. Wright testified that Chapin had said that Rountree shot at him and so he had to kill him. After additional testimony during December 1911, Chapin was acquitted, but the residents of the town named for him, which served as the seat of Hidalgo County, decided to call it Edinburg rather than Chapin.[34]

While Wright seriously wanted to become a Ranger again, he also had many always-changing responsibilities as a family man. William Berry "Bill" Wright, his fourth son, was born in April 1905, allegedly in the Floresville jail. He later privately published a small book on his life, in which he recalled that his mother handled most of the daily discipline for her children, and their large menagerie of pets, but his father was always ready to help her. He added drily, "Fortunately for us kids Papa's help was seldom needed." Bill knew well what that meant: once he made the mistake of calling a local merchant a "German SOB," and when the Sheriff learned of this, he chased his son down the street and, in public, administered the "damndest [*sic*] licking I was ever to receive." Five months after his fourth son was born, Wright's mother-in-law, Mary Reynolds Brown, died at Sutherland Springs in November 1905, leaving his father-in-law, Sanford N. Brown, alone at the age of seventy-five, after almost fifty years of marriage. He had eleven grown children, but they were scattered;

Charles B. Brown, for example, was serving on the border with Hughes' Ranger company by 1906. Fortunately for Wright, his father-in-law settled in Seguin with his oldest daughter, Sarah Lucinda Brown Sellingsloh, and her husband Charles, a German Texan who owned a truck farm. Wright lost a living link to his history when his grandmother, Rebecca Elizabeth Newman Tumlinson, the widow of Joseph L. Tumlinson, died in 1906. His son Dogie recalled that he was still very young when she died, but he remembered being "about half scared of her she was so old and wrinkled sat in a rocking chair, with her clay pipe I would go by and she would reach out with her cane and hook me and pull me to her. she [*sic*] knew the Indian language and believe me could tell some scary stories." While Dogie was apparently leery of his great-grandmother, he enjoyed the tales told by his grandmother, Ann Elizabeth Tumlinson Wright, who after her mother's death moved into the jail at Floresville with her son, his wife Mollie, and their five children. Sadly, the Wrights about this time also endured the loss of another son, who died in infancy sometime during the first decade of the twentieth century, after his father became a sheriff.[35]

On July 4, 1910, the residents of Sutherland Springs presented Wright with a pearl-handled, silver-plated engraved Colt .45 revolver in a ceremony at their town. While the gesture may have had less to do with gratitude and more to do with promoting land sales in their community, or with making amends for the mob that had threatened Wright two years earlier, it was a good moment for the sheriff, who had much weighing on his mind. In addition to Dionicio Martinez, the murderer who remained free in Mexico, and Taylor Reese and Dennis Richards, the wrongfully convicted African Americans who never got executive pardons, he also had unsolved cases such as the murder of an infant boy whose body, stabbed twice in the chest, was found in a well at Nockenut, north of Stockdale, in December 1909. The death of Quirl Carnes and the crippling of Pat Craighead certainly remained fresh in his memory. Adding to his concerns, the population of Wilson County had grown by about sixty percent since he was a young deputy in the 1890s. Developments such as that at Sutherland Springs during the first decade of the twentieth century brought even more problems; Wright had already investigated the stabbing of J. A. Berry, contractor for the hotel there, during a card game in March 1909. But if he wanted to remain a lawman in Texas, and support his family, being a sheriff was his best option, and he had become one of the most respected sheriffs in the state. He ran unopposed during the fall of 1910, eight years after he had first sought the office, and following yet another easy victory quietly continued as sheriff of Wilson County, making sure that he was worth his pay while watching for another good opportunity to become a Ranger again and add to his family's legacy.[36]

Chapter 4

Sheriff, 1910–1917

William L. Wright's last four terms as sheriff of Wilson County, like his first four, were filled with routine cases, but there were also those that challenged him and furthered his development as a law officer. There were several murders, most but not all of which he solved, and he impressed observers all over Texas with his investigation of a car theft ring. He was increasingly called upon by other sheriffs for assistance, and he became involved in what became known as the "Bandit War" on the Rio Grande border. He also became more engaged in social organizations and politics and was elected president of the Sheriffs' Association of Texas. In sum, if he were preparing to become a Texas Ranger again, he could not have written a better script for himself. After all, he not only wanted to prove he was worth his pay but also to uphold his family's tradition of Ranger service. As the twentieth century progressed, that required more skills in investigation and personnel management, which Wright steadily acquired as a sheriff.

During his last seven years as a sheriff, Wright increased the number of his deputies, few of whom he apparently paid and many of whom worked in communities far from his office in Floresville. Alfred B. "Burt" Carnes,

George A. Monkhouse, William B. "Will" Clements, and Thad J. Rees continued to work for him. In Floresville, Wright added John L. Allen, a store clerk, Alex Klaus, a bar owner whose parents and wife were born in Germany, and Robert G. "Bob" Seale, a bartender who was the younger brother of Eli C. Seale, the former sheriff of Karnes County. Bob Seale had the distinction of arresting a local woman for wearing pants in public. He had never seen that, and he just knew it had to be wrong. Wright chided his deputy about the dangers of arresting women and told him to release her. Northwest of Floresville, Adolfo G. Flores, a farmer and former constable, worked in Calaveras. After a bar fight at Poth, southwest of Floresville, Wright recruited Dionicio J. "Nicho" Acosta and Pablo "Paul" Casares. Acosta later served as a Ranger under Wright, and then returned to Wilson County and worked as a constable and later a deputy for Carnes, who succeeded Wright as sheriff. Even further afield, ranch manager William H. Patton handled situations for Wright in Pandora, while constable John J. Morris did the same in Stockdale.[1]

Acosta was not the only one of Wright's deputies who served under him after he returned to Ranger service as a captain in late 1917. Irish-born Thomas "Tom" Connelly, a constable at La Vernia who also worked for Wright while he was a sheriff, enlisted as well, as did Royal W. "Wade" Lorenz, a Stockdale native who apparently lived in the Floresville jail with Wright during his last few years as sheriff, sharing a room with his teenaged son, Emanuel A. "Dogie" Wright. Dogie wrote that Lorenz was his father's chief deputy, but several men actually held that post, including Seale and Carnes. Another was John J. "Johnnie" Edds, one of Wright's special projects as both a sheriff and Ranger captain. Edds, born in 1890 at Elmendorf in Bexar County, was the son of Jesse W. Edds, a Confederate veteran who died in 1905, and Gertrude C. M. Edds, a San Antonio native who insisted her ancestors were among the Canary Island settlers who arrived in 1731. Edds and Wright met one night in January 1911 when Wright responded to a call in an African American community northwest of Floresville. Edds lived near there, saw Wright ride by on his horse, and followed in case he needed help. Wright in fact did have a fight with Lee Roberts that ended with him shooting the drunken man in the heel, and he appreciated Edds' assistance.

Roberts spent a long time healing in the Floresville jail, while Edds became a deputy even though he was small, had no legal experience, was not yet twenty-one years of age, and walked with a limp due to an injury suffered while reloading shotgun shells at a store where he worked. Wright apparently appreciated his fluency in Spanish and readiness to fight with his fists or a gun, and he told Edds to just wait outside if any suspects went into a saloon before he was of legal age. Wright declared under oath during the 1919 legislative investigation of the Rangers that Edds was his chief deputy for four years, then departed in September 1915 to become a Ranger. At the time that he left, the *San Antonio Express* declared that Edds was "a splendid officer and a valuable man.... Sheriff Wright regretted very much giving him up." Edds later accepted an appointment as a mounted inspector with the United States Customs Service that Wright secured for him in March 1916, and then became the sergeant of Wright's Ranger company.[2]

Wright had other special charges beside Edds, and he took care of them as well. Halford Pace, an African American, became an undercover deputy for Wright, providing information while serving as a watchman in Floresville, where he was born. Fluent in Spanish, he was, like Edds, well known within the Tejano community. One day in January 1918 he got into a fight with Collie Dykes and killed him. During his trial, Wright revealed that in fact Pace was his deputy, and that he considered Pace had done a good job. The judge decided the best option was to continue the case to the next term, providing Pace with time to join the army, which was rapidly expanding since the United States in 1917 had joined the Allies for World War I. Fortunately for this plan, Halford, who was twenty-nine years of age, had already registered for military service the previous year, when he wrote that he was a laborer for the telephone company and farmed in Poth. He left on a ship for France in June 1918 as an infantry private and upon his arrival was assigned to the 369th Regiment, which became famous as the Harlem Hellfighters. He returned briefly to Floresville in May 1919, then went to work for Shudde Brothers in Houston as a hatter.[3]

One problem Wright faced by 1910 was the deterioration of his jail, where both the prisoners and his family lived. He did his best to treat his inmates well with the money provided by the state; for example, in 1911 he fed them a "big turkey dinner" at Christmas. He was also flexible in meeting various needs. That same year Ernesto Gonzales, a Mexican accused of killing Antonio Rivas at Canada Verde in Wilson County, was converted to the Mexican Methodist Church in the jail on December 30 by José Policarpo Rodriguez, an eighty-two-year-old itinerant Mexican Methodist minister whom Wright permitted to visit his prisoners. Wright witnessed the ceremony along with the Rev. A. W. Wilson of the Floresville Methodist Church. Five days later, Gonzales was acquitted by the Texas district court jury. But some inmates did not appreciate Wright's hospitality, and he had his first escape in 1910. The escapee was David Gee, who had been arrested for stealing a horse and buggy. One night, before the jailer came upstairs to see that everyone was in their cells, Gee arranged his bed so that it looked like he was in it, and then hid in a corner. While the jailer peered into the cells, Gee slipped through the cell block door, down the stairs, and out through the front door, almost trampling Dogie, who was coming in with an armload of kindling. Dogie watched dumbfounded as Gee bolted down the street and disappeared. Wright found Gee living with some of his relatives in Mississippi months later. He traveled by train to retrieve him in August 1911 and brought him back to Floresville. Gee was among the inmates who got a nice dinner that Christmas, then was convicted of bail jumping in January 1912 and sentenced to two years in the state penitentiary system. Of greater concern to Wright was when Fred Light, a prisoner in the Floresville jail for eleven months after being convicted of theft, dug his way to freedom through a brick wall in the summer of 1912.[4]

A spectacular escape brought much-needed renovations to Wright's aging jail. During October 1915 three stores were burglarized in Floresville, as well as a handful of homes. Residents lost money, jewelry, clothing, a suitcase, and even a parasol. Wright realized that an energetic and talented thief was in town. He and Monkhouse went first to San Antonio, telling pawn shop owners to watch for the stolen goods. Acting on a tip from a Tejano, Wright intercepted the suitcase there, stuffed with many other items, which had apparently been shipped from the Floresville railroad depot to Eagle Pass. The clerk at Floresville remembered the transaction because there was a parasol attached to the suitcase. Wright followed the contraband to Eagle Pass and then patiently waited four or five days for someone to claim it. He did, and Wright arrested him on October 23 with many of the stolen items in his hands. The prisoner proved to be A. Emiliano Sopra, who in mid-October had been sentenced to seven years in jail by the district court at Corpus Christi for two burglaries. Soon thereafter he escaped from several local officers, jumped from a third-story window in the courthouse, climbed aboard a freight train, and arrived in Floresville, where his illicit activities attracted Wright's attention. Sheriff Mike B. Wright of Nueces County, a cousin to William L. Wright, retrieved Sopra and took him back to complete his trial in Corpus Christi, then returned him to Floresville, where another district court jury added twelve more years to his prison sentence for his second crime spree.[5]

Sopra was determined not to serve his sentence. In January 1916 he and two comrades, one Mexican and one African American, used iron pieces from the cots in their cells at the Floresville jail to enlarge an existing hole in the concrete floor of the upstairs block, as well as the sheet-iron ceiling below it. After several days of hard work, they dropped through the opening and walked out of the front door of the jail at about eight at night on a Saturday. Wright's wife, Mary Ann "Mollie" Brown Wright, his mother, Ann Elizabeth Tumlinson Wright, Dogie, and his sister Zora Belle were sitting and talking by the fireplace in a front room. Mollie later said she heard the escapees but thought it was just some of the usual people coming in and out. Dogie recalled that it was cold, and Sopra stole a coat as he departed. He also took the jail keys from their hook on the wall by the telephone and unscrewed the lightbulb from the socket in the hallway. He threw away the bulb and keys in the prison yard but kept the coat. Albert, an African American man who had "charge of the little unfortunate white boy who is confined in the jail," discovered the escape when he and his charge returned from attending a nearby "tent show." Wright and Deputy Seale arrived home from Austin by train at midnight and went directly to work. By two in the morning the Mexican inmate had been captured near Calaveras, and by Tuesday the African-American escapee had been arrested on a freight train at Rosenberg, near Houston. Both were allegedly sent to the state penitentiary, while Sopra was apparently never recaptured. It took Wright more than a year after funds were subsequently provided, but a remodeling of his jail was completed in May 1917.[6]

Wright also upgraded his transportation at about the same time that he remodeled his jail. For his first twelve years as sheriff, he often rode a saddlebred, gaited horse given to him by Emanuel M. Tom. The dark bay had a star on his face, so he was easily identified as the sheriff's horse, and he held his head low as he traveled, which caused some people to claim that he was tracking criminals, like a bloodhound. But as automobiles became available, Wright during emergencies would have someone drive him to the scene of a crime. Finally, in November 1915, he bought a "Ford touring car." During one of his first test drives, he ran off the road and hit a fence, so he had his oldest son Charley H. "Pat" Wright chauffeur him initially, followed by Dogie when Charley left to become a Ranger in May 1916. This was a dubious honor; the Floresville newspaper reported in November 1916 that Dogie broke his arm trying to crank his father's car. Wright claimed that he could not think and drive at the same time, unlike when he was on horseback, but he could not deny that his newfound mobility was useful. For example, during the first week of December 1915 he was advised by Deputy Patton that Enrique Mata, who had shot and killed his girlfriend, fourteen-year-old Susana Gaitán, after a quarrel in Laredo in May 1913, had been spotted near Pandora, twenty-four miles from Floresville in the northeastern corner of Wilson County. Wright and a "Mexican deputy" arrested Mata and "whisked" him to the Floresville jail in Wright's car. Returned to Laredo, where Wright testified in his district court trial, Mata was sent to Huntsville for fifteen years, although he served a little less than four before being pardoned by Governor William P. Hobby in March 1920.[7]

Wright almost lost a deputy in a bloody brawl that resulted in a murder in Wilson County not long after his fifth election as sheriff. It erupted at a grocery in Poth, just seven miles from Floresville, on July 29, 1911. Deputy Allen, responding to a report that trouble might be brewing, searched several Mexicans after being told that one carried a knife. Florencio Lara then approached and, leaning against Allen, "invited him to take a drink." Allen declined and asked Lara to surrender the knife he could feel in his clothing. When Lara refused and a struggle ensued, Allen was cut on the hand but took the weapon from Lara. After arresting four Mexicans, including Lara, Allen was leaving with them when someone attacked him from behind. He drew a pistol, but it was taken from him after his right arm was broken in two places. Proprietor Joe Ludwig tried to rescue Allen but was slashed to death, while German farmer Rudolph J. Woellert "was badly cut" in the hip. Wright later told a newspaper reporter that he believed the mob would have killed Allen and those trying to help him except that a traveling photographer, who weighed about 250 pounds, waded into the fight with a piece of "scantling," knocking people aside and causing others to run. Wright believed the unnamed man saved Allen, as well as others, and deserved a medal. Meanwhile, hearing about the melee, Wright with other deputies and Dr. John V. Blake, the county physician, raced to Poth from Floresville, completing the trip allegedly in nine minutes in a "two cylinder chain-drive Buick" owned and driven by William O. Murray, a Texas state senator. Six culprits were soon arrested. Lara denied everything, saying the knife had been put in his waistband by Elberto Chaverrea and that, after being knocked unconscious by Allen, he remembered nothing else. Lazaro Arranda was convicted for killing Ludwig and went to Huntsville, but he was pardoned by Governor James E. "Pa" Ferguson in July 1916. Lara, Chaverrea, Gregorio Cortenas, and Reyes Flores were all indicted for attacking Allen. Chaverrea, Cortenas, and Flores posted bonds and disappeared, while Lara's fine of $300 and jail sentence of one year were dismissed by the Texas Court of Criminal Appeals.[8]

The Allen affair prompted Wright to complain about the violence within the growing Mexican population of Wilson County. Benidena Carrasco was shot twice and killed at a "Mexican dance" six miles from Floresville in October 1911. While Wright and some of his deputies, with Blake, went to the scene and began looking for suspects, Malecio Gilan, the shooter, arrived at the jail and surrendered to Mollie. He explained that the shooting came after a dispute persisted for several weeks. Nemencio de la Zerda, a thirty-nine-year-old Tejano farmer, was convicted of manslaughter in May 1912 and served twenty-one months in the state penitentiary for shooting Pablo Nunes in a Floresville saloon. Cesario Martinez, a fifty-two-year-old Mexican farmer, was sentenced to five years for murder in January 1914 and served a little more than four years. Ramon Martinez shot and killed Ben Morales in a fight over a mule in September 1915 at a farm near Stockdale. Ramon's brother, Florencio, was badly slashed by Morales before he was shot. Both surrendered to Deputy Clements and Constable Morris, and Wright escorted Ramon to the jail in Floresville. Deputy Acosta shot and killed Alejos Morales at a Poth restaurant in late September 1915 after Morales tried to stab him while being arrested. In March 1916, Petronilo Romo, a Mexican laborer on a farm twelve miles west of Floresville near Fairview, killed his wife by stabbing her in the stomach with a pitchfork and in the back with a knife. Wright offered a reward of $50, and a suspect was apprehended in Atascosa County, but he was the wrong man. Romo was arrested near Canada Verde in Wilson County by Deputy Flores, who was joined by Carnes for the trip to the jail. Romo had been in Atascosa County but heard his wife might not be dead and returned home, hoping it was true. The state district court sentenced him to life in prison, but he was pardoned by Governor Miriam A. "Ma" Ferguson in December 1926. Bartolo Garcia was arrested in February 1916 for shooting Jose María Ramirez in the head with a shotgun at a farm near Floresville, ending a fight that had begun at a dance the night before. He was sentenced to two years in the state penitentiary. Wright posted a notice in the *San Antonio Express* in April 1916 that he was looking for "a Mexican named Lionocio Obiaye," declaring, "I want him for murder. Boys, give this your best attention." This suspect was apparently never found. In November 1917, an "old feud" led to a bloody confrontation at the railroad depot in Floresville, where Alfonso S. and Luis Coy were shot in the head and stabbed while Antonio and Elijio Castro each suffered multiple knife wounds. Alfonso Coy died, and Antonio Castro, a forty-seven-year-old Tejano farmer, was sentenced to two years for manslaughter in December 1917, just before Wright rejoined the Rangers. Castro was pardoned by Pa Ferguson after serving less than a year in the state prison system.[9]

Most of the violent cases involving Mexicans in Wilson County during Wright's tenure as sheriff, some of whom were perhaps Tejanos, were not interracial conflicts, but there were a few exceptions. One evening in early 1917 Wright's wife Mollie got a telephone call at the jail that there was trouble at the railroad depot in Floresville. She had Dogie retrieve Deputy

Seale in Wright's Ford automobile, and they raced toward the depot only to stop suddenly when their lights revealed a man lying in the road. It was Isaac R. P. "Zack" Mills, who was well known to be a heavy drinker. He was obviously dead, having been stabbed repeatedly. Nearby was a surrey with a Mexican father and two sons sitting in it, and the latter readily confessed that they had done it, stabbing Mills as he ran in a circle until he finally died. It was simply the result of an alcohol-fueled argument. Seale of course arrested them, and both Roberto and Antonio Salas were indicted in May 1917 for killing Mills, but no further record concerning their case has been found. Conversely, John Britton, a twenty-nine-year-old African American, shot Santos Riojas, a native of Mexico, to death at La Vernia in May 1916. Arrested in a "road camp" near Stockdale, Britton was convicted by a district court jury in June and sentenced to ten years for murder. He served less than six years in the state penitentiary system before he was freed in January 1922. According to the *Floresville Chronicle Ledger*, two other African Americans were also implicated in the death of Riojas and arrested, but no further information concerning them has been found.[10]

While many fatal cases led to arrests and some convictions, sometimes there was just not much for Wright to do, no matter how tragic the circumstances. Theodor Erdmann, age sixty-five, murdered his grown son, Alex Erdmann, and Alex's wife Linda at the breakfast table in the family home at Beauregard Ranch on January 9, 1913. After shooting his son in the back of the head and his daughter-in-law in the back with a Winchester rifle, Erdmann seated himself at the table and shot himself in the mouth with the same weapon. Just before the shootings, he scrawled "come over and help bury the dead" across the bottom of his will and gave it to a Mexican hired hand to carry to his son-in-law, Henry M. Noll. The man said the gunshots erupted as he fled the house. The children of a neighbor, John Bielefeld, saw the bodies first, but Noll and Arthur Erdmann, another of Theodor's sons, arrived soon after Noll was given the bizarrely embellished will and called the authorities. Wright and Edds, with Constable Henry J. Price and Justice of the Peace James F. Henson of Floresville, "motored" to the crime scene, thirteen miles to the southwest of Floresville between Poth and Falls City, and Henson quickly declared the affair to be a murder/suicide.[11]

George W. Parks was found dead in the road near his home at Smiley on September 30, 1914, shot behind the left ear. A wealthy rancher, he had been traveling to Nixon on business. Two African- American men, George Dawson and Johnnie Jones, were arrested and confessed, but they implicated others. While the crime occurred in Gonzales County, Wright led the investigation at the request of Solomon Parks, the victim's brother, with the assistance of Houston B. "Hugh" Hanley and Marshal Norman D. Cone of the town of Gonzales. What he discovered led him to arrest Lonnie L. Parks, the victim's twenty-year-old son, who hired the killers. The younger Parks, in his confession to Justice of the Peace Ben S. Fisk of San Antonio, said that he sold some of his father's cattle without telling him, and when he learned that the latter intended to have him arrested for theft, he went to Chris F. House, the former city marshal of Nixon, who told him that Dawson would kill his father. Young Parks gave a note for $325 to House, who later told him that he gave Dawson a pistol for the shooting, then had him return it. Jones, apprehended at Columbus, confessed to District Attorney Lester Holt at Seguin. He said that he had been employed by Dawson to shoot the elder Parks for $325, with the assurance that House would mislead investigators. Jones shot Parks when he dismounted from his horse to open a gate. He then betrayed himself when he wrote to Dawson, telling him that the four dollars and fare to San Antonio that he had actually received were not enough. Jones was in Columbus when he heard that the younger Parks and Dawson had been arrested. He hid in the woods but was found by San Antonio policemen Al S. Mussey and Dave S. Coy. Wright with Phillip H. Tom, who knew Jones, took him to San Antonio and then the Gonzales jail, where he joined Parks. Meanwhile, Dawson confessed to Justice of the Peace H. DeWitt at Gonzales, saying he was promised $1,000 for the murder by the younger Parks and House. He got a note for $325, with the balance to come after the deed was done. He tried to get a Mexican to do it for $325, but he refused, as did another Mexican and two African-American men before Jones. Solomon Parks died of heart disease five weeks after his brother's murder, so he never knew that Lonnie Parks and House were acquitted despite Wright's testimony, nor that his sister-in-law Lucibe may have asked her son to kill his father. Dawson and Jones were sentenced to five and twenty-five years respectively in the state penitentiary system.[12]

The Parks case was not the only time that Wright as sheriff assisted with a case outside of his own county. Brothers Lewis and Herbert Dodd robbed the First National Bank at Marble Falls, in Burnet County, on October 26, 1915. Two employees were inside the bank when the Dodds entered: assistant cashier Herbert Tate and bookkeeper Robert H. "Robbie" Heinatz II. The two robbers demanded money and, when Heinatz refused to cooperate, shot him in the shoulder and stomach. He died the next day. Seeing his fellow worker lying mortally wounded on the floor, Tate opened the vault, and the Dodds took almost $3,000 in cash. The pair then left the scene on horseback, riding for the cane breaks along the San Marcos River. Sheriffs from eight counties helped search the brush country near San Marcos, but they could not find the suspects. In addition to Wright, the posse included John W. Tobin of Bexar County (with his chief deputy, James W. Galbreath), Albert R. Mace of Lampasas County, James C. Wall of McCulloch County, Hugh Miller Jr. of San Saba County, Horace F. Pirtle of Hays County, H. William Adams of Comal County, and George S. Matthews of Travis County. The Dodds were finally captured at Clarksville, in Red River County, in April 1916. A district court judge in Burnet County sentenced Lewis to ninety-nine years for killing Heinatz; sent to Huntsville, he was paroled in February 1932. Judge Nathaniel T. Stubbs had Herbert's trial moved to Travis County, stating that a jury could not be empaneled in Burnet County because of "widespread interest" in the case. Convicted and sent to Huntsville for fifty years, Herbert laughed in court and declared he could do that time standing on his head. He escaped in June 1919.[13]

Wright put Felix J. Tudyk, a forty-one-year-old farmer, in the Floresville jail in November 1915 after he was arrested in Wilson County and failed to make bond. He was convicted on New Year's Day, 1916 of assault to murder and sentenced to two years in the state system. When Tudyk appealed his conviction, interesting details emerged in the testimony. First, he did not employ an attorney at his original trial, but his relatives did to file an appeal after he was found guilty. Second, he claimed that he was hunting rabbits near La Vernia with a young lady named Lucy Ciomperlik, who was just fifteen years old. When they spotted two young men in a watermelon patch, she suggested firing a shot to scare them; when he did, number four shot showered fourteen-year-old John Olenick, one of the two teenagers. Although he was not fatally wounded, Olenick was peppered with pellets from his head to his knees. Tudyk insisted that shooting Olenick was an accident, but Ciomperlik and the two youths told a much different story. She declared that she never asked Tudyk to shoot, but when she approached Olenick and started talking to him, Tudyk first threatened and cursed Olenick, then shot him. The Texas Court of Criminal Appeals upheld the original verdict, and Tudyk went to Huntsville in June 1916, although he was pardoned by Governor James E. "Pa" Ferguson in December, just six months later.[14]

Wright's son Dogie many years later told a story that was strangely similar to the Tudyk case to an interviewer and added to it in handwritten notes that remain in his papers. He recalled that a "kinda sickly-lookin' feller" came to Floresville, and Dogie earned a dime by guiding him to a hotel and carrying his bag for him. Spotting him later near the hardware store, Dogie stayed close, hoping for another job to earn more money. Suddenly Newt Kale exited the store with a shotgun, confronted the stranger, and shot him in the stomach. It is not clear if the stranger died, but Dogie claimed he had nine buckshot in him. Wright immediately arrested Kale, who stayed in the jail throughout his trial because he could not pay bail and went to the state penitentiary "for a short time." Dogie told the interviewer that there was no reason given for the attack except that the stranger and Kale, who had only been in Floresville a short time, knew each other from East Texas. His written account matches the interview in most details, but there are some intriguing differences. Dogie recalls that "Cale" shot the stranger because he was an ex-boyfriend of his wife and had come to Floresville to see her. He added, "I left there in high gear on my stick horse for home." Cale subsequently, according to this version, spent one year in jail before being acquitted by a jury.[15] Nothing has been found in newspapers or public records to corroborate Dogie's story.

During the first week of October 1916, a human hand protruding from the "muck" in a "hog pen" near Gonzales led to the discovery of the body of a Mexican man. Called to the scene, Wright discovered that the hogs had already chewed the fingers off, and it smelled horrible. He decided that Florencio Compian, another Mexican who had been working on the place, had killed this man, buried him in the hog pen, and placed the feed trough over him. Over time, the trough shifted, and the body surfaced. Dogie brought the two deputies from Poth, Acosta and Casares, in Wright's car to assist with the case. They went to Gonzales and then Lockhart, where they waited several days, having been told that their suspect would be coming to take care of business on Saturday (as many did). An informant that day pointed out Compian's wife and children, and that night they followed her wagon out of town, hoping she would lead them to her husband. Again, they waited until midnight, when Wright decided to arrest her and hold her in Floresville, hoping that Compian would try to contact her. He never did, and no record has been found of her prosecution, indicating that Wright dropped the charges against her. Governor James E. Ferguson offered a reward of $100 for Compian's apprehension, but he was never found. Wright did identify the victim in the hog pen: Catarino Flores, a horse trader who somehow ran afoul of Compian.[16]

Wright lost a close friend when William T. Matlock, a wealthy rancher and officer for the First National Bank in Floresville, was killed near his Wilson County home on March 5, 1917. He arrested Anton Bohuslav almost immediately, who was denied bail and taken to the jail in San Antonio. As the investigation progressed, a strange tale emerged. Matlock was a good friend, but he had a bad temper. A change that upset some locals was the division of old ranches and farms, which were being bought in smaller parcels by Germans, Poles, and Czechs. They did not cause problems, but they were different in mannerisms, speech, and dress. Bohuslav bought a tract next to Matlock's ranch on the San Antonio River, and a dispute developed between them over a fence. On the day Matlock was killed, he and his son, Lee H. Matlock, encountered Bohuslav on the road, in his wagon, and a heated discussion ensued. The "Bohemian" became frightened of Matlock and shot him with his double-barrel shotgun. Everybody expected a hanging, but Bohuslav got good attorneys: Benjamin W. Fly, a county judge and city attorney from Victoria, his partner James W. Ragsdale, and, when other lawyers in Floresville would not take the case, Milton H. West, a former Ranger who had passed the bar just two years earlier. He was known by many locals as "Leche" West, because as a boy he carried milk to town in a two-wheeled cart and sold it door to door, calling out "Leche" to announce his arrival. As a young man he had accompanied Wright and others to San Benito to recover his wounded brother after he and other lawmen were ambushed in the summer of 1910. West and his partners failed to obtain a change of venue, so the trial was held at Floresville during May 1917. The courtroom was crowded, but when the jury acquitted Bohuslav, "you coulda heard a pin drop." He had acted in self-defense, and his attorneys had proven it. Fly and Wright quickly hustled Bohuslav out of the courtroom, through the back yard of the jail, and into Fly's Packard automobile, in which he left town immediately. West relocated soon afterward to Brownsville, whence he was elected to the legislature and Congress, while Bohuslav apparently died peacefully in Wharton County in 1942.[17]

While Wright hanged no one in Wilson County during the second half of his tenure as sheriff, he did assist other law officers with that grim duty, accompanied by Eli C. Seale, who had stepped down as the sheriff of Karnes County in 1910. They first stood on the gallows for the hanging of Albert Varner on February 16, 1912. Varner, an African American, had escaped after serving five weeks of a forty-year sentence for burglary. He raped Maria Campbell, a white farmer's wife, in Colorado County in October 1911, and was captured soon afterward. After he confessed and pleaded guilty, he was hanged at the Guadalupe County poor farm. Sheriff Phil P. Medlin of Guadalupe County pulled the lever; other sheriffs with him were E. B. Mayes of Colorado County and Jim F. Brown of Karnes County. The next hanging attended by Wright and Seale was particularly hard. Porfirio Torres shot Ike Hill at the La Salle County home of Brigida Potino in October 1913. Hill had come to retrieve his laundry from Potino, and when Potino said she was afraid of Torres, Hill confronted Torres and was shot by him at close range with a Winchester. On the day of his execution—August 14, 1914, at Pleasanton in Atascosa County—Torres asked for a delay, claiming he expected a reprieve from the governor. Refused, he cursed the priest who came to administer a blessing and Sheriff John H. Winn as he read the death warrant, kicked and bit the deputies who escorted him to the gallows, struggled as one man tried to secure him, tried to bite Wright when he put the noose on him, and screamed curses as the trapdoor sprang open. Wright recalled, "if anyone ever hung a raving maniac, we hung him that day." Finally, Wright was one of seven sheriffs at the hanging of Will Hemphill on February 26, 1915, again at the Guadalupe County poor farm. Hemphill, an African American, had raped a white woman, Annie Dittmar, in April 1913. The district court jury at Seguin convicted him and he was sentenced to death, but the Court of Criminal Appeals in November 1913 ordered another trial. Condemned again, with that verdict confirmed in October 1914, Hemphill was executed, with Sheriff William F. Neubauer of Guadalupe County pulling the lever.[18]

Wright's obituaries in 1942, many years after he served as sheriff, pinned a label of "unofficial executioner" for South Texas on him. This apparently originated with Robert B. "Bob" McCracken, a Corpus Christi journalist with whom Wright was working on a biography of himself. McCracken added details such as Wright always using the same rope. These tales resurfaced in several Texas newspaper accounts of Wright's life that appeared just after his death, but there is little evidence to corroborate them. Wright did not have his own rope—he borrowed one to hang Refugio Jaureque at Floresville in June 1909. There were nine hangings in Wilson or adjacent counties during Wright's term as sheriff. He probably attended six, including Jaureque, although he may have been among the many lawmen who provided security during the hanging of Henry "Monk" Gibson at Cuero in June 1908. He was certainly one of five sheriffs present at the execution of J. Williams for murder at San Antonio in July 1908. His participation in the hangings of Varner, Torres, and Hemphill has been noted. Other than Jaureque's execution, Wright played a prominent role in only one other hanging, that of Torres. The actual role of executioner was usually left to the resident sheriff, in support of whom the others attended. Wright attended a half dozen executions but, except in Wilson County, he was not the executioner. He was there, along with other law officers, to provide security and support for a fellow sheriff involved in a grim duty. Wright apparently inflated his participation in hangings when he spoke to McCracken, or the newsman may have engaged in his own exaggeration, but considering there were ninety-four hangings in Texas while Wright was sheriff, he played a relatively small role in executing prisoners.[19]

Wright also rarely drew his gun while he was sheriff. Perhaps that was because he had deputies, notably Edds, who seemed to get into the line of fire first. In August 1912 Edds tried to arrest a man at the Floresville depot for riding on a baggage car. When the man, whose name was not reported, drew a pistol, Edds shot and wounded him, arrested him, and later escorted him to San Antonio, where he had outstanding warrants. Two "hobos" robbed a Calaveras farmer at gunpoint in February 1915 and then hopped aboard a Southern Pacific freight train. Edds and night watchman William Batchelor met the train at the Floresville depot. When confronted, the younger robber, Charles F. Hydinger, fired several shots at Edds and Batchelor, then escaped as Edds returned fire, leaving the older fugitive to be taken into custody. Hydinger was arrested several hours later in Karnes City. He had a bullet in his leg, which was removed at a San Antonio hospital, while Edds found a bullet hole through his own coat pocket. Hydinger proved to be sixteen years old, and when a district court jury convicted him at Floresville, he was sentenced to four years in the State Juvenile Training School at Gatesville. No more information has been found about his partner, nor has anything more been discovered about an intriguing remark made by Wright to the legislative committee investigating the Rangers in 1919. Asked about Edds' proclivity for violence, Wright declared that he killed only one man, an African American, while he was a deputy, and that was in self-defense. It happened in a Floresville restaurant, and the man fired at Edds first.[20]

Not all of Wright's interesting cases during his final four terms as sheriff were violent. During November 1911 he was contacted by James H. Bain, president of the First State Bank in Stockdale, who reported that he had gotten two letters from a man telling him to leave $4,000 in a bag under the local bridge over Cibolo Creek on the night of November 18, a Saturday, or he would harm his family. Wright and two deputies, Clements and Rees, accompanied Bain to the drop site, where they left a bag filled with "bogus money" hanging on a cord underneath the overpass, as instructed. At the right time a man approached the bait. When Wright yelled at him to stop, he ran, and the lawmen began shooting. The man reached his horse, but Wright shot and wounded it, leaving the fugitive afoot. They finally arrested him at his nearby ranch house and took him to the jail in Floresville, where he insisted that he had been forced to blackmail Bain by another man, who threatened his family. Wright may have been astonished that his prisoner was D. Twing Wheeler Jr., a twenty-two-year-old Stockdale resident who was a distant relative of Mollie, the sheriff's wife. Since he used the mail to defraud Bain, Wheeler was arraigned in a federal court, where he had to post $1,000 in bail, and he was indicted in January 1912. Sentenced to a year and a day in the federal penitentiary at Leavenworth, Wheeler subsequently returned to Wilson County, where he and his wife had their second child in July 1915.[21]

A criminal problem that had vexed Wright earlier in his career as sheriff of Wilson County resurfaced in May 1917. An expert safecracker used nitroglycerine to blow open the safe at Earnest E. Perry's drug store in Sutherland Springs late one night. Unfortunately, Perry was not only the owner of the largest retail operation in the resort town, he also was vice-president of the Dove Mineral Water Company and secretary of the Commercial Club in the tiny community, which was making yet another attempt to revive itself. The culprit escaped on a stolen "railroad velocipede," which he abandoned near La Vernia. This was the second safe blasted in Sutherland Springs in two years; someone had done the same at the post office in 1915. Just as in 1908, when two safes were destroyed in La Vernia, and in 1915 when he went to San Antonio to retrieve two prisoners from lawmen there only to discover they had the wrong suspects, Wright had no conclusive answers. Perry angrily tried to sell his store in the fall of 1917, which would have been a great loss to Sutherland Springs, but he later changed his mind and continued to operate it until his death in 1934.[22]

In May 1916, just months after Wright bought his first automobile, Floresville had its first car theft when someone stole a five-passenger Ford. Wright posted a notice in the San Antonio newspaper, just as he often did about stolen animals, but no further information appeared concerning it. He got more attention with his quick resolution of yet another car theft at Floresville in December 1916. The thieves took a Ford touring car that belonged to Lee M. McDaniel, a prosperous farmer. A breakthrough in the case came when the two culprits boldly returned to Floresville to repeat their offense one month after the first theft, but their "peculiar actions" brought attention. They were detained by city marshal J. G. "Jack" Youngblood, and Dogie and others easily identified them because they had seen them steal McDaniel's car. The duo gave their names as S. W. Lee and J. M. Walker and provided a San Antonio address; when Wright visited the place, he found two young women who subsequently fled, but he had them arrested two days later in Wichita Falls. He then broadcast requests for information and gathered responses from all over Texas, building a strong case against the thieves and their female accomplices. They had been taking cars and reselling them in several Texas counties. Wright recovered automobiles, including McDaniel's vehicle, in locations as far apart as Anahuac and El Paso. The men, whose actual names were Charles Francis and J. M. Farmer, were each sentenced to two years in the Texas prison system for automobile theft in the first such case ever tried in the state district court at Floresville. Farmer was pardoned by Governor Hobby in September 1918, while Francis was not released until November 1921. A writer for the *Port Lavaca Wave* marveled at Wright catching the thieves in only one month when San Antonio officers had been investigating the ring for much longer, noting that Wright had thus earned "statewide" popularity. He claimed that Rogers, Wright's former captain, told him that Wright was the best sheriff in the state. Agreeing with Rogers, he added, "It has long been proverbial that if Will Wright gets after a man he might as well come in and surrender or commit suicide for he'll get him if it takes twenty years."[23]

Wright may have smiled when he read what Rogers allegedly said about him, but he also may have been frustrated at how often his investigations did not result in a culprit serving his entire prison sentence. For example, six men arrested by him or his deputies and convicted by the local district court from 1910 to 1917 were subsequently pardoned by the governor, while another three had their prison sentences overturned by the Texas Criminal Court of Appeals. One of the most frustrating cases took place during Wright's last year as a sheriff. Deputy Seale responded to a complaint from a distraught Tejano mother in early February 1917. She and Marcelino Galaviz lived together at Edward D. Young's farm, where Galaviz, and another man were helping to clear the property. But one afternoon Galaviz brutally attacked his girlfriend's nine-year-old daughter, Alfonza Martinez. Allegedly Galaviz, before assaulting the girl, dug a grave and told her that he would cut her throat and bury her there if she ever reported what he had done. Wright had Galaviz jailed in San Antonio and then escorted the girl and her mother to Beeville, where the state district court was in session. The grand jury quickly indicted the thirty-year-old Galaviz for rape, and Wright retrieved him from San Antonio for his trial. The jurors deliberated fifteen minutes before convicting Galaviz, and he was sentenced to five years in the Texas penitentiary. Less than eight months after Galaviz's trial, the Texas Court of Criminal Appeals set aside his conviction, declaring that since it could not be proven that he had actually sexually penetrated the girl, he could not be charged with, nor convicted of, rape.[24]

Of course, not every case resulted in an arrest while Wright was sheriff. One night, he and his wife Mollie were awakened by a man yelling. They at first thought it might be one of the prisoners but quickly realized it was someone outside. Fearing it might be a robbery or even worse, Wright dressed and hurried to investigate, followed by his three older boys—Pat, Jack, and Dogie. Jack and Dogie had shotguns, just in case. As Dogie went through the gate in the white picket fence that surrounded the jail, arriving on the street in total darkness, he heard two gunshots to his left, followed by the sound of Jack firing both barrels of his gun to the right. Startled, Dogie fired two rounds from his own weapon in the direction of the bank, which seemed a logical target for a nighttime robbery. But that was not what was happening. Wright had already checked the bank and continued to a general store, where he saw flames and smelled smoke. He had fired two shots from his Winchester to raise the alarm, and Jack did likewise after learning what was afoot. They could still hear someone yelling and eventually found a Greek fellow, high atop an adjacent wall, who had smelled smoke in his bedroom on the second story of the store and fled in his "underclothes" from a window onto the wall, where he was stuck. He said that he heard someone come and go from the store, using a key, and had thought little of it until he smelled smoke. There is no record of an arrest in the case.[25]

Wright as sheriff of Wilson County became increasingly engaged in social organizations. He had joined the International Order of Odd Fellows about 1900, while he was a Texas Ranger, thus following in the footsteps of his father, Little Berry Wright. But Wright was also surrounded by Masons, including his father and grandfather, Joseph L. Tumlinson. His father-in-law, Sanford N. Brown, was a member of the Brahan Lodge at La Vernia in Wilson County, and three of his sons, Wright's brothers-in-law, were also Masons: Charles B. Brown, Frederick H. "Fred" Brown, and Robert S. "Rob" Brown, who painted the murals in the Brahan Lodge to honor its centennial. Wright became a master mason in Floresville Lodge Number 515 on New Year's Eve in 1914. The degree team from San Antonio failed to arrive because of heavy rain and mud, so another team was assembled from nearly one hundred attending Masons from Karnes County. The *Floresville Chronicle Journal* reported that "Sheriff Wright rode 'the goat' in great style," a humorous archaic reference that meant he did well in his initiation ceremony. Indicating the overlap in Texas social organizations at that time, especially in rural areas, the same writer reported that a "sumptuous supper" was served afterward in the Odd Fellows Hall, while the Woodmen of the World band played. Wright not only belonged to the Odd Fellows but was a Woodman as well. Of course, "good fellowship reigned supreme until a late hour." Wright later joined Chapter 160 of the Royal Arch Masons at Floresville, serving at least one term as an officer, and he took the degrees for the Knights Templar. Finally, he became a charter member of the Old Time Trail Drivers Association, organized at San Antonio in 1915 with John R. Blocker, one of Wright's former employers, as president.[26]

Wright's work in Wilson County led him to become active in the Sheriffs' Association of Texas. In January 1909 the legislature debated a bill to stop paying sheriffs with fees and put them all on a salary. Many prominent sheriffs converged on Austin to lobby against the idea, including Wright, whom the *Austin American* described as one of the most highly regarded sheriffs in the state. Wright provided some colorful quotes, such as "We might be able to arrest the legislature if it came to a showdown, but it's a fact that a sheriff can't talk. We are having a hard time making silvery tongued speeches to the committees." He added, "Of course we've got

Captain Rogers as a representative and he is right with us, but the captain has been a ranger all his life and he can't talk. I guess though that we will succeed in explaining things so that the representatives will see where the bill would put us on the blink." The fee system continued, and in February 1911, as a member of the Legislative Committee of the Association, Wright was one of sixteen sheriffs who returned to Austin and again lobbied for more money to care for prisoners. By 1910 he also became the unofficial chaplain of the Association, which required him to sit at the head table during meetings despite his protests. He was elected vice president in 1913, and in 1914, when Edds and Rees accompanied him to the annual meeting, he became the president. These were honorary titles, but they came in recognition of his service, and local newspapers each time, in Austin and Corpus Christi, contained warm praises for him. But Wright did not apparently enjoy public speaking. His duties as the outgoing president in 1915 at Waco included delivering an address, but he had J. W. Israel, the minister of a Baptist church in Cuero, speak in his place. The *Floresville Chronicle Journal* declared that "Rev. Israel delivered a most powerful speech" on the "relationship of the church to the law" that "drew enthusiastic applause." Deputy Rees and Floresville city marshal Youngblood probably knew Israel well, since he had pastored the Baptist church in Floresville when Wright became sheriff, but they may have been disappointed when he spoke in place of their colleague, whom they accompanied to the 1915 meeting.[27]

Since Texas sheriffs were elected and had many political duties, it was a short step for Wright to become more deeply involved in politics. During elections, he chaired the Registration Board for Wilson County, serving with other officials such as the county clerk and his longtime ally, Health Officer Dr. John V. Blake. Wright appointed all the registrars for the eight precincts in Wilson County, then delivered the ballot boxes to the polling places. He would hire a "hack," and it would take four or five days to deliver the boxes and collect them after the balloting. He often took some of his sons with him and make a fun trip out of it, camping if the weather was good, staying with people if it was not, and hunting along the way. A caucus at Floresville in August 1913 chose Wright to be among the 55 delegates that it sent to the state Democratic convention at San Antonio. During the summer of 1914, Thomas H. Ball, a staunch prohibitionist trying to win the Democratic nomination for governor, visited Floresville. As a pre-event, the former president of the Sheriffs Association of Texas (and incumbent state treasurer), Sam Sparks of Austin, spoke in Floresville during the first week of July, and Wright, then the incumbent vice president of the Association, chaired the reception committee that greeted him. Just two weeks later, when Ball arrived by train, Wright was among a committee of one hundred prominent citizens who greeted him. Unfortunately for any future political aspirations that Wright may have entertained, Ball was soundly trounced by James E. "Pa" Ferguson in the Democratic primary, and Ferguson also easily won the governor's race that year.[28]

Only a month after he stepped down as president of the Sheriffs' Association of Texas, Wright went to Brownsville, where alarms were being raised as the Mexican Revolution spilled across the Rio Grande. Concerned about an invasion after the discovery of the "Plan de San Diego," which called for an attack on Anglos in Texas in early 1915, and a flurry of raids along the border in July of that same year, federal authorities had Army troops join Texas lawmen in scouring the brush for raiders and bandits. Wright accompanied Texas Adjutant General Henry Hutchings and other lawmen, who apparently welcomed his knowledge of the border region. They accomplished nothing, so Wright returned home, where he was working when W. Henry Edds, a cousin of his deputy who was visiting in Floresville, received a notice in late August 1915 that Mexican raiders had ransacked his ranch in Jim Hogg County, driving away the foreman and engaging in a gunfight with Sheriff Oscar Thompson and Texas Ranger James P. N. "Pat" Craighead, the son of former Wilson county sheriff John S. Craighead, who had served as a deputy for Wright before losing his left leg in an ambush on the border in 1910. Sheriff Wright, Deputy Seale, and Robert A. Wiseman rode with Edds as he hurried by train to Hebbronville, thence drove forty-two miles overland to check on his home. They found, perhaps fortunately, that the raiders had gone.[29]

Wright did later play a slightly larger role in the so-called Bandit War, as the outbreak of border violence after the appearance of the Plan de San Diego came to be known. During the spring of 1916, it was reported that

José M. Morín, who claimed to be an officer for Pancho Villa but in fact had become a brigadier general for Venustiano Carranza, was in San Antonio making arrangements to implement the Plan de San Diego in South Texas. Saspamco, Calaveras, and Poth, all in Wilson County, were among the many towns that allegedly had agents working for Morín. When he boarded a train one evening in May 1916 to travel south from San Antonio, William M. Hanson and Howard P. Wright also climbed aboard. Hanson was a former federal marshal who had been expelled from Mexico as a suspected operative and worked as a security officer for the San Antonio, Uvalde, and Gulf Railroad, while Wright was an agent of the federal Bureau of Investigation. When Morín attempted to leave the train just before midnight near Saspamco, the lawmen arrested him peacefully in the smoking car. Sheriff Wright, who as a Ranger had earlier worked with Hanson in Laredo but apparently was not related to the federal agent with whom he shared a last name, joined the group at Floresville along with Carnes, his deputy. The four officers and their prisoner arrived quietly at Kingsville, where Morín was jailed. Kingsville newspaper editor Eulalio Velazquez and Victoriano Ponce, a local baker who reportedly was one of Morín's minions, soon became prisoners as well. After the Wilson County officers departed, Velazquez was released, but Ponce and Morín, who were accused of being involved in several deadly events, were given to several Rangers, who were supposed to take them to Brownsville but instead shot the two men on May 22, 1916, and claimed that they tried to escape. Subsequent protests led President Woodrow Wilson to require that no more Mexican prisoners be surrendered to Rangers.[30]

Wright returned home from Kingsville to find Floresville in chaos. Dogie recalled that many other suspected revolutionaries had been arrested all over South Texas, and that his father's jail was "full of 'em." Having so many Mexican prisoners in Floresville, along with the rumors of an impending border war, upset many locals. A large group, after Wright climbed on the train for Kingsville, occupied the jail, sending Mollie, the sheriff's protesting wife, and her family to stay with relatives and friends in Sutherland Springs. Wright restored order without apparently losing any prisoners, unlike the notorious case he left behind in South Texas, and in July 1916 he wrote to Rogers, his old captain who had gotten a commission as a federal marshal, that he believed there was little chance of an uprising on the border, despite the persistent fears of others. He explained that the Tejanos and Mexicans in Wilson County supported him in keeping the peace, and that the latest enlistments in the U.S. Army from his area were all Mexican Americans. These peaceful comments were published in the *Austin American*, while Wright posted a reassuring circular in the *San Antonio Express*. Written in English and Spanish, it asked both communities, Anglo and Hispanic, to cooperate in keeping the peace during the turmoil. Wright also advised everyone to "refrain from any unnecessary remarks and actions in regard to the Mexican situation." As this came during the time that the Army had launched the Punitive Expedition, sending troops into Mexico in response to Villa's raid on Columbus in New Mexico, Wright was asking a lot of his fellow Texans, and he perhaps realized that. But similar letters were issued by other Wilson County officials, including district clerk Nemencio R. de la Zerda, who had previously been a deputy for Wright, and Salvador T. Rodriguez, a former county commissioner.[31]

After the Punitive Expedition ended in early 1917 with the withdrawal of American troops from Mexico, the United States entered World War I when President Wilson asked for and got a declaration of war against Germany. Wright suddenly found himself involved in new tasks, such as enforcing the draft, while his family also became engaged in the war effort. His first son, Charles H. "Pat" Wright, had joined the Rangers in May 1916, at the age of twenty-two, but he returned home to enlist in Battery D of the 131st Field Artillery Regiment, 36th Division, which organized at Floresville. By the time the war ended, Pat had become a sergeant and was serving in France. Pat's brother Maurice H. "Jack" Wright, who was just over one year younger than him, joined his older brother in the same company. Wright's mother, at the age of seventy-seven, drew much attention for her energetic work with the Red Cross at Floresville in support of the soldiers. Among other things, she knitted more than one hundred pairs of socks for them.[32]

By late 1917, after fifteen years in Wilson County, Wright had become one of the better-known sheriffs in Texas, if not the best-known. Time had lessened his family concerns: his mother-in-law and grandmother passed during his second term as sheriff, while his father-in-law died in 1916.

His mother and grown daughter, Zora Belle, were able to help his wife, Mollie, with her tasks, while the number of sons at home dropped when the two oldest departed for military service. That left only two at home: William Berry "Bill" Wright and Houston Tom "Simp Tom" Wright, allegedly born in the Floresville jail during April 1905 and January 1915 respectively. The latter's name and nickname honored Wright's friend Hugh Simpson "Simp" Tom, a Confederate veteran and former Ranger, as well as a banker and rancher in Floresville, who died just one month after his namesake was born. By this time, Wright had apparently decided that a Ranger captain's pay, which was $125 per month in the fall of 1917, could be as good as what he collected in fees as a sheriff. His reputation certainly allowed him to consider trying once more to become a Ranger captain, a goal he had failed to secure earlier but had never abandoned. Texas Assistant Attorney General C. C. McDonald in late 1916 had forwarded a letter from Wright to Adjutant General Hutchings asking about new opportunities to be a captain. McDonald wrote, "He has for many years been one of the best sheriffs in Texas and actively identified with the sheriffs' association of the state … I know he would make good in the position." He added that Wright's inquiry should be confidential—if there was no position available, he "might want to seek re-election as sheriff of Wilson County." Hutchings never appointed Wright to the Rangers, but his successor, hard-pressed to find a solution to many problems along the Mexican border, would make Wright a captain in the late fall of 1917. Having earned his pay many times over as a sheriff, Wright would finally get a chance to do the same as a captain in the Rangers, where he would add much to his family legacy.[33]

Joseph L. Tumlinson (*Courtesy of Dolph Briscoe Center for American History, University of Texas, Austin*).

Rebecca Elizabeth Newman Tumlinson (*Courtesy of Dolph Briscoe Center for American History, University of Texas, Austin*).

Little Berry "L.B." Wright (*Courtesy of Dolph Briscoe Center for American History, University of Texas, Austin*).

Ann Elizabeth Tumlinson Wright (*Courtesy of Dolph Briscoe Center for American History, University of Texas, Austin*).

William L. Wright, ca. 1889 [image by Asa A. Brack, San Antonio] (*Courtesy of Dolph Briscoe Center for American History, University of Texas, Austin*).

Mary Ann "Mollie" Brown Wright [image by Stauffer Photo Service (F. F. Stauffer), San Antonio] (*Courtesy of Dolph Briscoe Center for American History, University of Texas, Austin*).

William L. Wright [on left] with Unidentified Colleague, ca. 1896 (*Courtesy of Dolph Briscoe Center for American History, University of Texas, Austin*).

Levi Old, William L. Wright, and Milam H. Wright [left to right] at Orange in 1900 (*Courtesy of Dolph Briscoe Center for American History, University of Texas, Austin*).

Company E at Cotulla in 1900 [left to right]: company cook, Jim Moore, William A. "Billy" Old, Henry G. "Harry" DuBose, William L. Wright, August Y. "Augie" Old, and Thomas C. "Creed" Taylor (*Courtesy of Texas Rangers Hall of Fame and Museum, Waco*)

William L. Wright and Deputies, ca. 1905: Wright stands second from the left, while Alfred B. Carnes and William B. Clements are on the far right, with Luke Davis seated in front (*Courtesy of Dolph Briscoe Center for American History, University of Texas, Austin*).

William L. Wright at Sheriff's Association of Texas convention at San Antonio in 1908: he is third from the right, with his daughter Zora Belle Wright in front of him [second girl from the right] (*Courtesy of Dolph Briscoe Center for American History, University of Texas, Austin*).

William L. Wright by William E. Crandal of Floresville, ca. 1911 (*Courtesy of Dolph Briscoe Center for American History, University of Texas, Austin*).

Charles H. "Pat" Wright in his Army uniform, ca. 1918 (*Courtesy of Dolph Briscoe Center for American History, University of Texas, Austin*).

Zora Belle Wright on Red Cloud, ca. 1914 (*Courtesy of Dolph Briscoe Center for American History, University of Texas, Austin*).

Company K, 1918 [left to right]: William B. “Bryan” Butler, Ferrell E. “Ex” Holloman, Harold W. Adams, Grover C. “Cleve” Oliphant, Dionicio J. “Nicho” Acosta, William S. “Sanders” Peterson, Marvin N. Butler, Robert B. “Bob” Sutton Jr., Wright C. Wells, Thomas “Tom” Connelly, M. Monroe Wells, and William L. Wright (*Courtesy of Dolph Briscoe Center for American History, University of Texas, Austin*).

M. Monroe Wells, Harold W. Adams, and William L. Wright in South Texas, 1918 (*Courtesy of Dolph Briscoe Center for American History, University of Texas, Austin*).

William L. Wright, John J. Edds, Wright C. Wells, and Thomas "Tom" Connelly [left to right] with chuckwagon, 1918 (*Courtesy of Texas Rangers Hall of Fame and Museum, Waco, TX*).

Company D, ca. 1919: standing, left to right, are Dionicio J. "Nicho" Acosta, William B. "Bryan" Butler, Harold W. Adams, and William S. "Sanders" Peterson; seated, left to right, are Wright C. Wells, Robert B. "Bob" Sutton Jr., William L. Wright, and Desiderio "Jesse" Perez (*Courtesy of Dolph Briscoe Center for American History, University of Texas, Austin*).

Marcus Hines, William L. Wright, an unidentified soldier, and L. C. McDuff, the Deputy Collector of Customs at Hidalgo [left to right] with contraband liquor at Pharr, December 3, 1920 (*Courtesy of Dolph Briscoe Center for American History, University of Texas, Austin*).

Frank Smith, Hubert P. "Red" Brady, John J. Edds, David C. "Jack" Webb, Charles H. "Pat" Wright, Juan C. Gonzalez, William L. "Bill" Miller, and William L. Wright (left to right) after capturing thousands of bottles of contraband tequila in November 1921 [image by Serrano Studios, Laredo] (*Courtesy of Dolph Briscoe Center for American History, University of Texas, Austin*).

Emanuel A. "Dogie" Wright in his Border Patrol uniform, 1925 (*Courtesy of Dolph Briscoe Center for American History, University of Texas, Austin*).

Company D, 1924: in the back [left to right] are John E. Hensley, Dan Coleman, William S. "Sanders" Peterson, William A. Dial, John W. Sadler, and William E. Burford; in the front [left to right] are Asa Light Townsend, William L. Wright, Thomas G. "Tom" Brady, and William B. "Bill" Wright (*Courtesy of Texas Rangers Hall of Fame and Museum, Waco*).

Company D supply truck on right; on horseback [left to right]: William L. Wright, Stanley M. Morton, David C. "Jack" Webb, and Hubert P. "Red" Brady (*Courtesy of Dolph Briscoe Center for American History, University of Texas, Austin*).

William L. Wright (left) with new recruits for Company D, 1924: [left to right] Dan Coleman, William A. Dial, Thomas G. "Tom" Brady, John W. Sadler, and J. Warren Smith [image by Serrano Studios, Laredo] (*Courtesy of Dolph Briscoe Center for American History, University of Texas, Austin*).

William L. Wright, ca. 1928 (*Courtesy of Dolph Briscoe Center for American History, University of Texas, Austin*).

Company A, 1932 [left to right]: Thad Tarver, Henry D. Glasscock, William L. Wright, and J. Warren Smith (*Courtesy of Texas Collection, Baylor University, Waco, TX*).

Company A near Marfa, 1932 [left to right]: William L. Wright, J. Warren Smith, Robert E. Poole, William E. "Earl" Young, Fred E. Griffin, Harold Slack, and Thad Tarver (*Courtesy of Texas Collection, Baylor University, Waco*).

John R. Hughes with William L. Wright at Ranger Headquarters, Texas Centennial State Fair, 1936 [image by William "Frank" Rogers] (*Courtesy of Dolph Briscoe Center for American History, University of Texas, Austin*).

William L. Wright with Lyndon B. Johnson at Corpus Christi, 1941 (*Courtesy of Dolph Briscoe Center for American History, University of Texas, Austin*).

Wright family, 1941 [left to right]: Maurine Wright (Maurice H. "Jack" Wright's daughter), Mary Ann "Mollie" Brown Wright, Sam Lane Fore (Zora Belle Wright Fore's son), Zora Belle Wright Fore, JoNelle Wright (Maurice H. "Jack" Wright's daughter), William L. Wright, Elizabeth Brown (Charles B. Brown's daughter), and Maurice H. "Jack" Wright (*Courtesy of Dolph Briscoe Center for American History, University of Texas, Austin*).

Houston Tom "Simp Tom" Wright displays the United States flag, made by Dutch prisoners, that he and his fellow American inmates raised over the Japanese prison camp where they were held in August 1945 (*Courtesy of Dolph Briscoe Center for American History, University of Texas, Austin*).

Zora Belle Wright Fore watches as her niece and namesake, Zora Belle Wright Whitfield (daughter of Emanuel A. "Dogie" Wright) places a wreath on the memorial to William L. Wright at its dedication, June 1967 (*Courtesy of Dolph Briscoe Center for American History, University of Texas, Austin*).

Chapter 5

Captain, 1917–1919

James A. Harley of Seguin inherited a crisis on the Rio Grande when he left the Texas Senate in 1917 and became the Adjutant General of Texas, appointed by William P. Hobby after he took office as governor following the impeachment of James E. Ferguson. Efforts to address persistent problems with violence and theft as the Mexican Revolution continued were complicated by the entry of the United States into World War I. Deserters began crossing into Mexico as the federal government implemented a draft to expand its military operations. The Texas Council for Defense pressed Hobby for solutions, and he in turn endorsed Harley's request to double the number of Ranger Force companies, from six to twelve, with most of the new commands assigned to the border. Harley dismissed all Special Rangers in late 1918, and recruited a much smaller number in subsequent years, but he appointed hundreds of the new Ranger Home Guards, popularly known as Loyalty Rangers, who monitored their home counties for disloyal activities. William L. Wright's deputy, George A. Monkhouse, became a Loyalty Ranger in Wilson County. Most important for Wright was that these changes provided him with an opportunity to be a Texas Ranger again, and he became the captain of Company K on the Mexican border.[1]

A writer for the *San Antonio Express* in November 1917 claimed that Wright's appointment as a Ranger captain was "unsolicited," but that was not entirely true. Wright wrote to Harley on October 4, asking to be appointed. He reminded the Adjutant General that they had known each other "for years" and that he should "know my reputation." Perhaps just as important, Wright claimed that Sen. Joseph W. Bailey, a prominent Texas Democrat, supported his application. Ranger captain John J. Sanders, under whom Wright's oldest son Charles had served, added his endorsement, declaring Wright was "one of the best officers in the state." By mid-November Harley appointed Wright as a Ranger captain, which the latter learned when a former Ranger telephoned him to ask if he could be in his company. Harley invited Wright to meet with him in Austin to discuss the appointment and gave him five days to decide about accepting, but instead Wright telegraphed his acceptance one day later, with a promise to send a formal letter forthwith. Wright was one of four captains announced by Harley that month. Another was Charles F. Stevens, the Bexar County constable and deputy sheriff who had worked with Wright when he was a sheriff and had also served as a U.S. deputy marshal under Wright's Ranger mentor, John H. Rogers. A writer for the *San Antonio Express*, regarding the appointments of Wright and Stevens, declared, "Those careless Mexican bandits down in the border are going to have a touch of real high life soon after the turn of the New Year." The *Guadalupe Gazette* explained that "Mr. Wright is known as one of the most fearless and capable officers in Texas and will make a fine Ranger," while the *Seguin Enterprise* added: "General Harley could not have found a more efficient man."[2]

Harley not only increased the number of Ranger companies but also authorized an increase in the complement of each one from ten privates each to fourteen, in addition to a captain and sergeant. When Wright's appointment as a captain was announced, he was "besieged" with letters from eager applicants all over Texas. He wrote to Harley in late November that he regretted the announcement in the *San Antonio Express* because, since its appearance, "I have done nothing but answer phones and I have been getting letters by the bunch." Most need not have bothered; Harley usually let his captains make their own choices, and Wright chose thirteen men whom he already knew, either personally or by reputation. Four of his appointees served as deputies under him in Wilson County. Another had been with him in the Frontier Battalion, while four others also had prior law enforcement experience. Four men were ranchers, two from Karnes County and two related to Wright. Two additional members of Company K, as Wright's new command was designated, were assigned to him by Harley, but one was a veteran peace officer who came from a law enforcement family, while Wright knew the other man's father, a fellow sheriff.[3]

Wright's nine recruits with law enforcement experience had a wide range of backgrounds. His former deputy, John J. Edds, became his sergeant, rejoining Wright after eight months of service as a Ranger in Henry L. Ransom's Company D and almost two years as a mounted inspector for the United States Customs Service. Dionicio J. "Nicho" Acosta enlisted while still serving as a deputy for Wright, as did Royal W. "Wade" Lorenz, a twenty-one-year-old native of Wilson County who–according to Wright's son Emanuel A. "Dogie" Wright—lived in the Floresville jail at least part of the time that he was a deputy. Irish-born widower Thomas "Tom" Connelly, a forty-year-old constable from La Vernia, was probably what Dogie called a "pistol deputy," a peace officer who was not paid for the work he did for Wright while he was sheriff. Apparently, Connelly was an excellent cook and teamster, and he was willing to drive the chuck wagon. Sidney S. "Sid" Hutchison had served with Wright as a Ranger under Rogers; since that time, he had worked as a ranch hand, including one summer with Dogie on a ranch in Karnes County. Grover C. "Cleve" Oliphant, age thirty-three, was an ex-deputy sheriff from Karnes County, as was fifty-four-year-old Thomas N. "Tom" Pullin, who as a young man had seen his father shot and killed in a street fight. He had since served twenty years as a deputy. James P. "Paul" Perkins, age forty-three, a native of Beeville, had been a constable and deputy sheriff for Bee County. The most impressive legal credentials belonged to William S. "Sanders" Peterson, a fifty-three-year-old rancher from Mission who had been an Arizona Ranger for four years and subsequently served as a deputy sheriff in Gila County, Arizona, and Kerr County, Texas. He was also a distant cousin of Wright.[4]

Wright had been raised in a ranching culture, and he respected the work ethic and skill set of ranch hands. He knew many ranchers in Karnes County, and there he enlisted two recruits: Marvin N. Butler, twenty-three years old, and W. Bryan Butler, twenty-one years of age. Both were Karnes County natives, and each described his occupation as "stockman," but Marvin had also been a star football player for Texas A&M College (now University). William's father, Sykes C. Butler, was Marvin's uncle and a well-known rancher who served as a Special Ranger for one year, beginning in January 1918. Two additional recruits were ranchers related to Wright. Madison Monroe Wells, age thirty-one, was Wright's first cousin, the son of his mother's sister, Martha Elizabeth Tumlinson Wells, and her husband, William W. Wells. He enlisted in Kerr County, where he was raised. Wright C. Wells, a more distant cousin to Wright born in Mississippi, joined Company K on Christmas Day 1917 in Wilson County. He was forty-seven years of age, but he was a good cook and a "great storyteller" that "kept everybody in a good humor." Wright later assigned him to drive the chuck wagon after Connelly left the Rangers.[5]

The two recruits selected by Harley did fit the pattern of Wright's other enlistees. Harley in December 1917 reported that Ferrell E. "Ex" Holloman had been assigned to Company K and needed to know where and when to join his command. Holloman was a twenty-five-year-old "peace officer" from Seguin, Harley's hometown, in Guadalupe County. His father, Tom H. Holloman, had served as a U.S. marshal in Texas. Harold W. Adams, a twenty-one-year-old bookkeeper from New Braunfels, enlisted in mid-January 1918 and was sent to Company K as its last original recruit. He had been working in a bank, but his father was H. William Adams, who as the sheriff of Comal County had participated with Wright in the pursuit of the men who killed a clerk during a bank robbery at Marble Falls in October 1915. The elder Adams had also been president of the Sheriff's Association of Texas, as had Wright.[6]

During its first year on the border, Wright's Company K did not have many significant changes in personnel. Pullin was the first to leave, resigning in May 1918, followed by the resignations of Perkins in October and Marvin Butler in December 1918. Holloman was discharged at the end of his first year as a Ranger. Wright had mixed results with their replacements. He must have been very pleased to accept the enlistment of his son, Dogie, in June 1918, but the seventeen-year-old "Ranger boy," as his father described him in a letter to a fellow Ranger, Lon L. Willis, developed "typhoid fever" within a few months and went home, whence he submitted his resignation. Robert B. "Bob" Sutton Jr., a twenty-one-year-old cowboy from Stockdale, enlisted in La Salle County in August 1918, presumably in place of Dogie. He may have been a member of the family who owned the Karnes County ranch where Dogie and Hutchison briefly worked together. Desiderio "Jesse" Perez of San Antonio was forty-nine years of age in mid-November 1918 when he transferred from Company G, which was commanded by Stevens. Perez had been a law officer all his adult life, including working as a constable in Hidalgo County, deputy sheriff in several counties, police officer in San Antonio, and Ranger under three of the four Great Captains—John R. Hughes, William J. McDonald, and James A. Brooks—as well as several others. Wright wrote about him in his enlistment papers: "I have known Jes Perez for many years and know that he is a fine officer and man."[7]

While recruiting Company K, Wright lobbied to be assigned to the Mexican border. District Attorney John A. Valls of Laredo, a feisty longtime political leader known as the "stormy petrel of the Rio Grande," asked for Wright to be posted in his city, and Wright forwarded the request to Harley. He did not mention the gunfight that had erupted the first time he had visited Laredo as a Ranger under the command of Rogers in 1899, but perhaps that was best. He had gone there several times while he was sheriff, most recently in the summer of 1915, with no violent conflicts. Most important, Valls wrote to Wright, "I have assured several persons that you are not an enemy of the Mexican people," and told him to have prominent Mexicans in Wilson County write to their friends in Webb County, for which Laredo served as the county seat, on the same subject. Getting no response from Harley, Wright contacted him again on December 6, 1917: "I see from the papers that they have already had some disturbances on the river, that makes me want to go." He wrote to Harley once more on December 11 that "there must be something [w]rong," adding, "General I am in this work for the good of Texas, I know rangers have done more good for the State than any other one thing in the way of preserving law and order, but I tell you they are [*sic*] lots of talk about the way they do now, I tell you this as a friend and for the good of Texas." He assured Harley that he wanted to be on the border, where he could address the obvious problems that had developed. By December 19, Wright knew that his headquarters would be in Laredo because he had a carbine shipped there. In late December, as he prepared to depart for Laredo, the county clerk of Wilson County, Nemencio R. de la Zerda, a former deputy for Wright, wrote to his counterpart in Webb County to assure him that he was the right choice for protecting Hispanics there.[8]

Wright was particularly worried about reports from the Marfa area concerning the activities of Ranger Captain J. Monroe Fox on the Rio Grande, and there were wealthy stockmen there who shared his concern. T. C. Mitchell congratulated Harley for appointing Wright, an "efficient and fearless officer" who was "familiar with the ways of the Mexican people and understands thoroughly how to handle them." His sentiments were seconded by H. B. Holmes, who explained that he did so because "I believe him to be a man that will always stand up for the right things and that he is not afraid to inforce [*sic*] the law." Both ranchers wanted Wright to replace Fox at Marfa. Presidio County judge William W. Bogel opposed the change, however, arguing that Fox had been effective in keeping the peace. Harley left Fox at Marfa, which led to the bloody tragedy of the Porvenir Massacre in January 1918, when Fox's Company B cooperated with ranchers and U.S. Army troops in the execution of fifteen men and boys of Mexican descent. Infuriated and politically embarrassed, Governor William P. Hobby had Company B disbanded and pressured Fox into resigning, but no one was prosecuted for the killings. This contributed to demands for a legislative investigation and reforms, into which Wright would be drawn. An interesting comment on the situation was offered by William M. Hanson, the former U.S. marshal and railroad security agent who was hired by Harley as captain of the Headquarters Company of the Ranger Force and often served as his personal investigator. Sent to Marfa in February 1918, Hanson wrote that those who wanted Wright at Marfa thought he would support his friend A. Mathis Avant, the former Atascosa County sheriff who had relocated there and was becoming involved in politics. Hanson concluded, "I think [they] figured wrong in this, for if Wright was stationed there, no one could control him, and he would always be found executing the law as he understands it, and without fear or favor. This is his religion."[9]

Wright's assignment to Laredo met with approval there and elsewhere in the state. When he visited the border city during December 1917 to arrange living quarters for his company, "The people in Laredo met me with open arms[;] it made me feel good to know that they was so glad to see me and that I was comeing there [*sic*]." The *Laredo Weekly Times* gleefully announced the impending arrival of Wright's Rangers and that Captain William M. Ryan, a former law enforcement officer from Luling, would command Company I in Laredo as well. This would make the city "immune from visits of bad men from the Mexican side of the Rio Grande." Too, criminals from the United States would stay far away, "for if there is anything a real lawless character is actually afraid of that is a Texas Ranger." The writer added that the latter were a "godsend in preserving law and order in a community." Closer to Wright's home in Floresville, the *San Antonio Express* was more specific in defining Wright's new targets: "[Pancho] Villa followers are advised to give [the Rangers] a wide berth as they are 'plumb pizen.'"[10]

The residents of Wilson County certainly were not pleased to have the sheriff they had elected eight times leave them, but they showed their gratitude for his service. In 1910 those in Sutherland Springs had given him a .45 caliber engraved Colt revolver with pearl grips; in 1917 others gave him a "magnificent bay horse as a Christmas gift." The new mount, which Wright named Jack, was a quarter horse raised by the noted horse breeder Crawford Sykes, who lived in Wilson County near Pandora. Wright as sheriff had traced horses stolen from Sykes all the way to Louisiana, where he recovered and returned them to the relieved rancher. In gratitude, Sykes had then given Wright a mare named Nelly. Now he and other supporters outdid themselves; Jack had a lineage that could be traced to Steel Dust, the progenitor of every quarter horse and thus true Texas equine royalty. Wright later had his picture taken at Laredo, astride Jack with the engraved Colt in a holster on his hip. It became a frequently reproduced image of Wright, which is appropriate since he often worked at that time on horseback in the thick brush along the Mexican border, usually riding Jack and carrying a short-barreled carbine like the one he had in the picture along with his revolver. In a more somber moment, Wright's resignation was accepted by the Wilson County commissioners on December 31, 1917. Alfred B. "Burt" Carnes, his former deputy, resigned as a county commissioner at the same time and was appointed to succeed Wright as sheriff. Wilson County had suffered a "great loss" in the departure of its "widely known and honored sheriff," but Wright was eager to be a Ranger again.[11]

By the time Wright resigned as sheriff, most of his local recruits for Company K had departed for the Rio Grande. He wrote to Harley on December 26: "I got my men off this morning bright and earley [*sic*] for Laredo, they all are in fine shape and well mounted." He confessed, "I could hardly stand to see them go with out [*sic*] going along, I love the work." Wright's "advance guard" traveled on horseback, accompanied by a new chuck wagon and pack mules. The group included everyone except Wright, Edds, and Adams, who all joined the company later at Laredo. Pullin led the new Rangers on their first long ride, during which they apparently met with no problems. Wright briefly detoured to Kenedy, where on the evening of January 2, 1918, he became a Knights Templar, then went a few days later, presumably by train, to Laredo, ready to begin patrolling his district, which stretched along the Rio Grande downstream from Laredo, while Ryan patrolled upstream with his company.[12]

Wright's men and his superiors both quickly learned that his appointment had been a great choice. Wright took care of his Rangers—he tried to make sure they were paid and reimbursed in a timely fashion, and when someone did not get a paycheck, Wright was known to loan him the money. He also broke with long-standing custom concerning reimbursements for food for his men and forage for their animals, which they had to provide. Ranger captains customarily received all the money for food and forage from Austin, purchased these items themselves, issued them, and then pocketed any savings. Wright refused to do this, instead having expense money from Austin sent directly to his men. Hanson commented to Harley in late February 1918 about Wright's Company K: "He has a fine lot of men, the best I have seen, and they are under perfect controll, and dicipline, [*sic*] and I believe will prove a great honor to our force. Such men are hard to get and but for his personality think it would be impossible to get togather [*sic*] such a force of men." Harley, slowly realizing the mistake he had made with Fox, must have been reassured to read about one of his newest captains at Laredo, "He is in full accord in everything with your ideas as to the management of the border and her people." Within the political, economic, and social turmoil in South Texas generated not only by the Mexican Revolution but also the infusion of new residents from both the United States and Mexico, Wright emerged as one of the most durable and effective Ranger leaders on the lower Rio Grande.[13]

Ranger service for Wright in early 1918 was relatively quiet until as many as twenty "Texans, Mexicans, and Slackers," as an eyewitness later described them, raided the headquarters of the San Antonio Viejo Ranch, a sprawling operation in Jim Hogg and Starr counties southeast of Laredo. The owner of the property was Tom T. East, who had married Alice Gertrudis Kleberg, granddaughter of Richard King, in 1915 at the King Ranch. In March 1916 another forty raiders had occupied San Antonio Viejo Ranch and held Alice hostage until Sheriff Oscar Thompson and a dozen Texas Rangers arrived from nearby Hebbronville. Now yet another group stormed onto the property about supper time on March 7, 1918, and again took prisoners. The latter included Alice, her driver Terry Downs, foreman William P. Franklin and his wife, their son William C. Franklin and his wife, their nephew Stephen L. Franklin, J. Claude McGill of Santa Rosa Ranch and his driver Rosendo Garcia, and some Tejano ranch hands. Stephen Franklin and McGill had the bad luck to arrive in an automobile owned by Thompson and driven by Garcia just after the raiders occupied the property. East himself had been with his wife and Downs in a similar situation in their car, but he got out to open the gate, spotted several intruders crossing the fence line, and hurried to his automobile while the other two continued to the house. He drove to one of his cow camps, where he told a hand to ride to Hebbronville and get help. Meanwhile, the raiders looted the store at his ranch and discussed hanging William C. Franklin, whom they mistook for Dudley V. "Duncan" Stilwell, one of East's employees who had been a deputy sheriff, constable, and Ranger whom they hated, but Franklin's mother convinced them not to do that.[14]

Having ransacked the main facilities of San Antonio Viejo Ranch for supplies, guns, saddles, and horses, the raiders revealed that they intended to rob the bank in Hebbronville. Apparently, none of them knew the way to the town, nor could they drive, so they drafted Garcia and William C. Franklin to take them in the automobiles owned by East and Thompson. Franklin's mother again protested, but he explained to her that the intruders only wanted him to go because he knew the man who had the keys to the bank. With both cars packed with raiders, with those who could not fit following on horseback with some ranch hands as hostages, the raiding party departed for Hebbronville about eleven at night. After a journey of several hours, they arrived near the town, where the raiders questioned Garcia about local security and learned that Wright was there with his Rangers. Deciding not to attack since expected Tejano reinforcements had not appeared, they returned to East's ranch by about three in the morning, packed everything they could carry, and rode away. Freed from having to worry about retributions, the erstwhile captives at San Antonio Viejo Ranch sent Downs to Hebbronville in Thompson's automobile to join the ranch hand East had already sent there. They were not the only ones to sound the alarm; the raiders had kidnapped Salvador Salinas at his father's ranch, Las Escobias, on March 7 and, despite their dire warnings, his younger brother José Salinas Jr. had raced to tell the authorities about the abduction, although in fact Salvador was released before the intruders reached San Antonio Viejo Ranch.[15]

Wright had left Laredo on March 3 with six Rangers and settled near Hebbronville at the ranch of W. Henry Edds, a cousin of his sergeant, John J. Edds, who had a commission as a Special Ranger. A "Mexican" arrived before sunrise on March 8 to tell him about the raid at San Antonio Viejo Ranch, and Wright was on his way there a few hours later. With him rode James P. N. "Pat" Craighead, who had succeeded Thompson as sheriff. Craighead and Wright knew each other well; the latter had served as a deputy for the former's father, John S. Craighead, when he was sheriff of Wilson County, and Wright as sheriff accompanied the elder Craighead to retrieve Pat when he was ambushed on the border in 1910 and lost his left leg. They traveled in cars with Edds and Thompson, who like

Henry Edds was a Special Ranger; a pair of inspectors for the Cattle Raisers Association of Texas, Special Ranger William T. "Tom" Moseley and John C. Draper, a former Special Ranger; rancher and former Special Ranger Alex H. Reed; and two of Wright's Rangers. Their saddles were piled into a truck provided by Thompson, while Ranger Wright C. Wells followed with horses and mules. Arriving at San Antonio Viejo Ranch, Wright's posse was reinforced by the addition of Stephen Franklin, who was also a Special Ranger, and Stilwell, Wright sent Henry Edds and Thompson in a car to Rio Grande City to get the three Rangers posted there, then saddled up when Wells arrived with the horses and mules and hit the trail. While the pursuers traveled on horseback like their quarry, Wright used a driver with a car provided by Henry Edds as a courier to keep in touch with potential reinforcements.[16]

The chase lasted for two days, punctuated, according to newspaper accounts, by a series of bloody clashes. Reports claimed that at least five raiders, who outnumbered Wright's party, were killed on March 8, and official records do confirm that Wright led his original posse of eight men in a skirmish on that date at El Javali (or El Jabali) Ranch in La Salle County near Encinal, south of Cotulla. The *San Antonio Express* declared that Wright recovered seven horses with saddles (some bloodstained), hats, and Winchesters, along with plunder from San Antonio Viejo Ranch. Henry Edds rejoined Wright at El Javali with the three Rangers from Rio Grande City, bringing the total number from Company K to seven: Wright, Connelly, Hutchison, Perkins, Pullin, Monroe Wells, and Wright Wells. Riding through the night, Wright's reinforced posse attacked again on March 9 near Salineno, a Mexican settlement on the north bank of the Rio Grande about thirty-five miles west of Rio Grande City. The remaining raiders scattered and crossed into Mexico. Again, according to several Texas newspapers, Wright and his men suffered no casualties while killing as many as fifteen raiders. The *San Antonio Express* later amended the story, claiming one day that the fifteen had been shot during a running fight in thick brush, then the next day that Wright's men captured the fifteen but had to shoot them when they tried to escape. The second writer added, "What the bandits need is an English primer that will advise them that while a camel may pass through the eye of a needle, a Texas Ranger will tackle hades [*sic*] with a single bucket of water." The body count of fifteen appeared in the *New York Times* and persisted in popular accounts of the pursuit for decades. In fact, while testifying under oath before the legislative committee convened in 1919 to investigate the Rangers, both Wright and Thompson admitted that they had seen only one dead raider, the same number Wright included in his original report and Hanson confirmed in a later letter. That figure has been accepted in recent historical accounts. The rest escaped into Mexico, for which Wright blamed East, who seemed more interested in tending his cattle than forwarding fresh horses for the posse as he had promised.[17]

Not all calls for help ended in such excitement for Wright and his Rangers. The commissioners of Atascosa County in the summer of 1918 had a dispute with their treasurer, Hugh L. McKenzie, and asked him to resign, which he refused to do. A meeting was arranged between the disputing parties, and the commissioners asked for Rangers to attend in case things went terribly wrong. Wright and Special Ranger Stephen Franklin accompanied Friedrich H. "Frank" Burmeister, a former Texas legislator who had known Wright when he served as a district attorney, to Atascosa County and sat for two long days in July 1918 doing nothing before McKenzie agreed to quit. Wright wrote to Lon Willis, his friend who was then serving as a Ranger sergeant in Company M, "They are having a hot time in politicks [*sic*] in Atascosa County … They had me and Franklin to stay in the Court while they was investigating him, we thought we was going to have some fun but we failed." Wright returned to Laredo but sent several of his men to Atascosa County, where they busied themselves helping local law enforcement officials gather evidence for other cases. They also enjoyed a bit of rest and recreation: "all my boys have them a girl in Charlot[te] except Peterson and Connally and they are two [*sic*] old." Wright added that he had joined a colleague at the park there and "watched the girls go around for awhile, but that is all the good it done us." Wright proved to be of more help when Burmeister asked him to help investigate cattle rustlers around Hebbronville that same summer. Men were arrested and the stealing stopped. Wright was also approached by rancher Adolph

Lorenz of Live Oak County, who told him "Socialists," or open range squatters, were poaching cattle near his home, but Wright told him that area was outside of his jurisdiction. Instead, Captain Ryan was sent from Laredo with some of his Rangers, and they arrested five or six men, including two brothers of Sheriff Charles L. Tullis. Wright and Ryan in September 1918 attended the district court in Pearsall, in nearby Frio County, at the request of James Callan, president of the Cattle Raisers Association of Texas, when the grand jury reviewed the rustling cases. Again, despite concerns about impending violence, they apparently enjoyed a quiet session.[18]

Ongoing efforts to win the war in Europe led to other new tasks for Wright. He noticed that a significant number of "slackers" who wanted to avoid being conscripted were leaving Texas for Mexico. He asked the various draft boards in Texas counties to forward names and descriptions of the offenders so he could be more effective in finding them. Commenting on Wright's initiative, a writer for the *San Antonio Express* reported that Wright declared there was a "cavayard," or herd, of draft dodgers on the border, and that if local boards would send names, he would round them up. The writer opined that Wright would certainly find the offenders if he got the information he needed. Lists were sent, and Rangers hung copies in post offices and carried them in their pockets. Wright and other Rangers were not the only ones concerned about the wartime influx of strangers along the Rio Grande; Judge James B. Wells, a political boss in Cameron County who usually supported the Rangers, reported that the roads across the Rio Grande into Mexico were filled with Mexican citizens and their families who were trying to avoid the draft, as well as many genuine shirkers and deserters, and even German spies. Wright later reported that his men captured a total of twenty-five draft evaders at Rio Grande City, where he posted Sergeant Edds because he was bilingual. At Laredo, Wright recounted that he caught at least the same number. And Wright even arrested a possible German spy in September 1918. All these prisoners were forwarded to the Army for disposition, while several counterfeiters Wright's Rangers arrested in Laredo and Rio Grande City were transferred to federal custody. Conversely, Wright had to dispatch Adams to investigate hateful graffiti, such as "Slacker," that was scrawled on the houses of George Druschel and E. Pinkney Moxley in

La Feria, a small town in Cameron County. Apparently the two refused to buy Liberty Bonds. Adams noted that Druschel, who had two sons in the army, later invested $500 in the bonds.[19]

Border politics consumed much of Wright's attention in the fall of 1918. Archer Parr, a wealthy rancher known as the "Duke of Duval County," had established a powerful political machine based upon his control of Hispanic voters, who were a majority in his county. A challenge by another Democratic politico in 1912 led to gunfire and the deaths of three Tejano officials before a state judge intervened to restore Parr's hold. Subsequent battles in court were hampered by a mysterious fire that destroyed key records in the courthouse in 1914, the year Parr was first elected to what became a twenty-year term in the Texas Senate. David W. Glasscock defeated Parr in the 1918 Democratic primary with the support of Governor Hobby and the votes of the Anglo majorities, including many newly enfranchised women, in the other counties in Parr's district. But the stage was set for another underhanded political victory for Parr. Glasscock was a lawyer and former legislator from McAllen, in Hidalgo County. Anticipating a debacle at the Democratic district convention, he asked Hobby to have Rangers investigate the election returns in Hidalgo, Duval, and Cameron counties. Wright went to Hidalgo County to collect records and take depositions, while as anticipated the district caucus, led by Judge Wells, Parr's ally who controlled Cameron County, declared Parr to be their candidate. Glasscock led a walkout and became the nominee of a portion of his district's delegates. When the Texas Democratic convention endorsed Glasscock, Parr sued and was declared the primary winner by a state district judge, who disallowed all women's votes as unconstitutional. Amid this turmoil, Wright had some of his Rangers guard the polls in Hidalgo County, as he had during the primary, and he temporarily moved his headquarters there, to Mercedes. Parr won the election, and Glasscock protested, leading to a Texas Senate investigation in which the legislators by a narrow margin endorsed Parr rather than Glasscock.[20]

While the Texas Senate investigated the 1918 election conflict between Parr and Glasscock, Wright and his Rangers shifted from guarding the polls to gathering information about what happened. They interviewed 190 people concerning the voting at multiple sites in Hidalgo and Starr counties during both the primary in July 1918 and the regular election in November. Wright led a team of Rangers—Acosta, Adams, Bryan Butler, Edds, Perez, and Loyalty Ranger Juan C. Gonzalez—who worked with officials in ten communities: Havana, Hidalgo, Los Ebanos, Mercedes, Mission, Penitas, Raymondville, Rio Grande City, Sam Fordyce, and Santa Maria. According to the published testimonies, Wright was able to talk with those who said they could not speak English, so he spoke Spanish. Many times, the Rangers heard a variation of what one woman told them: "I don't know what I voted, just like the rest, just like a bunch of burros." Sergeant Edds, immediately after completing the task of taking depositions, wrote to Ranger Captain Roy W. Aldrich at Austin: "We made a thorough canvass of Hidalgo Co. It was 'rotten' to say the least." Two years later, assigned to guard that polls once more in Hidalgo County at the request of the "Independents," Wright, who had perhaps learned a hard lesson in 1918, reported that all went well and the Democrats, including Parr, were big winners. Asked again by local political activists in 1924 to guard the polls in Hidalgo County, Governor Pat M. Neff declined to send any Rangers.[21]

Accusations of improper behavior by Rangers during the electoral battle between Parr and Glasscock added to a groundswell of protest about the law enforcement agency. Calls for reforming or even abolishing the Rangers had resurfaced during the turbulent administration of Governor James E. "Pa" Ferguson, with much of the unsavory evidence against them coming from the border with Mexico. Wright himself had protested in November 1917 about Captain J. Monroe Fox, whose notoriety for posing with dead Mexican raiders in photographs after the Las Norias raid in August 1915 had been far eclipsed by his role in the massacre of fifteen men and boys at Porvenir in January 1918. Harley in June 1918 disbanded Fox's Company B, among whose members was J. Boone Oliphant, the younger brother of Grover Oliphant in Wright's Company K. Harley also quickly discovered, as numerous people already suspected, that many of the problems along the border originated with the Special Rangers, who often did not have professional law enforcement experience and were not supervised as intended by regular Rangers enrolled in standing companies. Wright four months after arriving at Laredo wrote to Harley, "I would consider it a special favor if you would not appoint any more Special Rangers from here, without my passing on them, as there are some in the service now, who should not be." There were hundreds of Special Rangers, and Harley dismissed them all in December 1918.[22]

Wright and Company K emerged unchanged from Harley's reorganization of the Ranger Force in 1918, primarily because most of them had never been accused of any improprieties, and when the Texas legislature launched an investigation of the Rangers in 1919, Wright became a star witness. The inquiry began at the request of José T. Canales, a veteran legislator with a law degree from the University of Michigan who lived in Brownsville. He had always supported the Ranger Force, had obtained a Special Ranger commission for his brother Albino T. Canales, and was a friend of Ranger captains John H. Rogers and John R. Hughes. But the excesses of Rangers on the border during the Mexican Revolution led him to doubt their integrity, and an angry clash with Ranger Francis A. "Frank" Hamer, who threatened him, convinced him that something must be done. Canales complained to Governor Hobby, who referred the matter to Harley, whose dismissive responses in turn further angered the Tejano legislator. When the legislature convened in January 1919, Canales submitted a bill to reform the Ranger Force by reducing it in number, requiring recruits to have two years of law enforcement experience and post a bond against any transgressions, allowing local officials to have Rangers removed from their county, and making it possible to sue Rangers for their actions. This prompted heated debates and a request from Harley that an investigation be launched into the reasons for Canales' proposal. The reform bill failed, but a joint legislative committee organized to review a variety of allegations about the Rangers, including nineteen specific charges by Canales.[23]

Wright was never under negative scrutiny from Canales or his fellow legislators. When Canales testified, he declared that while the Rangers had declined, Rogers, Hughes, and Wright were "some of the noblest men and best men that I know." Cameron County lawyer William G. B. Morrison described Wright as a "very fine gentleman." Wealthy oilman and land developer Alba S. Heywood of San Benito in Cameron County, a former vaudeville comedian, had much to say about local corruption and some Rangers' transgressions. But he insisted that since Wright and Charles F. Stevens arrived on the border, relations between Rangers and Mexicans had improved. Sheriff Will T. Vann, who supported Canales' demands for Ranger reform and had even called for abolishing the agency, agreed with Heywood about Wright, whom he said was a "prince." Judge Wells made his opinion clear: "I don't think every Tim, Dick and Harry ought to be appointed a Ranger, and I think there [are] entirely too many Special Rangers, Loyalty Rangers and God knows what all." But he also said that Wright was "A good officer and a good man, like some of the rest of us he gets his head a little set sometimes, but he don't get far off." Calixto E. Valle, a prominent Rio Grande City businessman, testified that Wright was a "fine man" about whom he had heard no complaints. J. Claude McGill was very complimentary in his account of Wright's actions after the raid on Tom T. East's San Antonio Viejo Ranch in March 1918. However, not everyone liked Wright. Virginia Yeager, who described herself as the leading suffragette in Duval County, submitted multiple denunciations of Rangers, including Wright. Among her claims was that men went to Mexico to avoid the draft not because they hated the United States, but because they wanted to avoid "inevitable unwarranted assault and arrest by the Rangers." She reported that Wright and his Rangers had illegally invaded her San Diego home. Other witnesses who knew Wright, Friedrich H. "Frank" Burmeister and Oscar Thompson, responded that Yeager had already admitted in a deposition for a lawsuit that Wright and his men had never entered her residence. The legislative committee, rather than censure Wright, appointed him as one of three Rangers responsible for securing witnesses during its investigation.[24]

While Wright did not have to worry about himself during the legislative inquiry, he did have a serious problem with John J. Edds, his former deputy and the sergeant of Company K. While Morrison testified that Edds had a "good" reputation in Cameron County, Canales specifically mentioned him in his complaints to Harley. And when Canales on January 30, 1919, presented his first list of five charges against specific Rangers, three of them accused Edds of violent crimes. In chronological order, the first was the murder of Jose Maria Gomez Salinas on September 2, 1918, by Frederico López and Sabás Ozuna in Jim Hogg County, which Canales declared had been done "under the orders and at the request of" Edds. The second was having "tortured and brutally treated" Jesus Villareal on September 4, 1918. The third was killing Lisandro Muñoz, at the home of Jesus Sánchez, near Roma on October 5, 1918. Historian Evan Anders has declared that this incident was one of two specific incidents that pushed Canales to demand the reform of the Rangers. Harley initially responded that neither he nor Hanson, whom he had sent to investigate both homicides, had done anything wrong in not punishing Edds, who was indicted for Munoz's death. Canales disagreed, and in fact he and Hanson had argued about Edds during a railroad trip from Brownsville to Austin in October 1918, with the exchange leading Canales to leave that train and take another. It apparently mattered little to Canales, whose primary focus was on the mistreatment of Mexicans and Tejanos, that Edds was a proud descendant of the Canary Island settlers of San Antonio, and so he would be considered Hispanic under twentieth-century guidelines.[25]

Edds' testimony to the legislative committee concerning the death of Salinas, which included responses to questions from Canales, did reveal a lapse in judgement, but his culpability in the crime could hardly be proven beyond a reasonable doubt. Eduardo Yzaguirre, a rancher in Jim Hogg County with a commission as a Special Ranger, called Edds in Rio Grande City from Agua Nueva Ranch to ask for his help in arresting Salinas, who had stolen a horse and fled. Edds agreed, and Yzaguirre with a cousin went to Rio Grande City in an automobile and brought Edds and Hutchison back to Agua Nueva Ranch. The two Rangers rode about thirty miles up the Rio Grande, where they thought Salinas might try to cross, while Ozuna and Lopez, who worked as ranch hands for Yzaguirre, followed the fugitive's trail. After failing to intercept Salinas, Edds and Hutchison were taken back to Rio Grande City by Yzaguirre, and they were resting there when another telephone call came from Yzaguirre, who reported that his men had Salinas. The Rangers faced a dilemma: they were witnesses in a trial before the state district court, and officials were adamant that they had to be there. They were given one day's leave by the judge to hurry to Agua Nueva Ranch and deal with Salinas. The two drove to the ranch, arriving late at night, and decided to let Ozuna and Lopez take Salinas to Hebbronville, where he would be given to Perkins of Wright's company and Special Ranger Thompson, the former sheriff, along with a note of explanation from Edds. Salinas never arrived in Hebbronville—Ozuna and Lopez claimed that he tried to escape, and so they had to shoot him about four miles from their destination early on the morning of September 2, 1918.[26]

When Edds heard about the death of Salinas, he sent Hutchison with Yzaguirre to Hebbronville to report to Wright. They found that Wright was in the field, but a telephone call from Connelly to him at Torrecillas conveyed the bad news. Wright of course ordered Connelly to arrest Ozuna and Lopez, but they posted bonds of $500 apiece with the endorsement of Thompson and returned to Agua Nueva Ranch, whence they later traveled to Austin with Yzaguirre to testify before the legislative committee investigating Edds. Neither man was indicted for killing Salinas. When Wright returned to Hebbronville by train on September 3, the two ranch hands had already departed, but he and Hanson investigated as best they could. There was nothing to be seen at the site of the killing because many others had already walked over it, and Salinas had already been buried. They interviewed both Ozuna and Lopez, who said that Salinas tried to escape by spurring his horse into the brush alongside the road, which contradicted witnesses who said they saw his lifeless body lying in the road, handcuffed and shot in the back. In his testimony before the legislative committee, Wright declared that he still had confidence in his sergeant because he did nothing wrong in following the lead of Yzaguirre, who chose the two men to escort Salinas. Hanson provided more details in his report to Harley. He insinuated that a foreman at Agua Nueva Ranch, whom he did not name, had conspired with Salinas to steal horses and told Ozuna and Lopez to kill their prisoner to cover his tracks. Hanson added that Salinas allegedly participated in the March 1918 raid on the San Antonio Viejo ranch, Edds made a bad decision and became tangled in an "unfortunate occurrence," and Wright had now ordered his Rangers to transfer prisoners only to a "duly authorized officer."[27]

Canales remained convinced that Edds had instructed Ozuna and Lopez to kill Salinas. Edds denied giving such an order and insisted he did not handcuff Salinas; that was done by the two ranch hands. As for being directly involved in the murder, he and Hutchison had already departed for Rio Grande City when Ozuna and Lopez started with Salinas for Hebbronville. Asked why he had sent the prisoner to Hebbronville instead of taking him to Rio Grande City, Edds confessed that he knew Judge Wells would release Salinas on a bond, while Edds wanted the suspect to remain in custody while he investigated other charges against him. As for giving prisoners to civilians, Edds responded that he had relied upon citizens many times and never had a problem until the killing of Salinas. Yzaguirre in his testimony to the legislators largely corroborated what Edds said, with one interesting exception: he claimed that Edds handcuffed Salinas and gave the key to Lopez. Canales in his testimony concerning the Salinas matter insinuated that the Rangers in Hebbronville had "protected" Ozuna and Lopez by arranging a low bond of $500 apiece for them, and he again repeated that Edds told the two ranch hands to kill Salinas.[28]

Canales and others next questioned Edds about Villareal's claim of being abused on September 4, 1918, just two days after the killing of Salinas. Edds' testimony, along with that of U.S. Army Scouts Royal Collins and N. Lee Dickens, provided the committee with a fairly complete account of what transpired. Edds and Hutchison, with Collins, Dickens, and two prisoners, were returning to Rio Grande City about three in the morning when their automobile quit about six miles west of the town. A quick examination revealed there was no water in the radiator, which made the car overheat. Dickens went with a jug to find a house and get water, but he came back standing on the running board of another car driven by Villareal, who had three young men with him. Told by Dickens that these travelers should be questioned, Collins talked first with Villareal, who said he was a Duval County constable. Collins was surprised when Villareal, who had been drinking heavily, declared that he did not know the three young men in his car. Asked by Collins if he had been paid to transport them, Villareal said no. Collins next removed one of the young men from the car, who gave his name as Pedro Garcia and said his uncle, the father of Guillermo Benavidez, one of the other passengers, paid Villareal seventy dollars to take him across the Rio Grande. Benavidez added another detail when questioned separately—that his father wanted Villareal to convey them over the river so they could avoid the draft. Asked about this, Villareal emphatically denied the story, then declared that as a constable he should not be detained. Edds was angry that a law officer would help shirkers escape, and it did not help Villareal that the young men had full suitcases and were less than a mile from a popular ferry across the Rio Grande. Edds and the Scouts concluded their testimony to the legislators by reporting that they delivered Villareal and his passengers to military authorities at Fort Ringgold in Rio Grande City about an hour after Dickens had initially encountered them.[29]

Villareal told a very different story to the legislative committee. He testified that on September 3, 1918, he went by car to Rio Grande City to transport his nephew, Miguel Villareal, to be married at Falfurrias. Having accomplished that mission, he agreed to convey three other young men—Guillermo and Eulalio Benavides, and Ramiro Ramos—to Roma to buy goats. At one in the morning on September 4 he was stopped by a Ranger. After asking where he was going, the Ranger asked Villareal to give him a ride back to his stalled car. Villareal did, but when they arrived there were other Rangers who arrested him and his passengers. The Rangers choked Villareal, trying to get him to admit he was taking the boys across the river to avoid the draft, but he stubbornly refused, insisting they were going to Roma. After putting a cocked pistol in his mouth several times, the Rangers loudly discussed how they were going to kill Villareal, but he did not change his story. He also recalled that, taken to the Rangers' camp and then to a magistrate in Rio Grande City to post bonds, the four men had appeared in the federal district court on December 2, 1918 and were all dismissed without indictments despite the testimony of Edds and Collins. Villareal admitted that the younger men said they were going across the Rio Grande to avoid the draft, but he insisted that they did so only after being "tortured."[30]

Edds emphatically denied putting a gun in Villareal's mouth, or anyone choking him or sitting on him while he was lying down. Problems with the Duval County constable's testimony gave the benefit of doubt to the Ranger. Several days after they were left at Fort Ringgold, the three young men were again questioned by military authorities, with Collins present, and all signed statements that corroborated the story provided by Edds and the two Scouts, without Villareal's embellishments. It was apparently at that time that "Pedro Garcia" confessed that his real name was Eulalio Benavides. But when they appeared with Villareal and attorney John R. Monroe (a former legislator from Rio Grande City) before a federal commissioner for a pretrial hearing, they declared they had been threatened and guns had been put in their mouths. It was also then that Villareal introduced such details as Ramos being a nephew who was going with him to Roma to be married the day they were stopped (apparently just like Miguel Villareal in Falfurrias), and that the other two were traveling to Roma to buy goats. Collins told the legislators that Villareal on the night he was detained never mentioned his nephew or a wedding. He also denied any of the four were ever struck or threatened with a gun, or even came close to being harmed, except when Villareal stuck his hand in his pocket, saying he was going to give Collins his knife and money. When he did that, Edds immediately stepped up and had Collins talk to another boy while he questioned Villareal, who continued to say he did not know the three young men. Edds added that the two young men were too well-dressed to be shopping for goats, which he believed was a story invented by Monroe. Finally, each of the Benavides brothers had a suitcase, and there were initials on the luggage and letters inside that corroborated their ownership. It also helped Edds that he had been investigated by Sheriff Gustavo A. Guerra of Starr County, Robert Oosterveen as the Starr County attorney, and Justice of the Peace Emilo Naranjo after Villareal's accusations surfaced, and none of them had filed charges against him.[31]

The legislative investigators were understandably puzzled by one singular fact: there had been no criminal charges filed against any of the four men Edds and his colleagues had taken to Fort Ringgold. In fact, Ramos was apparently both a Mexican citizen and had a draft registration card, and while Edds and the Scouts told him he was not under arrest, he may have accompanied the others to Fort Ringgold because he had no other transportation options. As for the other two young men, the legal deadline for registering for the draft was more than a week after they were stopped, so they had not yet violated the law. Edds argued that he intercepted them in the process of avoiding registration by fleeing to Mexico, which was the infraction, and he noted that they were only released by a local magistrate after posting bonds. Of course, the fact that none of them were convicted for anything was outside of his authority as a law enforcement officer. Interestingly, Wright remained silent about this case in his testimony to the legislative committee. He certainly wanted to support Edds, and he may well have known Collins and Dickens. The former was a native of Wilson County and by 1919 had become the Chief of Scouts at Fort Ringgold, while the latter was from Carrizo Springs in Dimmit County, the home of at least seven Rangers to whom Wright was related or with whom he served. Given the confusion surrounding these charges—the San Antonio *Evening News* printed conflicting accounts exonerating and condemning Edds in the same issue—Wright may have decided it was best just to let this issue pass unchallenged. After all, unlike the Salinas and Munoz incidents, Harley had not ordered an official inquiry, and no one was calling for Edds' arrest in the Villareal case.[32]

Wright had actually approved Edds' plan of action that led to his killing of Muñoz, the focus of the most serious charge by Canales against the Ranger sergeant. Edds had contacted Wright from Rio Grande City, presumably by telephone, and told him that he had information about Alonzo Sánchez, a deserter whose name appeared on a list provided by the local draft board. Edds said he had been told that the fugitive periodically came back from Mexico and stayed near Roma at the home of his father, Jesus Sánchez. Most important, he planned to cross the Rio Grande that night. Wright accepted Edds' proposal to take two privates from Company K, Lorenz and Monroe Wells, and make a dawn raid on the Sánchez house. The Rangers arrived about daylight on October 6, 1918; Edds posted Wells on the road that ran along one side of the house, while he placed Lorenz twenty yards away, on the street in front of the home, to stop anyone leaving by the front door. Edds then went to the other side of the house from Wells, found a gate in the fence that surrounded the back yard, and went through it into a small area enclosed by poultry netting adjacent to the house. In this enclosure were two unarmed men, sleeping on cots. He had been told that Alonzo had a black mustache, while his brother was clean-shaven; the two men matched that description. Waking the man with a mustache by saying "Alonzo" several times, Edds identified himself as a Ranger, said he wanted to talk to him, and asked his name. The man stood up and, rather than sit back down as asked, grabbed Edds' rifle, which he had cocked. As they wrestled for the gun, Edds called for Wells, but there was no gate on that side of the house and Wells did not get over the fence before Edds, who was smaller than his antagonist, pulled his pistol and shot the alleged deserter. Seriously wounded in the groin, the man with the mustache fell, still holding the rifle, and died despite the efforts of the Rangers and the man in the other cot to save him.[33]

Edds quickly learned from Alonzo's father Jesus and younger brother Zaragosa, the clean-shaven fellow who had been sleeping in the other cot before he was rudely awakened, that the man he shot was not Alonzo but Lisandro Muñoz, his cousin. Alonzo had indeed come to his father's home earlier that night after crossing the Rio Grande just three hundred yards away with others to attend a dance and visit with their families, but he left shortly after midnight. Edds had Lorenz and Zaragosa Sánchez try to call the county judge, Higinio Garza Jr., but he could not be reached. Lorenz and Sánchez then telephoned Wright, Sheriff Guerra, and an unnamed justice of the peace, after which the Rangers stayed with the body so no evidence would be altered. Wright arrived with a justice of the peace and deputy sheriff (Guerra was unavailable). After he had investigated the site, Wright declared that he believed his sergeant told the truth and was justified in using deadly force. Understandably, Harley asked Hanson to investigate; the latter wrote, after talking to Wright and others, that he was "thoroughly convinced that Sergeant Edds was compelled to kill this man in order to save his own life." His deadly action was "unfortunate" and "greatly regretted," but justified. Wright wrote his own letter in support of Edds to Sam D. W. Low, the acting Attorney General of Texas, who also got reports that exonerated Edds from Sheriff Guerra and Starr County Attorney Oosterveen, as well as Justice of the Peace Naranjo.[34]

Canales in his questioning of Edds before the legislative committee focused primarily on the killing of Muñoz, for which Edds had been indicted by early 1919. The Tejano legislator emphasized the fact that Edds had no legal warrant for Alonzo Sánchez. Edds in response declared that the Rangers operated under the authority of a proclamation from President Woodrow

Wilson and never obtained warrants for deserters because they were not needed. He later claimed that the Rangers often did not officially file cases against men they were hunting, and thus acquire warrants, because that provided a warning to their targets and allowed them to escape. Edds' failure to secure a warrant had prompted Judge Wells to write to Hanson earlier that the sergeant was guilty of manslaughter. Canales and Wells had quarreled bitterly as political competitors, but they united in demanding that Edds be convicted of manslaughter and denouncing Hanson for agreeing with Wright that the killing of Muñoz was "Perfectly justifiable." Hanson stood his ground, arguing that "I do not believe that there is a jury in the United States that would convict him for anything in connection with this." Ultimately, he proved to be correct. A Texas district court jury at Alice in late January 1919 took just ten minutes to decide that Edds was not guilty of manslaughter in the killing of Muñoz. As for the legislative committee, the members decided that Edds's actions at the Sánchez house were negligent but not criminal.[35]

Edds was never tried for his role in the death of Salinas or the alleged abuse of Villareal, and he was acquitted for killing Muñoz. However, he was suspended from the Rangers during February 1919 pending the outcome of the legislative investigation. Wright welcomed him back as his sergeant when the suspension ended, which may have puzzled some observers. But Wright's testimony provided some explanations as to why he retained his former deputy. First, it was difficult to recruit good Rangers, and Wright still believed Edds was "one of the best men ever on the Ranger force." Questioned by Canales about violent incidents that occurred during the time that Edds was his deputy in Wilson County, Wright declared that Edds' killing of a black man and wounding of a white man were acts of self-defense. Edds, on the recommendation of Wright, also worked as a mounted inspector for the Customs Service under the direction of Frank Rabb, the controversial collector at Laredo who dabbled in politics on both sides of the border. Called before the legislative committee, Rabb said Wright was "one of our best officers in Texas" and praised Edds highly. Rabb and Wright both emphasized that the Spanish-speaking Edds was particularly adept at working with Mexicans and Tejanos. What neither man mentioned, and Canales apparently did not know, was that while working for Rabb in the late summer of 1916, Edds had written a letter to Wright reporting that he had shot and killed a "cattle smuggler" after the man pulled a knife and attacked him while being questioned in a house near Zapata. After a "bloody knife scuffle," Edds shot his attacker. Edds posted a $500 bond, but apparently no further legal action was taken against him. Wright also did not mention Edd's service with Captain Henry L. Ransom, whose killing of Mexican prisoners and other excesses on the border was a source of much well-deserved controversy. Wright did declare that Edds was not at fault in the killing of Salinas and Muñoz, and when cross-examined by Canales he reminded him that none of his men had participated in any of the depredations recounted by the Tejano legislator. Wright believed Edds had done nothing wrong and in fact was quite useful, so he kept him.[36]

Others agreed with Wright about Edds, if sometimes reluctantly. Hanson reported to Harley that there was a division of opinion in Starr County regarding Edds. Many thought he was doing a good job, but prominent people involved in illicit activities such as smuggling alcohol and harboring deserters were loud in their criticism of him. Calixto E. Valle told the legislative committee that Edds' clashes with Starr County leaders came after he caught one of them with cattle that carried someone else's brand, a charge that echoed Hanson's negative opinion of those who called for Edds's removal. Judge Wells, the political boss who wanted Edds convicted of manslaughter, reported that Edds could be "dictatorial and overbearing," and after "people" at Rio Grande City protested, he had spoken with Wright about Edds. But Wells in his testimony to the committee admitted that people thought well of the Ranger sergeant. Captain Harry H. Dunn of the Thirteenth United States Cavalry praised Edds highly for his assistance and "tact, foresight, and thoughtfulness." Finally, when Wright's old commander, Rogers, testified, he was repeatedly asked about Edd's guilt and refused to condemn him, saying several times that circumstances sometimes led men, including some Rangers he had known, to make tragic mistakes. Historian Robert M. Utley perhaps described Edds best when he wrote that he had a "solid record" and earned praise from almost everyone, but his "pugnacious" nature led him to be a target for reformers like Canales.[37]

Canales and Wright bitterly split over the latter's testimony before the legislative committee, beginning with the material on Edds, continuing with their opposing opinions on Hanson, and finally concluding with Wright's refusal to endorse Canales' general denunciation of the Rangers. Canales in his official charges wrote, "there are now, and have been for some time, in the State Ranger force men of desperate character, notoriously known as gunmen, their only qualification being that they can kill a man first and then investigate him afterward." When challenged by the legislative committee to name such men, Canales included Edds in a short list of particularly abhorrent villains. Wright of course did not agree, and he made that clear. Among the charges later added by Canales was that Hanson in his investigations sought to protect Rangers, not find the truth. Again Wright, who had first worked with Hanson many years earlier as a Ranger in Rogers' company, disagreed. Canales subsequently claimed that Wright told him about Mexican children hiding under their beds when Rangers came to their towns, then became frustrated when Wright repeatedly denied saying that. Wright must have appreciated the kind words Canales had for him when the legislative investigation began, but that did not persuade him to join in criticizing his fellow Rangers, especially when he did not think they had done something wrong. The legislative investigators agreed with him in their final report, generally praising the Rangers even as they laid the groundwork for reforming the Ranger Force. As for Canales, he never again ran for a seat in the legislature.[38]

Edds stayed with Wright, but many other members of Company K left during the turmoil of the legislative investigation. Grover Oliphant was discharged in mid-January 1919, while four of Wright's men resigned in March: Dionicio Acosta, Bryan Butler, Royal Lorenz, and Monroe Wells. Acosta and Lorenz had been deputies for Wright in Wilson County, while Wells was his cousin; losing them must have been particularly painful. Acosta became a constable and deputy sheriff again in Wilson County, while Oliphant later worked for the Customs Service. It is not clear when Thomas Connelly quit, but Wright in February 1920 asked for permission to rehire him, which did not happen. Company K did get three replacements in early 1919. Harrison L. Hamer, younger brother of Francis A. "Frank" Hamer, the more famous Ranger whose threat arguably provoked Canales into calling for reform, arrived in January 1919. A native of Fairview in Wilson County, he became a bodyguard, deputy sheriff, and game warden before joining Company F in October 1918. After he transferred to Company K, Harrison and his brother Frank often worked together on the border, catching as many as nine suspects in a single day in March 1919 (seven draft dodgers, a deserter, and a Mexican accused of participating in a raid on a ranch that left two American soldiers dead). Another arrival in January 1919 was Austin T. Hamilton, a farmer born in Lampasas County that also had previously joined Company F and then transferred to Company K. He stayed with Wright just six months before transferring again, then quit the Rangers in August 1919. The third transfer from Company F, thirty-six-year-old Junction City "peace officer" Sterling O. "Sod" Durst, left Company K just two months after his arrival in January 1919.[39]

Harley avoided being censured by the legislature, but he understood changes were needed. He began disbanding companies and dismissing Rangers in March 1919, with a fortunate few transferred to new commands. This reorganization added four men to Wright's Company K when Company A, led by Captain John J. Sanders (with whom Wright's oldest son had served), disbanded. The transfers included Samuel P. Chesshire, a forty-six-year-old ranch hand from Red River County with strong ties to Cesar Kleberg and the King Ranch; John E. Hensley, a Rockdale native who had joined Sanders at the age of thirty-seven after serving as a deputy sheriff in Coleman County; and Benjamin T. Tumlinson Jr., a Dimmit County native and Wright's cousin by virtue of being a great-great-grandson of John J. Tumlinson. His father worked for the Customs Service. The fourth new arrival from Company A, Earl Ray Wright, a Nueces County native who was another distant cousin of William L. Wright, did not stay long. He joined early in March 1919 but resigned in April, writing, "I am quiting [*sic*] to take something that offers more advancement." Wright almost lost another Ranger when he got an order to reduce his company to one sergeant and eleven privates. He initially dismissed Harrison Hamer, on the principle that the last man hired should be the first fired, but his brother Frank protested and enlisted Kleberg for support. Harley contacted Wright, and the younger Hamer was reinstated.[40]

Fortunately for Wright, while he was wrestling with the problems of being a Ranger captain, his wife, Mary Ann "Mollie" Brown Wright, managed their family affairs. His resignation as sheriff meant that they had to move out of the county jail in Floresville, where they had lived for fifteen years. Their two oldest sons, Charles H. "Pat" Wright and Maurice H. "Jack" Wright, left to serve in the Army, but their third son, Emanuel A. "Dogie" Wright, returned home after illness compelled him to resign from his father's Ranger company in the summer of 1918. Mollie prudently decided to stay in Floresville, where she rented a two-story house from Fredrich A. "Fritz" Skarke. She settled there with her daughter Zora Belle, who celebrated her twentieth birthday in September 1918, her two younger sons William B. and Houston Tom Wright, who were not quite thirteen and three years of age respectively when their father left for the border, and her mother-in-law, Ann Elizabeth Tumlinson Wright. Dogie of course lived with them when he was not working on the border, and Wright came when he could, such as a brief two-day visit during February 1919 after the legislative investigation, when he and Edds traveled together to Floresville. Such trips may have become a bit more important as the family circle continued to shrink: Wright and his mother, before he went to Austin to testify before the legislative committee, traveled to Victoria to attend the funeral of his sister, Cornelia Elizabeth Wright Cline, a victim of the Spanish Flu who died in early January 1919 at the age of fifty-seven.[41]

While many historians might agree with Utley that the legislative investigation in 1919 was "inept" and generated little real reform, it provided Wright with another hard lesson in the politics of being a Ranger when it led to the demise of Company K. The final version of the bill passed and signed in March 1919 reduced the Ranger Force to four companies of fifteen privates each, plus a sergeant and a captain for each one. Effective July 1, it also provided for a Ranger quartermaster and a headquarters company of six men led by a "senior captain." The governor would nominally make all appointments, with preference given to military veterans. There were no clear provisions in response to those who wanted recruits with more law enforcement experience, nor any effort to reduce the impact of politics on the Rangers, but salaries were raised across the board to attract better men:

captain's pay increased from $125 to $150 per month, while private's paychecks rose from $50 to $90. Companies got expense accounts, and the governor could call more of them into the field, but again the legislature controlled all budget matters. Governor Hobby retained Wright as one of his captains that summer, and he assumed command of Company D. A few months later, Harley resigned, and Wright got a new boss: Adjutant General Wesley D. Cope, who had been Harley's assistant adjutant general. Hired by Harley as part of an effort to improve the Rangers, Wright had done much to advance his own reputation in less than two years while enduring a political firestorm and watching many of his Ranger colleagues leave the service. He had added to the family tradition of Ranger service, and he had earned his pay. He would continue to do just that and hope for better circumstances.[42]

Chapter 6

Captain, 1919–1927

After the legislative investigation instigated by José T. Canales, William L. Wright and his new command, Company D, were posted in Brownsville, where Canales lived and a previous Company D, led by Captain Henry L. Ransom, had committed some of the transgressions that led to a reform of the Ranger Force. Efforts to replace Ransom with Charles F. Stevens, Wright's friend from San Antonio, and William W. Taylor, Wright's cousin with whom he had worked during his first term as a Ranger, did not lessen Canales' complaints. In fact, ongoing violence that claimed the lives of Ranger Sgt. Delbert Timberlake and Fred Tate, a United States Customs Service officer, contributed to the angry clash between Canales and Francis A. "Frank" Hamer, who succeeded Timberlake as Taylor's sergeant. Wright's Brownsville assignment may have been in response to the praise accorded him during the legislative inquiry, but Adjutant General James A. Harley also received letters from South Texas ranchers such as W. Henry Edds urging him to keep Wright on the border. When Pat M. Neff took office as governor, and Thomas D. Barton succeeded Harley as Adjutant General, Wright continued in service, chasing Prohibition-era liquor smugglers along the Rio Grande. Wright patrolled on horseback but adopted modern methods when it made him more effective, cooperated with federal agents to enforce prohibition, and had his men dress professionally when circumstances warranted. Under the reforms adopted in 1919, Ranger Force captains had sole discretion over the men assigned to their companies; as Ranger quartermaster Roy W. Aldrich explained to an applicant, "Captain Wright will not have a man unless he asks for him himself." Wright used that power well; he never had a man killed or wounded in action, was never accused of abusing prisoners, and his company confiscated more liquor than any other. Wright thus continued to earn his pay and uphold his family legacy well during his six years as the captain of Company D.[1]

Wright had eleven men when he took charge of Company D in June 1919, and this number only increased by two during his first year at Brownsville. The original group included five from Company K: John J. Edds (who remained Wright's sergeant), Harold W. Adams, Sidney S. "Sid" Hutchison, William S. "Sanders" Peterson, and Wright C. Wells. Robert B. "Bob" Sutton Jr., who joined Wright in August 1918, also remained in the ranks, as did Desiderio "Jesse" Perez and Harrison L. Hamer, who transferred in November 1918 and January 1919 respectively. The three transfers from Company A also remained: Samuel P. Chesshire, John E. Hensley, and Benjamin T. Tumlinson Jr. Hamer resigned in late December 1919 after working undercover for several months, Wells left two months later when asthma made it impossible for him to continue, and Sutton left in May 1920. Five recruits replaced them, increasing Wright's complement to thirteen. Three joined in December 1919: Juan C. Gonzalez, a forty-five-year-old naturalized citizen who had been a sheriff for Starr County and a Loyalty Ranger in World War I; Stanley M. Morton, a forty-two-year-old former Bureau of Immigration officer from Kentucky who had occupied a variety of public offices in Brownsville; and Roy L. Hearn, a twenty-nine-year-old farmer from Karnes County who served in the same artillery company as Wright's oldest son, Charles H. "Pat" Wright, during World War I. A writer for the *Houston Post* declared in an article on Company D that Gonzalez was a "noted river man;" his recruitment meant that of the four Hispanic Rangers serving when Pat M. Neff took office as governor, three were with Wright. Robert D. Brown, a forty-one-year-old Goliad

County native who had been a constable, Customs Service inspector, deputy sheriff, and police chief at Mission, joined in January 1920. Wright noted that he was a "good officer" who spoke "good Spanish." David C. "Jack" Webb joined in February 1920. A native of Wilson County, born in 1886, he served in Company A from 1915 to 1917, then in the Navy before he wrote to Wright from Carrizo Springs in Dimmitt County and asked to join his company. As a bonus, Webb's comrades discovered that he was the "finest law enforcement cook of all time," at least according to Wright's son William B. "Bill" Wright, who drove the chuck wagon truck. Wright had another recruit, but he did not remain long: twenty-four-year-old Army veteran Darwin E. "Buck" Singleton of Angelina County came during July 1919 and resigned four months later.[2]

While William P. Hobby served as governor, concerns were expressed about the persistent decline in the number of Texas Rangers. A report in the *San Antonio Express* in December 1919 noted that while the statutes provided for 119 officers and men in the agency's seven companies, there were in fact only 75 Rangers. The same newspaper reported in September 1920 that the total had shrunk to 63. A close look at Wright's company would have proven their point. Wright patrolled the Rio Grande from Starr County through Cameron County, as well as all adjacent counties. But at his headquarters in Brownsville in September 1920, a visitor found only eleven on duty, including Wright. The missing two were Perez and Brown, both of whom had resigned in July. Wright struggled to keep his company at an effective strength, but his men were often sent to distant posts; for example, in March 1920, five went to Wichita Falls. Turnover of course continued: Hutchison was discharged in December 1920, and Adams resigned that same month. Matters improved somewhat when Hubert P. "Red" Brady, a twenty-five-year-old Wilson County native, joined Company D in October 1920 after declaring he did not want to serve in any other unit. Brady had previously served in Company A before joining the Navy and then becoming a "peace officer."[3]

The election of Neff as governor brought more recruits for Wright even as the Ranger Force continued to shrink. The agency was reorganized again in February 1921 to a headquarters company and four "line" companies, with an authorized force of seventy-five officers and men. Wright, one of the three captains who continued in service, got three new rookies in early 1921. Peter B. Winn Jr., a twenty-eight-year-old Atascosa County native and distant cousin of Wright, had experience as a Webb County deputy sheriff. Robert A. "Abe" Boyd, a Llano County native born in 1894, enlisted at Mission, where he was a rancher. The most interesting newcomer was Hayes M. Wallis, a thirty-year-old stockman from Edwards County. Wallis had been a sergeant in the Corps of Intelligence Police for the Army, then served as a Special Ranger for four months beginning in September 1918. He left during May 1922, was a Railroad Ranger from July to October 1922 during the national strike, rejoined Company D in December 1922 for eight more months, and then became a Special Ranger again as a railroad security guard. Wright also enrolled three Ranger veterans. Pelton B. "Pell" Harbison, a thirty-four-year-old rancher from Goliad County, transferred from Company C, in which he had served since December 1919. Jesse Perez rejoined Wright in March 1921. After Morton contracted malaria and left in May, followed by Hearn and Harbison in August (the latter became the sheriff of Jim Hogg County after James P. N. "Pat" Craighead died in office), William L. "Bill" Miller transferred from Company C. A rancher from Gonzales County, Miller had been a Ranger since October 1918, when he enlisted at the age of fifty-five after serving as an "Express Guard" with a commission as a Special Ranger.[4]

Wright's recruitment drive was short-lived. When the legislature cut the Ranger force to fifty in the late summer of 1921, Wright had to make hard choices, beginning with his most recent acquisitions. He wrote that he had to keep Miller because he owned an automobile and was thus too useful to drop. Perez was the Ranger he assigned to work with District Attorney John A. Valls at Laredo, who was always complaining that he did not get enough support. Wallis was Wright's best Ranger at Rio Grande City. Peterson and Boyd worked together at Mission—to drop one and leave the other alone "would not be right." After all, they had just raided a gambling den in San Juan, arresting seven. But there was Winn. Wright wrote about him that he was "a good man but is high-tempered. He has been taught from a child not to take anything off a Mexican." Because the "Mexicans in

Laredo have never been taught to respect Americans," conflict was perhaps inevitable, and Winn got into a fight with a Mexican over a roping contest. So Winn had to go, as did Chesshire, who had made it evident that he wanted only to work at Las Norias, a King Ranch property. Sadly, among the Rangers dismissed from other companies was Wright's son, Emanuel A. "Dogie" Wright. Edds, Wright's sergeant who had been a primary target of the Canales investigation, resigned in December 1921. Canales and others had continued to watch Edds, and apparently the lawman finally went too far. Dogie obtusely recalled that Edds, who moved from Rio Grande City to Laredo with Perez in the spring of 1921, "had a little difficulty." He got "mixed up with the wrong crowd," and Wright had to "split the blanket" with him. Edds, however, told Aldrich, with whom he remained friends, that he left because circumstances had become unbearable. Within weeks, Edds became a district supervisor for the United States Customs Service. Jack Webb succeeded him as sergeant for Company D, which included only ten Rangers by early 1922.[5]

In 1922, Wright struggled to retain enough men in Company D to patrol the Rio Grande. Two more resigned: Wallis in May 1922 and Boyd in November 1922. Wallis returned in December 1922, and Wright filled the other vacancies with new recruits. While he was in Floresville on leave in the spring of 1922, he enlisted a deputy sheriff and former constable with an unusual name and interesting pedigree: Grenade Donaldson "Don" Gilliland. A native of Wilson County, he was a cousin to Jack Webb, Wright's sergeant, and a nephew to Sheriff Alfred B. "Burt" Carnes of Wilson County, who had been a deputy for Wright when he was sheriff. Two of Gilliland's uncles, Carnes' brothers, were Quirl B. Carnes, who was killed while serving as a Ranger on the Mexican border, and ex-Ranger Herff A. Carnes, who was working as a Customs Service officer on the Rio Grande. Another new man who claimed ties to Wright's past was Asa Light Townsend, a forty-nine-year-old Colorado County native who was a Kingsville peace officer when Hensley recruited him in September 1922 to be a Railroad Ranger. Townsend as a young man had been involved with the Reese-Townsend feud at Columbus, during which Captain John H. Rogers provided security with several members of his company, including Wright. According to Townsend,

Rogers intercepted and disarmed him, and he was so impressed by Rogers' mannerly but firm demeanor that he resolved to become a lawman. Townsend became a Regular Ranger in February 1923, succeeded Webb as sergeant of Company D, and was later a captain.[6]

More of Wright's men left in 1923: Gonzalez and Perez in January, Tumlinson in April, Brady in June, Webb in August, and Miller in December. The discharge of Miller, which was done in response to yet another reduction in the Ranger Force, left Wright with no man permanently stationed at Laredo; the loss of Miller's car was temporarily solved by the use of a confiscated automobile. Part of Wright's problem may have been the expansion of the federal presence on the border—at least twelve men who served under him during this period became federal officers, who were paid better and did not have to worry about Texas politics. Some, like Wright's son Dogie, enjoyed lengthy careers in national service. To replace his losses, Wright during April welcomed the transfer of Howard N. "Happy" Hall, a thirty-six-year-old Army veteran and former deputy sheriff from Karnes County with three years of prior Ranger experience, while Gonzalez returned in May. Hall was unhappy at Mission and resigned during August. Wright had more luck with six other men. William E. Burford, a thirty-nine-year-old "peace officer" in Yoakum but a native of Colorado County, joined in February upon the recommendation of state senator Isaac E. Clark. Chell M. Baker, a thirty-one-year-old rancher from Travis County, was a Railroad Ranger during the 1922 strikes before Wright recruited him in July. William A. Dial also worked as a Railroad Ranger, then joined Wright in August. Only twenty years of age, although he claimed to be older, Dial had been a peace officer in his hometown of Greenville. Too, Wright in August recruited Edgar B. Harrell, a twenty-five-year-old "cowboy" from Arkansas. Jack Webb's younger brother, Lake T. Webb, a 28-year-old rancher who had served in the Army overseas during World War I, joined at Carrizo Springs during September. Wright noted that he had known Lake "all his life" and that he was "all OK in every respect." Three months later, Wright recruited a veteran from Rogers' Frontier Battalion company: Dan Coleman. He had been a Ranger from January 1893 to July 1895, then resigned at his wife's request and became a deputy sheriff in Karnes County.

After chasing Gregorio Cortez Lira, he obeyed her again and became an unhappy farmer. She died of cancer in 1922, and so at the age of fifty-four he became a Railroad Ranger, then joined Company D. Finally, when Baker left in November after serving just four months, Wright asked his son, Bill, to join him. While his applications were denied because there were no vacant positions in the reduced Ranger Force, Bill stayed with Company D for about a year and also worked undercover in San Antonio. He does not appear in official rolls, but neither does Perez's son and namesake, an Army veteran of World War I who worked with his father in Company D and the Bureau of Immigration.[7]

During 1924, his last full year as captain of Company D, Wright lost three Rangers—Harrell quit in January, then Lake Webb in February and Dial in July. Wright then recruited five, one of whom quit within a few months, giving him a total of twelve by November. This was only one more than he had four years earlier, which a journalist had then denounced as too few. Two enlisted in January 1924: Thomas G. "Tom" Brady and John W. Sadler. Brady was a twenty-two-year-old "peace officer" born in Wilson County, just like his older brother Hubert or "Red," who had left Company D in the summer of 1923. Tom was "Discharged for cause" in July 1924. Sadler, who had served briefly in 1918, joined Wright when he was thirty-seven. A rancher born in Pearsall, with four brothers who were also Rangers, he became a sergeant before leaving the agency in January 1933. J. Warren Smith, a twenty-three-year-old ranch foreman born at Carrizo Springs, enlisted during March. Like Sadler, he served for nine years and became a sergeant. Wright reported that Smith spoke Spanish, adding "I am certain [he] will make a good Ranger." Wright recruited another Spanish speaker, Eugene H. Tumlinson, a cousin of Benjamin T. Tumlinson Jr. and thus of Wright, in October. A veteran of World War I with a Purple Heart, the thirty-two-year-old Tumlinson, a native of Carrizo Springs, was already a lawman when he joined the Rangers. Wright noted his military service and wound, as well as his language skills, but he also wrote that Tumlinson was "Borned and raised on a ranch." Finally, thirty-three-year-old Samuel C. "Sam" Mayes joined Company D in November. Born in Hays County, he was also a wounded veteran of World War I.[8]

Wright as the captain of Company D from the summer of 1919 to early 1925 never had more than fourteen Rangers under his command, but to maintain an effective strength he recruited a total of thirty-seven in six years, including those who served previously in Company K but exclusive of his son Bill and Jesse Perez Jr. All but four were born in Texas, and one of those, Wells from Mississippi, was among his three cousins whom he enrolled. The other three non-Texans were from Arkansas, Kentucky, and Mexico. Among the Texas natives, almost half came from Wilson or neighboring counties, and the rest mostly came from central and western Texas. Few enlisted with Wright directly from a ranch or farm. Most had prior law enforcement experience, as reformers had demanded in 1919: twenty-three had been Rangers before joining Company D, while sixteen had previously been law officers (Gonzalez had been a sheriff). Three had been federal agents, while nine served in the military during World War I. In sum, the Rangers recruited by Wright during this period were almost all well acquainted with Texas and its culture, especially its rural aspects, and most were familiar with the demands of a law enforcement career. Apparently the most significant problem Wright had with them was turnover, but that appears to have been neither his fault nor theirs. Instead, the turmoil of state politics and legislative stinginess took a toll.

Part of the problem in maintaining Company D was that recruiting did not always go as planned. Wright thought he found a recruit in August 1922 at Gainesville, north of Dallas in Cooke County on the Oklahoma border, where he and others from Company D were sent during the railroad strike. Charles F. Cochran, a forty-seven-year-old native of Georgia, was a sheriff in Oklahoma for five years before he moved to Gainesville, where he was elected as constable. He ran for the office of sheriff in Cooke County in July 1922 but lost in the Democratic primary, which prompted him to approach Wright about becoming a Ranger. With ten years of experience as a lawman, Cochran must have appeared to be a fine candidate, but he only got a commission as a Railroad Ranger. Wright left town without his recruit, despite early reports to the contrary, and Cochran became a constable again after the railroad strike ended. Too, not everyone was excited to have a family member join the Rangers. Oscar S. "Sonny" Warnke was driving a bread truck in

San Antonio in 1925 when he encountered Coleman at the Southland Hotel. Coleman knew Warnke from Karnes County, and he told him there was a vacancy in Company D. Warnke jumped at the opportunity, accompanied Coleman to meet Wright and enlist, went with his new comrades to a pawn shop to buy a Colt .45 revolver like the others, returned his truck to Richter's Bakery, and finally rushed home to tell his wife Clara that he was leaving for Laredo. She angrily declared that he was signing his own death warrant and told him that if he left, she would not be waiting for him when he returned. Dejected, Warnke told Coleman and Wright that he would not be a Ranger. Instead, he talked his boss at the bakery into rehiring him. Interestingly, he later served for many years as a peace officer in San Antonio, and Clara stayed with him for sixty-five years.[9]

The first months at Brownsville in the summer of 1919 apparently passed quietly for Wright and Company D. He insisted that his Rangers had to wear coats and ties when they were in town, and they had to conceal their guns. There was time to respond to requests for assistance from other parts of Texas. When prominent Atascosa County rancher John W. Lowe shot and killed his son-in-law William G. Tullos and William's brother S. Calvin Tullos on the main street of Jourdanton in the middle of the day on November 3, 1919, the community was understandably outraged. The two victims, whose brother George had previously served as the local sheriff, were unarmed, and so Lowe was refused bail by the state district judge, Covey C. Thomas. The venue was moved from Atascosa to Wilson County, where Thomas presided in December 1919 at Floresville. He asked for Wright and three other Rangers from Company D—Chessire, Hensley, and Sutton—to provide security during the proceedings, which attracted much attention and resulted in two life sentences for Lowe. As for Wright, he may have enjoyed visiting with his wife, children, and mother, all of whom still lived together in Floresville. He provided security for Lowe's first trial, then returned in late December 1919 as a witness when Thomas presided over a hearing to review the defense counsel's demand for a retrial, which the judge denied. The Texas Court of Criminal Appeals affirmed the verdict in June 1920, but no record of Lowe's arrival at Huntsville has been found. Instead, a 1933 obituary for his son Pogue Lowe, who was ironically shot to death by his father-in-law for abusing his wife, notes that the Lowe family (which included Tullos' widow, Lallie Ethel Lowe Tullos) moved from Floresville to Crystal City, in Zavala County, during the 1920s.[10]

An observant reporter for the *Houston Post* noted that the Rangers on the border traveled and were assigned to towns in pairs by December 1919, indicating that not all remained tranquil on the Rio Grande. Wright probably began having his men operate in pairs after he was attacked in Brownsville on November 21, 1919, by a drunken local, Jose Corona, wielding a knife. The Captain was leaving the Post Office in the Federal Building when two U.S. Army soldiers stopped him and reported that a man was throwing bottles at passing automobiles driven by military personnel. Wright, wearing a coat and tie but carrying his revolver, found Corona and told him to desist. Clearly intoxicated, Corona pulled a knife and lunged at Wright, stabbing him in the left side of his chest. Wright responded by drawing his pistol and shooting his attacker in the leg. Knocked to the ground, Corona regained his feet and advanced again, only to be shot point-blank in the face. He expired in five minutes. Wright survived primarily because his men had given him a "can" of tobacco, which he was carrying in his left breast pocket along with rolling papers for cigarettes. Corona, whom some accounts described as a "marihuana addict," stabbed Wright just as Refugio Jaureque had done on the gallows a little more than a decade earlier, but this time a tobacco tin saved the Captain. Henry J. Kirk, as justice of the peace and coroner, presided over an inquest, and the jury exonerated Wright. Kirk wrote on Corona's death certificate that Wright shot him "While in the discharge of duty and self defense." The story, of course, was reported all over Texas.[11]

While the Rangers spent much time chasing thieves of all sorts, Prohibition added a difficult, and dangerous, task to Wright's responsibilities. A statewide law took effect in Texas in May 1919, while the national statute took effect on the first day of 1920. The almost total ban on legal liquor sales created a bonanza for smugglers in South Texas. When Prohibition began, a quart of tequila or mescal cost as little as fifty cents in Mexico, while it could be sold on the Texas side of the Rio Grande for three dollars and in San Antonio for ten dollars. This differential increased as Prohibition continued, providing a strong temptation to load fifty to eighty quarts per donkey, mule, or horse, in wicker baskets or burlap sacks, and cross the border. Mexicans who previously earned thirty to fifty pesos in a month could now make four hundred U.S. dollars in the same timeframe. Such profits attracted many unsavory characters, some of them former combatants in the bloody revolution that wracked Mexico beginning in 1910. Wright and his Rangers worked closely with Customs Service officers on the border, especially from Laredo to Brownsville, the section with the greatest amount of smuggling. What made that region so attractive to "horsebackers," as Wright liked to call them, was the thick brush laced with trails and hundreds of miles of river that could be easily crossed in many places. Their destination was San Diego, where Archer "Archie" Parr, the "Duke of Duval," profited from allowing illegal businesses while he demanded cuts in the Ranger Force as a Texas legislator. At San Diego, bottles were transferred from pack animals to automobiles for transport further north. Despite the protests of some historians that Mexican smugglers were peaceful, patrolling this area was a deadly business for both state and federal lawmen, who in turn killed a significant number who decided to fight rather than flee. Many Rangers regarded chasing Prohibition violators as "distasteful duty," but they understood that smugglers often cut fences, disrupted efforts to control agricultural pests, and even killed people.[12]

Wright's Rangers patrolled on horseback, often from remote camps deep in the brush. Aldrich wrote to Townsend, when he joined Company D, that he had better bring a saddle and tack with him because "Captain Wright stays in the field most of the time." Several ranches in the area provided facilities that became semipermanent bases, including San Antonio Viejo and Agua Dulce in Jim Hogg County, and Los Ojuelos in Webb County. As Wright explained to Aldrich, using these places put him "in the center of the horsebacker country." Los Ojuelos had substantial rock buildings and good surface water, so it became his favorite. Pack mules proved to be the best solution to the challenge of supplying his camps. Bill Wright recalled that his father had three "large missouri mules:" Lizzie (who belonged to Wright), Monk, and Poly. Wright also had two smaller "mexican mules," Spider, and Rat. Poly took the lead, with the others following in order: Lizzie, Monk, Spider, Rat. They knew their job—they followed the Rangers without fail, and if any shooting erupted, they huddled around Monk, a veteran that carried loads for twenty years. Wright supplemented them by using automobiles whenever possible, either his or one that belonged to another Ranger. In early 1921 he began begging Aldrich to send him a truck so more supplies could be hauled into the brush for longer patrols. One year later he got a one-ton truck, which he appreciated—as Aldrich wrote to Wallis, "Bought Captain Wright a truck yesterday so I guess he will be happy for a while now." But when historian Walter Prescott Webb visited Wright's camp in the summer of 1924, he saw that the mules were still being used, perhaps because the truck "consumed a world of gasoline." They seemed to really like Jack, Wright's favorite horse that was given to him by friends in Wilson County when he resigned as sheriff. Perhaps the mules followed him closely because Wright was very protective and would not let them be abused. He apparently never knew that Lake Webb's favorite device to keep them moving was a slingshot.[13]

Living in the brush for long periods brought more than just logistical problems. Wright by early 1923 declared he would no longer recruit married men into his company because the extended patrols made them "discontented." At least that is what Aldrich wrote to a Ranger who wanted a transfer to Wright's command so that his wife and child could enjoy the drier climate on the border. While Wright did hire three more married men during 1923 and 1924, twenty-one of those who served under him in Company D were single and four were widowers, or about two-thirds of his Rangers. The eleven who were married usually had specific skills, such as the ability to speak Spanish, or more experience in law enforcement or military service. At least one, Hensley, made an interesting arrangement to reduce the problem of being separated from his wife. Apparently divorced when he joined Company D in 1919, he married Lyna Wright in 1923, and she recalled living with him and his colleagues in the field, where she tended horses rather than cook or wash. Wright was of course married, but like his older colleagues such as Gonzalez and Perez, he had been in law enforcement on the border for a long time, so he and his wife must have had an understanding. Darwin E. "Buck" Singleton, who served in Company D for only four months, was not so fortunate. His wife, the former Edna Crumpler, hated South Texas, and when he was posted at Alice, she stayed in Lufkin. Singleton's transfer to Mercedes, where Wright had his headquarters, did not suit her any better, and so Singleton resigned after his request for a furlough to visit Lufkin in November 1919 was denied.[14]

Sergeant Edds was among the first of Wright's men to encounter liquor smugglers after the passage of statewide prohibition in 1919, which added to his ongoing conflict with Canales. The latter filed a suit against Edds after he arrested four Mexicans who had robbed G. W. Edgerton, a physician in Rio Grande City. All confessed to Starr County Attorney Robert Oosterveen, but they later contacted Canales and claimed that their confessions were coerced. Edds responded by declaring that the Guerra family, who had long been the Democratic political bosses of Starr County and allies of Canales, were "among the greatest smugglers" in the area. Edds later reported that Sheriff Gustavo A. Guerra was supporting the operation of long-running fiestas, during which all sorts of illegal activity took place. He never arrested the sheriff, but he did begin nabbing smugglers. In November 1919, Edds and Gonzalez captured seven smugglers with 243 quarts of illegal alcohol. Edds continued his campaign in February 1920, arresting ten smugglers and confiscating 650 quarts of contraband alcohol. Wright's son, Charles H. "Pat" Wright, returned from the Army after World War I and, after failing to become a Ranger in spite of a long list of recommendations due to reductions in the agency, enlisted as a mounted inspector with the Customs Service. He joined Edds during January 1921 to arrest a bootlegger at Fowlerton in La Salle County, and they later confiscated 174 quarts of mescal near Roma. Evidence of the involvement of a prominent rancher came with their capture of a man who carried letters documenting the activities of Eduardo Yzaguirre in smuggling mescal, while their prisoner's partner was detained in Laredo with two cars filled with illegal alcohol and drugs that belonged to Yzaguirre. Customs agents arrested Yzaguirre for smuggling liquor and opium, but his associates fled to Mexico. They must have taken the evidence with them; Yzaguirre was arrested and had to post bond, but there is no record of a conviction.[15]

Wright's operations during the first year of national prohibition, 1920, yielded relatively few arrests or confiscations, at least in comparison to subsequent years. Accompanied by two Rangers, Morton and Peterson, and three Customs officers, he captured a wagon with 300 quarts of "Mescal wine and all sorts of Mexican booze" at Donna in Hidalgo County in January 1920. The intervention was peaceful, but the five Mexicans he arrested were all carrying Colt .45 automatics, while one wore "the uniform of a Mexican army officer." Ben Tumlinson reported the capture of 350 quarts of "booze" in May 1920 and another 150 in August. Wright resurfaced during September when he battled a dozen liquor smugglers, four of whom he captured with their cargo, on one of Tom T. East's ranches. His son Pat and Edds were scouting on horseback near Hebbronville in November 1920 when they spotted two Mexicans who had car trouble. Approaching to help, the officers spotted nine sacks in the back seat. They arrested the two luckless smugglers and confiscated their car and two hundred bottles of liquor. Later that month, Wright with Louis C. McDuff, deputy collector of Customs at Hidalgo, and Marcus W. Hines, an ex-Ranger employed as a mounted inspector for Customs, followed a tip and searched bales of hay loaded on a railroad car at Pharr in Hidalgo County. They found four bottles in each bale, including tequila, scotch, and rye. Two weeks later, Wright with three of his men—Hearn, Morton, and Jack Webb—intercepted four Mexicans smuggling 274 bottles of mescal on horseback near Agua Dulce ranch, 65 miles north of Rio Grande City. The Rangers sent their prisoners and contraband to Customs agents. When a writer for the *San Antonio Express* visited Wright's camp that December, he reported that "Capt. Wright with his usual congeniality and hospitality was well and heartily supported by his fine boys." The correspondent assured readers that the Rangers were "ready to back the captain upon any proposition, whether it be to afford his friends pleasure or to scatter and punish his enemies—the evil-doers."[16]

Despite the happy chatter of the newspaper reporter, not all the Rangers in Company D did as Wright asked, and so they had to be dismissed. Wright returned to Mission from a scout in December 1920 only to be told by Peterson that Hutchison had been drunk for three days. The Ranger apparently had confiscated three trunks filled with liquor, some of which he kept when he gave the rest to Customs agent Hines to be destroyed. This must have been hard news for Wright; Hutchison had served with him in the Frontier Battalion, worked with his young son Dogie at a Karnes County ranch, and was one of the first to enlist under him in 1917. Further investigation by Wright, however, revealed that Hutchison was a troublemaker. Wright wrote to Adjutant General Wesley D. Cope that he had been duped but fixed the problem by discharging Hutchison. Writing to Aldrich to inquire about his final paycheck, Hutchison declared angrily, "I certainly hated to quit my job, but there is a limit to human endurance and I certainly had had mine put to a test. I don't know how I've been reported as getting out of the service. But I have a clear conscience and know better than anyone why I quit." Aldrich in his response ignored the complaint and told Hutchison that he would probably do better as a civilian since there was no money for the Rangers. In fact, it took more than a year, and some research by Aldrich, to provide Hutchison with all the funds that the state apparently owed to him.[17]

Wright got new bosses in 1921, which seemed to bode well for his Rangers. Governor Neff announced a campaign "to down the uplifted hand of the outlaw," as he described it in his memoir. He regarded the Rangers as one of his best weapons in his attack on vice, and to prepare them properly he asked any Ranger who gambled or drank alcohol to resign immediately. In response to an inquiry from Peterson of Company D, Aldrich declared that Neff really meant it—"any Ranger who takes even one drink, and it comes out on him, is a gone gosling." Neff also appointed Thomas D. Barton, a longtime member of the National Guard and a decorated combat veteran of World War I, as his Adjutant General. Neff probably anticipated Barton's hands-on approach and drive for political advancement would bring improvements to the Rangers, who appreciated his efforts on their behalf. Unfortunately, legislative cuts in Ranger appointments and refusal to increase funding for salaries and travel funds curtailed many of Neff's, and Barton's, ambitious plans, but Wright did not yet know this in early 1921, when he made several new appointments and patrolled aggressively in the South Texas brush.[18]

During 1921, the amount of alcohol confiscated by Wright escalated, along with arrests. He collected 700 quarts of whiskey near Mercedes in Hidalgo County during February, then later that month captured eight heavily armed Mexicans and more than 600 quarts northwest of San Diego in Duval County. He expected a fight from the latter group, but they never fired a shot. Again, despite the complaints of state officials such as District Attorney John A. Valls at Laredo, Wright gave his prisoners to federal authorities, who had stiffer penalties. Wright and his men settled at Rio Grande City in March, when they arrested twenty bootleggers and investigated a prostitution ring. Three months later, he captured six men transporting hundreds of quarts of tequila in Duval County. In July, Wright arrested Crecensio Olivares near Bruni in Webb County. Olivares was one of several smugglers who had engaged in a running gunfight with American lawmen a year earlier; he survived, but several of his comrades did not. He had been indicted in absentia by a Texas grand jury but not arrested until Wright caught him and sent him to Laredo. Brady accompanied Wright in stopping Pedro Gonzales and Arturo Trevino in August; both were arrested, and the Rangers confiscated their car and 141 bottles of tequila. Edds and Perez joined Wright in pursuing eight Mexican smugglers, and Edds shot and killed Ygnacio Serna in a confrontation on September 12 at Cheri Muscos Ranch, forty miles from Cotulla. Edds wrote to Aldrich: "One of them thought he would learn us [*sic*] how to shoot so I naturalized him (made an American Citizen out of him don't you know)." The Rangers arrested six of the smugglers—Guadalupe Garcia, Bonifacio Serna, Federico Villareal Serna, Mateo Serna, Jose Villareal, and Martin Villareal—and they confiscated 550 quarts of tequila. Three local deputies escorted the prisoners to the jail in Cotulla, where Customs agent Robert S. "Bob" Rumsey Jr., who was also in the gunfight, directed the smashing of all the contraband bottles against a nearby mesquite tree while a crowd watched. As the summer ended, Wright's son Pat, with fellow Customs officer W. Frank Smith, an excellent tracker whose brother J. Warren Smith later joined Company D, and Ranger Gonzalez captured three men with an automobile and two hundred bottles of "Mexican liquor" near Hebbronville after an "all-night chase of nearly 100 miles."[19]

The September 12 skirmish was the opening engagement in a three-month campaign by Wright and seven Rangers: Edds, Brady, Gonzalez, Miller, Perez, Sadler, and Jack Webb. Three Customs agents—Hearn (who previously served under Wright), Smith and Pat Wright—assisted, as did three ranchers—W. Paul Cotulla, Duncan A. Barter, and Roland A. Gouger—probably because they knew the terrain. Wright must have known Gouger because he was a nephew of Judge Henry B. Gouger of Wilson County and had earlier served as a Ranger and mayor of Cotulla. Two days after the September 12 fight, Wright nabbed three hundred bottles of tequila and six prisoners without firing a shot. A series of smaller incidents followed, with the contraband including two cars and two trucks. The climax came with three gunfights in five days in Zapata, Starr, and Jim Hogg counties. On November 17, Wright grabbed three smugglers and 800 quarts of tequila, and the next day he got three more. These men he sent to the jail in Laredo while Smith and Pat Wright destroyed the alcohol. The third clash came on November 22 at Barronena Ranch, twelve miles north of Hebbronville; Wright captured no prisoners, but he got 2,750 quarts of tequila and 250 quarts of aguardiente, all smashed by Smith and Pat Wright. During this fight, Wright charged sixteen smugglers at dawn with two federal officers, five Rangers—Edds, Brady, Gonzalez, Miller, and Jack Webb—and Texas folklorist J. Frank Dobie, who wrote to his wife that he thoroughly enjoyed himself. After a brief burst of gunfire, the Mexicans fled, leaving blood trails that indicated some were wounded. Wright wrote to Barton that his Rangers "showed pluck and daring. In fact every one came up like old Rangers and stood the test without the least hesitation." He estimated that his men had confiscated more than 10,000 bottles in 1921 and arrested 25 smugglers. Regarding those whom he did not catch, he concluded, "I am very sorry all those men escaped but they will have something to remember the Rangers by." As a bonus, he captured 95 horses that year; since Rangers got a 25% commission on their sale, this helped offset the miserly $25 per month car allowance from the state.[20]

Most newspaper accounts mention only one Mexican killed by Wright and his team in 1921, and Wright did not add to this number in reports to Barton. But Henry B. Yelvington, a Wilson County native who often worked as a journalist, provided a different perspective on Wright's fall campaign in an article published several years later. He claimed that Wright's team on November 18 killed three Mexicans and arrested four while confiscating 1,000 bottles. Wright's final pursuit, according to Yelvington, ended on November 22 when the Rangers saw a Mexican carrying a rifle and leading a pack horse out of a thicket. The Texans were nervous, having found an empty watering trough at a windmill, which indicated there were substantially more smugglers than usual in the group they were chasing. When men concealed in the woods suddenly began shooting, Wright and his men charged, holding their fire until after they had dismounted at the edge of the trees. In the ensuing gunfight, four Mexicans were killed and four were captured, two of whom later died from their wounds. The Texans confiscated three thousand bottles of alcohol, thirty-two pack horses, and sixteen rifle scabbards, which indicated the smugglers numbered sixteen. Yelvington, who had been a deputy sheriff, Customs agent, and Special Ranger, as well as a friend of Wright, thus indicated that nine Mexicans had been killed in just one week by Wright and his associates. While it is puzzling that he is the only contemporary to record these numbers, it should be noted that he had a good reason to inflate Wright's prowess. Yelvington was writing when Governor Daniel J. "Dan" Moody was rebuilding the Ranger Force in the spring of 1927, and so he may have exaggerated to impress upon readers the necessity of returning "El Capitan Diablo," as he labelled Wright, to the border, which was done. In another article that appeared two months after Yelvington's account, Texas historian Walter P. Webb repeated his numbers and his opening line about Wright, "El Capitan Diablo cabalga otra vez."[21]

Aggressive efforts by some of his Rangers to intercept contraband led to some legal headaches for Wright, but he generally supported his men. Brady of Company D, together with a Customs officer, stopped a car driven by S. H. Woods, the district attorney at Alice, in February 1921. They searched the vehicle, then let him go, but he angrily protested to Wright. In response, Wright declared that he would continue to vigorously pursue lawbreakers, and that he expected Woods's support. As for searching a car, Wright said he did not think warrants were necessary on public roads, but to make sure things were done properly, his Rangers always had Customs agents with them, as Brady did. On March 7, 1921, Edds apparently got into another tangle. He stopped a car at Rio Grande City in which three armed men, two of them Anglos, were riding. After a heated exchange, during which one drew his gun, Edds arrested all of them, taking two to the local jail and releasing the other at his wife's request. The three later filed a formal protest, with one claiming that he was a deputy constable and therefore could carry a weapon, which was not true. Captain Howard W. Houghton of the U.S. Army, who was present during the incident, came forward to say that Edds had handled the situation well. Wright again defended his former deputy, and the matter apparently went no further.[22]

Edds was not the only Ranger under Wright's command who was accused of using excessive force. Ben T. Tumlinson Jr., working with two Customs officers in Duval County in April 1921, captured three men with 550 quarts, four horses, two pistols, and a truck in three raids. Later that month the trio found a still near Alice. Then a wealthy rancher, Edward C. Lasater accused Tumlinson and the federal agents of beating a young Mexican, Elidio Villareal, to get information about liquor smugglers. Aldrich demanded an explanation from Tumlinson, who reported that they had arrested Villareal late one night on horseback with a "sack of 9 bottles of booze." He admitted slapping Villareal while questioning him, but insisted he did not break his ribs, as Villareal claimed. Tumlinson also wrote that Lasater's concern was a ploy to gain Tejano votes in his effort to supplant Parr as the chief politico in the county. Wright maintained a public silence, but Lasater dropped his allegations after a conversation with Tumlinson, who stayed in Company D for another two years. He handled several difficult cases at the request of Aldrich, including the rape of the fifteen-year-old daughter of an Episcopal minister, Jay S. Budlong of the Church of the Epiphany at Kingsville, in the fall of 1921. He became a cattle inspector after he left the Rangers but died from a gunshot wound two months after leaving Wright's company. His death certificate declared the fatal wound was accidental, but some questioned this.[23]

Prohibition did not consume all of Wright's time in 1921. In addition to the prostitution ring in Rio Grande City, he and his Rangers investigated many other matters. In January reports surfaced that Mexican generals Antonio Irineo Villarreal and Pablo González Garza were both in Texas and plotting a return to power in Mexico. Wright with his son Dogie, several Rangers, Eugene H. Parker of the federal Bureau of Investigation, and Jesse Perez and his son from the federal Bureau of Immigration, joined in capturing Villarreal with two of his colleagues near Rio Grande City on January 8. They delivered their prisoners to the Army at Fort Ringgold and resumed chasing Garza, arriving at Benavides in Duval County after nightfall on January 9. While the others waited, Perez and Gonzalez went into the town, found a house with a light showing, and talked with F. Benavides, who insisted he did not know where Garza was until Gonzalez claimed to be an ally of Villarreal, after which Benavides became very friendly and offered to drive them to the Oliveira Ranch, where they would find Garza. When Perez had him stop to get Wright and the other officers in their cars, Benavides realized something was wrong and refused to go further. They took him back to his house, where he found an almost full bottle of tequila and quickly drank it, forcing the lawmen to wait several hours until he regained consciousness. After the sun rose, Benavides was convinced to take Wright and his team to Oliveira Ranch, where they arrested Garza and his wife. Wright deliberately thanked his reluctant guide for his help while standing in front of the two prisoners. He took Garza to Rio Grande City, then escorted him, Villarreal and the others to Brownsville. Both generals were soon back in Mexico, where Villarreal became Secretary of Agriculture for President Álvaro Obregón. Despite this triumph, Perez had to leave Immigration because he was too old, so he rejoined Wright as a Ranger.[24]

Mexicans and Tejanos played a variety of roles in the cases Wright investigated in 1921. In May he and Wallis were sent to San Benito after the lynching of Salvador Saucedo, who was accused of being one of several Mexicans who raped and killed a teenager named Marie Schroeder. Two other suspects were sent to San Antonio for safekeeping after law officers allegedly took Saucedo to the crime scene and let white vigilantes kill him. When reports surfaced that he was innocent, the Mexican government protested to Secretary of State Charles Evans Hughes, and Texas officials were told to arrest those who were responsible for Saucedo's death. Wright interviewed Joe Ballinger, Joe Taylor, and Ray Wade, who claimed they only took Saucedo into the brush to question him but had to shoot when he tried to run. A possible witness, Joe Schaffer, insisted he was too far away to see anything much, and his line of sight was blocked. Wright reported what he learned to Barton, but there is no record of any further action. Some historians have written that it proved to be two white men who murdered Schroeder, but in 1923 Alfredo Luna told a woman, whom he kidnapped after murdering her husband, that he killed Schroeder. A posse rescued her and killed Luna. In October 1921, Wright sent Gonzalez with Sheriff Tomas Munoz of Starr County to investigate reports of drunken American soldiers from Fort Ringgold terrorizing local Tejanos. They found a handful of soldiers at two ranches and recorded testimony about an attack on a Tejano family. Of course, they could do no more than provide this information to Army officers. While Gonzalez was away, Wright sent Wallis to Weslaco, where he joined Peterson and Boyd in arresting thirty-five men at a gambling house. Three were white, but most were Hispanic, including a deputy sheriff and a constable. One Mexican drew a pistol and pointed it at the back of Peterson's head, but he dropped his weapon when he realized two other men were ready to shoot him. All the prisoners paid a minimal fine for gambling, and even the would-be shooter was free by the next day.[25]

Wright spent much of 1922 involved in non-Prohibition matters. J. W. Minner was shot and killed at his farm near Mercedes on the evening of January 13. His assailants, two Mexicans, escaped across the border. Minner had heard hoofbeats, went out of his house into his back yard, and asked the riders what they wanted. He was answered with a "fusilade [*sic*]" of bullets at close range. Wright led a group of law enforcement officers in "scouring" the countryside for the killers, but they found only signs indicating that they crossed into Mexico. Two months later Wright briefly became a border diplomat. He was scouting along the Rio Grande with Jack Webb, Boyd, and Perez when they heard gunshots. Backtracking, they found Mexican law officers who said they wanted to meet with Rangers, specifically Wright. The Texans directed the Mexicans to a nearby boat, and they crossed the river to the American side and had a long talk with Wright and the others. Wright remarked in his report on the meeting to Aldrich that they were "the best looking officers I ever saw on that side." The visitors told Wright that "their government" had instructed them to find him because he would give them a "fair deal." Wright agreed to work with them, get them anything they needed, and allow them to work with the Rangers on the Texas side of the Rio Grande, and the Mexicans reciprocated. Wright concluded that he planned to join them for a scout in Mexico soon, but there is no evidence that he did so, or that Texas authorities pursued this opportunity for cooperative law enforcement on the border.[26]

While Wright did not catch many liquor smugglers in 1922, he did lead a sweep in Zapata County in March that resulted in ten arrests and the confiscation of 800 bottles of liquor. Too, many of the men in his company busily enforced Prohibition. For example, Peterson wrote to Aldrich from Mission that he, along with Perez and several federal agents, captured five smugglers during the last week of May. He was even more excited to report that a few days later they arrested not only a pair of "Bootleggers" but also six "stiff collars having a Beer Drinking on the River." He claimed the group included the district clerk of Hidalgo County, the court stenographer, the Mission postmaster, the editor of the newspaper, a barber, and a "millionaire." He added, "You ought to have seen them run but we caught every one of them and filed charges against them." Peterson's tone was far less jubilant in his next letter to Aldrich, when he reported that another five men he arrested for gambling were all released without penalty because the justice of the peace who had jurisdiction refused to let the cards and chips they were using be introduced as evidence. The fact that local officials not only supported but also owned local vice establishments compounded Peterson's frustration.[27]

Wright was called in July 1922 from Corpus Christi, where he had been sent to guard the polls against threats of violence, to join most of his Rangers in dealing with a railroad strike. In September 1920, Wright had, with the support of prominent South Texas ranchers, convinced Cope to reverse an order that assigned him and some of his Rangers to Galveston, where Hobby had declared martial law in response to a dock strike. But this time a nationwide strike involved as many as 400,000 workers, with Denison, a shop town on the Oklahoma state line, becoming the principal focus in Texas.

There more than one thousand strikers on July 11 beat two dozen strikebreakers and exiled them to Oklahoma. As the violence continued, and the number of victims approached one hundred, local officials insisted they could handle the situation while railroad executives, faced with an almost complete shutdown, begged for more assistance. Governor Neff did not want to intervene before the Democratic primary, but after he won, and federal authorities threatened to send Army units, he sent the Ranger Force to Denison on July 23 under the Texas Open Port Law, adopted after the dock strike in 1920. Three days later, Neff declared Denison to be under martial law. Five hundred National Guard troops garrisoned the town, along with forty-four Texas Rangers and more than four hundred Railroad Rangers, recruited and paid by the railroad companies but commissioned by the state specifically for the crisis. Most of the Rangers, camped in Forest Park, soon discovered that the show of force had quieted the strikers; Ben Tumlinson on July 28 wrote to Aldrich, "The strike is not as serious as the news papers would make it [*sic*]." The lawmen still patrolled, however, to protect equipment and electric lines from possible sabotage.[28]

Neff added sixteen more railroad towns to the list of those under the Open Port Law in late July, and he took advantage of the armed truce in Denison to send Rangers to most of them. While the men of Company D went to rail towns all over the state, Wright moved to Cleburne, where he took charge of a dozen Rangers, and he also worked in Gainesville and Temple. He and his Rangers slept in a Pullman railroad car at Cleburne and walked to a boarding house for meals. One day a group of strikers tried to intimidate Wright and Jack Webb by yelling at them as they went to eat. As they walked by the yelling men, Jack Webb suddenly smacked one of the loudest in the head with a pistol barrel. Wright never said a word as the two kept walking, but there were no more threats. Matters were not so simple in Gainesville, where seven strikebreakers were assaulted. Three of them—M. J. Hassell, W. E. Stone, and Otis Lester—were kidnapped and whipped. Wright with four Rangers arrested six men by August 9, and on September 29 four railroad workers—C. M. Shorter, Everett R. Franks, Percy Gandillion, and Lewis Crowe—were sentenced to thirty days in jail by federal district judge W. Lee Estes for violating a court injunction by attacking Hassell, Stone, and Lester. Wright was one of thirty witnesses who testified in the case. These sentences were relatively light, but because about three hundred people were arrested in the rail strike and few were ever convicted, the convictions at Gainesville were a significant achievement for the Rangers. Wright's service on the railroads ended in early October, when he went home sick; as Aldrich explained to Peterson of Company D: "His stomach is giving him lots of trouble lately."[29]

Most accounts of the Denison railroad strike say that every Ranger went there except for three: Aldrich, one fellow with a broken leg, and a third who was left in Mission to take care of Wright's horses and mules. The Ranger at Mission was Gonzalez, who handled more than just his company's mounts. He joined with federal agents in patrols along the Rio Grande, and early one morning in September he was jarred awake by a fire alarm. Someone had set the mail car ablaze at the Mission depot. Gonzalez arrested Clarence Lamb, who had been sleeping in the car and was supposed to be guarding the mail. Lamb insisted that a white man in a mask, not him, started the blaze. Townsend, then a U.S. deputy marshal with a commission as a Railroad Ranger, and four federal agents arrived on the noon train along with Perez, Gonzalez's comrade in Company D who had been assigned to Kingsville since August. Gonzalez transferred Lamb to the federal agents, since destroying mail was their jurisdiction, but he and Perez went searching for the mysterious white arsonist. Within a few days they arrested Ernest L. Barker, who failed to post a $10,000 bond and went to the county jail in Edinburg while Lamb and his wife were taken to Corpus Christi for additional interviews. No further disposition of this case has been found. Meanwhile, Perez returned to Kingsville, where he worked alongside another member of Company D, Hensley. They had been briefly joined by Peterson in August after he had been sent from Mission to Alice to Corpus Christi to Denison, all in just two weeks. He subsequently traveled to George West in Live Oak County, to provide security during a murder trial, then to Greenville, where he had to settle disputes between federal officers and the local police and sheriff's departments. Aldrich planned to send the four of them to Denison in October, but Perez reported to him that "the horse backer[s]" were "getting very thick" in the "back country." Peterson also wrote, "I wish this strike was all over so we could all go back to the Border. I like it better down there." Aldrich relented, and by late October Company D was once more on the Rio Grande, where Wright rejoined them.[30]

Wright's return to the border was delayed by a murder in Corpus Christi. He had traveled to Denison from Corpus Christi in July 1922, and he hurried back to the port city in mid-October. His summer task had been guarding the polls during the Democratic primary, when violence was expected due to conflicts between the faction led by state district judge Walter F. Timon, a Democratic boss who relied on votes from African Americans and Tejanos, and challengers supported by the Ku Klux Klan. The resurrected Klan had spread rapidly after the first Texas chapter organized at Houston in October 1920. Many Rangers had mixed feelings about the Klan, but the laws had to be enforced. Samuel J. "Fred" Roberts, a prominent realtor and Klansman in Corpus Christi, clashed with Sheriff Frank G. Robinson and Constable Tilford L. "Lee" Petzel, both incumbents seeking reelection on Timon's ticket in July. Wright brought five Rangers, and they joined with others under the direction of Francis A. "Frank" Hamer, the captain of the Headquarters Company. Hamer was a native of Fairview in Wilson County, his brother Harrison served under Wright in 1919, and Wright's son Dogie worked with Hamer in 1921, but Wright later claimed he first met Hamer when he recruited him as a Ranger on the border when he was much younger. Since Hamer began serving as a law officer while Wright was the sheriff of Wilson County, it is doubtful that this was anything more than a tale told by Wright to dazzle newspaper reporters. In any case, the July primary proceeded quietly and, while Robinson and Petzel were both nominated, Roberts was so grateful at the lack of violence that he started a fund drive to buy engraved Colt revolvers for Wright and Hamer. But Roberts never delivered his gifts. Instead, Wright returned in October with Hamer to investigate his murder.[31]

Roberts and others had complained that the primary returns were fraudulent, but their charges were dismissed by the Democratic committee for Nueces County. On October 14, a lawsuit was filed to remove Petzel from the ballot. Robinson was furious, and he went that same day with deputy Joseph A. "Joe" Acebo to Klansman Gustavus E. "Gus" Warren's store, where the Sheriff confronted Warren and slapped him. A crowd gathered, and Warren's wife Dove called the chief of police, J. Monroe Fox, the former Ranger captain dismissed after the massacre at Porvenir. Fox arrived and questioned Robinson, but he refused to arrest him unless Warren submitted an official complaint. Robinson and Acebo, joined by Petzel and Cleve Goff, loitered at the drug store across the street as Fox left, then saw Roberts, whom Warren had called, return to his car after talking with Warren inside his store. Robinson quickly crossed the street and shot the unarmed Roberts three times while he was sitting in the driver's seat of his car; Acebo also shot Roberts once through the passenger window. Petzel and Acebo then fired at the crowd that quickly gathered, including Warren. Fox returned, arrested Petzel and Acebo at the scene and Goff and Robinson at the sheriff's office, and then left them with a deputy at the courthouse. Fearing chaos, Mayor Peter G. Lovenskiold and County Judge Hugh R. Sutherland asked Neff to send Rangers. The first to arrive were Aldrich and Hamer, who took charge. Finding the prisoners at the courthouse were now guarded by thirty to fifty armed men who sympathized with them, Hamer boldly confronted the group alone, took the four men to jail, and handed them warrants he had acquired after finding that Fox had never done so. It was the first of many times Hamer loudly criticized Fox that month.[32]

Wright was recuperating in Floresville when he heard about Roberts, but he climbed on a train and arrived the day after the murder at Corpus Christi, where Perez and Hensley joined him. Officially, Wright was there for a two-week campaign against alcohol smugglers in the area, in cooperation with federal agents. Reinforced with Jack Webb and Ben Tumlinson, Wright's sweep resulted in forty-six arrests, including Acebo for gambling, and the confiscation of hundreds of gallons of beer, wine, and liquor from a cosmopolitan mix of Anglos, Mexicans, Italians, and Assyrians. Meanwhile, Wright also assisted in the investigation of the murder of Roberts, carefully recording the testimony, for example, of Howard Grant, a deputy constable who went with Petzel to Warren's store and saw Robinson shoot Roberts. Wright also retrieved a bullet from the undertaker, who found it in Roberts' clothes.[33]

Robinson, Acebo, and Petzel left office before their trials for the killing of Roberts, which were held in Laredo in January 1923 after they, along with Goff, secured a change of venue. They trusted that the state district judge there, John F. Mullally, a longtime Democrat and ally of Timon, would do his best to secure the verdict they sought, and they proved right. No fewer than 167 witnesses testified, about evenly divided between the prosecution and defense. Wright was among them. But the key testimony came from Robinson, who said that as he came out of the drug store, he saw Roberts in his car motion him to come closer. As he did, Roberts extended his right arm across his chest, as if he was reaching for a gun, so Robinson stepped back and shot him three times, while Acebo fired another bullet from the far side of the vehicle. No one apparently considered that if Roberts tried to shake hands with the sheriff, that is exactly the motion he would make. Robinson and his accomplices were acquitted, and Acebo, Petzel, and Goff were likewise acquitted by a San Antonio jury in November 1923 on assault to murder charges for the shots they fired at Warren. Like Robinson, they pled self-defense. Robinson, who had been acquitted in Duval County in 1912 as one of three men who shot and killed three Tejanos during a dispute over local politics, subsequently moved to Mexico and later settled in Laredo. Goff, after being indicted in March 1923 for killing Francisco Lozano, got another change of venue and left Corpus Christi for good. Acebo, who in 1915 had perjured himself and shot and killed a Mexican railroad worker during a voting scandal trial in Corpus Christi that involved Timon, stayed in that port city and was shot to death in 1925 by Julian Esparaza, who pled self-defense and was acquitted. At least one reporter applauded the verdict as a fitting end for Acebo. Only Petzel salvaged his career, advancing from constable to deputy sheriff to chief of police for Corpus Christi in the 1930s.[34]

Wright played one last sad role in the drama of Roberts' murder. There is no record that he attended Roberts' funeral, although thousands did, and he was not present when a new hospital in Corpus Christi was named in honor of Roberts. But Roberts' widow was determined to complete her husband's promise of giving pistols to Wright and Hamer. A biography of the latter described the gun given to him as a "silver-plated .45 caliber Colt single-action revolver." It bore the date of July 22, 1922, the day that voters cast their ballots in the Democratic primary without anyone getting hurt. Notes in Dogie's personal papers indicate that Wright got a similar weapon, which he gave to his son Bill, who accompanied him in Corpus Christi during the fall of 1922. Roberts had raised much of the money to purchase the pistols before his death, and his widow delivered them to the Rangers who protected him and later tried to bring his killer to justice.[35]

Wright reported to Barton in early November 1922 that Corpus Christi was quiet, so he was ordered to Cleburne, where he found the railroad strike had ended, and then returned to the border. The reassignment of Rangers and other matters had left the Rio Grande unguarded, and Wright had been anxious to resume his patrols in South Texas for most of the year. As early as February, when some of his company had scattered across the state in anticipation of the railroad strike, he pestered Aldrich for their return to the border. His anxiety, and anger, intensified when his friend, Customs agent Rumsey, was killed by smugglers near Laredo in August 1922. He wrote to Barton, "I would sure like to go after a bunch of those armed horsebackers again." With any luck, he would locate the "low down murderers" who shot Rumsey, which would be a "grand meeting." In early October, before the murder of Roberts in Corpus Christi, he and Aldrich discussed his return to the border, and the quartermaster even offered to send Wright a pair of Thompson submachine guns, since the situation was understood to be especially bad. Wright declined the offer because he had one, which Jack Webb liked to carry, but for patrolling the South Texas brush Wright required his men to carry a rifle in addition to their pistol. He and others preferred what was known as "Tumlinson Carbines," shortened Winchesters sold to the Rangers by Jacob H. Petmecky from his sporting goods store in Austin. Reflecting again on South Texas, Wright told Aldrich, "Mexican horsebackers have my country now but they didn't have it when my boys and myself left that country. We were still cock of the walk. We never went backwards; we always went forwards." His company had not arrested any smugglers since May, when Perez, Gonzalez, Perez Jr., and Smith of Customs captured 750 bottles and a prisoner after a fight at Las Rucias Ranch near Rio Grande City, but in late October it resumed operations along the river. Miller and Dial drove their truck into the brush to establish a base camp, whence Wright, Sergeant Townsend, Baker, Jack Webb and Harrell patrolled on horseback, looking for smugglers and bandits.[36]

Wright returned to Floresville from the brush so he could consult his doctor about his recurring stomach ailment, then went in mid-November to investigate the lynching of Elías Villareal Zarate at Weslaco. Once more, the Mexican government had protested the killing of Mexican citizens and people of Mexican descent in Texas, claiming that the death toll had reached as high as twenty in the past three months. When the story appeared in papers throughout both the United States and Mexico, Secretary of State Hughes again demanded that the Texans do something, and Wright went to Weslaco. He found that Zarate had been arrested after a fight with a fellow construction worker, an Anglo named J. Frank Sullivan whose arm was broken by Zarate with a piece of lumber. Zarate was put in a "small building" to await his trial. The Mexican consul at Weslaco received a threat and warned local officials, but they did nothing. Two carloads of men kidnapped Zarate from the make-shift jail during the night of November 9, and his body was found two days later with multiple gunshot wounds six or seven miles from Weslaco. When the consul demanded an inquiry, he was threatened, and Wright had difficulty in investigating what he wrote was a "cold-blooded affair." The witnesses were "scattered everywhere … some in farms and some in the brush grubbing," but he gathered a few statements, which Perez translated. Wright declared that the consul's reports about threats were "Imaginary," but he also remarked that "the American people seem to be very indifferent in this matter." Sheriff Anderson Y. Baker, a former Ranger, arrested Marshal Thomas J. Buckow, Deputy Marshal George T. "Tol" Humphries, and local farmers S. L. Henson and Jim Davidson, but all posted bonds and were released. No one was prosecuted for Zarate's death. When the Mexican government submitted a claim from his widow, Aldrich sent Wright's report and other materials to federal authorities, but her suit was disallowed on the grounds that Zarate was an American citizen and thus Mexico had no standing in the case.[37]

Wright resumed chasing smugglers a few days after leaving Weslaco. He led seven Rangers and two Customs officers in capturing four in a gunfight on November 18, 1922, forty miles east of Laredo; several who escaped were wounded. The next month, he led six Rangers—Jack Webb, Brady, Gilliland, Peterson, Perez, and Ben Tumlinson--along with Frank Smith of Customs on a patrol. They found three man camped on Las Animas Ranch in Jim Hogg County on December 19. Wright did not want his heavily armed quarry to escape. He placed two men on one side of the road leading away from the campsite, he and another man settled on the opposite side, and the rest formed a line across the road, creating a pocket into which Wright hoped the smugglers would ride and, being surrounded, surrender. But one of Wright's party fired early and the smugglers scattered, forcing the Rangers and Smith to chase them in the brush and, when fired upon, shoot and kill them. Wright himself, after being peppered with rock fragments from a near miss, killed one with a shot that broke his neck. Another was found dead with his rifle cut in half by a bullet. The dead men were Leandro Villareal, Gerónimo García, and Silvano Gracia, all of whom had Winchester rifles and Colt revolvers. Wright's team smashed 650 bottles and allowed locals to bury the bodies where they fell. Interestingly, the smugglers became tragic heroes in Tejano folklore, remembered in a *corrido*, "Los Tequileros," as unarmed victims of Rangers who, according to historian George T. Diaz, stalked, ambushed, and murdered them, perhaps in revenge for the killing of Rumsey. But even Diaz admitted García and Gracia were veteran smugglers, and it seems highly unlikely they would not be armed. Gracia's brother Aristeo, a smuggler known as "El Pajaro," or "The Bird," for his ability to avoid capture, declared a few months later that he was going to cross the Rio Grande with ten to twenty men and kill Wright. Silvano was the second Gracia brother to be killed while smuggling, and Bird became the third in October 1924. Meanwhile, García's father filed a suit against the U.S. government that brought no result.[38]

Henry B. Yelvington in the *Austin Statesman* in 1941, in a post-retirement review of Wright's career, included an account of yet another operation that must have been in December 1922, about the time of the fight at Las Animas. Juan Pena was a smuggler who had continually eluded Customs agents. Wright had his team assemble singly or in pairs at a South Texas ranch, where Pena was allegedly hiding. With him were six law officers, other than himself: Customs agents Hearn, Pat Wright, Smith, Hines, and Henry B. O'Neill;

and Zapata County livestock inspector John Rathmell. Of five other men with Wright, William A. "Alonzo" Taylor was a cousin who had served as a deputy sheriff and Ranger, and Walter W. Musgrave was a World War I veteran who later worked for Customs. Ed McNabb, J. B. Moore, and Tim Oden may have simply served as guides since they appear to have been local ranchers or ranch hands. In a noon gunfight, after weeks of tracking smugglers, they killed one Mexican and confiscated 1,660 bottles of liquor. The reporter did not make it clear whether Pena was the man killed, or if he was one of those who escaped, some of whom were wounded.[39]

After his re-election, Governor Neff called his Ranger Force to Austin during late December 1922 for a mass meeting to discuss a push for Prohibition in coordination with federal authorities. Forty-one Rangers attended; Wright brought seven of his men with him. Asked how much illegal liquor he had confiscated so far, Wright quipped that he "[felt] safe in estimating that the amount [was] sufficient to fill a deep well and overflow some." He added to that total during the first months of 1923 when he and his Rangers intercepted fifteen smugglers in Zapata County in February and arrested forty-five men on alcohol charges at Weslaco in April. The latter group of detainees included two Customs agents: O'Neill, who had worked with Wright in December 1922, and Robert D. Brown, who had previously served in Company D. All of those arrested at Weslaco were fined the usual amount by the local justice of the peace, twenty-five dollars, and released, but by May the liquor traffic in most areas on the border had greatly declined. Webb, Hensley, and Peterson made arrests, but those who had alcohol only carried a few bottles each. Moving farther afield, Wright with his son Pat and several Rangers were led to a small still on the B (Bar B) Ranch in Refugio County by Bee County Sheriff Walter Malone in August. They found it and "two or three barrels of prunes" being tended by Adolph P. Jurek, who was apprehended. Wallis and Hensley, with Customs agent Brown whom their colleagues had earlier arrested, engaged in a confusing battle with smugglers in November near the international bridge in Brownsville. They were chasing one group of culprits but collided with another; many escaped, but four were arrested, including a thirteen-year-old boy, and the officers confiscated two "bladders" filled with four gallons of mescal, twelve bottles of tequila, and four quarts of whiskey.[40]

Wright was not always eager to cooperate in every scheme that federal officials concocted, even if it involved an old ally. William M. Hanson, who had worked with Wright many times during his career and strongly supported him before and during the Canales investigation, pitched a proposal to Governor Neff in May 1923 for a joint task force to stop illegal immigration across the Rio Grande. After reporting that he had made a personal reconnaissance of the border and found hundreds of people from southern Europe trying to cross illegally, Hanson decided the best solution would be a thirty-day sweep by a team of four Rangers and twenty-four federal agents. Asked to respond, Aldrich instructed Wright to send two more of his men to Laredo, where two were already posted. Hanson assured Aldrich that Wright approved the operation, but District Attorney Valls disagreed. In a letter to Adjutant General Barton, Valls praised Wright for "his loyalty, his efficiency, and his splendid courage and integrity," then added, "He was somewhat perturbed a few days ago when he received instructions to co-operate with the immigration officials in the exclusion of aliens." Valls explained that the Rangers were already doing enough in this matter; in fact, thanks to the support of local law officers, and a three-dollar bounty paid by the county for every illegal alien arrested, the Laredo jail was full of them. Aldrich assured Valls that Wright would not be required to have his Rangers work full time for Hanson, concluding, "I, too, have a high regard for Captain Wright and his ability and energy as an officer, and know that he is on the job day and night and all the time."[41]

Wright was ordered in January 1924 to conduct yet another special investigation, this time in Corpus Christi, where Rangers continued to have trouble, some of it self-inflicted. Duncan S. "Dunk" Wright, a thirty-five-year-old native of Karnes County who had joined the Ranger Force in May 1923 after serving as chief of police for Corpus Christi, went to a local restaurant with fellow Ranger Roy R. Bledsoe and accosted police officer M. T. "Mike" Pena. They took his gun, ripped up his commission when he showed it to them, and beat him in the restaurant and at the jail. Rumors flew that the same pair had beaten a Mexican boy several months earlier, and Bledsoe had in fact been investigated in May 1923, when he was a Customs agent, for harassing civilians in Corpus Christi, though Aldrich discounted the allegations. Pena was officially jailed by the two for carrying a sidearm, which was illegal if he was not a lawman, but the local police released him the next day without charging him. Barton suspended Duncan Wright and sent a clear order to Captain Wright: "Please go to Corpus Christi at once and make a thorough investigation. You know the bitter feeling that exists between the factions there." After the Captain submitted his report, Duncan Wright was reinstated, but he and Bledsoe were transferred in February 1924 to another company, from which Duncan Wright resigned ten months later.[42]

Company D also had conflicts with locals. Sergeant Townsend on March 5, 1924, received a report that three Mexicans would be leaving Donna, in Hidalgo County, that night in a car carrying 260 quarts of tequila. He took Dial and Hensley with him, but before they reached the point on the road where they intended to establish a roadblock, a car approached from behind. The Rangers stopped, and Dial stepped into the roadway, waving a light for the other driver to halt. At first the driver "aimed for Dial" with his car, then one of the occupants began firing a pistol, to which Dial responded with his rifle. As the attackers drove away, the three Rangers followed them to Falfurrias, where they finally stopped. Townsend furiously demanded to be told why they had not halted earlier, and in fact had fired at Dial, only to be told by the occupants of the car, both of whom were Anglo males, that they feared being hijacked. The driver, who gave his name as Arbuckle and said he lived in the Orient Hotel in Dallas, and his companion E. D. Graham, who did the shooting, later filed a formal complaint against the three Rangers, but there is no record of disciplinary action.[43]

Efforts to enforce Prohibition on the border continued in 1924, with some evidence that the Rangers were having an effect. In April, Gonzalez and Perez, along with Perez's son, Customs agent Pat Wright, and Immigration agent Roy Harrell, arrested Florentino Martínez and captured 350 bottles of tequila, three horses, two saddles, and a boat on the river near Rio Grande City. The next night, they captured two smugglers and 250 quarts at another river crossing. Wright bragged to Aldrich, "I've cleaned this country from top to bottom. Mexicans are leaving by the dozen. We've been raiding day and night. People are tickled to death."

He and his Rangers raided several stills at Crystal City in August, when Townsend reported a two-month tally of fifteen smugglers and a thousand "quarts of booze," then Wright intercepted an interesting party of smugglers fifteen miles southwest of Hebbronville in September, after tracking them for two weeks. He had Rangers Smith and Sadler with him, along with Customs agents Smith, Hearn, Jack Webb, and Thomas C. "Creed" Taylor. Hearn and Webb were both veterans of Company D, while Taylor was Wright's colleague (and cousin) from the Frontier Battalion. They located three Mexicans escorting a covered wagon drawn by six mules but captured only two men with the wagon and 600 quarts of tequila. District attorney Valls prosecuted the case, which resulted in sentences of 366 days for the driver of the wagon and ninety days for his escort. Meanwhile, Wright with the same team captured 900 more quarts of tequila in a raid on a "Mexican farm two miles from Hebbronville," and then followed that with another arrest of a smuggler with 300 quarts of tequila in September. Two raids during October 1924 netted a total of eight hundred bottles and one prisoner, with another Mexican killed in the second fight. The last gunfight of the year came in Starr County on November 14. After following smugglers for one hundred miles, thanks to Customs officer Smith and Ranger Eugene Tumlinson who "trailed to a fare-the-well," Wright and his men approached their camp and killed a picket who decided to fight rather than run. His comrades fled, leaving their liquor and horses to be confiscated.[44]

Historian Walter Prescott Webb visited Wright's camp at an "abandoned ranch" in Starr County during August 1924. On his way there in the company of Aldrich, he was told by William W. Sterling, who joined the two at Laredo, that Wright had been killed by smugglers, which proved to be incorrect. Webb was fascinated with the camp, which looked just like he imagined a Ranger campsite from the nineteenth century would have looked. The only modern convenience was the truck. Wright told Webb that he slept with a horsehair rope laid on the ground around his cot to deter rattlesnakes, which may have been a jest at the expense of the visiting scholar. Wright also took his visitors to the nearby site of the Las Animas fight. There, he recounted his gunfight at a range of 150 yards with a Mexican smuggler. Webb later wrote: "'I missed him,' said the Captain, 'but he cut down on me and hit a rock right by me, stinging my face with fine gravel. I said, "Good God, I've got to shoot," and I went down on them sights....'" Wright explained how he had placed his men, how he left the dead laying where they fell until a justice of the peace pronounced them dead, and that he and his men destroyed 800 bottles of sotol, tequila, scotch, and rye.[45]

While Wright was entertaining Webb, two members of Company D took a break from chasing smugglers to investigate a murder. Meyer Redman, a forty-one-year-old Jewish peddler who had emigrated to Houston from Poland with his family four years earlier, came to Mission to sell goods. He hired a local deputy sheriff, Canuto Silva, as his guide and driver, which proved to be a fatal mistake. Silva conspired with at least two associates to kill Redman, steal his money and goods, and dump his stripped car into the Rio Grande with the corpse tied to the steering wheel with barbed wire. When the car was found, without the body which had washed away, Peterson, at the request of Redman's brother, joined the investigation and arrested Silva and Gerardo Samora, both of whom confessed. Sergeant Townsend also came to Mission to work with Sheriff Baker, who had been challenged by Peterson in the Democratic primaries in July and apparently would not cooperate with him, but tensions eased when Peterson left to tend his dying father. A third suspect fled to Mexico but was later apprehended, yet the case never resulted in a murder conviction. According to a participant in the investigation, the killers removed the body from the car when it became visible as the river shifted. They never revealed where they buried Redman, so without a body they were tried for theft, not murder, and "sent to prison for several years." Meanwhile, having completed his part in the investigation, Townsend joined Hensley and two deputy sheriffs in a raid on a gambling house near Mercedes, where some got away with a "car load of booze" but they arrested forty-seven men and confiscated a lot of money.[46]

On January 16, 1925, Barton, after conferring with Texas Attorney General C. A. Wheeler, ordered his captains in the field, including Wright, to suspend operations. This came in response to an injunction issued one day earlier by Texas district judge R. B. Minor at San Antonio. The lawsuit that led to the injunction came after Rangers were sent to San Antonio more than a year earlier, commencing a law enforcement campaign that resulted in the arrest of over three hundred people, including Mayor John W. Tobin, who had previously served as sheriff for more than twenty years. But few substantial punishments were imposed by local courts; for example, no one went to Huntsville for an infraction of the Prohibition laws, according to Neff, and only one went for gambling, and he got a pardon. The suit was filed by attorney Dennis B. Chapin, on whose behalf Wright had testified at his murder trial in 1911. Since that time, as Peterson of Company D reported to Aldrich, Chapin had added extortion, theft, and more violence to his record, but no one in South Texas was apparently brave enough to testify against him. Chapin spent more than a year preparing and presenting his case against the Rangers, with John E. Elgin as his plaintiff. Elgin, angered by the raids on gambling dens and bootleggers, contended that the Ranger Force operated in violation of the Texas Constitution and federal Bill of Rights. Minor agreed that the laws of 1901 and 1919, which established and defined the Force, were unconstitutional.[47]

The injunction came at a particularly hard time for Wright. For a year, he had been complaining about an increase in cattle rustling along the border. In 1924 Townsend and Hensley had nabbed Pedro Trevino, considered to be one of the masterminds for a series of livestock thefts, but it seemed to make little difference. Concerned, Neff ordered an additional Ranger company to South Texas. Part of the problem was technology: the thieves were using trucks to transport livestock quickly. The popularity of automobiles also contributed to the situation: absentee owners no longer lived on many ranches, which were worked by reduced crews unable to watch every pasture. Finally, Wright's company had a familiar dilemma: his twelve Rangers had to patrol the Rio Grande from Laredo to Brownsville, a total distance of about 350 miles, and they could not protect every sector all the time. The arrival of another company led to a decline in rustling, but the problem persisted. After Judge Minor issued his injunction, criminal activity on the border spiked. Wright told the new Adjutant General, W. Mark McGee, that Paolo Leon Villers with fifteen men and twenty pack mules loaded with three thousand bottles had entered Texas on their way to San Diego. McGee, a World War I veteran and American Legion officer who had been appointed by the new governor, Miriam A. "Ma" Ferguson, sent twenty more Rangers to the Rio Grande and told Wright to do what was necessary. McGee had decided that the injunction prevented him from spending money, not commanding the Rangers, so he instructed his captains to keep working and hope that they would be paid. Wright chased Villers out of Texas, and he did get a paycheck after Chief Justice William S. Fly of the Texas Circuit Court of Appeals removed the injunction on February 25, 1925. But he was not happy about the situation at all.[48]

Matters became even worse for Wright when McGee, on orders from Ferguson after the Texas legislature cut the Ranger Force budget in half, reduced the agency from fifty-one men to twenty-eight in late January 1925. The Governor claimed this was part of her broad program to reduce the state budget, but many believed it was the culmination of her campaign promise to curtail Ranger operations. Wright was not only concerned at the reduction of the Ranger Force but also believed that her election meant a return to a policy of freely issuing pardons to convicted criminals, for which Ma Ferguson's husband, Governor James E. "Pa" Ferguson, had been notorious before he was removed from office. Wright and others proved correct. James Ferguson issued 2,253 pardons during his three years as governor, allegedly in return for lots of money, while his successors signed far fewer: Hobby granted 1,518 in a little more than three years, while Neff's total was 199 in four years. Ma Ferguson pardoned about 1,200 during her first year as governor, while her two-year total reached 2,147 and became the source of much controversy. McGee quit as adjutant general at the end of 1925; Wright, who had been appointed captain for the first time as part of the effort to clean up some of the mess Pa Ferguson created, left long before that.[49]

McGee tried to keep Wright in the Ranger Force but failed. He recommended a reduction plan to Ferguson that included retaining Wright, Thomas R. "Tom" Hickman, and Roy C. Nichols as captains, along with twenty-five Rangers, most of whom were assigned to the border. Instead, Wright resigned. He was tired of trying to do too much with too little. The prospect of having even fewer dollars and men infuriated him. In his letter of resignation, he wrote that a "grave error" was being made in reducing the Rangers at a time when the number should be increased to meet a rising level of crime. The ruling that lifted the injunction also contained the admonition that Rangers should be sent only when local officials asked for them, an idea embraced by Ferguson but rejected by Wright and many other Texans. Finally, Wright had sharply criticized some of the Ranger captains appointed by James Ferguson, and he had not been pleased with some of the selections made by his successors. His worst fears were confirmed when Miriam Ferguson assigned Fox, infamous for the massacre at Porvenir, to command Company A, while William M. Ryan, Wright's former colleague at Laredo whom he had asked Aldrich to discipline in 1921, took command of Company D. Historian Robert M. Utley has argued that Ryan was better "than later critics conceded," but Sterling, who succeeded Ryan as the captain of Company D, dismissed him as a "tallow faced ex-bartender whose principal experience in riding had consisted of straddling beer kegs."[50]

Wright resigned in late March 1925, with an effective date of April 1. By that time, most of Company D had already left the Ranger Force or would soon do so. Mayes, who in November 1924 had become the last man hired by Wright, wrote to Aldrich in January 1925 asking for his support "as we are all poor boys and need the position," but there was little the Ranger quartermaster could do. Three of Wright's eleven Rangers were discharged in February: Peterson, the last member of Company K who still served under Wright; Hensley, who was second only to Peterson in his length of service with Wright; and Gonzalez, who returned to Company D in July 1925 and served two more years. Three more resigned in six months: Eugene Tumlinson in March, Burford in April, and Coleman in August. Only five continued in service for a significant amount of time under Ferguson: Gilliland, Mayes, Sadler, Smith, and Townsend. Two, Mayes and Smith, rejoined Wright when he returned as a Ranger captain in 1927, after Ferguson was no longer the governor.[51]

Wright did not leave quietly in 1925. His resignation letter to McGee was widely quoted and sometimes reproduced in full. In it, he declared that reductions in numbers and restrictions on actions would render the Rangers "useless" and nothing more than "figure heads." He did not want to work for such an organization. In early April, having rejoined his family in Floresville, he was interviewed for the local paper. He recalled that his role during the railroad strike was to bring peace through cooperation, not by "bulldozing," which was a thinly veiled criticism of some Rangers with whom he had worked. Wright then declared, "As far as prohibition goes, it does not prohibit." He added, "The prohibition law should be enforced as long as it is on the statute books. If it is going to be ridiculed as it now is in so many places, why not lift the ban and let liquor in? I guess you might call me an anti, but I want to make it clear to you that my personal feelings in the matter did not interfere with my duty. I tried to uphold the law to the best of my ability." Having said that, Wright explained that he thought the greatest threat to peace in Texas was the Mexican bootlegger, "armed to the teeth" and using cars for mobility. Law enforcement had changed because automobiles were impossible to track on new hard-surface roads, and the criminals driving them, who were very violent men, could be much further away before being discovered. Aldrich continued as the Ranger quartermaster under Ferguson, but Wright still considered him a friend to whom he could speak, or write, freely. Still angry, Wright wrote to Aldrich in June 1925, ostensibly to settle some outstanding charges but also to again address the situation. He exploded, "My whole mind was on my work trying to pay the State for what I was getting payed [*sic*]. I gave the State my whole time and brains [.] Of course I could have stayed in Camp and done nothing and drew my pay like lots of others have in other words drew a pension from the State and gave nothing in return, in other words lay around the Court House and went with Deputy Sheriff's and what they done sent in reports that I done it, I could have done that." If Aldrich responded, his letter does not survive.[52]

Wright's departure did not go unnoticed. He was certainly missed in Laredo, where he had been posted for much of his term as captain. In February 1924, he and his Rangers rode in the Washington's Birthday parade in Laredo, and city officials presented them with a silver cup in appreciation for their service. J. Will Falvella, in the September 1924 edition of the popular magazine *Frontier Times*, praised Wright for being "as brave and fearless as ever was in the service." The *Hebbronville News*, on the date that Wright's resignation officially became effective, lamented his departure as the loss of "one of the State's most noted and respected officers." The writer added, "The name of Will L. Wright will go down in Texas history among the greatest peace officers Texas has ever had." In a much larger market, the *San Antonio Express* referred to Wright as the "dean" of the Ranger Force in an article that explained to anyone who did not yet know him: "He has the satisfaction of quitting the service with a clean record of duty efficiently performed, frequently when life was hanging in the balance." A writer for the *Corpus Christi Caller* was clearly not a great fan of all Rangers, but he declared Wright was "of the breed that has made [the] history of the ranger force [sic] a glorious one." The Force, he added, had "lost one of its best leaders" with the resignation of Wright.[53]

The family that Wright rejoined in Floresville had changed much during his time with Company D. In 1921, his daughter, Zora Belle Wright, married Blake D. Fore, a drug store owner whose father, Samuel L. "Sam" Fore, was the publisher of the local newspaper. The couple of course had their own home, where by 1926 Wright could visit two grandsons. His mother, Ann Elizabeth Tumlinson Wright, who lived for many years in Wright's home, died in October 1923. The next year, Wright's crippled brother-in-law, Charles P. Warren, who had become a widower with three children when his wife, Wright's sister Zora, died in 1898, passed away in nearby Sutherland Springs, where he had been the postmaster for a long time. Four of Wright's five sons were grown and away from home. Three had followed in their father's footsteps; Bill had become an inspector for the United States Public Health Service in Laredo, while, after serving as Rangers, Pat worked for Customs and Dogie was recruited into the Border Patrol by Grover C. Webb, chief of the Customs Office at El Paso and a former Ranger whose brothers, David C. "Jack" Webb and Lake T. Webb, served in Company D. Wright's second son, Maurice H. "Jack" Wright, worked as a mechanic in San Antonio, In sum, Wright and his wife, Mary Ann "Mollie" Brown Wright, with their youngest son, Houston Tom "Simp Tom" Wright, could live wherever they wished, so they decided to leave Floresville.[54]

Wright joined the police force of Robstown, near Corpus Christi in Nueces County, in the fall of 1925 as the deputy city marshal. The marshal who hired him was James W. Galbreath, who had been a Ranger under John H. Rogers, like Wright, before serving as the chief deputy sheriff in Medina and Bexar counties. Wright had worked with Galbreath when he was the sheriff of Wilson County and in 1917, when the Ranger Force expanded, had endorsed Galbreath's unsuccessful application to be a captain, writing "He is worth his weight in gold as a gentleman and as an officer." On his first day in Robstown, Wright arrested Juan Recio for having nineteen bottles of French brandy, which he apparently intended to sell in his store. Wright observed his "peculiar movements" as he drove into town, arrested him, and confiscated his "would be joy spirits." Recio was arraigned and sent to the jail in Corpus Christi to await his appearance before a federal grand jury. Wright ran for sheriff in Nueces County in August 1926 but was narrowly defeated in the Democratic primary by the incumbent, Ben D. Lee, who emphasized the brevity of Wright's residency in the county during the campaign. Wright won Robstown, where he lived with his wife and son, but he lost the overall race by 342 of 5,186 votes cast.[55]

Wright by the fall of 1926 was fifty-eight years of age. He had commanded two companies as a Ranger captain and could look back on more than fifteen years of service as a sheriff. Given his strong showing in the election, there was no reason not to expect that he would be either marshal of Robstown or sheriff of Nueces County before his final retirement. But he wanted to be a Ranger captain again and add to his legacy and that of his family. He had more than earned his pay on the border, having arrested more men and captured more contraband than any of his Ranger contemporaries without losing a man. If Texas politics allowed, he deserved another chance, and he would get it in 1927.

Chapter 7

Captain, 1927–1939

William L. Wright spent almost all the last dozen years of his law enforcement career serving as a Texas Ranger. He refused to be a Ranger while Miriam A. "Ma" Ferguson was governor, but he apparently had no reservations about serving under Daniel J. "Dan" Moody, her attorney general, who succeeded her as chief executive of the Lone Star State. This may have been because Moody had a strong law-and-order reputation for his prosecutions of Ku Klux Klan members, and he pushed investigations of the Fergusons to recover misspent state funds. In any case, after Moody took office, he received requests from South Texas to reinstate Wright as a captain in that region, and Robert L. Bobbitt of Laredo, the Speaker of the Texas House of Representatives, added his endorsement as well. Moody appointed Wright as a captain in May 1927, and he served until January 1933, when Ma Ferguson fired all the Rangers after she won a second term as governor. True to form, when she was not re-elected, Wright again became a Ranger in February 1935 upon the appointment of Governor James V "Jimmy" Allred, another former attorney general for Texas who was concerned about law enforcement. Wright seriously wanted this last Ranger commission; as he wrote to Smith, his former sergeant, "I am working all my strings," which meant he had talked to a lot of people. This time, however, Wright became a private. Many newspapers honored him by continuing to refer to him as a captain, but he never again commanded a company. Transferred with his fellow Rangers into the Department of Public Safety during August 1935, Wright served for four years before he stepped down on September 1, 1939, more than four decades after he first enlisted.[1]

Wright returned to the Rangers in 1927 as part of an attempt by Moody to revitalize the agency after two years of criticism and neglect under Ferguson. After a flurry of appointments and transfers, Wright took charge of Company A in place of J. Monroe Fox. Thomas R. "Tom" Hickman succeeded William W. Sterling in command of Company B, while Sterling became the captain of Company D in place of William M. Ryan, who had succeeded Wright in 1925. John H. Rogers, Wright's original commander, took charge of Company C, in place of Roy C. Nichols. Francis A. "Frank" Hamer, who had remained in the Rangers after Ferguson became governor, resumed command of the Headquarters Company, while Roy W. Aldrich continued as the quartermaster. In sum, there were many friendly faces around Wright, who went to Marfa with his company. Robert L. Robertson, a longtime member of the National Guard, took office as adjutant general with instructions from Moody to give special attention to the Rangers. Generally, while Moody could not convince the legislature to expand the Ranger Force, he appointed good leaders in place of bad and improved its organization. As a further boost to morale and recruiting, he persuaded the legislators early in his second term to increase the pay of Rangers to $225 per month for captains, $175 for sergeants, and $150 for privates, although the total number of Rangers remained low at thirty.[2]

Hamer's biographer, John Boessenecker, has written that Moody's appointments provided a "huge boost to Ranger morale and a clear public statement that the new force would return to the time-honored traditions of the horseback era: character, fairness, honesty, tenacity, and courage." Wright's appointment clearly fit such criteria, and it was certainly welcomed by his contemporaries. It was at this time that Henry B. Yelvington published several articles that pinned the title of "El Capitan Diablo" on Wright in an effort to generate public support for his appointment. The *Austin Statesman* hailed Wright as an "officer of the old frontier type," while the *Hebbronville News* a few weeks later declared that he was "possibly one of the most beloved and respected of border peace officers." Texas District Attorney John A. Valls congratulated Moody for appointing Rogers, Hamer, and Wright, expressing regret only that Wright had not been assigned to Laredo. Wright wrote to Moody thanking him "from the bottom of [my heart]," adding, "I am certain you will never have cause to regret." His assumption of command was interrupted by a medical condition that required surgery and a hospital stay of three weeks during the summer of 1927, but by the fall he was in Marfa "looking fit as a fiddle and stepping about according to his old form." As reports of his activities began to appear again, the *Hebbronville News* exulted that Wright was once more "at his old trade in the Big Bend—much to the discomfit of evil-doers."[3]

Wright's Company A in 1927 included at least one distant cousin. His sergeant was William W. "Bill" Taylor, grandson of Walter Riley and Elizabeth Tumlinson Taylor, Wright's great-aunt. The violent death of their son, Bill Taylor's father, William P. "Buck" Taylor, in 1868 allegedly initiated the infamous Sutton-Taylor feud in which Joseph L. Tumlinson, grandfather to both Wright and Taylor, played such a prominent role. More important, Taylor had extensive experience as a peace officer, including time in Ranger service. A native of DeWitt County born in the same year as Wright, 1868, Taylor had already served two terms as sheriff of Kimble County, 1898 to 1904 and 1906 to 1910. During his first term, he cooperated with Wright to keep order during the disastrous land rush at the Junction City courthouse in March 1902. Taylor first joined the Rangers in February 1918, advancing to captain by August of that year. He left the Rangers a few months later as a result of budget cuts and once again served as sheriff in Kimble County, but he re-enlisted as a sergeant in 1925 and worked in several companies before he joined Company A in August 1927. Wright benefitted from his cousin's expertise only a short time before Taylor again left the Rangers in June 1928 and returned to his ranch, but Wright worked once more with him from 1931 to 1933, when Taylor became a Special Ranger.[4]

Seven of the thirteen other men who served in Company A from 1927 to 1933 were veteran Rangers. Pinkney F. "Pink" Dyches had joined Company A at the age of thirty-five in December 1919 at Marfa. A Williamson County native, he had previously been an assistant constable at San Angelo, Texas, and city marshal at Toronto, Kansas. He resigned in January 1928 to become a peace officer in Coleman County. Robert W. "Bob" Sumrall, an Army veteran from Ballinger, had been a Ranger for eight years, six years in Company A, when he re-enlisted with Wright. He resigned to be a deputy sheriff in Coleman County but rejoined Company A in September 1931 (one month before his thirty-seventh birthday). J. Warren Smith originally enlisted with Wright in March 1924, stayed in Ranger service and transferred to Wright from Company D, and succeeded Taylor as sergeant. Emanuel A. "Dogie" Wright, who joined his father-in-law enforcement, remembered Smith as a "tip-top officer, one of the best offhand shots I have ever seen." Samuel C. "Sam" Mayes had joined Wright in November 1924, then remained a Ranger like Smith and transferred from Company D to Wright's new command, serving until January 1931. Clarence M. Ezell was twenty-eight when he joined Company C in July 1924. A native of Alabama, he had been a city police officer and Railroad Ranger in Marshall, and he returned there to serve as police chief after he resigned from Company A in February 1928. Jack T. Laughlin was a sixty-three-year-old former rancher from San Marcos who served under Rogers from 1907 to 1909, then became city marshal for Austin and a U.S. deputy marshal before again serving as a Ranger from 1921 to 1923, when he became the city marshal of Del Rio in Valverde County. He was briefly in Wright's company in 1927 before rejoining Rogers, for whom he became a sergeant. William E. "Earl" Young, a forty-four-year-old cowboy from La Grange, worked as a Ranger from November 1919 to May 1927, then re-enlisted in July 1928 and served almost five years with Wright.[5]

Most of the six whom Wright recruited into Company A who had not previously been Rangers did have law enforcement experience. J. C. Parker joined in May 1927 and resigned in February 1928. Thirty-three years of age, he had been born in Karnes County and was city marshal at Nixon when he enlisted. Con Cecil "C. C." Wren, an ex-constable from Marlin, served under Wright from February to May 1928. He became the assistant police chief for McCamey, where Wright's company was posted while he was a member, and he died there in January 1929 after being "slashed" in the chest while trying to end a fight. He was just forty-one years of age. Thad Tarver, a Cotulla native, had been a constable and deputy city marshal there before he joined Wright in July 1928. Robert E. Poole, an ex-sheriff from Lampasas County, served from October 1927 to February 1931 with Rogers, then joined Wright during October 1931 at the age of sixty-one. Fred E. Griffin was forty-three years of age and a Wilson County "peace officer" when he enlisted in Company A in January 1932 for a term of service that totaled only eleven months. The only exception to this list was Harold Slack, a twenty-one-year-old rancher from Brownsville who enlisted in Company A in September 1931.[6]

Wright quickly learned that Ranger service had changed rapidly during his time with the city police in Robstown. More smugglers had switched from mules and horses to automobiles, shifting the enforcement target to retail outlets away from the Rio Grande. During his first months back in South Texas, he concentrated on cattle rustlers at Marfa, where he also assisted in corralling drunken soldiers, but Robertson had him refocus on oil-boom towns, rough communities that appeared wherever oil was discovered. The crisis in West Texas was enhanced by legal crackdowns in North Texas towns such as Borger, which pushed the troublemakers to seek new locations. Wright soon found a variety of illegal operations in at least eight towns, especially gambling and bootlegging. One such community was Wink, which appeared in Winkler County after the discovery of oil on a local ranch. By the summer of 1927, thousands lived there. With them came businesses, both legal and illegal, but Wright had to establish his headquarters at Fort Stockton, seventy-four miles to the south, because Wink did not have lodging for him and his Rangers. When he first visited Wink during the fall of 1927, locals greeted him warmly and his inquiries revealed nothing. Returning to his headquarters, Wright dispatched Taylor, who had more success. He arrested seventy-five men in an illegal gambling house and located a still, which he destroyed along with some liquor and 900 gallons of fermenting mash. Allegedly 100 men and women were told to leave Wink after this raid. A writer for the *Hebbronville News* could not resist a clever comment on Taylor's success: "Capt. Wright winked at the news."[7]

Wright must have reflected on how his career had changed yet again; in 1906, when he was a sheriff, he had made his first sweep of gambling dens in Wilson County, making arrests that resulted in fifty indictments. In late November 1927, he and Taylor led a campaign in West Texas oil-boom towns that eclipsed his earlier numbers. His initial raid at Wink netted 105 gamblers, with a similar number arrested by his Rangers at Pyote in Ward County, which local attorney Lee J. Marks described as "the common gateway to Wink and Winkler County, traversed by many highwaymen, bootleggers, burglars, thugs, and law violators." Wright reported that anything could be bought, but what was more alarming was that other law officers claiming to be Rangers were confiscating money, liquor, and other goods for their own use. He returned to Wink at the request of the Winkler County attorney but found nothing. Wright proudly told Robertson in January 1928 that bootlegging was on the decline in his district, but he proved to be too optimistic. That month, Wright and three of his Rangers—Taylor, Parker, and Sumrall--cooperated with Captain Rogers and Ranger Henry D. Glasscock, along with Sheriff William P. Rooney and a pair of United States Customs Service agents, in a raid on Grube, another oil boomtown in Pecos County. The lawmen arrested two dozen men for gambling and seven for selling alcohol, mostly tequila. They smashed bottles, gaming tables, and slot machines, and gave all the money they confiscated to Texas District Attorney Joe G. Montague. Within a few weeks after more pressure from Wright, the population of Grube had dropped by half, and many businesses were closing.[8]

In February 1928, Wright assembled a team for a coordinated attack on illegal activities in Wink, which was earning a reputation as "about as tough an oil town as ever sprang into existence overnight." He mustered six Rangers, including four of his own—Taylor, Mayes, Smith, and Wren—and two from Rogers: Glasscock and Laughlin. Wright also recruited Hugh Gillespie, a deputy sheriff in Upton County where, after a series of complaints prompted an investigation by Governor Moody, Wright had recently moved his headquarters to McCamey, yet another oil town that boomed like Wink. Gillespie in January 1928 had been involved in a shootout in which two bank robbers had been killed, so Wright must have regarded him as a reliable addition. Wright cooperated with another team of lawmen led by Jay D. Reeder. A former inspector for the Customs Service and then chief of police for El Paso, Reeder had become the "chief of prohibition enforcement for the southwest division." His teammates were Sheriff Rooney and three of his Pecos County deputies. Wright prepared for the operation by sending Mayes to Wink as an undercover agent to gather information, but he discovered that he could not trust many local officials, and spies were everywhere, so Mayes apparently accomplished little.[9]

A murder investigation briefly delayed Wright's raid on Wink. Murl Burzette, a twenty-year-old oilfield worker from Iowa, was shot in early February at a filling station near McCamey and died at the local hospital the next day. Wright, with Parker and Smith, assisted Upton County Sheriff J. O. "Bud" Barfield in making an arrest in the case within twenty-four hours of the shooting. Will Brake was later sentenced to six years for killing Burzette, while Brake's wife, who was arrested with him, was released in return for her testimony. Meanwhile, having arrested the Brakes, Wright launched his attack on Wink during the last week of February. He focused on gamblers, while Reeder concentrated on alcohol. In a late-night raid on the Quality Lunch, which had been identified as a prime location for illegal activities by Mayes, Wright and his lawmen detained 131 patrons for gambling—including three deputy sheriffs and Homer E. Pace, brother of the mayor of Borger—and confiscated $6,996 from six tables owned by four men. All the gamblers were fined and released, while Rooney escorted the four table owners—Clarence L. "Heavy" Brecheen, Cecil Byrd, Henry C. Fields, and Lem Wallace—to his jail in Fort Stockton. Reeder and his officers arrested seventeen for alcohol violations and confiscated a lot of liquor. Allegedly hundreds were again warned to leave town before sundown "or else." All those detained on liquor violations were subsequently indicted on state or federal charges, as were the four table owners. While reporting that Wink had become "as quiet as a graveyard," the *Hebbronville News* lavished praise on Wright. Taking aim at the critics who apparently said he was too old, at sixty, to be a Ranger, a reporter declared that "For an old-timer, Captain Wright is still a young man, full of pep and ready at any time for a fight or a frolic."[10]

Wright's relocation to McCamey had unexpected consequences: he became involved in the scandal concerning Gillespie's gunfight with bank robbers in January 1928. After watching for three nights, Gillespie, Sheriff

Barfield, and another deputy, Clarence Shannon, waylaid two men when they burgled the First State Bank at Rankin. One of the suspects began shooting, and both died in a hail of buckshot. The Texas Bankers Association offered rewards of $5,000 apiece for dead bank robbers, so Barfield and his deputies expected to get $10,000. Instead, in March Hamer announced that he believed the shooting was one of several scams in which unwitting would-be criminals were ambushed for the sole purpose of collecting bounties. Challenged by Barfield and others, Hamer came to Upton County, enlisted Wright and others for an investigation, and with them testified on April 5 before a grand jury, who refused to indict the three lawmen. Hamer finally secured indictments for all three in June 1931, but these were dropped just a few months later. Meanwhile, another of Wright's men, Sumrall, left to be a deputy sheriff in Coleman County, and he got $5,000 for killing a bank robber near Santa Anna in January 1930. While the dead man again fired first, as at Rankin, other circumstances were different: the suspect was one of four partners who had robbed two banks, Sumrall tried to arrest them at a local farm, and a chase on foot in thick brush ensued. Interestingly, Sumrall's wife allegedly shot an escaping prisoner a few months later and also got a cash award. Wright welcomed Sumrall back to Company A in September 1931, but there is no evidence that he worked with Gillespie again.[11]

While working with Hamer, Wright continued his efforts to clean up Wink and its environs. Just across the New Mexico line was the community of Jal, which proudly displayed a big sign that said it was "eight miles from the Texas Rangers," for anyone who needed that information. The "chief prohibition enforcement officer" for the federal government in West Texas, former Ranger and Army veteran Rufus C. Van Zandt, did not appreciate this. He arranged for Wright and four of his Rangers to be deputized as federal officers for a raid on Jal. Reeves County Sheriff Edgar B. Kiser brought Wright's men to Pecos for the formalities on March 17, 1928, then all the raiders—Van Zandt, his partner Walter J. Knight, Sheriff Kiser, Wright, Taylor, Mayes, Smith, and Wren—drove to Jal. When they arrived, they were confronted by angry locals, but the Rangers' sharp answers and Thompson submachine gun discouraged any would-be foes. Among those disarmed was Emerald Allen "Two-Gun Dick" Herwig, a former lawman who had been in the Oklahoma penitentiary for murder. He had already been driven out of two Texas oil-boom towns where he operated illegal businesses: Borger, by Hamer (after raids by Van Zandt), and Wink, by Wright. Herwig, who reportedly owned the saloon where the defiant sign hung, allegedly protested that he was a law officer only to be told by Wright, "You ain't nothing." The Rangers raided several gambling rooms and, outside of town, found a still operated by some of Herwig's associates. The Texas lawmen destroyed the still, sixty gallons of whiskey, and thousands of gallons of mash before returning to Texas with two trucks filled with furniture, sugar, rye, and other contraband. They also took five prisoners to Pecos to be arraigned. New Mexico Governor Richard C. Dillon protested, and allegedly met personally with Wright, but the state executive could not undo what the "federals" had done.[12]

Prior to the Jal raid, Wright found another still in Wink with a capacity of 1,500 gallons, which he told Robertson was the "largest still I ever saw," and arrested the operator: Homer E. Pace. But Wright's task was becoming more complicated that chasing gamblers and bootleggers. Wink secured permission to incorporate in the late spring of 1928, and Wright and his company were assigned to guard the polls when residents voted on a town charter in May. Winkler County officials opposed the incorporation of Wink because it would reduce their opportunities for illicit profits by creating another level of possibly corrupt bureaucracy, but the measure passed and local merchant Julian R. Ostrom became the mayor, with Bob Williams as police chief. Williams quickly discovered, as he told a grand jury in October 1928, that Winkler County had fallen under the control of "two distinct rings … a dope and a liquor ring." He told the jurors that he had served as the police chief of Norphlet, an oil town in Arkansas, but had come to Texas looking for a new job when that place became too quiet. He did well in Wink against the drug dealers, arresting seven men and confiscating a lot of drugs. But he got no support from county officials, and suspicions surfaced that Ostrom, who allegedly made a good income from fines levied on oilfield workers for minor offenses, was also cooperating with criminals in protection schemes. Chief among these was Brecheen, who had previously operated bars and gambling houses in Borger and continued to do so in Wink, despite Wright's efforts.[13]

In July 1928, Governor Moody sent an assistant attorney general, David J. Pickle, to aid Wright and his Rangers in Wink. Wright had asked for additional help in combatting gambling and bootlegging, which continued to escalate along with related violence and theft. He had tried a direct assault again, raiding several well-known drinking establishments as well as "dope nuisances," but they reopened after he returned to his headquarters at McCamey and Winkler County Sheriff William A. "Bill" Priest filed an official protest against the Rangers. Pickle, a former Travis County judge, took charge upon his arrival. The careful groundwork for a new wave of arrests was laid by having plainclothes agents circulate in Wink for two weeks, gathering information. Under the direct supervision of Pickle, Wright returned to the oil town during the first week of August with three Special Rangers. They arrested at least 25 men for gambling, bootlegging, and vagrancy in a week-long sweep. Pickle then left for Austin, and Wright once more returned to McCamey, hoping for the best.[14]

Wright could not have anticipated the next chapter in the troubled history of Wink. Texas District Judge Charles L. Klapproth received a petition in September 1928 asking him to remove Sheriff Priest for eighteen counts of "official misconduct." It is not clear whether Priest cooperated with the criminal rings in Wink or was simply intimidated by them, but residents wanted him gone. At the same time, other citizens sued a long list of local officials, including Priest and Mayor Ostrom, and a special prosecutor appointed by Klapproth reported irregularities in the selection of grand jurors in Winkler County. When his district court met during October 1928, Klapproth listened to testimony for a few days, including a detailed complaint from Chief Williams, then declared the town's incorporation void, throwing Williams and Ostrom out of office. This left local law enforcement in the hands of Priest and Wright. When one of Priest's deputies celebrated the ruling by "shooting out the lights of the town," Wright arrested him, indicating who had the upper hand in disputes over authority. Perhaps realizing this, Priest decided to cooperate with Wright, who continued his investigation of the sheriff until the summer of 1929, when Priest resigned and Wright left Wink.

At the same time, Ostrom continued to act as the mayor of Wink, although the town had no charter, and he soon appointed a new police chief, Rufus N. Gilbreath, in place of Williams.[15]

While Wright battled to enforce the law in Wink, some locals did their best to have him fired. Victor Wagner, editor of the *Borger Herald* until the Rangers ran him out of that town, edited the *Wink Times*, a weekly owned by Mayor Ostrom and others, in the summer and fall of 1928. Wagner declared that Wright and his men had only driven away the good people who might testify against real criminals. This allowed even more violence against those who wanted crime eliminated from Wink. C. A. Davis, who claimed to be a "special" correspondent for "several leading daily papers" in Texas, told Governor Moody that law enforcement efforts in Wink had been ineffective because at least two Rangers there were taking bribes from the criminal rings. He even claimed that Rangers would sit in their cars in front of a place they intended to raid for a half hour before they acted, deliberately allowing the guilty parties to escape. He added that Sheriff Priest was cowed by criminal leaders and had stopped enforcing the law, allowing a still owned by Fields and Brecheen to operate openly. Understandably agitated, Moody asked Davis to send him the names of Rangers who were guilty of such behavior. There is no further correspondence concerning Davis, so the Governor must have decided his allegations were spurious. What may have convinced him was a note from Wright saying that Judge Klapproth wanted to remove Priest and had offered to appoint him as sheriff, but he declined because "I know those people up there don't want me, or anyone like me."[16]

Rangers and federal officers raided thirty "alleged gambling halls and vice resorts" at Wink in December 1928, and arrested twenty men, after yet another strange event. Paul C. "Denver Blackie" Burcham, a Wink café owner who claimed to have been an associate of Al Capone, disappeared and was reportedly found, after a two-day search, wandering deliriously in northern Winkler County. He had been kidnapped by rivals when he would not divulge the location of a cargo of liquor that he stole from them. Ostrom ordered Gilbreath to investigate the "gangs" vying for control of Wink, and he discovered that Burcham and his colleagues had taken $500,000 in alcohol that was being conveyed from Ciudad Juarez to Wink for a cartel that included H. E. "Battling Red" Heaton, the leader of the "Big Mitt" gang, and L. M. "Rickers" Rikle. According to Burcham, Heaton's men kidnapped him, tied him to a fence rail with rope, barbed wire, smooth wire, and fishing line, and lowered him into an empty water tank that was fourteen feet in depth. Burcham burned through the rope, undid the wire and fishing line, and climbed out of the tank, but then became lost and very thirsty. Deputy Sheriff Walter Wood found him, and Sheriff Priest cooperated fully in the sweep that ensued, personally arresting half of the twenty-five men detained for Burcham's abduction. When Heaton and his associates were arrested for the kidnapping, Priest had to take Heaton to the jail in Pecos after a mob gathered in Wink to kill the man responsible for abducting Burcham. In a strange turn of events, Heaton accused Burcham of hijacking, a federal offense, so Burcham's associates were arrested and Heaton and his men were released. Van Zandt later recalled that Burcham was sentenced to seven years in jail and paid a fine of several thousand dollars.[17]

Understandably frustrated, Wright growled at a newspaper reporter that the stories of "aimless wandering" and "wholesale arrests" were "all a myth." Instead, it was a simple case of being "hijacked and tied up." Burcham in fact was lucky—another rival of Brecheen, George Helmer, was shot to death on December 22, 1928, by John H. "Toughie" Northcutt, a gunman who had been chased out of Borger and then convinced locals in Wink that he would make a fine Special Ranger. Just days before Northcutt forced his way into Helmer's boarding house, claiming that he was pursuing four escapees from Wink's flimsy jailhouse, and then shot Helmer as he allegedly opposed the illegal entry, Wright had received a request to do what he could to have Northcutt commissioned and assigned to Winkler County. Instead, he had to watch with others as Northcutt was freed on a $2500 bond the day after the shooting, while Helmer's family demanded a thorough investigation. There is no evidence that Wright ever seriously considered having Northcutt appointed as a Ranger. Instead, Northcutt continued to ply his career as an enforcer in Wink until Brecheen killed him with a shotgun blast in November 1929. Of course, a local jury ruled the killing was self-defense, and Brecheen went free again.[18]

Wright and his Rangers left the murder cases to local officers in Wink. Instead they, often with the assistance of others from Rogers' company, detained many locals for prohibition violations during the first months of 1929. Wright wrote to Robertson, "I'm tired of fooling with them. I'm coming after them with blood in my eyes," but he made little progress. In May, Wright with two of his men, Young and Tarver, closed a new gambling den, arresting twenty men. Ostrom meanwhile continued to push for incorporation to secure his status as mayor. Without completing the first objective, he won an April election for mayor, only to be sued by the other candidate, who succeeded in having another election held but lost again as Brecheen's men for a second time barred those who would vote against Ostrom from the polls. Two months later, state district court grand jury foreman W. C. Freeman filed a lawsuit for libel against Ostrom and Smythe H. Lindsay, the new editor of the *Wink Times*, after Lindsay printed an article that referred to the grand jury's angry condemnation of the town's financial system as a "lie." Lindsay eventually left town, but Ostrom remained as mayor although Wink was not incorporated again until 1933. In the meantime, Wright welcomed the help of his son, "Dogie" Wright, in keeping peace. After serving as a Ranger with his father and as a U.S. deputy marshal, as well as doing Ranger undercover work in East Texas oil towns, Dogie had joined the new Border Patrol. Posted in Hudspeth County, he joined his father in raids with the excuse that there could be illegal aliens. The Wrights once found a large tin shed with 500-gallon tanks of mash fermenting inside. No one would admit owning the place, so they destroyed it. Captain Wright did not always find what he wanted. Spotting a likely place near Wink during the summer of 1929, he decided there had to be liquor inside. But when he and Smith entered, they found jars of nitroglycerin and other explosives for oil wells. A reporter wrote: "Sensing danger immediate and certain, these redoubtable custodians of the law gently rolled their flivver to a safe distance and if they exceeded the speed limit in their retreat who is there to blame them." The next day, that same building exploded.[19]

While Ostrom remained the nominal, if not quite legal, mayor of Wink, the office of police chief proved much more volatile. Williams' replacement, Gilbreath, died of a gunshot wound at the Wink jail on May 31, 1929. Wright believed that Gilbreath was Ostrom's "henchman" in criminal activity, and he was determined to find the truth behind the incident, which was said to be an accident. But no one said anything, and no good evidence surfaced, while Wright in June had to be hospitalized for an unidentified illness. Meanwhile, Williams, who had worked as a patrol officer under Gilbreath, resumed the role of police chief. Wright grumbled to Robertson that Gilbreath was "as near nothing as anyone could find," but he found someone even worse nearby. Wright must have been absolutely stunned in July 1929 when he learned that Williams was an escapee from the Oklahoma penitentiary. His real name was Joe Rachate, and he had allegedly been in the Henry Starr gang, participating in thirty bank robberies and many train hold-ups. Sentenced to twelve years, Rachate escaped after ten months and went to work in Norphlet, where he supported town officials in their fight to secure incorporation against the opposition of the oil companies, who did not welcome new taxes. After he left Norphlet, he was a police officer in Kilgore, Texas, before he arrived in Wink. Williams, who by all accounts was an "efficient officer," was arrested by his fellow Wink police officers on orders from Wright. The Ranger captain took him to Pecos to await the arrival of officials from Oklahoma, who escorted him back to their state prison. Meanwhile, Williams' wife was in the hospital with typhoid fever, unaware of what had happened to her husband. Sadly, Williams' rearrest ended his efforts at law enforcement; he died while resisting arrest after a bank robbery in Louisiana.[20]

After a year-and-a-half of hard work, Wright finally got to leave Wink, which continued to be wracked by lawlessness and violence. He returned there only once before leaving the Rangers again in 1933. He was working in 1931 with other local and state officers, most notably Sheriff Jess Slaughter of Howard County, to derail an automobile theft ring operating in five West Texas communities. Wright was also cooperating for the first time with Edward A. Gormley, the manager of the Dallas office of the National Automobile Theft Bureau, a not-for-profit corporation allied with the insurance industry. The trail led to Wink in May 1931, when lawmen arrested two men and recovered eight stolen vehicles. By that time, Wright's efforts in Wink and other West Texas towns, as well as Jal in New Mexico, had firmly established his reputation in the region as an effective law officer. While a newspaper reporter in 1928 had described him as a "quiet looking, harmless appearing man of sixty," in less than two years another noted that he had "brought law and order to the oil field territory" and hailed him as "Perhaps the most noted Ranger captain in West Texas." Because of budget cuts and political infighting, he had done this with just five men in his company, not the fourteen he led only a decade earlier.[21]

Wink of course was not the sole focus of Wright's activities in 1928. He assisted Reeder during the fall, raiding gambling houses and bootleggers in the oil towns of Crossett and McCamey, in Upton County, and Grube, in neighboring Pecos County. During November, he arrested four men in the latter county for cattle rustling. Later that same month in Fort Stockton, the seat of Pecos County and the site of his new headquarters, he helped retrieve three prisoners who attacked Deputy Sheriff C. I. Miller and escaped from the local jail. The trio, after asking Miller to light the stove in their cell, overpowered him, "pried open their cell door," and fled. Originally J. P. Bridges and Howard Savage, two of the four men arrested by Wright, were believed to be two of the escapees, but Leon O. Bridges, the attorney for Garza County, reported that they had posted bonds one week earlier and were now in Post, more than two hundred miles away. Wright learned that Van Leach Finchum, one of his rustlers, had in fact bolted with Clyde Stone and Tom Mack Jones, jailed for a "liquor law violation" and burglary respectively. Finchum surrendered on December 1, reporting that he found it impossible to reach Mexico. He also said that Stone had been shot in the leg—apparently Miller fired three times during their escape and hit Stone. Meanwhile, the ringleader of the captured rustlers, James William "Dutch" Luman, who was wanted for murder and cattle theft, remained in jail. Luman in 1927 had walked into a theater in Post and shot Marvin Breeding, whom he said had insulted his wife, the former Ola Faye Finchum. In December 1928, a jury accepted Luman's claim that Breeding tried to shoot first and sentenced him to only three years in jail. That same month a grand jury indicted Luman and his wife Ola for cattle theft along with Bridges, Savage, and Finchum. The charges against Ola and Bridges were quickly dropped, but Luman had two years added to his original sentence. No verdict has been found for Savage and Finchum. Reporting the original four arrests, Wright remarked that the men were "Docile as a lot of lambs," but "Their women, bad ones, reared and pitched like tigers."[22]

Wright was similarly busy in 1929 when he was away from Wink. He and his men raided liquor and gambling places in San Angelo in January and arrested twenty men, including Police Chief James C. Bates and former Tom Green County sheriff Gerome W. Shields (along with several other members of the Shields family). Bates, a former Ranger captain, ultimately resigned his office and was sentenced to eighteen months in the federal prison at Leavenworth, Kansas. In February, the Rangers returned to Pecos County to focus on Fort Stockton and Iraan. Wright in August got a telephone call from Jackie Mae Whiteside in Crane, the seat of adjacent Crane County, who asked him to come there. When he and Young arrived at her café, they learned that she resented several apparent discrepancies in local law enforcement. With the information she provided about her rival, the two Rangers went to a brewery in town that had a "fine" front parlor, a well-stocked saloon filled with customers, and "several notorious women" who kept private rooms. There Wright arrested "Mrs. Jewel Hodges," who was probably Jewel P. T. Hogan. In September, Wright got a change of scenery. He accompanied Rogers to El Paso, where a planned prize fight failed to occur, and then, upon the order of Governor Moody, escorted a reluctant informant, E. G. Tarlton, from Monahans to Borger for a conversation with Hamer about the murder of Texas District Attorney John A. Holmes. Tarlton apparently wanted to talk only if Moody gave him the reward he had offered of $500 in advance, while the frustrated chief executive, who would soon declare martial law at Borger, understandably wanted information before giving money to anyone.[23]

In March 1930, the "nude and partly decomposed body" of Henry M. Polan was found floating in the Pecos River at a bridge near Imperial, about thirty miles northeast of Fort Stockton. Later that year Fred L. Moutray was indicted in Ector County for the murder, but he had already fled the area. Sheriff Reeder Webb of Ector County had statements from eyewitnesses who saw Moutray and another man dump Polan's body into the Pecos. Webb joined Wright for an investigation that initially took them to Houston, Goose Creek, and Baytown. They subsequently tracked Moutray to Europe, the east coast of the United States, Chicago, and Tulsa, where they arranged for his arrest during the spring of 1932 and brought him to the Ector County jail. Once in custody, Moutray quickly identified Roger F. Thompson as his partner and implicated Ruby Taggart in their crime. Wright located Thompson in the Washington State Prison at Walla Walla, where he had been jailed for burglary, and in October 1932 he went with Smith and James G. Rooney, a thirty-nine-year-old rancher from Alpine who served several terms as a Special Ranger, to escort him back to Texas. Thompson and Moutray were brought to Sterling City, the seat of Sterling County where Polan had been murdered, and indicted. Thompson was tried first, with Moutray as the main witness, in May 1933. He was sentenced to fifty years in the penitentiary at Huntsville. The trial of Moutray was delayed to the next term of the district court, when he was sentenced to four years in the state prison system as an accessory in the killing of Polan.[24]

The story that emerged during the trials of Thompson and Moutray was sordid and reinforced Wright's already low opinion of Ma Ferguson. Polan, a gambler from Montana, had come with Taggart to the Cattlemen's Convention at San Angelo in March 1930. They left town together on March 22 and disappeared. What Polan did not know was that he was the target of a nasty plan. Moutray had been working in McCamey when Thompson came to see him. The two had first met while they were serving long sentences in Huntsville, whence they were released after being pardoned by Ferguson. Thompson took Moutray to see Taggart, who told them that "she knew a Jew with a big roll of money." The plan was for Taggart to convince Polan to leave San Angelo for Lubbock, and Thompson would follow them in Moutray's car, with Moutray waiting for them to return. But when Thompson and Taggart returned, he was in Polan's car, while she was driving Moutray's car with Polan's body in the trunk. Thompson told Moutray that things had gone awry when Polan tried to pull a revolver, and Thompson shot him twice. Deciding to dump the body in the Pecos River, Moutray and Thompson drove to McCamey, where they bought whiskey to fortify themselves, and arrived at the river, where they cut Polan's clothes from his body, burned them to hinder identification, then tossed the corpse into the water. They then drove from Texas through Kansas to Chicago, where they parted.[25]

While Thompson was convicted, primarily on the testimony of Moutray, and Moutray likewise stayed in jail, no one had seen Taggart since the day of the murder. She had also been released from Huntsville by Ma Ferguson, in March 1925 after serving two years of a five-year sentence for armed robbery. That incarceration resulted from a scheme in which she led two men, her companion and his friend, into a similar trap at Wichita Falls. Unfortunately for her, she was caught in bed in a Fort Worth hotel with one of the robbers, with some of the two victims' belongings in their room. After the murder of Polan, and between the trials of Thompson and Moutray, lawmen captured Taggart on June 7, 1933, in Kilgore, Texas, and brought her to San Angelo, where she was questioned and released. Apparently, no evidence to support Moutray's story about her could be found, while witnesses saw Thompson and Moutray disposing of Polan without Taggart. She did not appear again in Texas records, at least under the name of Ruby Taggart, but by the summer of 1933 she was arrested while using at least two aliases. Wright must have been disappointed that she eluded justice in the Polan case, and his frustration was greatly compounded by the dismissal of Thompson's conviction by the Texas Court of Criminal Appeals. Wright believed that Thompson was also guilty of the murder of a woman and her young daughter, whose bodies were discovered in the Pecos in February 1930, one month before Polan was found, but he was never tried for that crime.[26]

Wright for most of 1930 kept his headquarters in McCamey but sent Rangers as far south and west as Presidio and Hudspeth counties to chase cattle rustlers and other thieves. In May 1930 he had Smith and Young join the manhunt for Ira McKee, who had killed William R. Billingsley while robbing a gas station in Dawson County. The Rangers captured McKee three days after they joined the chase, and Wright with Tarver accompanied them to provide security at McKee's trial in Lamesa, 130 miles north of McCamey. McKee was later executed in the electric chair at the state penitentiary in Huntsville. Closer to McCamey, Wright became more active in Crane County, a thinly populated area just to the west that had not been fully organized until 1927, forty years after it was created. Until then, residents depended on nearby counties for law enforcement. Changes came with the discovery of oil, when the population exploded from less than one hundred to several thousand in just a few years. Newcomers built drinking and gambling establishments, creating problems that had to be addressed. Wright led Smith, Tarver, and Young in a midnight raid on a "road house" known as the "Light House" on Sunday, July 13, 1930. The popular establishment held about forty "highly intoxicated" customers who "greeted" Wright and his men when they arrived. The Rangers arrested the proprietors and appropriated "some 500 bottles of home brew." Ten hours later, Wright led a raid on a bogus laundry in McCamey and confiscated more beer. In the fall, when Wright moved his headquarters again to Fort Stockton, he continued to police oil towns. He returned to Crane County with several Rangers and found a still in the brush. The owner was absent but had hidden barrels of peach mash in a trench. The Rangers poured the contents of kerosene lanterns they found on the property into the barrels and quietly left, leaving the proprietor to make a nasty discovery. When local authorities wanted extra security during the June 1931 trial of Jack Hall for killing prominent local rancher Thomas C. Barnsley, Wright returned again to Crane County. Ironically, after two trials and at least one successful appeal, Hall was shot to death in another dispute.[27]

Wright survived the transition of power in the governor's office from Moody to Ross S. Sterling in January 1931 without any apparent disruptions. Governor Sterling replaced Robertson with William W. Sterling. The new adjutant general, who had been a civilian scout for the Army on the Rio Grande and a Texas National Guard officer before becoming a deputy sheriff and Ranger captain, wanted to raise the number of Rangers and have only Ranger veterans as captains. The four field companies thus came under the command of Wright (A), Thomas R. "Tom" Hickman (B), Asa Light Townsend (C), and Albert R. Mace (D). Hamer remained in command of the Headquarters Company, while Charles O. Moore became the Rangers' quartermaster. Wright's reappointment was not a surprise to him. He had been concerned that, as the oldest captain, he might not be chosen to continue in service, but Sterling told Blake D. Fore, Wright's son-in-law, to tell him not to worry because he "never had a better friend than the new adjutant general." In spite of the Great Depression, which had already created financial havoc elsewhere, Texas, which had oil money to delay the full impact of the crisis, employed seventy Rangers by the fall of 1931, even more than either of the Sterlings had envisioned, and the Rangers had more money in their operating budget, including funds for every company to have several automobiles. Among the Rangers, Wright was not only the oldest but also the only one with a mustache, a singular fact that the *Longview Daily News* noted.[28]

By 1932, the Great Depression affected many parts of Texas, and crime increased. The primary trouble for the Rangers came in the East Texas oil fields, but Wright remained busy in Winkler, Crane, and Upton counties, arresting bootleggers and gamblers while patrolling for cattle rustlers. In May, he raided a "dance hall and gambling house" three miles from McCamey with Smith and Young, along with Special Rangers Taylor and Rooney and a local deputy sheriff. Just after midnight, with seventy cars in the parking lot, the Rangers "Punched down [the] back door of [the] gambling house." They arrested twenty-seven gamblers as well as the bartender, the "notorious" Keet Hogan, and the proprietor, Slim Goodwin, whom they had nabbed the previous year on similar charges. Sheriff W. C. Fowler of Upton County took Goodwin and Hogan to Pecos County to be arraigned on federal charges. Hamer warmly congratulated Wright, writing to him that "lots of good citizens are tickled to death with the work you have done in cleaning up this place." Wright used trickery in July 1932 to keep his quarry from bolting during a raid on another operation near McCamey. Ordinarily, there were lookouts and a buzzer to give the alarm if lawmen approached. Wright flanked these by having three ranch hands pose as robbers. They mingled with customers and then staged a robbery. Miraculously, no one shot them, and Wright with Taylor arrived after the "bandits" secured their victims. Politely knocking on the door, Wright and Taylor were admitted by their accomplices. The customers were at first happy to be rescued but quickly changed their minds when a local justice of the peace arraigned them right there in the bar. Thirty were charged with state gambling violations and fined, while three were held on federal prohibition charges.[29]

Wright and two Rangers, Smith and Poole, accompanied Sheriff Frank Kuykendall of Gaines County in June 1932 to a private sanitarium in Wichita Falls, where they arrested Oscar M. Herring, former county attorney for Palo Pinto County, and confiscated about $32 in coins.

It was the strange culmination of an investigation of an armed robbery of the First State Bank in Seagraves, in Gaines County, on May 27 by a rather inept cast of characters. Herring was their leader; other charges of forgery and embezzlement indicate that he had money troubles, and so he decided robbing a bank might be the solution. He recruited Elmer Slaughter, a farmer from Terry County who said he knew someone who could be their gunman: Jodie Edwards of Motley County. The other two bank robbers were Edmond Meredith of Seagraves, Herring's twenty-one-year-old brother-in-law, and James W. Baker, the principal of Seagraves High School. After the robbery, Wright came north from Marfa, where he had established his headquarters in September 1931, with his two men to join Kuykendall and Edgar T. Neal, a Ranger with an interesting history. Born in 1869 at Fairview in Wilson County, Hamer's hometown and the county where Wright was sheriff for fifteen years, Neal served in the Frontier Battalion under Rogers before Wright enlisted, then was twice elected sheriff of San Saba County. Disgusted with the Ku Klux Klan, he resigned from law enforcement in 1925 and was selling real estate when Moody convinced him to be a Ranger again in 1930. Neal was put in charge of criminal investigations, which is what brought him together with Wright and the others in West Texas.[30]

After Herring's arrest, most of the others were apprehended quickly. Meredith was detained at Herring's home, where $60 in loot was found in a barn on the property. Baker had enrolled as a student in summer school at Texas Tech College (now University). When he was arrested, he led several officers to $390 in stolen money hidden at his residence, and then to a "quart fruit jar" filled with $80 in coins and buried at the foot of a telephone pole. Slaughter had also been apprehended by the time a Texas district court grand jury indicted all five robbers at Seminole in mid-June 1932. Only Edwards, whom the lone bank clerk identified as the gunman, had not been caught, but he was in custody before the trials began during the fall of 1932. When the court convened, many questions remained unanswered since only Meredith and Edwards were in the bank during the robbery. And since Meredith had been locked in the bank's vault along with the clerk by Edwards, who then fled in an automobile with an unknown driver, prosecutors were not certain they could convict anyone but Edwards, who had several witnesses ready to testify that he was in Paducah, Texas, 175 miles from Seagraves, when the bank was robbed.[31]

The district court tried Baker first, during December 1932, and his trial resulted in a hung jury. Frustrated, the judge agreed to a change of venue, to Terry County, where Baker could be retried and the other four would face their first juries. Being tried twice must have rattled Baker, because he was very talkative when he took the stand again in February 1933. He declared that Herring and Slaughter planned everything, with Slaughter enlisting Edwards as the gunman. Meredith and Baker were to be in the bank as Edwards came in, after having been signaled by Herring that there was only a single clerk present, then Slaughter would drive the getaway car. Meredith and Baker would serve as witnesses to testify later, if necessary, that Edwards was not the gunman. The plan unfolded without a hitch, with one change. Baker entered the bank about noon, lingered for a short while, then left, having perhaps lost his nerve. Meredith then came and was the only customer when Edwards arrived with a gun and bag. Giving the bag to Meredith and the clerk, Edwards told them to fill it, then herded them into the vault and closed the door. He then departed with Slaughter. Baker claimed to be an unwitting dupe who discovered the details of the scheme only after he accompanied Herring to a division of the spoils in Slaughter's barn one day after the robbery. To reinforce this, he recalled that Slaughter asked why he was there, and whether he was part of the plan. He also insisted that he did not know the source of the money being given to him until reports of the robbery appeared. He did not say anything then because he was threatened, and he drove Edwards to Lubbock to avoid investigators, hoping that he would soon leave the country, and all would be quiet again.[32]

Baker perhaps should have pled guilty; clearly the jury and judge were not impressed with his protestations of innocence, which were filled with contradictions. He was convicted in February 1933 and sentenced to twenty years in the Texas penitentiary. Edwards also insisted that he was innocent to no avail, even with the support of people who said he was in Paducah when the bank was robbed. He was sent to the state penitentiary for fifteen years. Herring then decided to plead guilty and received a sentence of ten years, while Slaughter also pled guilty and received a sentence of just eight years in the penitentiary. Meredith, the youngest suspect, had his trial delayed; no further action has been found. Wright must have been furious to learn that in April 1933, about two months after he was convicted, Herring returned home after being paroled for ninety days by Ma Ferguson. His release allowed him to arrange for the dismissal of charges of embezzlement and forgery, but it also prompted a petition to Ferguson from two hundred people in Palo Pinto County asking that Herring not be pardoned for the robbery. He stayed in prison until September 1940. As for the loot, newspaper reports indicated that less than 20% of the $3,298.89 stolen from the First State Bank in Seagraves was recovered.[33]

Wright's service as a Ranger captain ended after Ma Ferguson took office for her second term as governor. He had not grown to like her any more than he did in 1925, when he resigned after her first election as governor, and most other Rangers also opposed her. Adjutant General Sterling met with several senior Rangers who had been sheriffs, including Wright, and planned for raids in East Texas in August 1932 that were intended to disperse what they said was a large number of illegal voters brought in by the Fergusons for the fall election, but Governor Sterling told him to stop. Ma Ferguson narrowly won the Democratic primary in a runoff marked by obvious fraud, but when Hamer and Wright brought a detachment of Rangers to provide security at the state convention at Lubbock during September, the alarmed delegates still would not invalidate the balloting, nor did a lawsuit from Governor Sterling undo Ferguson's nomination. After taking office, Ferguson dismissed every Ranger in January 1933. Many of her replacements were political appointees, while the Special Rangers again swelled in number to over 2,300, over five times more than Sterling appointed. She also issued 1,055 pardons during her first six months back in the office. Wright during her two-year term was a deputy sheriff along with Albert R. Mace in Nueces County. They worked initially for Sheriff James W. Galbreath, a veteran lawman who died in March 1933 after only a few months in office. Galbreath as city marshal of Robstown had hired Wright when he refused to work for Ferguson in 1925, and then in the 1932 sheriff's race he defeated Ben D. Lee, who outpolled Wright when he campaigned to be the Nueces County sheriff in 1926. After he died, Wright and Mace worked for Sheriff Paul E. Cox, a Wilson County native and longtime friend of Wright's who had previously served as the tax collector.[34]

Cox led Wright into his only maritime adventure. The sheriff, Wright, and Deputy Leonidas L. Nusom boarded a grounded pleasure boat, the *Jacopin*, off Bird Island in late July 1933. Armed with search warrants, they scoured the craft for illegal liquor and arrested several of the crew. Cox took the prisoners ashore while Wright and Nusom began transferring cases of beer to another boat. When the captain volunteered to move the *Jacopin* to the Pleasure Pier in Corpus Christi, the lawmen agreed, but instead the boat motored toward Port Aransas. When Wright and Nusom protested, armed crewman surrounded and disarmed them. The owner of the *Jacopin* subsequently tried to file formal complaints against the law officers, specifically charging Wright with assaulting one of the crew, while Wright and the others, with the support of the local district attorney, submitted a request for an injunction that would prevent the *Jacopin* from operating for a year. Apparently neither party succeeded in suing the other, for there is no notice of this case in newspapers or official records except for a single report in the *Corpus Christi Caller-Times*.[35]

As Wright may have expected, the remainder of his service as a deputy in Nueces County proved uneventful, although in 1934 he did have his remaining teeth pulled. An old friend, Daniel Boone Choate, who had already had his teeth extracted, became Wright's self-appointed mentor throughout the ordeal. Wright and Choate had been boyhood friends in DeWitt County, where they "rode stick horses and killed lizards together," and their paths had crossed again when Choate's bungled Spanish translations as a deputy led to the deadly gunfight between Sheriff William T. "Brack" Morris and Gregorio Cortez Lira in June 1901. Since that time, Choate had served as a Loyalty Ranger in Karnes County during World War I and by the early 1930s was an inspector for the Customs Service in Nueces County at Robstown, where he could visit Wright after each session with the dentist. Choate was a faithful buddy, promising Wright that he would "keep this up until his plates are made and he learns how to use them, even to the extent of biting a nail in two." Wright apparently did appreciate the support of his old friend.[36]

The *Brownsville Herald* celebrated Wright's final return to duty as a Ranger in February 1935 as part of "Governor Allred's program of taking Ranger badges away from politicians." James V "Jimmy" Allred, who at the age of thirty-six was just three years older than Moody, the youngest person ever to be elected governor of Texas, had served as attorney general with Governor Sterling from 1931 to 1933. He ran for governor on a platform that promised to improve law enforcement in Texas, then appointed Carl E. Nesbitt, the former commander of the American Legion in Texas, as his adjutant general. Nesbitt dismissed all but three of Ma Ferguson's Regular Rangers and every one of her Special Rangers, then hired a new Ranger Force, one-third of whom were pre-Ferguson Rangers. The purpose once more was to combat Ma Ferguson's influence—she had once more reduced the Ranger Force and left it riddled with scandals—and create a professional, modern law enforcement organization. Wright was identified as one of the "old-time, hard riding, straight shooting rangers who are returning to duty." He was also the only active Ranger in 1935 who had served under seven Texas governors—Joseph D. Sayers, William P. Hobby, Pat M. Neff, Moody, Sterling, and Allred, as well as briefly, and unhappily, twice under Miriam A "Ma" Ferguson.[37]

Wright returned to duty in 1935 as a private, which has been criticized by contemporaries and historians alike. Former Adjutant General Sterling wrote that Wright's "vast experience as a leader was lost to the state," while historian James R. Ward later declared the appointment was a "grievous oversight." There is no evidence that Wright protested his lower rank—after all, he was sixty-seven years old and had worried that he would be entirely overlooked because of his age in 1931. He served in Company D, the unit he led from 1919 to 1925 but in 1935 was commanded by Captain William W. "Bill" McMurrey. Born in DeWitt County in 1890 but "educated in Floresville," McMurrey had become a Special Ranger in January 1918, when he was a foreman for the Las Norias branch of the King Ranch. That appointment ended when all Special Rangers were dismissed pending the legislative investigation initiated by Jose T. Canales. Since that time, McMurrey had worked briefly for Customs and then settled on his ranch at Hebbronville, where he again had a Special Ranger commission from 1929 to 1933. As a full-time captain, McMurrey made his headquarters at Hebbronville and proved to be a great leader. For the Texas Centennial, Paramount Studios employed him as the model for a bronze statue of a Texas Ranger that was unveiled in Dallas in conjunction with the local premier of the movie produced from historian Walter P. Webb's landmark study of the Rangers.[38]

Wright's fellow privates in Company D in 1935 had an interesting array of backgrounds. Alfred Y. Allee II's father and grandfather had both served as lawmen and met violent ends. Alonzo W. Allee, his father, was a Special Ranger in 1916–1917, but a few months after resigning his commission he died following a fight in Crystal City in which he killed his opponent. This was in fact the second time he had killed a man, with the first occurring a few years before he became a Ranger. Alfred Y. Allee, Alonzo's father, was killed by Marshal A. Joseph Barthelow at Laredo in 1896, five years after he shot Walter C. and William J. Bowen on a train at Cotulla, adding to the cycle of violence that Wright found there as a young Ranger. Before all this, during the 1880s, the elder Allee had served as a deputy sheriff in Karnes County. Alfred Y. Allee II was born in La Salle County in 1905, three years after Wright left to become a sheriff in Wilson County, and he became a game warden and deputy sheriff before joining the Rangers in 1931. He left the service during Ma Ferguson's second term, then returned when Allred took office and served more than three decades. Wright was certainly aware of Allee's family history, but he had much more in common with another member of Company D who returned to Ranger service in 1935: Edgar T. Neal, who had raided roadhouses with Wright during the summer of 1932. He had also left the Rangers when Ferguson became governor in 1933, then joined McMurrey's company for a final term of three years, while Wright stayed almost four years.[39]

The other privates in Company D in the first half of 1935 had little or no prior service as Rangers, but at least one quickly won lasting fame. Leo H. Bishop, a native of Kimble County, was a rancher at Del Rio in May 1932 when he enlisted at the age of twenty-nine. He lasted eight months, until Ma Ferguson took office, then had a commission as a Special Ranger during her term. He rejoined in 1935 and was assigned to San Augustine, where he participated in a law enforcement campaign that led to nineteen convictions for murder. Fred D. Holland, a former Fort Worth police officer from Johnson County, first became a Ranger in January 1933 as one of Ma Ferguson's replacements. He joined the Headquarters Company four months after his enlistment, then left the service in January 1935. One month later, he re-enlisted and remained with Company D for a year. Martin E. Trejo, a San Antonio native working as an investigator for the Bexar County attorney's office, joined McMurrey's command in February 1935 at the age of thirty-three. He had never served as a Ranger prior to that time, but he did well, transferred to the Narcotics Division in 1937, and remained a Ranger for a total of eight years.[40]

Levi Duncan, a twenty-nine-year-old native of Hondo, joined Company D in August 1935, the month that the Rangers officially became part of the new Department of Public Safety. It was his first enlistment as a Ranger, but he proved to be a long-term recruit, serving until his death in 1966. After Holland left the Rangers in February 1936, Joseph H. M. Bridge joined Company D the following month. A native of San Angelo, the forty-five-year-old Bridge also had no previous service as a Ranger, but he stayed until his death in 1956. McMurrey had less luck with his next recruit for Company D, although he had prior service as a Ranger. Powers R. Fenner, a native of Beeville born in 1894, served as a Railroad Ranger for four months in 1922, then as a Special Ranger from April 1934 to January 1935. As a deputy sheriff, he also worked with Wright at Laredo in the early 1920s. Appointed as a private in September 1936, his service came to an end after he arrested a private investigator during a complex investigation near Kingsville and hustled him to Brownsville to avoid complying with a writ of *habeas corpus*. Cited for contempt, he became angry and waved a pistol in the courtroom when a newspaper photographer took his picture. The published image of the gun-wielding Ranger required a public response, so Fenner was discharged in August 1937 and apparently later worked as an electrical contractor.[41]

The end of national prohibition let Texans endorse a local option law in August 1933 that only allowed beer with a low alcohol content. It was not until August 1935 that Texans voted to repeal state Prohibition, which led to a statewide return to local option for the sale of all alcoholic beverages. Allred, responding to the reluctance of many local officials to enforce state Prohibition, in March 1935 ordered a sweep by the Rangers of places violating laws against gambling and alcohol. The Rangers conducted raids in Austin, Fort Worth, Dallas, Houston, and Galveston, as well as in Starr and Duval counties along the Rio Grande. They arrested 2,389 people on March 17 and made more arrests on subsequent days. From his headquarters at Hebbronville, McMurrey directed the raids in Starr and Duval counties. He and Wright, with four Special Rangers and one Customs Service officer, personally raided the Rainbow Club in Rio Grande City on March 17, seizing gallons of illegal liquor and arresting the proprietor, J. J. Guerra. At about the same time, others from Company D arrested seventeen people at San Diego and confiscated even more illegal whiskey and gambling equipment.[42]

The campaign against liquor and gambling led to a conflict between the Texas Rangers and local officials at Corpus Christi in late March 1935. Privates Allee and Neal of Company D had been sent there to participate in the statewide sweep. Allee arrived first and arrested Dave Allen. Exiting the city police station, he was confronted by Maxwell P. Dunne, a political leader and funeral director who was Allen's friend. A fight ensued, and Allee arrested Dunne. By the time Neal came to Corpus Christi a few days later, Dunne had been released on bond and was charging Allee and police detective Ed Flint with false arrest, while Police Chief Albert R. Mace, recently appointed after serving as a Nueces County deputy with Wright, arrested Allee for assaulting Dunne. Allee posted a fifty-dollar bond, but Nueces County Sheriff William E. Shely, a former Ranger, and Mayor William Shaffer of Corpus Christi demanded that Nesbitt send the two Rangers elsewhere before "bloodshed" ensued. Nesbitt instead told McMurrey and Wright of Company D, along with Zeno A. Smith and Maro W. "Wiley" Williamson of Company A, to join Allee and Neal in providing security during the upcoming elections at Corpus Christi. The polls were remarkably quiet while the Rangers patrolled with, according to the *Austin Statesman*, pistols, rifles, and submachine guns. They harmed no one, but neither did Nesbitt acquiesce to the demands of local officials that they be removed. And there is no evidence that Allee was convicted of assault; in fact, Mace, who became a Ranger captain again in late 1935, later told Nesbitt that Dunne attacked the Ranger, which may explain the low bail required of Allee.[43]

Wright's duty station became Harlingen as McMurrey posted his Rangers all over the lower Rio Grande Valley to extend Allred's campaign against alcohol and gambling. Wright in May 1935 led a raid in Harlingen on a place owned by well-known restauranteur Dan Heslop, arresting the popular American Legion officer for selling liquor. The team led by Wright included local law officers and Customs agents. Months later, in November 1935, Wright with two Highway Patrol officers, Sam Estes and Dan Abbott, raided the White Kitchen Café in McAllen. There he arrested Will White and Lewis R. Hammerly for running a gambling operation. Their bonds were set at $500 each, while three of their customers were fined one dollar each plus court costs and released. Days later, McMurrey and Smith invaded sites in McAllen and Mercedes, completing a trio of raids by Rangers in South Texas. Once more controversy emerged when Wright angrily told a Brownsville newspaper reporter that local lawmen warned White and Hammerly that a raid was imminent. Wright added that a police officer was found in their place but released on his own recognizance by his colleagues, without paying a fine or posting a bond. Texas District Attorney Rogers C. Kelley of Hidalgo County, infuriated at Wright's allegations, ordered a court of inquiry to review Wright's claims, but the justice of the peace who directed the investigation was T. J. "Jud" Powell, who had released White and Hammerly, as well as their customers, on low bonds. There is no record of any further action on Wright's complaint.[44]

Allred during his campaign had advocated reforming the Rangers and combining them with the Highway Patrol, and that officially happened on August 10, 1935, when the Department of Public Safety (DPS) began operations. The idea did not originate with Allred; by 1931 the Highway Patrol Division of the Texas Highway Department, created in 1929, had grown to 120 officers and privates, and Governor Sterling began discussing a merger. The legislature hired Griffenhagen and Associates of Chicago to produce a multi-volume audit of the entire state government, with the intention of streamlining it, but their report, which appeared in early 1933, did not interest Ma Ferguson. She did, however, approve a reduction of the Ranger Force to thirty-two officers and men and a decrease of its budget by about one-half. Allred's initiative combined the Griffenhagen report with recommendations from the Texas Senate, Sheriff's Association of Texas, and Ranger captain Thomas R. "Tom" Hickman, who surveyed police forces elsewhere in the United States. The legislature began considering a bill soon after Allred's inauguration, and he signed it while Wright and others were enforcing his prohibition campaign. Within the new Texas Ranger Division of the DPS, the five companies kept their captains. Salaries and expense budgets increased, but their number remained small; for example, there were two dozen captains and privates in December 1935, when McMurrey had three men. This greatly reduced effectiveness when the Rangers adopted the model of scattering men at duty stations; Wright, for example, worked alone at Harlingen. Another problem for the Rangers was that the DPS leadership did not immediately stabilize. Complaints prompted the removal of Louis G. Phares, the first director, while his successor, Horace H. Carmichael, served only briefly before dying of a heart attack. Homer Garrison Jr. became the director in 1938 and ultimately remained in that office for thirty years.[45]

Wright and his colleagues became the focus of protests in the fall of 1935 when they gathered at Corpus Christi to keep order during a longshoreman's strike that turned violent. The passage of the National Industrial Recovery Act led to the resurgence of the International Longshoreman's Association (ILA). In Texas, the number of chapters more than doubled within a year, and strong growth continued through the eve of World War II. This expansion was accompanied by strikes as ILA leaders counseled their members to resist unfair practices by corporations. Tensions also mounted because the ILA was segregated, and blacks and Tejanos were excluded from both jobs and relief efforts during stoppages. In October 1935 workers in Corpus Christi joined in a Gulf Coast strike that included employees as far east as Pensacola. When seven non-union strike breakers were beaten—one died from being hit in the head with a brick—Allred at the request of the city council sent Rangers to investigate, as well as to guard job sites and anyone who wanted to work. Allee, who had helped bring a farm worker strike to a peaceful end at Laredo during the spring of 1935, and Wright arrived first in Corpus Christi. They arrested two African American strikers of a group of five who had trapped two African American strikebreakers in a local store. The confiscation of three pistols by the Rangers at the same time indicated that a tragedy may have been averted. In November, non-union worker Bibian Solís was shot in the back as he fled from an automobile that had been attacked by pipe-wielding picketers. The four ILA members arrested for assaulting Solís and his companions were charged with disturbing the peace and released on bonds of ten dollars each; only the suspect in the shooting of Solís stayed in jail. This prompted the arrival of three more Rangers—Captain McMurrey; Everard M. "Pappy" Davenport Jr., an ex-sheriff from Jackson County who had joined Company A; and Jerome B. Wheatley, a former Potter County sheriff and police chief from Amarillo who had served for many years with the Headquarters Company. The five Rangers began an investigation while also providing armed escorts for busloads of strikebreakers coming from San Antonio and Houston.[46]

An "interracial group" of seventeen ILA longshoremen submitted official complaints about "inappropriate treatment" by Allee and Wright during their inquiry into the murder of Solís. The two Rangers allegedly "interrogated and harassed" dock workers, yet accounts of specific incidents never mentioned Wright by name. In fact, most of the complaints seem to be about Rangers talking in a rough manner to longshoremen. When these statements were sent to Allred with a request to withdraw the Rangers from Corpus Christi, the Governor did not respond. ILA wives carried copies of allegations in a door-knocking campaign to get locals to sign a petition for the removal of the Rangers, but few people signed. The Houston Labor and Trades Council of the American Federation of Labor, which had official representatives in Corpus Christi, sent a telegram to Allred and once more got no response. Gilbert Mers, a white ILA longshoreman, later wrote in his autobiography that the Rangers routinely chose one picketer to beat each week, and they always had their guns ready when confronting pickets. He again never mentioned Wright by name, though he did complain repeatedly about Allee. He also noted that most of his armed comrades quit carrying guns when the Rangers arrived, and strikebreakers escorted by Rangers arrived safely at work. Since fifteen men were killed during the strike, only one of whom was a member of the ILA, this seems to have been an important achievement for the Rangers. After violent incidents at Port Arthur and Orange, Texas, and Lake Charles, Louisiana, federal officials negotiated an end to the strike.[47]

During 1936, with prohibition repealed at both the state and national levels, Wright focused his efforts on gambling houses in South Texas, although he got little support from local officials. He made a Saturday night raid on a gambling operation halfway between Donna and Weslaco in late September, arresting the proprietor and eleven customers. The owner paid a fine of $50, while the gamblers were fined $10 each. Wright with other Rangers and Highway Patrol officers raided two gambling houses in Corpus Christi in October, arresting five men at the Dragon Grill but no one at the Casino Night Club. The law officers confiscated and destroyed several black-jacks and dice tables, as well as other gambling equipment, in both places, while all confiscated money was donated to the Salvation Army. Later that month, Wright and Highway Patrolman Dan Abbott raided more gambling places with slot machines in Harlingen and Combes late one Saturday night, arresting three men.[48]

Wright was assigned to a case in the summer of 1936 that revisited some unpleasant memories for him. In April 1936 Wilbur Garton, a liquor dealer in Corpus Christi, was arrested for the murder of his first wife, Leta Belle Garton, and her ten-year-old daughter from a former marriage, Joyce Glen Roberts. Wright remembered both Garton and the murders well, but he had never connected them. Garton had been arrested at Wink, where he was working as a pharmacist, in February 1929. Charged with killing two men in Oklahoma City, he had been scheduled for extradition but escaped from the Wink jail. He resurfaced in Oklahoma City in June 1929, where he surrendered to authorities and was freed on bail. No record of a trial has been found, and within a year he was back in Texas, where he allegedly beat and strangled his estranged wife and her daughter and dumped their bodies in the Pecos River. Wright had long believed another man, Roger F. Thompson, was guilty of this heinous crime, but Garton became the focus of his new investigation more than six years after the murders were discovered. Unfortunately for the aging Ranger, there was no tidy legal resolution for this case. Released on bond again, thanks to the continued support of some of his Wink associates, Garton was indicted but remained free while his trial was apparently delayed several times. Writing to Smith, his former sergeant, about the case during July 1936, Wright sourly remarked that "Wink is the same old thing."

Later that year, Garton was indicted in Kansas on federal liquor charges, but he still lived and worked in Corpus Christi when he shot himself to death in September 1941.[49]

Wright got another break from arresting gamblers in the fall of 1936, but it also did not prove to be a welcome interlude. On November 18, Luther Blanton and his son John disappeared while poaching ducks on the El Sauz division of the King Ranch in Willacy County. When local lawmen failed to find them, state officials were contacted, and Wright interviewed Myrtle, Luther's wife, and led several posses in combing the area for the missing men. He found nothing, as did McMurrey, who conducted his own investigation. By November 22 an angry, and armed, crowd had gathered at the King Ranch fence near the Blanton's house, and it was only with difficulty that McMurrey and Bridge of Company D convinced them not to storm onto the property and seek either the lost men or revenge. Many stories circulated about others, Anglos and Tejanos, who had ventured onto King Ranch lands to hunt and were attacked or never seen again. McMurrey and Bridge confronted two of Myrtle's sons in the Willacy County courthouse later that week, and they faced an armed mob in the county seat, Raymondville, nine days after the Blantons had disappeared. McMurrey subsequently offered a personal reward of $500 in addition to $4,000 offered by the state, county, and other individuals for any information that led to an arrest. Despite weeks of investigation, and the personal intervention of Carmichael as the DPS director and Captain Manuel T. Gonzaullas as the chief of the DPS crime laboratory, no bodies were ever found.[50]

After the disappointment of the Blanton case, Wright returned to chasing gamblers. District Attorney Joe P. Hatchitt of Brownsville during January 1937 decided to raid places that had "galloping dominos" (slot) machines. Just one week after taking office, he ordered Cameron County Sheriff J. A. "Art" Goolsby to shut down the operations, but he refused. So Hatchitt brought in three Rangers—Wright, Bridge, and Fenner—as well as Wright's son, Customs agent Charles H. "Pat" Wright, and Highway Patrol officers Abbott and Jerry Modesette to conduct raids on a Saturday night. As they got underway, local officials called Carmichael in Austin, and he contacted McMurrey and ordered him to stop his Rangers. It was not clear if the gambling machines were illegal, since Carmichael understood the state comptroller was collecting taxes on them. The law officers had targeted four places, with one going in each to announce that every man playing the machines would be detained for questioning while any woman could leave. Rangers Wright and Bridge went to the White Kitchen, while Fenner raided the Travelers' Confectionary, and Hatchitt began interviewing the two dozen or so customers that they detained in those two places. Meanwhile, a large crowd gathered in the business district; among those who pushed into the White Kitchen was Texas Representative Augustine Celaya. While Hatchitt was recording statements there, the phone rang: it was McMurrey, who wanted to talk with Bridge. He told him not to take any machines on which state taxes had been paid, and he repeated this to Hatchitt, who insisted on speaking to him. As the Rangers prepared to leave, Hatchitt asked Wright if he would make a statement, which he declined to do after explaining that the Rangers were no longer involved in the raids. After a few more tense moments, Hatchitt prudently decided to leave with the Rangers.[51]

Hatchitt continued to press his attack on those who had "galloping dominos" and other "slot machines" in their places of business, declaring he would have them prosecuted if they failed to remove them. He was furious at Carmichael, declaring it was the first time that Rangers had been "withdrawn during a raid on orders from the state capitol." He pointed out that he had issued the same warnings to slot machine operators in Corpus Christi, and almost all of them had removed the offending items. But when he warned Brownsville operators, he was ignored. According to Hatchitt, the "galloping dominos" machines, unlike pinball machines, were clearly gambling devices, and that is why he targeted them and not pinball machines. Reminded by a newspaper reporter that pictures had been taken of slot machines in a Corpus Christi business, indicating that they had also ignored Hatchitt's warning, he explained that the place was a "novelty shop" and the machines were not actually being used. He had sent Wright to investigate, and that is what the Ranger told him. As far as the issue of state taxes being paid, Hatchitt insisted that did not protect illegal machines from being confiscated.[52]

Wright continued to support Hatchitt in his campaign against gambling in his district, arresting dozens during the summer of 1937, but he also had more interesting cases. Harlingen Justice of the Peace F. D. Nance claimed that Wright was so anxious to lead a raid on slot machine operators in May that he showed up a day early for the event. In August, Wright even raided a gambling house in the "negro section" of Corpus Christi, arresting six men and confiscating a dice table. Then G. H. Brooks stole several hundred dollars from a floor safe in an Alice theater in the fall. Wright, with Deputy Sheriff Halsey Wright of Jim Wells County, learned that Brooks would be telephoning a friend in Alice. After arranging to have the call taken at the DPS local headquarters, the two contacted law officers in Lake Charles, Louisiana, whence the call came, and had Brooks arrested and extradited to Texas. Nine men escaped from the Nueces County jail in December 1937, and Wright was among the dozens of officers enlisted to find them. The escapees were led by a bank robber, Fremont L. McCollum, who remained at large after most of the others had been caught. The main body of lawmen pursuing McCollum was led by McMurrey and Nueces County Sheriff William Y. Shely, and it included Wright. Tensions were high because McCollum was considered to be armed and dangerous, especially because he did not want to serve the sixteen years to which he had been sentenced for robbing a bank in Orange Grove. When one morning a small coupe passed McMurrey and Shely's posse near Falfurrias in Brooks County, and the driver failed to respond to their demands that he stop, Wright fired a shot that lodged in the back of the driver's seat. The driver, clearly shaken but unharmed, stopped his car and identified himself as Serapio L. Sendejo, a local teacher. McCollum was finally arrested in May 1938 by federal agents at a relative's home in Detroit, Michigan. Sent to the federal penitentiary at Leavenworth, Kansas, he was transferred within a few months to Alcatraz Prison at San Francisco.[53]

Someone who participated in the "manhunt" for McCollum penned an interesting memoir that provides a great perspective on Wright as he approached his seventieth birthday while still working as a Ranger. The writer described Wright as "still going strong." He was a tireless talker, punctuating points with a jab in the shoulder of the nearest listener, leaving bruises as evidence of his enthusiasm. Trying to explain such energy, he added that Wright was a "living testimonial to the value of fresh air and solid food for keeping mentally and physically fit." He concluded gleefully, "He's the world's champion storyteller, and a manhunt and cup of coffee have the same effect on him as a dozen nickels in an automatic phonograph. Only Capt. Wright never runs down." That writer would not have been surprised to read a tale that appeared just two years earlier in a McAllen newspaper. Wright and H. Perry Clark regaled the reporter with a tale of how Wright had led other Texas Rangers on a raid on East Texas cattle rustlers, nabbing two. After filing the paperwork for the disposition of the prisoners and stolen property, Wright left the two men, both "killers," in the sole custody of Clark, then a young deputy sheriff for Colorado County. Clark was terrified until Wright gave him what he described as "explosive cartridges" for his gun. Reassured, Clark delivered his prisoners to the court on time, not realizing that the rounds in his gun were just ordinary bullets.[54]

Wright spent much of 1938 chasing gamblers and liquor violators in Corpus Christi. In January, he assisted Texas Liquor Control Board agents John McKay and H. E. Barnes in arresting two bartenders, Julius Green of the Marine Bar and Ruben Corbell of Joe's Place, for selling alcohol on a Sunday, and Alberto Valdez for having an untaxed bottle of whisky. During April, he became entangled in another gambling controversy. Allred, after many protests from merchants and their attorneys, ordered the removal of all marble and slot machines that had payoffs. Wright originally intended to remove all such devices whether they had payoffs or not, but Carmichael relayed the Governor's instructions and Wright modified the warning he sent to local businessmen. He wrote that he hoped merchants would remove the machines themselves "because it would take a six-mule wagon with high side-boards if I had to haul them myself." Having issued his warning on Tuesday morning, Wright raided two places on Wednesday night, the Trott Inn and Bohemian Village. He confiscated one slot machine at each, arresting Anthony Bellitt at the first establishment and a woman, F. Kneuffer, at the second. He and Ranger Walter E. "Ebb" Riggs then arrested twenty-one gamblers on May 3, all of whom were fined one dollar apiece plus court costs (nine dollars) by Justice of the Peace Jack Sutherland. Wright with Rangers Quincy J. Lowman and Hugh J. Phares raided a poker game at the

Nueces Hotel in June 1938, arresting the operator and eight other men. Four days later, the same trio of Rangers raided a "gambling room," arrested seven, and had them destroy "two dice tables, two poker tables and a three-gallon bucket of playing cards." Perhaps the extra punishment of destroying their own equipment was imposed because other gamblers escaped by smashing through a wall and running. Finally, Wright and Lowman with others confiscated three slot machines from the Star Novelty Company. The machines were destroyed, the money in them was given to the Red Cross, and J. E. Loyd was arrested.[55]

Wright was assigned to investigate one of his fellow Rangers in the summer of 1938. Higinio S. Gonzales, the 25-year-old son and namesake of a grocer in Robstown, where Wright had been a deputy city marshal, filed a $35,000 suit against four lawmen, alleging they had beaten and falsely imprisoned him. The accused men were Riggs, the Ranger who had worked with Wright in Corpus Christi, Robstown City Marshal William W. Ainsworth, Alice City Marshal George B. Clegg, and Sheriff Charlie W. Price of Jim Wells County. While investigating cattle thefts, the four apparently detained Gonzales, took him into the woods near Alice about midnight on Sunday, August 21, 1938 and beat him so badly that he needed four days of care for wounds to his back and face after his father brought him to Fred Roberts Hospital in Corpus Christi on Monday morning. Medical records revealed that Gonzales had a high fever and welts, and was spitting blood, when he was admitted. Riggs was a former Zavala County sheriff who had gone to Austin in February 1931 with his deputy, Allee, to join the Rangers together. Discharged by Ferguson in January 1933, he had re-enlisted in September 1937 after working as a U.S. deputy marshal. McMurrey joined Wright in the investigation, but no record of any further action has been found, unlike a similar case involving two of Wright's men in July 1931. Then a Mexican who had been sentenced to two years in jail for cattle rustling had accused Thad Tarver and J. Warren Smith of beating him into a confession. A grand jury had been empaneled to investigate the Rangers and exonerated them. In the 1938 case, Wright was not in charge, and there is no indication of a special grand jury. Riggs remained a Ranger for many years, while Ainsworth served as a deputy federal marshal for two decades before his death in 1962.[56]

Labor conflicts resurfaced at Aransas Pass, about twenty miles northeast of Corpus Christi, in September 1938 when perhaps 250 members of the local chapter of the United Cannery, Agricultural, Packing, and Allied Workers of America, an affiliate of the Congress of Industrial Organizations (CIO), picketed a shrimp cannery owned by the Rice brothers, Rob Roy and Stephen. When a "boatman" was killed on the waterfront during an attempt to force the strikers to return to work, Wright was sent with Lowman to provide security. A rancher from Gregory, James Dee Willis, intervened and convinced the strikers to return to work. According to Wright, "Willis raised every one of those shrimp peelers on his ranch," which was just ten miles from Aransas Pass. In the meantime, Wright and Lowman kept the waterfront, in Wright's words, "quiet as a church house." The dead man was James Thomas "Jim" Cole, who was shot by Christopher Clarisch, president of the "union of shrimp peelers and cannery workers," as the *Taft Tribune* called his CIO chapter. Clarisch was taken to the hospital in Corpus Christi, having been badly beaten and cut himself, and he was later sentenced to twenty years in the state penitentiary by a Texas district court despite the judge's request that the jury send the "foreign-born" labor leader to the electric chair. Clarisch appealed, but his sentence was upheld.[57]

Wright was assigned to what his obituary writers referred to as a "desk job" at Harlingen and Corpus Christi for his last year of service. Oddly, in July 1939 he was ordered to guard a "priceless" table on display in the lobby of the Corpus Christi National Bank. Said to have an actual value of $100,000, the table, which measured three feet by three feet, had a top that held more than 12,000 pieces of painted wood that represented all the varieties then available. It had been created for a meeting of the Texas Division of Painting and Decorating Contractors of America. Wright grumbled to a newspaper reporter: "Damndest thing ever happened in Texas … Sending the Rangers out to guard a little old table nobody would bother to run off with anyhow." He added that he "Never felt so silly in all my life," guarding that table while wearing his gun. Nueces County Sheriff John B. Harney Jr. was kind enough not only to sit with him but also to find him a spittoon. Since someone supplied Wright with cigars, the time passed pleasantly enough.[58]

Obviously, the stint in the bank lobby guarding a table was a publicity stunt, but it was not the first time the aging Wright was used for such a purpose. On Ranger Day at the State Fair in August 1936, when the centennial of Texas was being celebrated, Wright and many other Rangers were treated to a preview of the new movie, "The Texas Rangers," which was loosely based on historian Walter P. Webb's book about the organization, which had been published in 1935, the same year that they became part of the DPS. Directed by King Vidor, a native of Galveston, the film featured rising star Fred MacMurray in the leading role. Afterward, Wright declared that the Rangers in the movie were "slow" and "clumsy," and a colleague added they would not have a chance against real Rangers in a gunfight. Wright enjoyed even more being the honored guest and "color" commentator at the public premiere of another movie in 1938: "Under Western Stars," which featured Roy Rogers, in his first starring role thanks to a contract dispute between Gene Autrey and Republic Pictures, and Smiley Burnette. Although Wright grumbled that Carmichael "ordered" him to go, he rode to Dallas in a sleeper car, slept in a nice room at the Baker Hotel, and relished the attention of "a bunch of pretty girls." He laughed, "Why, they treated me like I was a lord or something." He was a prominent member of the party that greeted Rogers and Burnette at the Union Terminal, where Mayor George Sprague presented keys to the city to the movie stars and Wright. During the show at the Capitol Theater, he felt awkward with his pants stuffed in his boots and refused to wear a big hat, which he dismissed as "all soup and picture show stuff." He explained that he never wore one because it was not practical in heavy brush. He introduced the movie twice to a huge crowd and gave another speech at the banquet for the "movie stars" at the Baker. Wright later told a newspaper reporter that the Dallas officials who gave him a key to the city "took it back again after it was all over."[59]

Wright's last full year as a Texas Ranger, 1938, was in fact a dark period for him personally. His brother Milam H. Wright, his only male sibling to survive to adulthood and with whom he served in John H. Rogers' company, died of pneumonia on February 12 at Hotel Dieu, a Catholic hospital in El Paso. He worked for Customs after leaving the Rangers and at the time of his death was the sheriff of Hudspeth County. He was buried in Evergreen Alameda

Cemetery at El Paso in a service attended by William with his wife Mary Ann "Mollie" Brown Wright, daughter Zora Belle Wright Fore, son Charles H. "Pat" Wright and his wife Arlene Masters Wright, and niece Inez Warren Sheehy. The Captain endured an operation in May at Spohn Hospital in Corpus Christi, then a little more than one month later, on June 27, Pat, his oldest son, died of a heart attack in Eagle Pass at the age of forty-four. Pat had served for twenty years with Customs and was a sergeant at the time of his death. He was interred in the City Cemetery at Floresville after a Methodist service and graveside Masonic ceremony. Many of Wright's fellow Rangers and other law officers came to pay their respects to the fallen lawman's grieving parents and wife Arlene, whom he had married in January 1932. Among the pallbearers were two men who had been Rangers with Wright, Grover C. Webb and Roy L. Hearn. The younger Wright's passing was noted sadly in many South Texas publications, but no one mourned him more than his father. In a profile of the elder Wright in 1937, the writer had declared that his oldest son was "one of the biggest joys of his life." And then he was gone.[60]

A new governor took office in January 1939: William L. "Pappy" O'Daniel. He had some drastic solutions for the continuing depression, and in the summer, he cut the DPS budget by 20%. The reductions included the dismissal of eight Rangers, one of whom was Wright. Officially dismissed as a Texas Ranger effective on September 1, Wright left without a complaint.[61] After all, it was the fourth time he had resigned or been dismissed from the Rangers during a law enforcement career of almost forty-five years. He was seventy-one years old, the oldest Ranger still in active service, had served under eight governors as a Ranger, and he had learned long ago that angry letters usually had little effect. He must have realized that he added much to his family legacy, and he certainly knew that he had more than earned his pay during his last dozen years as a lawman, mostly as a Ranger. Having first gone into the field as a Ranger captain in 1918, when he was fifty years old, he had established a reputation that men half his age would envy. He was now more than twenty years past that mark, and his family circle had suddenly become much smaller. Perhaps it was time to rest and tell a few stories about the good cases to anyone who would still listen, while also coping with the memory of those investigations that had not produced a positive result.

Epilogue, 1939–1942

William L. Wright did not long survive his final departure from the Texas Rangers. Having submitted a letter in which he declared that he was "proud" that he had "served my beloved state as Captain of the Rangers," and that he had enjoyed the privilege of having "served with some of the best men on the border," Wright did not work in law enforcement again before his death in early March 1942.[1] But his departure did not go unnoticed by the people of Texas, and his funeral was attended by several notable dignitaries and hundreds of people who simply wanted to pay their respects. Twenty-five years after his death, the citizens of Floresville dedicated a monument in his honor with a service that again included prominent speakers as well as many appreciative citizens. Wright had worked hard to earn his pay and add to his family legacy, and he had raised sons who followed him in serving as peace officers, soldiers, and productive members of the communities in which they lived. But like most Rangers, his greatest accolades did not come during his lifetime.

While Wright never protested his dismissal from the Rangers at the end of August 1939, many of the people whom he had served did express great unhappiness, fulfilling the prediction of a newspaper reporter that "They are not apt to sit idly by and see such excellent and lengthy service go unrewarded without protest." Nueces County sheriff John B. Harney Jr., who sat with Wright guarding a table during his last summer as a Ranger, wired his angry protest to Governor William L. "Pappy" O'Daniel. In it, he explained: "I am addressing you as one sheriff in Texas who does not resent the presence and invaluable assistance of old-time Texas Rangers." The Governor needed to understand that Wright's "dismissal will be a severe blow to law enforcement in this section of Texas." According to Harney, Wright's record had "not one blemish," he was still very active, and he should continue as a Ranger. Contacted by a reporter from Floresville, Harney admitted that O'Daniel had not responded to him, adding "Cap is a kind of a guardian angel over us fellows. He's a good influence on every one of us, and it's going to be hard to see him go."[2]

Harney was much more restrained than others in expressing their outrage at Wright's removal. A writer for the *Corpus Christi Caller-Times* declared that he was "plain downright flabbergasted" at the decision to dismiss the former captain. Apparently growing angrier as he wrote, he added that "There's nothing in the rules of justice, efficiency, economy, or plain common sense to justify such an action." To him, Wright was a great exemplar of all that was good in the Rangers. Perhaps reflecting on the official silence surrounding Wright's departure, he continued: "That younger officers in positions of authority should hasten his departure is unthinkably stupid and cruel." If nothing else, Wright still had much to offer as a mentor and teacher. The writer mixed his denunciations with humor: "He can't be bought, he has never been beaten, and he's too tough to eat." Believing that Wright would find another job in law enforcement, he concluded with a simple question, "Why not let him keep his badge?" In his memoir published twenty years later, former Texas Adjutant General William W. Sterling, Wright's friend and former supervisor, bitterly recalled, "While counterfeit Rangers who were not worthy of blacking his boots were basking in the favors of those in charge, Captain William Lee Wright terminated his service patrolling the docks in Corpus Christi." Directing his subsequent comment to those further up the chain of command, Sterling added, "A politically motivated administration forced this outstanding gentleman to suffer this ignominy, and to end his long service in this shameful manner."[3]

Longtime Nueces County Commissioner Ferdinand V. "F.V." Arnim, who was just five years younger than Wright, joined Sheriff Harney in expressing his disapproval to Governor O'Daniel, but it was the protests of church leaders that actually provoked an executive response. Rose Bell Tobey Mangham, corresponding secretary of the Corpus Christi chapter of the Women's Christian Temperance Union, penned a letter of protest to O'Daniel in anticipation of Wright's dismissal on the same day that the Reverend Forrest R. Waldrop of the Central Church of Christ and two of his elders telegraphed him on the same subject. The Governor's secretary, Reuben Williams, responded to Mangham that O'Daniel was "not in a position to be of any assistance to Mr. Wright in retaining his job." A similar response went to Waldrop. At least one scholar, Professor Fred Gantt Jr. of the University of North Texas, later cited O'Daniel's response to Waldrop as an example of exemplary leadership because he left personnel decisions to the agency responsible for them, but that did not mollify those who resented Wright's sudden departure, even if it was done according to established procedures.[4]

Wright's decision to settle in Floresville after his forced retirement perhaps came as a surprise to no one. More than a decade earlier, when he was attending a federal district court session at El Paso in October 1928, he had declared that if he was about to retire, and had plenty of money, he would buy a "small citrus orchard" in the lower Rio Grande Valley because "That is the finest country in the world." But he did not have a lot of money—his monthly salary when he left the Rangers was $200, respectable but not enough to make him wealthy. He did run for sheriff of Wilson County in the spring of 1940, but poor health compelled him to withdraw from the race. For example, he was bedridden for ten days in April 1940. He became a Special Ranger on January 30, 1941, when Homer Garrison Jr., the director of the Department of Public Safety, signed a commission for him, but this was honorary and not because he had a job that required such credentials. Not only were his funds thus limited, but his family circle in Texas was also shrinking. All his brothers and sisters were dead, and his wife Mary

Ann "Mollie" Brown Wright had lost her first sibling, Charles B. Brown, in October 1939. The Wrights' oldest son, Charles H. "Pat" Wright, had died in June 1938, and none of their remaining five adult children lived in the Rio Grande Valley. So Wright retired to Floresville, where he and Mollie, who suffered a mild heart attack in July 1939, had many friends. It was also not far from San Antonio, where their son Maurice H. "Jack" Wright lived with his wife, the former Helen M. W. Gorden, and Corpus Christi, where their daughter, Zora Belle, had settled with her husband, Blake D. Fore, who worked in the oil and gas division of the Texas Railroad Commission, and their three sons.[5]

Wright battled failing health for a year, then appeared to contract influenza and suddenly had a heart attack. He died during the early morning hours of March 7, 1942, not long after midnight. He was attended by Dr. Jerry W. Oxford, a Louisiana native who relocated his medical practice from San Antonio to Floresville in 1911, when Wright lived there as the sheriff of Wilson County. Oxford thus knew the old Ranger well, and the fact that he cared for Wright during the last weeks of his life indicates the two men were close. So, while Oxford recorded that the official cause of death was coronary occlusion, he also wrote: "Present war, his baby is in Java, [therefore] worry" in the blank space provided for "Contributory Causes." Oxford was referring to Houston Tom "Simp Tom" Wright, the old Ranger's youngest son, who insisted upon joining the same unit in which his two brothers had served in World War I, the 131st Field Artillery Regiment of the 36th Division, and became a prisoner at Java when its defenders surrendered to a Japanese army on March 8, 1942, the day after his father died. "Slug," as his comrades called him, and other survivors of what became known as the "Lost Battalion" endured forty-two months of captivity, working for most of the time on the Burma Railroad in Thailand. According to his brother Emanuel A. "Dogie" Wright, when Tom enlisted, his father took him out in the back yard and told him that he had never had one of his sons dishonor him, and he wanted him to remember that. A picture taken on the hospital ship after his liberation in August 1945 shows the emaciated Tom flashing a big smile, holding a small U.S. flag he made in the prisoner-of war-camp and kept hidden. Wright received several notes from his son before he died, all of which were reassuring, but later reports concerning conditions in Japanese prison camps revealed how much Tom endured to sustain the family legacy.[6]

Wright was buried in the city cemetery at Floresville on March 8, the day after he died. The body was prepared by Murray Funeral Home, who had provided the same services for Wright's oldest son in 1938. The funeral service itself was held in the auditorium of Floresville High School, which could accommodate the huge crowd that assembled. Wright's mother, Ann Elizabeth Tumlinson Wright, and his son were buried with Methodist rites, but the Captain's service was conducted by Dr. Pierre B. Hill, a colorful Presbyterian chaplain for the Rangers who established at least five churches and wrote poetry, including the "Rangers' Prayer," that later led to his official appointment as a Poet Laureate of Texas.

Acting Lieutenant Governor Henry L. Winfield, who had practiced law in Floresville and knew Wright when he was a Ranger in Fort Stockton, attended the funeral. The chairman of the Texas Highway Commission, Robert Lee Bobbitt, a former speaker of the Texas House of Representatives and Texas attorney general, delivered the eulogy for Wright, whom he had warmly supported when they were both in Laredo in the 1920s. In the audience were Garrison and William O. Murray, a Floresville native who served as chief justice of the state court of appeals at San Antonio. The pallbearers included three Rangers who had served under Wright—W. Bryan Butler, J. Warren Smith, and Thad Tarver—as well as Smith's brother Frank, the former Customs Service agent who worked with Wright when he commanded Company D in the 1920s; Joseph T. Sheehy of Floresville, who was married to Inez, the daughter of Wright's sister Zora Lee and her husband Charles P. Warren, both long deceased; and Sam L. Fore Jr., longtime publisher of the *Floresville Chronicle Journal* and brother of Wright's son-in-law, Blake D. Fore. Wright's body was interred by his fellow Masons from Lodge Number 515 in Floresville, which he had joined almost thirty years earlier when he was the sheriff of Wilson County.[7]

At the time of his death, Wright was working with journalist Robert B. "Bob" McCracken of the *Corpus Christi Caller-Times* to write a memoir, which many people, including Sterling, urged him to do. Born in Marfa and educated in Floresville and Corpus Christi, with strong family ties to Wilson County, McCracken died in 1958, at the age of forty-seven, without completing a book on Wright. But he wrote one of the first, and best, obituaries of Wright, which declared that the former Ranger's death ended a "career studded with adventures stranger than fiction." In South Texas, the *McAllen Monitor* and *Harlingen Valley Morning Star* published identical memorials under the bold headline "Colorful Pioneer Valley Officer Dies Old Man's Death in His Bed." The first line read: "Scores of border badmen tried to get Capt. Will L. Wright in their gunsights, but he died a kind old man's death in his bed at his Floresville home late Saturday." Wright might have blushed to read that "He survived more border gun-fights than any other peace officer still alive, veteran officers assert." Most of the newspaper obituaries, including the more modest one that appeared in the *Floresville Record Chronicle*, featured one of Wright's most iconic and best photographs. Taken on the Rio Grande near Laredo in the 1920s, it showed him seated on Jack, the horse given to him by the grateful citizens of Wilson County, wearing on his hip the finely engraved Colt revolver given to him years earlier by admirers in Sutherland Springs.[8]

Garrison and Murray played more prominent roles in the dedication of a small monument to Wright in June 1967, twenty-five years after his death. Located on the grounds of the Wilson County courthouse in Floresville, it was near the old jail in which Wright's family lived when he was a sheriff. Wilson County Judge Dietrich R. "Dee" Voges served as the emcee for the ceremony, which featured speeches by Garrison, Murray, State Senator Wayne Connally (in place of his brother, Governor John B. Connally), and Dogie, the late Ranger's son. Murray regaled the large audience of about 350 people with his recollection of watching from a second-story window of the courthouse when Wright was stabbed by Refugio Jaureque on the gallows at Floresville in June 1909. Garrison ended his address by declaring that "for as long as there is a state of Texas, there will be Texas Rangers," a response to public demands for disbanding the agency after labor unrest in Starr County during May 1967. Wright's wife Mollie had died at a Corpus Christi rest home in April 1958 after living for years with their daughter Zora, and their son Jack had passed away in San Antonio in February 1960, but their youngest son Tom came from San Diego, California, for the event, and Zora unveiled the monument—a bronze plaque attached to a red granite boulder set atop a two-step base of Wilson County fieldstone. Dogie's daughter, Zora Belle Wright Whitfield, the wife of James L. Whitfield of Raymondville, then placed a "wreath of carnations" in front of the plaque, which Sheriff Asa G. Fuller Jr. read aloud. In part, the inscription praised Wright as "A stern leader, but gentlemanly and kind." Wright's grandson, the Rev. Sam L. Fore III, delivered the benediction, which was followed by a parade and traditional Texas barbecue.[9]

There have been other posthumous efforts to honor Wright. In addition to the monument at the Floresville courthouse, there is a Texas Historical Commission marker at his grave in the nearby city cemetery that describes him as "A fearless, colorful, cultured man whose honesty and diplomacy often prevented bloodshed." Robert W. Stephens dedicated his 1972 book, *Texas Ranger Sketches*, to Wright. And in 1983, during the centennial of the courthouse, Wright's granddaughter, Maurine Wright Maher, the daughter of Maurice H. "Jack" Wright and a popular San Antonio artist, donated a portrait of him that she had painted so that it could "be hung in a prominent place."[10]

Many people, including some historians, believe Wright was the model for *Frontier Battalion Ranger*, a bronze statue of a Ranger on horseback leading a pack mule sculpted by Richard O. Cook. This memorial, dedicated on May 1, 1983, in front of the Old Pioneer Museum in San Antonio, was funded by the Former Texas Rangers Association, who subsequently moved it to the Buckhorn Museum in 2011 and finally to the Texas Rangers Heritage Center at Fredericksburg in 2015. A smaller version is in the Austin headquarters of the Texas Department of Public Safety. Unfortunately for those who think that the statue honors Wright, Cook published an article in which he explained that the Association told him not to have it resemble any specific Ranger, so it is a composite of several, none of whom are Wright. There was an indirect connection to the former captain, however; Dogie and Alfred Y. Allee II, Wright's former colleague in Company A during the 1930s, were appointed by the Association as a two-man committee to review Cook's statue. Without their approval, which Cook did get, there would have been no commission. While there is, therefore, no statue of Wright in Texas, the Texas Ranger Hall of Fame and Museum in Waco has a large display of items related to him that have been donated by his family members. Since Wright was in the first group of twenty Rangers inducted into the Hall of Fame, that makes perfect sense.[11]

Wright was always mindful of his family's heritage in law enforcement, especially as Rangers. While he was proud of all his sons who survived to adulthood, he was very pleased that three of them worked as law officers. Charles, or "Pat," became a Ranger in 1916, then went to work for the Customs Service after he served overseas in the Army during World War I. He advanced to the rank of sergeant before his death in 1938. Emanuel, or "Dogie," served in a variety of law enforcement roles, including Ranger, Border Patrol, and sheriff of Hudspeth County, east of El Paso. When William L. Wright was mustering Company K during late 1917, Harrison L. "Harry" Moore, a former Ranger serving as the first sheriff of Hudspeth County, asked that the new captain be assigned to his county. Wright never served there, but his brother Milam H. Wright and son Dogie both later became Hudspeth County sheriffs, and the latter stayed in the office for sixteen years, one year longer than his father served in Wilson County. William B. "Bill" Wright was a deputy sheriff, deputy U.S. marshal, and a Ranger with his father before going to work for Standard Oil in California, with whom he remained for forty-two years. He published a small book about his family and experiences. Tom Wright worked for Standard Oil both before and after World War II; like Bill, he also settled in California, where he served on the city council and as mayor of Oceanside. The successful owner of a service station, he also became the commander of the local American Legion post. And while Maurice, or "Jack," like Tom never became a law officer, both joined the 131st Field Artillery Regiment of the 36th Division, serving overseas like their brother Pat. Jack settled in San Antonio, where he worked as an automobile repairman, laundry mechanic, and well driller. Like their father, Wright's sons always earned their pay. And Dogie, Bill, and Tom, along with other relatives and descendants, were very active in the Former Texas Rangers Association during their lifetimes.[12]

Wright never wrote an autobiography, and his accomplishments were quickly overshadowed by colleagues such as Francis A. "Frank" Hamer, who were flashier in manner and perhaps more fortunate in being assigned to more high-profile cases. But his persistence in pursuing a career with the Rangers, his old-fashioned morality, and his adaptability during an era when law enforcement, especially in the borderlands of Texas, was rapidly changing, made him an effective peace officer who stayed above the scandals that plagued some of his comrades. With Tumlinsons in his lineage, he was perhaps born to be a Ranger, but he had some fine mentors, such as John H. Rogers, he proved to be a quick study, and he capitalized on opportunities as they arose. Wright became a great Ranger captain, one of the best in the first half of the twentieth century, and for that he well deserved to be among the first inducted into the Texas Ranger Hall of Fame at Waco. To date, he shares that honor with only thirty other men, among the hundreds who have served in the Frontier Battalion, Ranger Force, and Texas Ranger Division of the Department of Public Safety. He in turn stands out from this exceptional group in that he is the only one who enlisted in all three organizations, serving as a Ranger four times in five decades, often in an effort to reform and improve the agency. Wright wanted to be a Ranger captain, he worked hard, and when circumstances provided him with the right opportunity, he became his family's greatest legacy to the Texas Rangers.

Abbreviations

Archives

AGC	Texas Adjutant General, Departmental Correspondence, 1846–1943, Texas State Library and Archives, Austin
AGSR	Texas Adjutant General, Service Records, Texas State Library and Archives, Austin
DBCAH	Dolph Briscoe Center for American History, University of Texas at Austin
FBC	Texas Adjutant General, Frontier Battalion Correspondence, Texas State Library and Archives, Austin
FBR	Texas Adjutant General, Frontier Battalion Records, Texas State Library and Archives, Austin
RFC	Texas Adjutant General, Ranger Force Correspondence, Texas State Library and Archives, Austin
RFR	Texas Adjutant General, Ranger Force Records, Texas State Library and Archives, Austin
TGC	Texas Governor, Correspondence, Texas State Library and Archives, Austin
TRHC	Texas Rangers Heritage Center, Fredericksburg

TRHFM	Vertical Files, Texas Ranger Research Center, Texas Ranger Hall of Fame & Museum, Waco
TSLA	Texas State Library and Archives, Austin

Newspapers

DMN	*Dallas Morning News*
FCJ	*Floresville Chronicle Journal*
SAE	*San Antonio Express*

Websites

FAG	Find a Grave
HOT	*Handbook of Texas*

Endnotes

Notes for Introduction and Acknowledgments

1. William Shakespeare, *Julius Caesar*, Act 3, Scene 2 [quote]; *Dallas Morning* News, June 3, 2020; Doug J. Swanson, *Cult of Glory: The Bold and Brutal History of the Texas Rangers* (New York: Viking Press, 2020); Doug J. Swanson, "The Horrible Truth of Love Field's Texas Ranger Statue," *D Magazine*, accessed June 9, 2020, https://www.dmagazine.com/publications/d-magazine/2020/june/texas-rangers-love-field-statue-jay-banks-frank-hamer/; Kendall Curlee, "Tauch, Waldine Amanda," *HOT*.
2. Robert M. Utley, *Lone Star Justice: The First Century of the Texas Rangers* (New York: Oxford University Press, 2002), 253; Robert M. Utley, *Lone Star Lawmen: The Second Century of the Texas Rangers* (New York: Oxford University Press, 2007), 202, 336; Ben H. Procter, *Just One Riot: Episodes of Texas Rangers in the 20th Century* (Austin, TX: Eakin Press, 1991), 8; Bruce A. Glasrud and Harold J. Weiss Jr., "In Pursuit of the Texas Rangers: The Twentieth Century," *Tracking the Texas Rangers: Twentieth Century*, ed. Bruce A. Glasrud and Harold J. Weiss Jr. (Denton: University of North Texas Press, 2013), 11; Harold J. Weiss Jr., "The Texas Rangers Revisited: Old Themes and New Viewpoints," *Southwestern Historical Quarterly* 97 (April 1994): 621 [quote], 632; Ben H. Procter, "Texas Rangers," *HOT*. See also "Texas Rangers," Bullock Museum, Austin, TX, accessed June 8, 2020, https://www.thestoryoftexas.com/discover/campfire-stories/texas-ranger.
3. For biographies of the Great Captains, see, in order of publication, Paul N. Spellman, *Capt. John H. Rogers, Texas Ranger* (Denton: University of North Texas Press, 2003); Spellman, *Capt. J. A. Brooks, Texas Ranger* (Denton: University of North Texas Press, 2007); Harold J. Weiss Jr., *Yours to Command: The Life and Legend of Texas Ranger Captain Bill McDonald* (Denton: University of North Texas Press, 2009); and Chuck Parsons, *Captain John R. Hughes, Lone Star Ranger* (Denton: University of North Texas Press, 2011). The published biographies of two of the Big Four are John N. Boessenecker, *Texas Ranger: The Epic Life of Frank Hamer, The Man Who Killed Bonnie and Clyde* (New York: Thomas Dunne Books, 2016), and Brownson Malsch, *"Lone Wolf" Gonzaullas, Texas Ranger* (Norman: University of Oklahoma Press, 1998). Excellent essays on all six of these Ranger

captains, as well as William L. Wright and many others, can be found in Darren L. Ivey, *The Ranger Ideal, Volume 2: Texas Rangers in the Hall of Fame, 1874–1930* (Denton: University of North Texas Press, 2018), and Ivey, *The Ranger Ideal, Volume 3: Texas Rangers in the Hall of Fame, 1898–1987* (Denton: University of North Texas Press, 2021).

4. Emanuel A. Wright to Mrs. Joe Shriber, Oct. 17, 1966, E. A. "Dogie" Wright Papers, DBCAH; William L. Wright to Roy W. Aldrich, June 14, 1925, Roy W. Aldrich Papers, DBCAH; *FCJ*, Apr. 10, 1925; J. Will Falvella, "Captain Wright, A Gallant Texas Ranger," *Frontier Times* (September 1924): 6–7 [first quote]; *FCJ*, May 6, 1927 [second quote]; Walter P. Webb, "Rangers Reorganized," *The State Trooper* 8 (July 1927) 13 [third quote, which translates as "The Devil Captain rides again."]. The popular website *Find A Grave* lists Wright as William Leonidas "Rattlesnake Willie" Wright, but the only contemporary use of a nickname like that is "Rattlesnake Will Wright" in a biographical paper written by the daughter of one of his Rangers. See Normadale Smith, "Captain Will Wright" (Manuscript, n.d.), James Warren Smith Sr. Papers, Texas Collection, Baylor University, Waco, TX. The impact of early newspaper accounts of Wright's work as a Ranger, which were often inaccurate, is reflected in a letter written by William M. Wallis, the father of Hayes M. Wallis of Wright's Company D, to a friend in March 1923. The elder Wallis forwarded a photograph of a group of Rangers at the Texas Capitol and commented on Wright, "I believe has killed more men than any one man in the Ranger service." See William M. Wallis to John Wilson, March 15, [1923], TRHFM: William Sanders Peterson, Francis A. "Frank" Hamer.
5. Walter P. Webb, *The Texas Rangers: A Century of Frontier Defense* (Boston, MA: Houghton Mifflin, 1935); Américo Paredes, *With His Pistol in His Hand: A Border Ballad and Its Hero* (Austin: University of Texas Press, 1958), 31 [quote].
6. Procter, *Just One Riot*, 8 [first and second quotes]; Dan E. Kilgore, *A Ranger Legacy: 150 Years of Service to Texas* (Austin, TX: Madrona Press, 1973), 65, 67 [third and fourth quotes]; Charles H. Harris III and Louis R. Sadler, *The Texas Rangers in the Mexican Revolution: The Bloodiest Decade, 1910–1920* (Norman: University of Oklahoma Press, 2004), 368 [fifth and sixth quotes], 341; Charles H. Harris III and Louis R. Sadler, *The Texas Rangers in Transition: From Gunfighters to Criminal Investigators* (Norman: University of Oklahoma Press, 2019), 12 [seventh quote]; Utley, *Lone Star Lawmen*, 97 [eighth and ninth quotes].

7. James A. Sandos, *Rebellion in the Borderlands: Anarchism and the Plan de San Diego, 1904–1923* (Norman: University of Oklahoma Press, 1992), 160–162; Benjamin H. Johnson, *Revolution in Texas; How a Forgotten Revolution and Its Bloody Suppression Turned Mexicans into Americans* (New Haven, CT: Yale University Press, 2003), 147, 155; Miguel A. Levario, *Militarizing the Border: When Mexicans Became the Enemy* (College Station: Texas A&M University Press, 2012), 17, 29–34, 114–117; Julian Samora, Joe Bernal, and Albert Peña, *Gunpowder Justice: A Reassessment of the Texas Rangers* (Notre Dame, IN: University of Notre Dame Press, 1979), 67–76; Nicholas Villanueva, *The Lynching of Mexicans in the Texas Borderlands* (Albuquerque: University of New Mexico Press, 2017), 171; George T. Diaz, *Border Contraband: A History of Smuggling Across the Rio Grande* (Austin: University of Texas Press, 2015), 100–103; Monica Muñoz Martínez, *The Injustice Never Leaves You: Anti-Mexican Violence in Texas* (Cambridge: Harvard University Press, 2018), 189, 198–202; Kelly Lytle Hernandez, *Migra! A History of the U.S. Border Patrol* (Berkeley: University of California Press, 2010), 30–31; Roger M. Olien and Diana D. Olien, *Oil Booms: Social Change in Five Texas Towns* (Lincoln: University of Nebraska Press, 1982), 133–136.
8. Emanuel A. Wright to Mrs. Joe Shriber, Oct. 17, 1966, Wright Papers; Emanuel A. Wright, "Memoir" (Typescript, n.d.), Wright Papers, 73, 142; Aldrich to Ben T. Tumlinson Jr., July 7, 1921, AGC [first quote]; Interview with Zora Wright Fore, Dec. 7, 1973, South Texas Oral History & Folklore Collection, South Texas Archives, James C. Jernigan Library, Texas A&M University at Kingsville; Texas Legislature, "Proceedings of the Joint Committee of the Senate and the House in the Investigation of the Texas State Ranger Force," 8 vols. (Typescript, n.d. [1919], DBCAH), 6: 1,139; *Corsicana Democrat and Truth*, Apr. 9, 1925; *San Patricio County News*, Apr. 30, 1925; *Harlingen Valley Morning Star*, Mar. 7, 1937 [second quote, seventh and eighth quotes]; *Corpus Christi Caller-Times*, Sept. 22, 1937, Mar. 8, 1942 [ninth and tenth quotes] Feb. 26, 27, 1953; *SAE*, Mar. 8, 1942; William W. Sterling, *Trails and Trials of a Texas Ranger* (Privately printed, 1959), 397 [third and fourth quotes], 398 [fifth and sixth quotes], 412–413; Harris and Sadler, *Rangers in Transition*, 49, 52; Kilgore, *Ranger Legacy*, 66; FAG: Oscar Newt Wright.
9. Emanuel A. Wright to Mrs. Joe Shriber, Oct. 17, 1966, Wright Papers; Wright, "Memoir," 62; *Junction Eagle*, July 21, 1922 [first quote];

Harlingen Valley Morning Star, Mar. 7, 1937 [second quote], Mar. 8, 1942; *McAllen Monitor*, Mar. 8, 1942 [third quote]; Sterling, *Trails and Trials*, 88–91.

10. Emanuel A. Wright to Mrs. Joe Shriber, Oct. 17, 1966, Wright Papers; William L. Wright to J. Warren Smith, July 30, 1936, James Warren Smith Sr. Papers, Texas Collection, Waco, TX; *Harlingen Valley Morning Star*, Mar. 7, 1937; *SAE*, Mar. 8, 1942, *Corpus Christi Caller-Times*, Mar. 8, 1942 [quote].
11. Wright Family Bible Record, Wright Papers; *SAE*, Sept. 24, 1920; *Austin American*, Jan. 8, 1924; Sterling, *Trails and Trials*, 399 ["Bud"]; Maude T. Gilliland, *Horsebackers of the Brush Country: A Story of the Texas Rangers and Mexican Liquor Smugglers* (Brownsville, TX: Springman-King Company, 1968), 39; James R. Ward, "The Texas Rangers, 1919–1935: A Study in Law Enforcement" (Ph.D. Diss., Texas Christian University, 1972), 35; Jim Coffey, "Will Wright: Rangers and Prohibition," accessed Feb. 16, 2020, https://www. texasranger.org/ wp-content/ uploads/2017/07/ BIO-Will-Wright.pdf.
12. AGSR: Carl G. Busch; Carl G. Busch, "The Incredible Mr. Busch," *Cinquapin* 2, No. 5 (1980), 50.
13. Texas Legislature, "Proceedings," 6: 1,139 [first quote]; Sterling, *Trails and Trials*, 397 [second quote], 399 [third quote]; Interview with Zora Wright Fore, Dec. 7, 1973; William L. Wright to Aldrich, March 24, 1937 [fourth quote], Aldrich Papers, DBCAH; Aldrich to William L. Wright, Apr. 5, 1937 [misfiled as 1927], Roy W. Aldrich Papers, Archives of the Big Bend, Bryan Wildenthal Memorial Library, Sul Ross State University, Alpine, TX; Kilgore, *Ranger Legacy*, 65 [fifth quote].

Notes for Chapter 1

1. William L. Wright to Roy W. Aldrich, June 14, 1925, Roy W. Aldrich Papers, DBCAH; *SAE*, Oct. 28, 1915; *FCJ*, Oct. 29, 1915; Dan E. Kilgore, *A Ranger Legacy: 150 Years of Service to Texas* (Austin, TX: Madrona Press, 1973), 47, 61, 62, 66–67, 74–77; Thomas W. Knowles, *They Rode for the Lone Star: The Saga of the Texas Rangers* (Dallas, TX: Taylor Publishing Company, 1999), 25; Sammy Tise, *Texas County Sheriffs* (Albuquerque: Oakwood Press, 1989), 270, 288, 295, 395, 547. William L. Wright's antebellum relatives in the Texas Rangers included his grandfather and two great uncles, four cousins (Peter F. Tumlinson's

sons Absalom T., Joseph, and William O. Tumlinson, and Littleton F. Tumlinson, whose father was James S. Tumlinson, the brother of John J. Tumlinson Sr.), and Creed Taylor, whose brother married Wright's great aunt and whose sister was the first wife of Wright's grandfather. Wright's relatives in the Frontier Battalion included his brother, brothers-in-law Gratz D. Brown and Charles P. Warren, and cousins Thomas C. "Creed" Taylor and Peter C. Tumlinson. His relatives in the Ranger Force included his three sons, brother, brother-in-law Charles B. Brown, and cousins Howard T. Cragg, Joseph A. Taylor, William A. "Alonzo" Taylor, William W. Taylor, Benjamin T. Tumlinson Jr., Eugene H. Tumlinson, Lott Tumlinson, Peter B. Winn, Monroe M. Wells, Wright C. Wells, Earl Ray Wright, and Thomas R. Wright. Five more cousins served as Special Rangers: Elmer J. Taylor, Thomas C. "Creed" Taylor, Eugene C. Wright, James B. Wright, and Oscar N. Wright. For a valiant effort at creating a family tree for William L. Wright, see Charles H. Harris III, Francis E. Harris, and Louis R. Sadler, *Texas Ranger Biographies: Those Who Served 1910–1921* (Albuquerque: University of New Mexico Press, 2009), 415–418, 425–427. It is worth noting that Dan E. Kilgore dedicated his book on the Rangers "To Dogie Wright Last of the Tumlinson Rangers A Credit to his Name and to his Calling." In this study, "Texas Ranger" will refer to antebellum mounted volunteers organized separately from the militia, as well as men in the Frontier Battalion and Ranger Force [both Regular and Special Rangers].

2. U. S. Bureau of the Census, Eighth Census, 1860, Free Population, Karnes County, TX, and Ninth Census, 1870, Population, DeWitt County, TX (Record Group 29, National Archives, Washington, DC); Genealogy Notes, Wright Family Bible Record, Marriage Certificate (Nov. 4, 1858), IOOF Certificate for L.B. Wright (June 19, 1869), Appointment of L.B. Wright as Deputy Inspector of Hides and Animals for Yorktown (Oct. 30, 1876), Matilda Wright to L.B. Wright, May 28, 1882, Emanuel A. Wright to Mrs. Joe Shriber, Oct. 17, 1966, Emanuel A. Wright to Mrs. Jack W. Rowland, June 21, 1969, Emanuel A. Wright to Secretary of Cameron Lodge, Feb. 28, 1985, E. A. "Dogie" Wright Papers; Texas Adjutant General, Muster Roll Index Cards, 1838–1900, TSLA; Texas Comptroller, County Tax Rolls, TSLA; Texas Death Certificates, 1890–1976: William Lee Wright, accessed Jan. 20, 2020, https://www.fold3.com/image/ 90346596; Tise, *Texas County Sheriffs*, 295; Chuck Parsons, *The Sutton-Taylor Feud: The Deadliest Blood*

Feud in Texas (Denton: University of North Texas Press, 2009), 109, 126, 132, 138, 140; Darren L. Ivey, *The Ranger Ideal, Volume 3: Texas Rangers in the Hall of Fame, 1898–1987* (Denton: University of North Texas Press, 2021), 1–2; Nellie Murphree, *A History of DeWitt County*, ed. Robert W. Shook (Privately printed, 1962), 18; FAG: Robert W. Wright, Matilda Watters Wright, L.B. Wright, William Leonidas "Rattlesnake Willie" Wright; "Our Family History: The Genealogy of Robert and Christina Barritt," accessed Jan. 20, 2020, http://tree.barrittfamily.net/getperson.php?personID=I473&tree=dyal_speckels. William L. Wright's siblings (with birth and death dates if known) were Robert (1859–1870), Cornelia Elizabeth "Neely" (1861–1919), Zora Lee (1866–1897), Mary H. (b. 1872), Joseph T. (b. 1875), and Milam Harper (1878–1938). See FAG: Cornelia Elizabeth Wright Cline, Zora Lee Wright Warren, Milam Harper Wright. Ivey includes an eighth sibling, Dollie Myrtle Wright, and someone entered dates for her (1880–1922) on the Ancestry website, but no further corroboration has been found. The Find A Grave website lists "Little Berry Wright" as buried in Sutherland Springs, but in fact he is in Upper Yorktown cemetery in DeWitt County; see FAG: L. B. Wright. A newspaper article gives Mary H. Wright's nickname as "Belle" and says she married a man with the last name of Johnson. See *FCJ*, Dec. 15, 1966.

3. *Corsicana Democrat and Truth*, Apr. 9, 1925; *FCJ*, Apr. 10, 1925; *San Patricio County News*, Apr. 30, 1925; "Our Family History."
4. Emanuel A. Wright to Shriber, Oct. 17, 1966, Wright Papers; Josiah W. Wilbarger, *Indian Depredations in Texas* (Austin, TX: Hutchings Printing House, 1889), 204; Knowles, *They Rode for the Lone Star*, 24; Kilgore, *Ranger Legacy*, 12–22, 26, 28–29, 33 [quote], 35, 36; Mike Cox, *The Texas Rangers: Wearing the Cinco Peso, 1821–1900* (New York: Forge Books, 2008), 25–31; Stephen L. Moore, *Savage Frontier: Rangers Rifles, and Indian Wars in Texas*, 4 vols. (Denton: University of North Texas Press, 2007–2010), 1: 8–10; Darren L. Ivey, *The Texas Rangers: A Registry and History* (West Jefferson, NC: McFarland & Company, 2010), 7, 250–252; FAG: James S. Tumlinson, Joseph A. Newman; Samuel H. Tumlinson, "Tumlinson, John Jackson, Sr.," *HOT*, Bobbie Rogers Thompson, "Tumlinson, James, Jr.," *HOT*; "The Tumlinson Family of the DeWitt Colony," accessed Jan. 20, 2020, http://www.sonsof dewittcolony.org/tumlinson fam.htm. John J. Tumlinson settled in what is now Colorado County, near modern Columbus; he was killed in what is now Guadalupe County, near modern Seguin.

5. Wilbarger, *Indian Depredations*, 204–205, 604–605; Kilgore, *Ranger Legacy*, 26, 34–39; Knowles, *They Rode for the Lone Star*, 24; Moore, *Savage Frontier*, 1: 10–12; Frederick Wilkins, *The Legend Begins: The Texas Rangers, 1823–1845* (Austin, TX: State House Press, 1996), 6; FAG: Joseph L. "Joe" Tumlinson; Samuel H. Tumlinson, "Tumlinson, John Jackson, Jr.," *HOT*, Samuel H. Tumlinson, "Tumlinson, Joseph," *HOT*; "Tumlinson Family of the DeWitt Colony."
6. Texas Comptroller, Republic of Texas Claims: John J. Tumlinson (#618), Joseph Tumlinson (#N/A), Littleton Tumlinson (#278), James Tumlinson (#5264), John Tumlinson (##5263), TSLA; Noah Smithwick, *The Evolution of a State* (Austin, TX: Gammel Book Company, 1900), 118–124; Wilbarger, *Indian Depredations*, 60–61, 220–222; John H. Brown, *Indian Wars and Pioneers of Texas* (Austin, TX: L. E. Daniell, 1896), 89–90; Kilgore, *Ranger Legacy*, 34 [quote], 38, 41–43; Knowles, *They Rode for the Lone Star*, 25, 30, 35–38, 40, 45; Wilkins, *Legend Begins*, 12–20; Cox, *Cinco Peso*, 48, 50–51, 55; Ivey, *Registry and History*, 12, 15, 16, 29, 31; Walter P. Webb, *The Texas Rangers: A Century of Frontier Defense* (Boston: Houghton Mifflin, 1935), 23–24, 34–39; Robert M. Utley, *Lone Star Justice: The First Century of the Texas Rangers* (New York: Oxford University Press, 2002), 20–21; Stephen L. Moore, *Eighteen Minutes: The Battle of San Jacinto and the Texas Independence Campaign* (Dallas, TX: Taylor Publishing Company, 2003), 80–83, 96, 179, 244–245, 443; Moore, *Savage Frontier*, 1: 10–12, 23–29, 54–55, 58, 74–81, 91–93, 100, 103–106, 117, 128, 291–292; Herbert C. Banks, *Daughters of the Republic of Texas Patriot Ancestry Album* (Paducah, KY: Turner Publishing Company, 1995), 277; FAG: James S. Tumlinson, Capt. John Allison York Sr.; Thompson, "Tumlinson, James, Jr.;" Bill Groneman, "Tumlinson, George W.," *HOT*; "Tumlinson Family of the DeWitt Colony."
7. Republic of Texas Claims: John J. Tumlinson (#618, #2091, #2092); Wilbarger, *Indian Depredations*, 1–4, 60–61; Brown, *Indian Wars and Pioneers of Texas*, 79–80, 108; Kilgore, *Ranger Legacy*, 43–44; Knowles, *They Rode for the Lone Star*, 76–77; Moore, *Savage Frontier*, 1: 120–121, 127, 171–173, 2: 96–97, 311–317, 319, 321, 3: 84–86, 90–95, 99, 311; Wilkins, *Legend Begins*, 83; Cox, *Cinco Peso*, 47–48; Webb, *Texas Rangers*, 58, 60–61; Utley, *Lone Star Justice*, 29; Ivey, *Registry and History*, 23, 47, 49, 54; Parsons, *Sutton-Taylor Feud*, 18, 33; Tumlinson, "Tumlinson, John Jackson, Jr.;" Ruby Farrar Pridgen, "York, John," *HOT*; FAG: James S. Tumlinson, Capt. John Allison York

Sr. The best study of the Linville Raid remains Donaly E. Brice, *The Great Comanche Raid: Boldest Attack of the Texas Republic* (Austin, TX: Eakin Press, 1987).

8. Republic of Texas Claims: Peter Tumlinson (#N/A); AGSR: Absalom T. Tumlinson, Joseph Tumlinson, Peter Tumlinson, William O. Tumlinson; Emanuel A. Wright to Shriber, October 17, 1966, Wright Papers; Kilgore, *Ranger Legacy*, 45–48, 55–56; Webb, *Texas Rangers*, 186, 188–190, 199, 202–216; Ivey, *Registry and History*, 92, 96; Harris, Harris, and Sadler, *Texas Ranger Biographies*, 426; Frederick Wilkins, *Defending the Borders: The Texas Rangers, 1848–1861* (Austin, TX: State House Press, 2001), 108, 115–116, 122–123, 140–141; William J. Hughes, *Rebellious Ranger: Rip Ford and the Old Southwest* (Norman: University of Oklahoma Press, 1964), 165, 171 [quotes]; Tise, *Texas County Sheriffs*, 160; Banks, *Patriot Ancestry Album*, 277; Essie Walton Martin, "Scurlock, William (1807–1885)," *HOT*; John Leffler (revised by Brett J. Derbes), "English, Levi," *HOT*; Samuel H. Tumlinson, "Tumlinson, Peter," *HOT*; FAG: Joseph Tumlinson, Peter Frank Tumlinson; "Tumlinson Family of the DeWitt Colony." Joseph Tumlinson, age 22, joined Company K of the Thirty-Sixth Texas Cavalry at San Antonio in March 1862, along with Peter, age 16, and William O. Tumlinson, age 21, who were presumably the sons of Peter F. Tumlinson and thus his brothers. Joseph and William somehow ingested arsenic at Fort Inge one month after their enlistment and were medically discharged in August 1862; Peter, who was underage, left the service at the same time. See United States Department of War, Compiled Service Records of Confederate Soldiers Who Served in Organizations from Texas (Record Group 109, National Archives, Washington, DC), Thirty-Sixth Texas Cavalry: Joseph Tumlinson, Peter Tumlinson, William O. Tumlinson.

9. Emanuel A. Wright, "Memoir" (Typescript, n.d.), Wright Papers, 146; Republic of Texas Claims: Holmes Byfield (#N/A), John J. Tumlinson (#618, #2091, #2092); Moore, *Savage Frontier*, 1: 160; Parsons, *Sutton-Taylor Feud*, 18; Kilgore, *Ranger Legacy*, 49; Dan E. Kilgore, "Two Six Shooters and a Sunbonnet: The Story of Sally Skull," *Legendary Ladies of Texas*, ed. Francis E. Abernethy (Dallas, 1981; reprint, Denton: University of North Texas Press, 1994); Tumlinson, "Tumlinson, Joseph;" Dan E. Kilgore, "Sarah Jane Newman Scull [Sally]," *HOT*; FAG: Joseph A. Newman, Elizabeth Newman Tumlinson; "Our Family History;" "Tumlinson Family of the DeWitt Colony." Joseph L.

Tumlinson donated the land for the first seat of DeWitt County at its organization in 1846, but Cameron, as the town was named, failed to develop. See Murphree, *DeWitt County*, 4–6, 26–27; Craig H. Roell, "Cameron, TX (DeWitt County)," *HOT*.

10. William L. Wright to Aldrich, July 16, 1936, Aldrich Papers, DBCAH; Interview with Zora Belle Wright Fore, Dec. 7, 1973, South Texas Oral History & Folklore Collection, South Texas Archives, James C. Jernigan Library, Texas A&M University at Kingsville; AGSR: Joseph Tomlinson [Tumlinson]; Kilgore, *Ranger Legacy*, 48–49, 54; Webb, *Texas Rangers*, 233, 235, 237, 290; Parsons, *Sutton-Taylor Feud*, 33–38, 52–59, 143, 204, 284, 290; Tise, *Texas County Sheriffs*, 160; Barry A. Crouch and Donaly E. Brice, *The Governor's Hounds: The Texas State Police, 1870–1873* (Austin: University of Texas Press, 2011), 294; C. L. Sonnichsen, *I'll Die Before I Run: The Story of the Great Feuds of Texas* (New York: Devin-Adair Company, 1962), 53–55, 57, 69–72, 84–89; Murphree, *DeWitt County*, 18; C. L. Sonnichsen, "Sutton-Taylor Feud," *HOT*; Thomas W. Cutrer, "Hall, Jesse Leigh," *HOT*; FAG: John Littleton, William P. "Buck" Taylor; "Our Family History;" "Tumlinson Family of the DeWitt Colony;" "John T. Littleton," Texas Legislators: Past & Present, accessed Jan. 21, 2020, https://lrl.texas.gov/legeleaders/members/memberdisplay.cfm?memberID=4549. William L. Wright's father, L.B. Wright, presided as justice of the peace over the inquests for the deaths of Jack Helm and at least two other men killed in the Sutton-Taylor Feud, and he sent a letter protesting the violence to Governor Edmund J. Davis. See Ivey, *Ranger Ideal, Volume 3*, 2.
11. Wright, "Memoir," 126, 142; *Harlingen Valley Morning Star*, Mar. 7, 1937; *Corpus Christi Caller-Times*, Mar. 8, 1942; *Pampa Daily News*, Mar. 8, 1942; *Abilene Reporter-News*, Mar. 8, 1942; *Marshall News Messenger*, Mar. 8, 1942; *Waco Tribune-Herald*, Oct. 2, 1977; William W. Sterling, *Trails and Trials of a Texas Ranger* (Privately printed, 1959), 407–408; Kilgore, *Ranger Legacy*, 57; FAG: Herman P. Eckhardt; H. Allen Anderson, "Blocker, John Rufus," *HOT*; J. Frank Dobie, "Wallace, William Alexander Anderson [Bigfoot]," *HOT*. Because Leander H. McNelly clashed with Joseph L. Tumlinson, while J. Leigh Hall was welcome in DeWitt County, William L. Wright, who would have been about ten years of age during Hall's operations, was most likely influenced more by Hall. The man who claimed to have seen Wright at the Ranger camp was William L. Rudd, who served

mostly under Hall and not McNelly. See AGSR: W. L. Rudd; *FCJ*, Dec. 15, 1966, Chuck Parsons and Marianne E. Hall Little, *Captain L. H. McNelly, Texas Ranger: The Life and Times of a Fighting Man* (Austin, TX: State House Press, 2001), 148–151, and Chuck Parsons, *Texas Ranger Lee Hall: From the Red River to the Rio Grande* (Denton: University of North Texas Press, 2020), 55, 64–65, 74, 87, 94–95, 104–105, 108–109; Ivey, *Ranger Ideal, Volume 3*, 2.

12. Genealogy Notes, Wright Family Bible Record, William L. Wright to Ann E. T. Wright, Feb. 24, 1890, Emanuel A. Wright to Shriber, Oct. 17, 1966, Leo E. Gossett to Emanuel A. Wright, Feb. 11, 1985, Emanuel A. Wright to Secretary of Cameron Lodge, Feb. 28, 1985, Historical Notes (Manuscript, n.d., probably written by Emanuel A. Wright), Sanford N. Brown, "Memoirs of Sanford Brown" (Typescript, June 2, 1916), Wright Papers; Wright, "Memoir," 142, 144, 149; AGSR: C. P. Warren, Peter Tumlinson; Compiled Service Records, Eighth Texas Infantry: Sanford N. Brown; *SAE*, July 18, 1916; *FCJ*, July 14, 21, 28, 1916; Sterling, *Trails and Trials*, 408, 409; Ivey, *History and Registry*, 87; Maude T. Gilliland, *Wilson County Texas Rangers, 1837 to 1977* (Privately printed, 1977), 33–34; FAG: Sanford Brown; "Our Family History." For more about Sutherland Springs when the Wrights lived there, see Richard B. McCaslin, *Sutherland Springs, Texas: Saratoga on the Cibolo* (Denton: University of North Texas Press, 2017), especially Chapter 3.
13. Bureau of the Census, Thirteenth Census, 1910, Population, Wilson County, TX [John J. "Pegleg" Tumlinson is listed as "Joe Tomlinson"]; Parsons, *Sutton-Taylor Feud*, 2147, 204, 284, 292; J. Frank Dobie, *Coronado's Children: Tales of Lost Mines and Buried Treasure of the Southwest* (Dallas, TX: Southwest Press, 1930), 70, 71, 73, 76; FAG: John Jackson Tumlinson, John Jackson "Pegleg" Tumlinson, Travis Elmo Tumlinson; "Tumlinson Saga," accessed May 3, 2020, https://www.desertusa.com/mb3/viewtopic.php?t=3339&start=40; "Legend of the Stone Maps," p. 68, accessed May 3, 2020, http://www.treasurenet.com/forums/superstition-mountain-legends/461199-legend-stone-maps-68.html.
14. William L. Wright to "Mr. Tuffly," March 1891, Historical notes [first quote], Wright Papers; Wright, "Memoir," 2, 143; *FSJ*, Jan. 11, 1918; *Pampa Daily News*, Mar. 8, 1942; *SAE*, Mar. 8, 1942 [second quote]; *Abilene Reporter-News*, Mar. 8, 1942; *Marshall News Messenger*, Mar. 8, 1942; *Corpus Christi Caller-Times*, Mar. 8, 1942; Tise, *Texas*

County Sheriffs, 546; FAG: Gratz D. Brown. William W. Sterling wrote that William L. Wright served as a justice of the peace in Wilson County before becoming a deputy sheriff, but there is no record that corroborates this. See Sterling, *Trails and Trials*, 408. Some sources claim that Wright first became a deputy in 1892, but again there is no documentation of that.

15. Compiled Service Records, Border's Regiment, Texas Cavalry: J. Craighead; *SAE*, July 18, 1916; *FCJ*, July 14, 21, 28, 1916; Tise, *Texas County Sheriffs*, 546; FAG: Sanford Brown, John Sutherland Craighead, Abner Hubbard Polley, Frances Marian "Fannie" Brown Polley. For more about the Polley and Sutherland families in the development of Sutherland Springs, as well in the Civil War, see McCaslin, *Sutherland Springs, Texas; Saratoga on the Cibolo*, and Richard B. McCaslin, ed., *A Soldier's Letters to Charming Nellie: The Correspondence of Joseph B. Polley, Hood's Texas Brigade* (Knoxville: University of Tennessee Press, 2008). John P. Border's cavalry battalion merged with other companies to form the regiment commanded by T. Scott Anderson. Border remained lieutenant colonel, and the regiment is officially listed under his name in the service records.
16. *Corsicana Democrat and Truth*, Apr. 9, 1925; *FCJ*, Apr. 10, 1925; *San Patricio County News*, Apr. 30, 1925; West C. Gilbreath, *Death on the Gallows: The Encyclopedia of Legal Hangings in Texas* (Fort Worth, TX: Wild Horse Press, 2017), 370–371; "The First Legal Execution in Wilson County," *Wilson County, TXGen Web*, accessed Jan. 22, 2020, http://hometownchronicles.com/tx/wilson/martinezm.htm.
17. Gilbreath, *Death on the Gallows*, 370–371; FAG: Jefferson McIntosh "Mack" Mason, H. B. Gouger; "First Legal Execution in Wilson County." According to Genealogy Notes, Wright Papers, the maiden name of the mother of Sanford N. Brown, William L. Wright's father-in-law, was Margaret Tom, so there may be a distant family relationship, by marriage, between the young deputy sheriff and the Tom brothers who served as trackers.
18. Wright, "Memoir," 137–138 [quote]; Obituary for William L. Wright, n.d., in in Scrapbook, Wright Papers; *Houston Daily Post*, June 13, 1895; *Corsicana Democrat and Truth*, Apr. 9, 1925; *San Patricio County News*, Apr. 30, 1925; *Corpus Christi Caller-Times*, Mar. 8, 1942, Dec. 16, 1947; Gilbreath, *Death on the Gallows*, 370–371; Ivey, *Ranger Ideal, Volume 3*, 3; "First Legal Execution in Wilson County."

19. *FCJ*, Jan. 2, 1925; Wright Family Bible Record, Emanuel A. Wright to Shriber, Oct. 17, 1966, Emanuel A. Wright to Rowland, July 2, 1978, Emanuel A. Wright to Secretary of Cameron Lodge, Feb. 28, 1985, Wright Papers; Wright, "Memoir," 142, 145, 150; William B. Wright, *Career Hunting: Texas Ranger vs. Standard Oiler* (El Cajon, CA: Privately printed, 1983), 4; Bureau of the Census, Twelfth Census, 1900, Population, Wilson County, TX; Maude T. Gilliland, *Horsebackers of the Brush Country: A Story of the Texas Rangers and Mexican Liquor Smugglers* (Brownsville, TX: Springman-King Company, 1968), 114; FAG: Zora Lee Wright Warren; "Our Family History."
20. William L. Wright to Thomas Scurry, Feb. 6, 1899, FBC; Sterling, *Trails and Trials*, 409; Tise, *Texas County Sheriffs*, 546; FAG: John Pyrimitt "Sheriff" Campbell, William Leonidas "Rattlesnake Willie" Wright; Arnoldo de León, "Ximenes, Manuel Jesus," *HOT.*

Notes for Chapter 2

1. Walter P. Webb, *The Texas Rangers: A Century of Frontier Defense* (Boston, MA: Houghton Mifflin, 1935), 457–461; Robert M. Utley, *Lone Star Justice: The First Century of the Texas Rangers* (New York: Oxford University Press, 2002), 253; Harold J. Weiss Jr., "The Texas Rangers Revisited: Old Themes and New Viewpoints," *Southwestern Historical Quarterly* 97 (April 1994): 632; Claudia Hazlewood, "Scurry, Thomas," *HOT*.
2. John H. Rogers to Thomas Scurry, Feb. 21, 1899 [oaths of Thomas C. Taylor, Feb. 18, 1899, and William L. Wright, Feb. 20, 1899, enclosed], FBC; Muster Rolls and Monthly Returns, Company E, FBR; AGSR: H. G. DuBose, Frank D. McMahan, Jim Moore, A. Y. Old, W. A. Old, T. C. Taylor, W. L. Wright; TRHFM: F. D. McMahan, J. W. (Jim) Moore; Allison Mayfield, *Biennial Report of the Secretary of State of the State of Texas, 1896* (Austin, TX: Ben C. Jones & Company, 1897), 218; *Pampa Daily News*, Mar. 8, 1942; *Abilene Reporter-News*, Mar. 8, 1942; *Marshall News Messenger*, Mar. 8, 1942; Andrew J. Sowell, *Early Settlers and Indian Fighters of Southwest Texas* (Austin, TX: Ben C. Jones & Company, 1900), 630; Utley, *Lone Star Justice*, 254; Paul N. Spellman, *Capt. John H. Rogers, Texas Ranger* (Denton: University of North Texas Press, 2003), 92; Charles H. Harris III, Frances E. Harris, and Louis R. Sadler, *Texas Ranger Biographies: Those Who*

Served 1910–1921 (Albuquerque: University of New Mexico Press, 2009), 374; FAG: Henry Gilpin "Harry" DuBose, Frank D. McMahan, Jim Moore, Augustus Yardley Old, William Anthony "Billy" Old; Thomas Creed Taylor. The first wife of William L. Wright's grandfather, Joseph L. Tumlinson, was Creed Taylor's sister, Johanna Taylor, while Wright's great-aunt, Elizabeth Tumlinson, married William R. Taylor, Creed's brother.

3. AGSR: McMahan, Moore, A. Y. Old, W. A. Old, Taylor, W. L. Wright; *Brownsville Herald*, Aug. 17, 18, 20, 1914; Spellman, *Capt. Rogers*, 24, 45–52; Sammy Tise, *Texas County Sheriffs* (Albuquerque: Oakwood Press, 1989), 39, 304; FAG: Henry Gilpin "Harry" DuBose, Francis M. "Frank or FM" Moore, James H. Moore, Jim Moore, William Anthony "Billy" Old, Thomas Creed Taylor, James Oury Taylor. Jim Moore's brother, Harrison L. Moore, who was also a Ranger, served as the sheriff of Hudspeth County, where William L. Wright's brother, Milam H. Wright, and son, Emanuel A. "Dogie" Wright, both later became sheriffs. See Tise, *Texas County Sheriffs*, 270, and Harris, Harris, and Sadler, *Texas Ranger Biographies*, 416–417.
4. Emanuel A. Wright, "Memoir" (Typescript, n.d., E. A. "Dogie" Wright Papers, DBCAH), 128–129, 154; Spencer Hutchins to Scurry, Mar. 9, 1899, Henry W. Locke to Scurry, Mar. 16, 1899, A. S. Fisher to Scurry, May 18, 1899, Locke to Scurry, May 26, 1899, Rogers to Scurry, Oct. 3, 1899, AGC; Muster Rolls and Monthly Returns, Company E; AGSR: Henry W. Locke, Edwin M. DuBose, S. S. Hutchison; TRHFM: Sidney S. Hutchison; *Uvalde Leader News*, Aug. 1, 1924; *FCJ*, Aug. 1, 1924; William W. Sterling, *Trails and Trials of a Texas Ranger* (Privately printed, 1959), 369–370; Harris, Harris, and Sadler, *Texas Ranger Biographies*, 93, 196, 227; Spellman, *Capt. Rogers*, 121–122; FAG: Edwin M. DuBose Sr., Sidney Sill Hutchison. Oddly, while Levi appeared in monthly returns and muster rolls for Company E, no file for him has been found in the service records of the Texas Adjutant General. Edwin M. DuBose was with his brother, Henry G. "Harry" DuBose, in the gunfight that resulted in the death of the latter, as well as the man who attacked them. See FAG: Henry Gilpin "Harry" DuBose, Gerhard John Schoenbohm Sr.
5. William L. Wright to Milam H. Wright, Aug. 16, 1899 [with enclosure], William J. McDonald to Milam H. Wright, Aug. 26, 1899, Wright Papers; Rogers to Scurry, Oct. 10, Nov. 20, 1899, AGC; Monthly Returns, Company E [second quote]; AGSR: Gratz Brown,

C. L. Rogers [[first quote], C. H. Sandherr, Milam H. Wright; Harris, Harris, and Sadler, *Texas Ranger Biographies*, 517; Spellman, *Capt. Rogers*, 92, 120–121; FAG: Curren Lee "Kid" Rogers, Charles H. Sandherr; "Our Family History: The Genealogy of Robert and Christina Barritt," accessed Jan. 20, 2020, http://tree.barrittfamily.net/getperson.php?personID=I473&tree=dyal_speckels. Curren L. Rogers died in a San Antonio hospital on July 24, 1902, a little more than a month before William L. Wright left the Rangers.

6. Rogers to Scurry, Dec. 8, 1899, May 23, 26, 1900, A. Y. Old to Scurry, June 6, 1900, W. A. Old to Scurry, Aug. 15, 1900, W. A. Old to W. W. Tunney [Turney?], March 2, 6, 1901, W. A. Old to Joseph D. Sayers, n.d. [received Mar. 8, 1901], Mar. 26, June 25, 1901, Charles Filleman to Sayers, Mar. 25, 1901, W. A. Old to Sayers, June 25, 1901, AGC; Muster Rolls and Monthly Returns [quotes], Company E; AGSR: A. Y. Old, W. A. Old, Milam H. Wright; FAG: Augustus Yardley Old, William Anthony "Billy" Old.
7. T. S. Smith to Sayers, May 24, 25, 1900, Rogers to Scurry, May 26, 1900, William L. Wright to Scurry, June 2, 22 [third quote], 1900, AGC; Muster Rolls and Monthly Returns, Company E; Records of Scouts, Company E, FBR; AGSR: Enoch Cook [second quote], H. G. DuBose, Joe C. Hudson [first quote], William L. Wright; Webb, *Texas Rangers*, 453, 457; Utley, *Lone Star Justice*, 271–272; Spellman, *Capt. Rogers*, 108–109; Chuck Parsons, *Captain John R. Hughes, Lone Star Ranger* (Denton: University of North Texas Press, 2011), 343; Bob Alexander, *Winchester Warriors: Texas Rangers of Company D* (Denton: University of North Texas Press, 2009), 304, 308; Bob Alexander, *Riding Lucifer's Line: Ranger Deaths Along the Texas-Mexico Border* (Denton: University of North Texas Press, 2013), 155–158; Harold J. Weiss Jr., *Yours to Command: The Life and Legend of Texas Ranger Captain Bill McDonald* (Denton: University of North Texas Press, 2009), 204, 205.
8. Rogers to Scurry, Mar. 5, June 1 [quote], 1901, AGC; Muster Rolls and Monthly Returns, Company E; AGSR: William M. Burwell, T. F. McKinney, Alex Ormand, William Steele; TRHFM: W. M. Burwell; Tise, *Texas County Sheriffs*, 321; Spellman, *Capt. Rogers*, 88, 96, 122; Charles H. Harris III and Louis R. Sadler, *The Texas Rangers in the Mexican Revolution: The Bloodiest Decade, 1910–1920* (Norman: University of Oklahoma Press, 2004), 23; FAG: William M. Burwell, Tolbert Fannin "Tol" McKinney, Alex Ormand, William Hutton Steele;

"Raid of 1878," accessed Jan. 24, 2020, https://historicdistrict.com/Genealogy/lasalle/raid.asp; "William M. Burwell," accessed Jan. 20, 2020, http://genealogytrails.com/tex/gulfcoast/jackson/jackson_biographies.html. John H. Rogers married Harriet Randolph Burwell at Cotulla in 1892; William M. Burwell was her brother.

9. J. W. Petty to Rogers, Apr. 1, 1901, AGC; Muster Rolls and Monthly Returns, Company E; Muster Rolls and Monthly Returns, Company C, RFR; "Brief Biennial Report of Co. C, RF"[quote], AGC [misfiled in Box 401–594, Folder 26: December 23–31, 1922]; AGSR: H. G. DuBose, T. F. McKinney, Jim Moore, J. W. Petty, Charles Sandherr, W. L. Wright; Utley, *Lone Star Justice*, 273; Spellman, *Capt. Rogers*, 117–118; Mike Cox, *Time of the Rangers: Texas Rangers from 1900 to the Present* (New York: Forge Books, 2009), 20–21.
10. Rogers to Scurry, Dec. 7, 1901, Aug. 11, 1902, Oscar Latta to Rogers, Dec. 18, 1901, AGC; Muster Rolls and Monthly Returns, Company C; AGSR: Oscar Latta (quote), Alex Ormand, William Steele, Thomas C. Taylor, Milam H. Wright, W. L. Wright; TRHFM: Oscar Latta; FAG: Oscar L. Latta.
11. Historical Notes (Manuscript, n.d., probably by Emanuel A. "Dogie" Wright), Wright Papers; Rogers to Scurry, Feb. 7, 1900 [quote], AGC; Monthly Returns, Company E; *Corpus Christi Caller-Times*, Mar. 8, 1942; *SAE*, Mar. 8, 1942; *Pampa Daily News*, Mar. 8, 1942; *Abilene Reporter-News*, Mar. 8, 1942; *Marshall News Messenger*, Mar. 8, 1942; Sterling, *Trails and Trials*, 370; Utley, *Lone Star Justice*, 253, 256; Spellman, *Capt. Rogers*, passim.
12. AGSR: Jim Moore, A. Y. Old, W. A. Old, Moore, W. L. Wright; Sterling, *Trails and Trials*, 376; FAG: Augustus Yardley Old, William Anthony "Billy" Old; "William Old," accessed Jan. 24, 2020, https://arizonagravestones. org/view.php?id=86496.
13. Rogers to Scurry, March 18, 1899, n.d. [July 1900], H. G. DuBose to Scurry, Mar. 28, 1899 [with enclosure: Report of Rangers Work at Laredo Texas From March 19th to March 25th 1899], AGC; Records of Scouts, Company E; *San Francisco* [CA] *Call*, Mar. 21, 1899; *El Paso Herald-Post*, Aug. 22, 1959; TRHFM: T. C. "Creed" Taylor; Sowell, *Early Settlers and Indian Fighters*, 630–631; Utley, *Lone Star Justice*, 269–270; Webb, *Texas Rangers*, 450–451; Spellman, *Capt. Rogers*, 96–99; Mike Cox, *The Texas Rangers: Wearing the Cinco Peso, 1821–1900* (New York: Forge Books, 2008), 372–373; Darren L. Ivey, *The Ranger Ideal, Volume 2: Texas Rangers in the Hall of*

Fame, 1874–1930 (Denton: University of North Texas Press, 2018), 473–474; John McKiernan-González, *Fevered Measures: Public Health and Race at the Texas-Mexico Border, 1848–1942* (Durham: Duke University Press, 2012), 127–132 [quote], 133–142; Howard E. Smith, *History of Public Health in Texas* (Austin: Texas State Department of Health, 1974), 45; Teresa Palomo Acosta, "Idar, Nicasio," *HOT*; Carlos E. Cuéllar, "Laredo Smallpox Riot," *HOT*; FAG: Adam Joseph "Joe" Barthelow.

14. Report of Rangers Work at Laredo Texas From March 19th to March 25th 1899, Rogers to Scurry, n.d. [July 1900], AGC; Muster Rolls and Records of Scouts, Company E; AGSR: Thomas Ragland; *Corpus Christi Caller-Times*, Feb. 26, 27, 1953, *El Paso Herald-Post*, Aug. 22, 1959) TRHFM: T. C. "Creed" Taylor; Spellman, *Capt. Rogers*, 99–100; Ivey, *Ranger Ideal, Volume 2*, 222; Charles H. Harris III and Louis R. Sadler, *The Texas Rangers in Transition: From Gunfighters to Criminal Investigators, 1921–1935* (Norman, University of Oklahoma Press, 2019), 6–7; Bob Alexander and Donaly E. Brice, *Texas Rangers: Lives, Legend, and Legacy* (Denton: University of North Texas Press, 2017), 333–335; FAG: Oscar Newt Wright.
15. Report of Rangers Work at Laredo Texas From March 19th to March 25th 1899, Rogers to Scurry, Mar. 18, 1899, n.d. [July 1900], AGC; Muster Rolls and Records of Scouts, Company E; AGSR: Thomas Ragland; TRHFM: T. C. "Creed" Taylor; *San Francisco* [CA] *Call*, Mar. 21, 1899; *Corpus Christi Caller-Times*, Feb. 26, 27, 1953; *El Paso Herald-Post*, Aug. 22, 1959; Ivey, *Ranger Ideal, Volume 2*, 222, 274; Spellman, *Capt. Rogers*, 99–101; Cox, *Cinco Peso*, 372–373; Tise, *Texas County Sheriffs, 526*; Cuéllar, "Laredo Smallpox Riot;" FAG: Oscar Newt Wright. Historian Andrew J. Sowell says the two men with Agapito Herrera were his brothers. See *Early Settlers and Indian Fighters*, 631.
16. Report of Rangers Work at Laredo Texas From March 19th to March 25th 1899, Rogers to Scurry, Mar. 18, n.d. [July 1900], AGC; Muster Rolls and Records of Scouts, Company E; Historical Notes, Wright Papers; AGSR: Thomas Ragland; TRHFM: T. C. "Creed" Taylor; Sterling, *Trails and Trials*; 375 [second quote]; *El Paso Herald-Post*, Aug. 22, 1959 [first quote]; Sowell, *Early Settlers and Indian Fighters*, 631; Ivey, *Ranger Ideal, Volume 2*, 474; Spellman, *Capt. Rogers*, 101–103; Cox, *Cinco Peso*, 372–373. The story of the fight at Laredo grew with each retelling; Wright's obituary said five

men were killed in gun battles the day after he arrived in the border town. See *Pampa Daily News*, Mar. 8, 1942; *Abilene Reporter-News*, Mar. 8, 1942; *Marshall News Messenger*, Mar. 8, 1942. The article in the *El Paso Herald-Post*, published on Aug. 22, 1959, is an interesting interview with Thomas C. "Creed" Taylor, the last surviving member of Company E who was in the Laredo fight.

17. John R. Hughes to Scurry, March 25, 1899, AGC; Historical Notes, Wright Papers; *San Francisco* [CA] *Call*, Mar. 21, 1899; *Laredo Times*, Apr. 1, 1899; Sowell, *Early Settlers and Indian Fighters*, 631; Utley, *Lone Star Justice*, 269–270; Spellman, *Capt. Rogers*, 102; Ivey, *Ranger Ideal, Volume 2*, 474; McKiernan-González, *Fevered Measures*, 124, 142–147; Cuéllar, "Laredo Smallpox Riot."
18. Rogers to Scurry, May 18, 22, 1899, AGC; Monthly Returns, Company E; AGSR: D. S. Barker; *Hallettsville New Era*, May 19, 1899; *Houston Daily Post*, May 19, 1899; Sterling, *Trails and Trials*, 337–338; Weiss, *Yours to Command*, 154–162; Tise, *Texas County Sheriffs*, 118; Paul N. Spellman, *Capt. J. A. Brooks, Texas Ranger* (Denton: University of North Texas Press, 2007), 108–111; C. L. Sonnichsen, *I'll Die Before I Run: The Story of the Great Feuds of Texas I (New York: Devin-Adair Company, 1962)*, 307–312; James C. Kearney, Bill Stein, and James Smallwood, *No Hope for Heaven, No Fear of Hell: The Stafford-Townsend Feud of Colorado County, Texas, 1871–1911* (Denton: University of North Texas Press, 2016), 87–92, 95–96, 170–171, 176; John H. Jenkins and J. Gordon Frost, "*I'm Frank Hamer:" The Life of a Texas Police Officer* (Austin, TX: Pemberton Press, 1968), 21–22; Robert W. Stephens, *Texas Ranger Sketches* (Dallas, TX: Privately printed, 1972), 22–23, 144–146; Harold J. Weiss Jr., "Sieker, Lamartine Pemberton," *HOT*; Bill Stein, "Colorado County Feud," *HOT*; FAG: William D. "Will" Clements, Samuel Houston Reese, Burrell Green Whittington "Dick" Reese, Dudley Snyder "Dud" Barker; "Texas State Cemetery: Lamartine Pemberton Sieker," accessed Jan. 25, 2020, https://cemetery.tspb.texas.gov/pub/user_form .asp?step=1&pers_id= 934; Bobbie Elliott and Bill Stein, "Colorado County District Court Records, Criminal Cause File Index, 1837–1930," accessed Jan. 25, 2020, http://library.columbustexas.net/history/Criminal%20Causes. htm.
19. Rogers to Scurry, n.d. [July 1900], AGC; Records of Scouts, Company E; TRHFM: T. C. "Creed" Taylor [quotes]; *El Paso Herald-Post*, Aug. 22, 1959; Sonnichsen, *I'll Die Before I Run*, 312; Stein, "Colorado County Feud."

20. E. M. Phelps to Scurry, June 11, 1899, William L. Wright to Scurry, June 9 [second quote], 10, 11, 1899, Scurry to Rogers, June 11, 1899, AGC; Records of Scouts, Company E; Historical Notes, Wright Papers; TRHFM: T. C. "Creed" Taylor [first, third, and fourth quotes]; *El Paso Herald-Post*, Aug. 22, 1959; Weiss, *Yours to Command*, 162–163; Kearney, Stein, and Smallwood, *No Hope for Heaven*, 92, 170–171, 176, 194.
21. William L. Wright to Scurry, June 18, 19, 26, 28, July 13, 22, 26, 1899, AGC; William L. Wright to L. P. Sieker, July 14 [quote], FBC; Monthly Returns and Records of Scouts, Company E; Texas Department of Criminal Justice, Convict Record Ledgers, 1849–1954: Duff Hines (#18293), TSLA; Historical Notes, Wright Papers; *El Paso Herald-Post*, Aug. 22, 1959; TRHFM: T. C. "Creed" Taylor; Weiss, *Yours to Command*, 160–163; Kearney, Stein, and Smallwood, *No Hope for Heaven*, 92, 170–171, 176, 194); Elliott and Stein, "Criminal Cause File Index." While there is no record of a disposition for William Stallion, the Convict Record Ledgers do report the case of Allen Small (#18295), a fifteen-year-old black laborer from Colorado County sentenced to eight years in the penitentiary for assault to rape during the same district court session. It is possible that he and Stallion are the same person.
22. Monthly Returns and Records of Scouts, Company E [copy of Records of Scouts for July 1899 also in FBC]; *Bryan Morning Eagle*, July 22, 23, 1899; *Houston Daily Post*, July 20, Aug. 6, 1899; TRHFM: T. C. "Creed" Taylor; Merline Pitre, "Burton, Walter Moses," *HOT*; Curtis Bishop, "Brazos Flood of 1899," *HOT*; FAG: Walter Moses Burton.
23. Rogers to Scurry, n.d. [July 1900], Aug. 19, 26, Oct. 2 [quote], 21, 25, Nov. 13, 1899, William L. Wright to Scurry, Sept. 26, 30, Oct. 1, 1899, AGC; Monthly Returns and Records of Scouts, Company E; United States Bureau of the Census, Twelfth Census, 1900, Population, Wilson County, TX, and Fifteenth Census, 1930, Population, Colorado County, TX (Record Group 29, National Archives, Washington, DC); Ivey, *Ranger Ideal, Volume 2*, 390–391; Spellman, *Capt. Rogers*, 106–107; Weiss, *Yours to Command*, 196–198; Richard B. McCaslin, *Sutherland Springs, Texas; Saratoga on the Cibolo* (Denton: University of North Texas Press, 2017), 185; Elliott and Stein, "Criminal Cause File Index."
24. J. E. Mills to Alvin Henderson, Oct. 30, 1899, Henderson to Scurry, Oct. 30 [first and second quotes], Nov. 1, 2, 3, 1899, A. Emden et al. to Sayers, Nov. 29, 1899, Warren H. Russell to Sayers, December 23,

1899, Citizens of Hempstead to Sayers, Dec. 6, 1899, L. P. Sieker to Scurry, Nov. 30, Dec. 2, 1899, R. E. Hannay to Scurry, Dec. 14, 26, 1899, Rogers to Scurry, Dec. 16, 1899, William L. Wright to Scurry, Dec. 20, 25, 28, 1899, William L. Wright to Seiker, Dec. 21, 1899, Mills to Scurry, Dec. 30, 1899, Jan. 20, 1900, General Order No. 19, Adjutant General's Office, Feb. 23, 1900, AGC; Monthly Returns and Records of Scouts, Company E; *FCJ*, Apr. 10, 1925; *Tise, Texas County Sheriffs*, 520.

25. Monthly Returns and Records of Scouts, Company E; *Weimar Mercury*, Jan. 20, 1900; *El Paso Herald-Post*, Aug. 22, 1959; TRHFM: T. C. "Creed" Taylor; Weiss, *Yours to Command*, 164–166; Spellman, *Capt. Rogers*, 109–115; Ivey, *Ranger Ideal, Volume 2*, 343–344, 476–477; Spellman, *Capt. Brooks*, 112–115; Kearney, Stein, and Smallwood, *No Hope for Heaven*, 99–108; Sonnichsen, *I'll Die Before I Run*, 308, 312–313; FAG: Arthur Lee Burford.
26. Rogers to Scurry, Sept. 18, 1899, Mar. 1, 1900, McDonald to Scurry, Sept. 27, Oct. 2, 7, 11, 14, 28, 30, Nov. 1, 2, 9, 22, Dec. 21, 1899, Apr. 12, 20, 22, 1900, P. F. Eastin, B. H. Norsworthy, and E. M. Davis to Scurry, Feb. 18, 1900, C. A. Teagle to Scurry, Feb. 20, 1900, A. Y. Old to Rogers, Feb. 23, 1900, William L. Wright to Scurry, Feb. 28, Mar. 3, 15, 16, 1900, Eastin to Scurry, Mar. 3, 1900, George F. Poole to Sayers, March 7, 1900, AGC; Monthly Returns and Records of Scouts, Company E; AGSR: Lawrence Fuller; *Houston Daily Post*, Jan. 14, Mar. 7, 1900; Thomas Scurry, *Biennial Report of the Adjutant General of Texas for 1899–1900* (Austin, TX: Ben C. Jones & Company, 1900), 22–23; *Weimar Mercury*, Mar. 24, 1900; Albert B. Paine, *Captain Bill McDonald, Texas Ranger: A Story of Frontier Reform* (New York: J. J. Little & Ives Company, 1909), 261–262; Ivey, *Ranger Ideal, Volume 2*, pp. 390–391; Weiss, *Yours to Command*, 198–200; Kearney, Stein, and Smallwood, *No Hope for Heaven*, 241; Cox, *Time of the Rangers*, 19–20.
27. George F. Poole to Scurry, April 6, 1900, McDonald to Scurry, May 8, 21, 22, 1900, William L. Wright to Scurry, Apr. 15, 1901, Rogers to Scurry, Apr. 9, 1901, Charles A. Hotchkiss to Scurry, Apr. 10, 1901, McDonald to Sieker, Mar. 19, 1902, AGC; Scurry, *Report of Texas Adjutant General, 1899–1900*, 23; *New Orleans* [LA] *Picayune,* Jan. 31, 1893; *El Paso Times*, May 28, 1900; Sterling, *Trails and Trials*, 338–339; Paine, *Captain Bill McDonald*, 408–409; Ivey, *Ranger Ideal, Volume 2*, 390–391; Cox, *Time of the Rangers*, 20–22; Weiss, *Yours to*

Command, 201; Alexander, *Riding Lucifer's Line*, 155–158; Clifford R. Caldwell and Ron DeLord, *Texas Lawmen, 1900–1940: More of the Good and the Bad* (Charleston, SC: Arcadia Press, 2012), 293–294; FAG: James A. Jett, Thomas F. Poole.

28. Monthly Returns, Company E; *Fort Worth Gazette*, June 5, 6, Nov. 17, 1891, Feb. 11, 13, 19, 20, 1892; *Galveston Daily News*, June 5, 9, 11, 23, 26, July 5, 1891, Feb. 9, 11, 13, 14, 1892; *Austin Statesman*, June 11, 18, July 2, Oct. 1, 1891, Feb. 18, 1892; *Brownsville Daily Herald*, Aug. 24, 25, 1896; *Brenham Daily Banner*, Apr. 13, 1898, *Houston Daily Post*, April 11, 1898, *Stephenville Empire*, May 26, 1898; *Halletsville Herald*, May 26, 1898; *Lampasas Leader*, May 27, 1898; "Editor Killing in Texas," *The Fourth Estate*, April 21, 1898; John P. White, comp., *Texas Criminal Reports, Volume 39* (Austin, TX: Ben C. Jones & Company, 1898), 320–322; *Southwestern Reporter, Volume 45: April 18 to June 20, 1898* (St. Paul, MN: West Publishing Company, 1898), 1013; *Rowell's American Newspaper Directory, Volume 32* (New York: Printer's Ink Publishing Company, 1900), 1017; Sowell, *Early Settlers and Indian Fighters*, 629; Tise, *Texas County Sheriffs*, 160, 321; Caldwell and DeLord, *Texas Lawmen*, 153–154; Spellman, *Capt. Brooks*, 101; Dan E. Kilgore, *A Ranger Legacy: 150 Years of Service to Texas* (Austin, TX: Madrona Press, 1973), 55–56; David Johnson, *The Cornett-Whitley Gang: Violence Unleashed in Texas* (Denton: University of North Texas Press, 2019), 194–195; Beatriz de la Garza, *A Law for the Lion: A Tale of Crime and Injustice in the Borderlands* (Austin: University of Texas, 2003), 121–125; Herbert C. Banks, *Daughters of the Republic of Texas Patriot Ancestry Album* (Paducah, KY: Turner Publishing Company, 1995), 277; FAG: Alfred Young Allee, Walter C. Bowen, William J. Bowen; "Cattle Trails from Wyoming Tails and Trails," accessed Jan. 26, 2020, http://www.wyomingtalesandtrails.com/cattletextrail2.html.
29. Rogers to Scurry, Feb. 22, 1899, AGC; Records of Scouts, Company E; *Houston Daily Post*, Dec. 23, 1898; Spellman, *Capt. Rogers*, 96; Ivey, *Ranger Ideal, Volume 2*, 342; Spellman, *Capt. Brooks*, 104–105.
30. Monthly Returns and Records of Scouts, Company E; *Fort Worth Daily Gazette*, Aug. 13, Sept. 1, 1886; *Galveston Daily News*, Aug. 8, 1886; *Austin Weekly Statesman*, Aug. 12, 1886; *El Paso Times*, Oct. 19, 1887; *Brownsville Daily Herald*, Oct. 29, 1900; *Alpine Avalanche*, Nov. 9, 1900; Sterling, *Trails and Trials*, 410; Spellman, *Capt. Rogers*, 92–94; Bob Alexander, *Whisky River Ranger: The Old West Life of*

Baz Outlaw (Denton: University of North Texas Press, 2016), 45–47; FAG: James R. Davenport. Historian Darren L. Ivey says William L. Wright's opponent in Cotulla was James R. Devenport, but his gravestone clearly says Davenport. See Darren L. Ivey, *The Ranger Ideal, Volume 3: Texas Rangers in the Hall of Fame, 1898–1987* (Denton: University of North Texas Press, 2021), 7–8.

31. Rogers to Scurry, July 24, Aug. 24, 1900, William L. Wright to Scurry, Oct. 25 [quotes], 1900, AGC; Records of Scouts, Company E; Historical Notes, Wright Papers; Transcript of J. Guy Smith article in *Isonomy*, dated only October 1900, in TRHFM: William L. Wright; *Alpine Avalanche*, Nov. 9, 1900; *Brownsville Daily Herald*, Oct. 29, 30, 1900; *Corsicana Democrat and Truth*, Apr. 9, 1925; *FCJ*, Apr. 10, 1925; *San Patricio County News*, Apr. 30, 1925; Scurry, *Report of Texas Adjutant General, 1899–1900*, 23–24; Sterling, *Trails and Trials*, 410–411; Spellman, *Capt. Rogers*, 109–110; Cox, *Time of the Rangers*, 22; Darren L. Ivey, *The Texas Rangers: A Registry and History* (West Jefferson, NC: McFarland & Company, 2010), 222; FAG: James R. Davenport, Joseph Warner Petty.
32. William L. Wright to Scurry, Oct. 25, 1900, AGC [first and second quotes]; Records of Scouts, Company E; *Alpine Avalanche*, Nov. 9, 1900; Historical Notes, Wright Papers; Transcript of Smith article in *Isonomy*, TRHFM: William L. Wright; *Brownsville Daily Herald*, Oct. 29, 30 [last quote], 1900; *Corsicana Democrat and Truth*, Apr. 9, 1925 [third, fourth, and fifth quotes]; *San Patricio County News*, Apr. 30, 1925; *N. W. Ayer & Son's American Newspaper Annual* (Philadelphia, PA: N. W. Ayer & Son, 1902), 840, 1293; *Pettingill's Newspaper Directory and Gazetteer* (New York: Pettingill & Co., 1903), 587; *N. W. Ayer & Son's American Newspaper Annual* (Philadelphia, PA: N. W. Ayer & Son, 1906), 863; *Rowell's American Newspaper Directory* (New York: Printer's Ink Newspaper Company, 1907), 1434; *N. W. Ayer & Son's American Newspaper Annual* (Philadelphia, PA: N. W. Ayer & Son, 1908), 872); F. B. Baillo, *A History of the Texas Press Association* (Dallas, TX: Southwestern Printing Company, 1916), 220.
33. Rogers to Scurry, Nov. 23, 1900, AGC; Monthly Returns and Records of Scouts, Company E; Historical Notes, Wright Papers; Sterling, *Trails and Trials*, 409–410; *Alpine Avalanche*, Dec. 21, 1900; Spellman, *Capt. Rogers*, 110; Tise, *Texas County Sheriffs*, 17; FAG: Abner Mathis Avant; "Joseph Eli Newman," accessed

Jan. 26, 2020, https://www.wikitree.com/wiki/ Newman-6224. For examples of newspaper accounts of Wright's gunfight with James R. Davenport, see the *DMN*, Oct. 26, 1900, *Fort Worth Morning Register*, Oct. 26, 1900, and *Brownsville Daily Herald*, Oct. 29 and 30, 1900. Thirty years later, Mabel B. "Tiny" Love married William L. Wright's son, Emanuel A. "Dogie" Wright, who became a lawman like his father. Allegedly her new mother-in-law, Mary Ann "Mollie" Brown Wright, told her, "Don't worry when they're out and you don't hear from them. Just remember that bad news travels fast." See *San Antonio Express-News*, June 2, 1984.

34. Monthly Returns, Company E; *Laredo Weekly Times*, Feb. 5, 1911 [quotes]; *DMN*, Jan. 15, Feb. 27, 1901; *Fort Worth Morning Register*, Feb. 27, Mar. 9, 1901; *El Paso Herald-Post*, Mar. 9, 14, 1901; *Houston Post*, May 10, 1901; Webb, *Texas Rangers*, 461; Mike Casey, "Joe Choynski: One Last Breath of Fire," accessed Jan. 26, 2020, http://www.boxing.com/joe_choynski_one_last_breath_of_fire.html.
35. Thomas H. Spooner to Sayers, Feb. 19, 1901, Rogers to Scurry, March 4, 1901, AGC; Records of Scouts, Company E; "Brief Biennial Report of Co. C;" *Cuero Daily Record*, Mar. 2, 1900; Houston Daily Post, Mar. 5, 1900; *La Grange Journal*, Mar. 8, 1900; *Albany News*, Mar. 23, 1900; Sterling, *Trails and Trials*, 411; Tise, *Texas County Sheriffs*, 27, 209; Candice DuCoin, *Lawmen on the Texas Frontier* (Round Rock, TX: Riata Books, 2007), 158–181; Ivey, *Ranger Ideal, Volume 3*, 9; FAG: Judge Thomas Harrison Spooner, Isaac Webster "Ike" Stevens.
36. J. W. Baker to Sayers, Apr. 16 [first quote], 29, 1901, William M. Hanson to Scurry, Apr. 17, 1901 [second quote], Rogers to Scurry, Apr. 24, May 2, 7, 1901, William L. Wright to Scurry, May 25, 1901 [third quote], AGC; Monthly Returns and Records of Scouts, Company E; "Brief Biennial Report of Co. C;" William L. Wright to Ann E. T. Wright, May 17, 1901, Wright Family Papers, TRHC.
37. "Brief Biennial Report of Co. C;" Sterling, *Trails and Trials*, 498–516; Spellman, *Capt. Rogers*, 114–116; Utley, *Lone Star Justice*, 274–275; Cox, *Time of the Rangers*, 25–26; Tise, *Texas County Sheriffs*, 210, 296; Michael Ariens, *Lone Star Law: A Legal History of Texas* (Lubbock: Texas Tech Press, 2011), 66–67; FAG: Richard Martin "R. M." Glover Jr., Henry John Schnabel; Cynthia E. Orozco, "Cortez Lira, Gregorio," *HOT*.
38. Emanuel A. Wright to Mrs. Joe Shriber, Oct. 17, 1966, Wright Papers; Wright, "Memoir," 3–4, 59; Records of Scouts, Company E; *Corsicana*

Democrat and Truth, Apr. 9, 1925; *San Patricio County News*, Apr. 30, 1925; *FCJ*, Apr. 10, 1925, July 9, 1926, Jan. 14, 1927; *McAllen Monitor*, Mar. 8, 1942; *Harlingen Valley Morning Star*, Mar. 8, 1942; *Corpus Christi Caller-Times*, Dec. 16, 1947; William B. Wright, *Career Hunting: Texas Ranger vs. Standard Oiler* (El Cajon, CA: Privately printed, 1983), 4; Sterling, *Trails and Trials*, 507; Spellman, *Capt. Rogers*, 114; Tise, *Texas County Sheriffs*, 17, 210, 270, 296; Maude T. Gilliland, *Horsebackers of the Brush Country: A Story of the Texas Rangers and Mexican Liquor Smugglers* (Brownsville, TX: Springman-King Company, 1968), 115–116; Arnoldo de León, "Ximenes, Manuel Jesus," *HOT*; FAG: Richard Martin "R. M." Glover Jr.; "Our Family History." The best discussion of making a folk hero of Gregorio Cortez Lira remains Américo Paredes, *With His Pistol in His Hand: A Border Ballad and Its Hero* (Austin: University of Texas Press, 1958).

39. Records of Scouts, Company C, RFR; "Brief Biennial Report of Co. C;" AGSR: A. Y. Baker, Alonzo W. Livingston; TRHFM: A. Y. Baker; Utley, *Lone Star Justice*, 274–276; Tise, *Texas County Sheriffs*, 296.
40. Rogers to Scurry, Nov. 14, 20, Dec. 10, 1901, AGC; Monthly Returns and Records of Scouts, Company C [quotes]; Twelfth Census, 1900, Population, Bandera County; *Austin Daily Statesman*, July 31, 1901; *El Paso Herald*, Aug. 3, 1901; *DMN*, Aug. 3, 1901; *Galveston Daily News*, Aug. 3, 1901, *Shiner Gazette*, Aug. 7, 1901; *Houston Daily Post*, Sept. 12, 19, 1901; *SAE*, Sept. 18, 1901; Tise, *Texas County Sheriffs*, 27; Marvin Hunter, *Pioneer History of Bandera County* (Bandera, TX: Privately printed, 1922), 279.
41. William L. Wright to Scurry, Dec. 30, 1901, Jan. 1, 8, 14, 27, Mar. 11, 1902, W. M. Burwell to Scurry, Jan. 29, 1902, Rogers to Scurry, Mar. 7, 1902, AGC.
42. "Brief Biennial Report of Co. C;" William W. Taylor to Scurry, Feb. 8, 1902, Rogers to Scurry, Feb. 17, Mar. 20, 1902, AGC; *Palo Pinto County Star*, Apr. 25, 1902; *FCJ*, Apr. 15, 1938; *Corsicana Daily Sun*, Apr. 22, 1938; *Kerrville Mountain Sun*, Apr. 28, 1938; Tise, *Texas County Sheriffs*, 307; FAG: William P. "Buck" Taylor; William W. Taylor.
43. Records of Scouts, Company C; *FCJ*, Apr. 15, 1938; *Kerrville Mountain Sun*, Apr. 28, 1938; *Corsicana Daily Sun*, Apr. 22, 1938; *Palo Pinto County Star*, Apr. 25, 1902; Thomas L. Miller, *The Public Lands of Texas*, 1519–1970 (Norman: University of Oklahoma Press, 1972),

200–201; FAG: William John Lee Fairchild, Mattie Elizabeth Melton Fairchild.

44. Mary Ann "Mollie" Brown Wright to Ann E. T. Wright, Dec. 8, 1901, Rogers to Scurry, Apr. 16, 1902, Emanuel A. Wright to Shriber, Oct. 17, 1966, Wright Papers; Rogers to Scurry, Apr. 29, 1902, AGC; Republic of Texas Claims: Elizabeth Tumlinson (#N/A), TSLA; *SAE*, Oct. 4, 1906. The Wrights' fourth child was a son, Emanuel A. "Dogie" Wright, who joined two brothers, Charles H. "Pat" Wright and Maurice H. "Jack" Wright, born in 1894 and 1895 respectively, and a sister, Zora Belle Wright, born in 1898.
45. William L. Wright to Sieker, Mar. 24, 1902 [quotes], A. Mathis Avant to Scurry, Apr. 9, 1902 [quotes], John A. Brooks to Scurry, Apr. 8, 1902, Rogers to Scurry, Mar. 31, 1902 [last quote], AGC; AGSR: Milam H. Wright, Oscar Latta, Alex Ormand, T. C. Taylor.
46. Rogers to Scurry, Apr. 29 [first quote], May 10, July 4, 11, Aug. 17, 25 [fourth quote], 29, 1902, John N. Garner to Scurry, Aug. 12, 1902 [second and third quotes], W. A. Old to Jim Moore, Aug. 21, 1902, AGC; Cox, *Time of the Rangers*, 26–27. Interestingly, John N. Garner wrote to a constituent in February 1899 that he was not only in favor of the "Ranger Force," he in fact wanted to increase it in size. This was two years before the official creation of the Ranger Force, about which he must have later changed his mind. See John N. Garner to J.C.B. Harkness, Feb. 9, 1899, FBC. Paredes stresses Garner's support for the abolition of the Rangers in *With His Pistol in His Hand*, 31, 80. This is repeated several times by Julian Samora, Joe Bernal, and Albert Peña in *Gunpowder Justice: A Reassessment of the Texas Rangers* (Notre Dame: University of Notre Dame Press, 1979), 13, 63.
47. Records of Scouts, Company C; Rogers to Seiker, Aug. 13, 1901, Rogers to Scurry, May 19, 27, June 2, 19, Aug. 11, 1902, William Duke to Scurry, July 14, 1902 [quotes], F. C. Weinert to Scurry, Aug. 12, 1902 [quotes], William L. Wright to Scurry, Aug. 10, 1902 [quotes], AGC.
48. AGSR: W. L. Wright; *FCJ*, Jan. 2, 1925.

Notes for Chapter 3

1. Emanuel A. Wright, "Memoir" (Typescript, n.d., E. A. "Dogie" Wright Papers, DBCAH), 3; Mary Ann "Mollie" Brown Wright to Ann E. T. Wright, Dec. 8, 1901, Wright Papers; *DMN*, June 18, 1901; *Houston Daily Post*, July 11, 1901; *SAE*, Sept. 4, 1902; *Corpus Christi Caller*,

Sept. 12, 1902; Sammy Tise, *Texas County Sheriffs* (Albuquerque: Oakwood Press, 1989), 546.

2. Emanuel A. Wright to Mrs. Joe Shriber, Oct. 17, 1966, Emanuel A. Wright to Mrs. Jack W. Rowland, July 2, 1978, Obituary for William L. Wright, n.d., in Scrapbook, Wright Papers; John H. Rogers to Thomas R. Scurry, Dec. 3, 1900, AGC; *FCJ*, Jan. 2, 1925; *SAE*, Oct. 4, 1906, Mar. 8, 1942 [quote]; *Corpus Christi Caller-Times*, Mar. 8, 1942; Robert M. Utley, *Lone Star Justice: The First Century of the Texas Rangers* (New York: Oxford University Press, 2002), 6; Thad Sitton, *The Texas Sheriff: Lord of the County Line* (Norman: University of Oklahoma Press, 2000), 82–85; FAG: Elizabeth Newman Tumlinson; "Our Family History: The Genealogy of Robert and Christina Barritt," accessed Jan. 20, 2020, http://tree.barrittfamily.net/getperson.php?personID=I473&tree=dyal_speckels.
3. Wright, "Memoir," 57–58, 63–64, 74, 97, 101; Sitton, *Texas Sheriff*, 79; *The Sons of the Republic of Texas* (Nashville, TN: Turner Publishing Company, 2001), 176; FAG: King George Wiley, Stephen Wiley, Samuel Wiley. The jail still stands in Floresville, and it is currently being renovated for use as a museum.
4. Wright, "Memoir," 60–61, 80, 87, 89; Interview with Zora Belle Wright Fore, Dec. 7, 1973, South Texas Oral History & Folklore Collection, South Texas Archives, James C. Jernigan Library, Texas A&M University at Kingsville; AGSR: Pat Craighead, George A. Monkhouse, Milam H. Wright; U.S. Bureau of the Census, Thirteenth Census, 1910, Population, Wilson County, TX (Record Group 29, National Archives, Washington, DC); J. R. Curl, *Biennial Report of the Secretary of State of the State of Texas, 1904* (Austin, TX: Gammel-Statesman Publishing Company, 1904), 199; W. R. Davie, *Supplemental Biennial Report of the Secretary of State, 1908* (Austin, TX: Von Boeckmann-Jones Company, 1908), 211; *Victoria Fact*, Sept. 23, 1904; *SAE*, Oct. 27, 1906, Sept. 12, 1910, Oct. 28, 1915; *Houston Post*, Sept. 12, 1910; *FCJ*, Oct. 29, 1915, Apr. 10, 1936; "January Bank Elections," *Texas Bankers Record*, 4 (Sept. 1914), 61; "New Corporations," *Industrial Development and Manufacturers Record*, 51 (Feb. 7, 1907), 118; Sitton, *Texas Sheriff*, 49 [quote]; Tise, *Texas County Sheriffs*, 546; Maude T. Gilliland, *Horsebackers of the Brush Country: A Story of the Texas Rangers and Mexican Liquor Smugglers* (Brownsville, TX: Springman-King Company, 1968), 79; Charles H. Harris III, Frances E. Harris, and Louis R. Sadler, *Texas Ranger Biographies: Those Who Served 1910–1921* (Albuquerque:

University of New Mexico Press, 2009), 74, 417; FAG: Alfred B. Carnes, William Barnett "Will" Clements, James Patterson Nelson "Pat" Craighead, George A. Monkhouse, Thad J. Rees, Andres Farias Trevino; Gene Maeckel, "Thad J. Rees: Farmer, Rancher Freighter, Trail Driver and Lawman," accessed Jan. 28, 2020, http://wilsoncountyhistory.org/Moments/Thad%20J. %20Rees.pdf. Thad J. Rees lived in Marcelina, midway between Floresville and Stockdale.

5. Wright, "Memoir," 60 [first quote], 63–64; *FCJ*, Jan. 25, 1918 [second quote]; Sitton, *Texas Sheriff*, 79, 84–85; Darren L. Ivey, *The Ranger Ideal, Volume 3: Texas Rangers in the Hall of Fame, 1898–1987* (Denton: University of North Texas Press, 2021), 12.
6. Wright, "Memoir," 82–83.
7. Cumulative information taken from the federal census and the Texas Department of Criminal Justice, Convict Record Ledgers, 1849–1954, TSLA.
8. *Hallettsville Herald*, Apr. 30, June 18, Nov. 12, 19, Dec. 3, 10, 1903; *Waxahachie Daily Light*, Dec. 5, 1903, *Houston Post*, Dec. 5, 1903; *Corsicana Democrat and Truth*, Apr. 9, 1925; *FCJ*, Apr. 10, 1925, *San Patricio County News*, Apr. 30, 1925; Tise, *Texas County Sheriffs*, 325; Clifton R. Caldwell and Ron DeLord, *Eternity at the End of a Rope: Executions, Lynchings, and Vigilante Justice in Texas, 1819–1923* (Santa Fe: Sunstone Press, 2016), 450–451; West C. Gilbreath, *Death on the Gallows: The Encyclopedia of Legal Hangings in Texas* (Fort Worth, TX: Wild Horse Press, 2017), 232.
9. *Houston Post*, May 31, 1905; *Galveston Daily News*, May 31, June 1, 1905; *Brenham Daily Banner*, June 8, 1905; *Palestine Daily Herald*, June 22, 1905; John G. Tod, *Biennial Report of the Secretary of State of the State of Texas, 1902* (Austin, TX: Von Boeckmann-Jones, 1902), 161; Ogden K. Shannon, *Biennial Report of the Secretary of State of the State of Texas, 1906* (Austin, TX: Von Boeckmann-Jones, 1907), 238; Tise, *Texas County Sheriffs*, 43; FAG: Perry A. Sammons, Alfred B. Carnes; Zelime Vance Gillespie, "Tobin, John Wallace," *HOT.*
10. *Beaumont Enterprise*, Oct. 4, 5, 19, 1905; *DMN*, Oct. 19, 1905; *SAE*, Oct. 19, 1905; William W. Sterling, *Trails and Trials of a Texas Ranger* (Privately printed, 1959), 340–347; Gilbreath, *Death on the Gallows*, 54, 95–96; Harold J. Weiss Jr., *Yours to Command: The Life and Legend of Texas Ranger Captain Bill McDonald* (Denton: University of North Texas Press, 2009), 229–242; Bruce McCandless III, "Gibson, Henry [Monk]," *HOT.*

11. *SAE*, Apr. 30, May 11, 15, 1906; Texas Convict Record Ledgers: Elojio Estrada (#26138), Melchior Ximenes (#26559, #32673).
12. Wright, "Memoir," 64–65; *San Antonio Gazette*, July 4, 1908; *SAE*, July 4, 1908; *Houston Post*, June 12, 1909; Rudolph Kleberg, comp., *The Texas Criminal Reports: Cases Argued and Adjudged in the Court of Criminal Appeals of the State of Texas, Volume 55* (Chicago, IL: T. H. Flood & Company, 1909), 222–227.
13. Wright, "Memoir," 65; *SAE*, June 11, 12, 1909; *Houston Post*, June 12, 1909; *Galveston Daily News*, June 13, 1909.
14. Wright, "Memoir," 66–67; Interview with Zora Belle Wright Fore; *DMN*, June 12, 1909; *Houston Post*, June 12, 1909; *SAE*, June 12, 1909; *Abilene Daily Reporter*, June 13, 1909; *Galveston Daily News*, June 13, 1909; *FCJ*, June 18, 1909; *McAllen Monitor*, Mar. 8, 1942; *Harlingen Valley Morning Star*, Mar. 8, 1942; Gilbreath, *Death on the Gallows*, 371–372; Tise, *Texas County Sheriffs*, 157, 296; Richard B. McCaslin, *Sutherland Springs, Texas; Saratoga on the Cibolo* (University of North Texas Press, 2017), 138; Ivey, *Ranger Ideal, Volume 3*, 15, 17; "John Edgar Trainer," accessed Jan. 29, 1900, http://losttexasroads.com/people/64-trainer-john-edgar. According to a newspaper reporter, Albina Olenick was happily married by the time her attacker was executed. See *FCJ*, June 18, 1909.
15. Texas Convict Record Ledgers: Joseph Clark (#23635), Tomas Reyes (#26173), Clemente Garcia (#26169); *SAE*, Oct. 27, Dec. 12, 1906; *Schulenburg Sticker*, Dec. 20, 1906; Shannon, *Biennial Report of the Secretary of State of the State of Texas, 1906*, 238.
16. *SAE*, Feb. 8, 1911; *Laredo Weekly Times*, Feb. 5, 12, 1911; *Galveston Daily News*, Feb. 7, 1911; *Austin Daily Statesman*, Feb. 22, 1941 [quote]; AGSR: S. V. Edwards, Robert Rumsey; W. B. Townsend, *Supplemental Biennial Report of the Secretary of State, 1910* (Austin, TX: Austin Printing Company, 1911), 188; Sterling, *Trails and Trials*, 88–91; Tise, *Texas County Sheriffs*, 321; FAG: Samuel V. "Pete" Edwards Jr.
17. AGSR: M.G. Delling, Louis E. Flach, Tom M. Ross, Milam H. Wright; TRHFM: M. G. "Blaze" Delling; *SAE*, Sept. 27, 1905; *DMN*, Sept. 28, 1905; Tise, *Texas County Sheriffs*, 321; FAG: Manoah George "Blaze" Delling, William T. Hill, Charles F. Stevens.
18. *SAE*, Sept. 27, 1905; *DMN*, Sept. 28, 1905; *Fort Worth Star*, Oct. 8, 1905; *Austin Daily Statesman*, Oct. 8, 1905; *Waco News-Tribune*, Nov. 27, 1927.

19. *Fort Worth Star*, Oct. 8, 1905; *Austin Daily Statesman*, Oct. 8, 1905, Feb. 7, 1909; *Waco News-Tribune*, Nov. 27, 1927.
20. *Investigation of Mexican Affairs*, Senate Document 285, Volume 1, 66th Congress, 2nd Session, p. 1223 (Serial Set 7,665); *SAE*, June 16, 18, 20, 30, July 20, Sept. 13, 1911 [quote], Jan. 28, 1914; *Galveston Daily News*, June 18, 1911; *Laredo Weekly Times*, June 25, 1911; Ivey, *Ranger Ideal, Volume 3*, 22–23; Tise, *Texas County Sheriffs*, 526; Charles H. Harris III and Louis R. Sadler, "The 1911 Reyes Conspiracy: The Texas Side," *Southwestern Historical Quarterly* 83 (Apr. 1980): 331–332, 335.
21. *Waco News-Tribune*, Nov. 27, 1927; *Investigation of Mexican Affairs*, 1223; Albert B. Paine, *Captain Bill McDonald, Texas Ranger: A Story of Frontier Reform* (New York: J. J. Little & Ives Company, 1909), 365.
22. Texas Convict Record Ledgers: Allie Taylor (#24915); *Austin Daily Statesman*, Dec. 2, 1907; *SAE*, Dec. 1, 8, 1907 [quotes]; *Liberty Vindicator*, Dec. 6, 1907; Ivey, *Ranger Ideal, Volume 3*, 14; FAG: Bettie Taylor, Cora Taylor, Stella Taylor Gibson. Stella died in 1910, just three years after the murders.
23. *San Antonio Gazette*, Sept. 5, Dec. 19, 21, 1908 ; *SAE*, Sept. 14, Dec. 26, 1908; *Houston Post*, Sept. 3, 1908. Historian Darren L. Ivey wrote that "sepsis from a urinary infection" killed J. D. Becton. See *Ranger Ideal, Volume 3*, 15–16.
24. *SAE*, Sept. 12, 1910, May 19, 1911; *Houston Post*, Sept. 12, 1910; Tise, *Texas County Sheriffs*, 44; FAG: Alfonso Newton Jr.
25. *Houston Post*, Jan. 26, Apr. 18, 25, 1907; *SAE*, Nov. 30, 1906, Dec. 20, 1906, Jan. 26, Apr. 18, 25, May 8, 1907; Texas Department of Criminal Justice, Conduct Registers, 1875–1945: Huntsville, TSLA; Texas Convict Record Ledgers, Oscar Smith (#27601) and John Taylor (#27602).
26. *SAE*, Mar. 22, June 2, 1906; *San Antonio Gazette*, Mar. 23, 1906; *Houston Post*, Mar. 23, 1906; Stanley D. Casto, "Texas Sportsmen and the Conservation of Bird Life, 1890–1915,"*East Texas Historical Journal* 44 (March 2006), 14–15.
27. *SAE*, June 30, July 1, 1907; *Austin Daily Statesman*, July 2, 1907; *Houston Post*, July 2, 1907; *Abilene Daily Reporter*, July 4, 1907; *Corpus Christi Caller-Times*, July 5, 1907; Ivey, *Ranger Ideal, Volume 3*, 13–14; Minnie B. Cameron, "Graytown, Texas," *HOT*.
28. AGSR: Oscar Latta; *Official Register of the United States, 1907*, 2 vols. (Washington: Government Printing Office, 1907), 2: 493, 633; *SAE*, Mar. 14, 16, 17, May 21, 23, 1908, Dec. 1, 1915; *Houston Post*, Mar. 16, 1908;

San Antonio Gazette, Feb. 28, Dec. 5, 1908; Tise, *Texas County Sheriffs*, 43, 258, 296, 406; McCaslin, *Sutherland Springs*, 175, 181; Ivey, *Ranger Ideal, Volume 3*, 14–16; David Johnson, *The Cornett-Whitley Gang: Violence Unleashed in Texas* (Denton: University of North Texas Press, 2019), 246; FAG: Henry A. Linne; "Henry Scott Sisk," accessed Jan. 29, 2020, https://www.geni.com/people/Henry-Sisk/6000000028147293357; "La Vernia Postmasters," accessed Jan. 29, 2020, http://losttexasroads.com/ people/46-la-vernia-postmasters.

29. *SAE*, Dec. 1, 1908, July 14, 1909; *Houston Post*, July 14, 1909; *Brooklyn* [NY] *Daily Eagle*, Sept. 22, 1909; Thomas Stringfield, *Captured by the Apaches* (Hamilton, TX: Herald Print, 1911); Mike Cox, "Two Braids," accessed Jan. 29, 2020, http://www.texasescapes.com/MikeCoxTexasTales/141TwoBraids.htm; Alfredo E. Cardenas, "Indian Raid Prompts Request for Soldiers," accessed Jan. 29, 2020, http://www.soydeduval.com/2015/04/indian-raid-prompts-request-for-soldiers/; "Thomas Wesley Stringfield," accessed Jan. 29, 2020, http://heathcock.org/genealogy/ps06/ps06_188.html.
30. AGSR: Desiderio Perez, James C. White; Vertical Files: Tom M. Ross; *Houston Post*, Jan. 18, 1907; *SAE*, Jan. 6, Feb. 1 [second quote], April 9 [third quote], 1907; *Fort Worth Star*, Jan. 19, 29, 1907; *DMN*, Jan. 31, 1907; Tise, *Texas County Sheriffs*, 157; Harris, Harris, and Sadler, *Texas Ranger Biographies*, 202, 304–305, 327–328; Charles H. Harris III and Louis R. Sadler, *The Texas Rangers in the Mexican Revolution: The Bloodiest Decade, 1910–1920* (Norman: University of Oklahoma Press, 2004), 27 [first quote]; Barbara M. Westbrook, "Rossville Brothers Served as Texas Rangers," accessed Jan. 29, 2020, http://atascosa county.blogspot.com/2008/04/rossville-brothers-served-as-texas.html.
31. Wright, "Memoir," 135; Frank Johnson to J. O. Newton, Aug. 8, 1910, AGC; AGSR: Quirl B. Carnes; TRHFM: Quirl B. Carnes; *Alice Echo*, Aug. 4, 1910; *FCJ*, Nov. 25, 2004; *San Antonio Light*, Aug. 1, 2, 1910; Harris and Sadler, *Bloodiest Decade*, 41–42; Harris, Harris, and Sadler, *Texas Ranger Biographies*, 54, 74, 399; Bob Alexander, *Riding Lucifer's Line: Ranger Deaths Along the Texas-Mexico Border* (Denton: University of North Texas Press, 2013), 221–225; Maude T. Gilliland, *Wilson County Texas Rangers, 1837 to 1977* (Privately printed, 1977), 41–47; Ivey, *Ranger Ideal*, *Volume 3*, 18–20.
32. Wright, "Memoir," 134–135; AGSR: Herff A. Carnes, Quirl B. Carnes, Charles A. Craighead, Pat Craighead, J. E. Gilliland, David Cornelius Webb, Milam H. Wright; TRHFM: Herff A. Carnes, J. P. N Craighead;

Alice Echo, Aug. 4, 1910; *SAE*, Aug. 4, 1910; *San Antonio Light*, Aug. 1, 2, 1910; *Brownsville Daily Herald*, Aug. 2, 5, 1910; *El Paso Herald*, Aug. 24, 1911; *FCJ*, Dec. 9, 1932, Nov. 25, 2004; Alexander, *Riding Lucifer's Line*, 225–226; Harris and Sadler, *Bloodiest Decade*, 42–43; Harris, Harris, and Sadler, *Texas Ranger Biographies*, 53–54, 74, 400; Charles H. Harris III and Louis R. Sadler, *The Texas Rangers in Transition: From Gunfighters to Criminal Investigators, 1921–1935* (Norman: University of Oklahoma Press, 2019), 415; Gilliland, *Wilson County Rangers*, 47, 48, 121–122; Gilliland, *Horsebackers*, 79–81; FAG: Alfred B. Carnes, Herff A. Carnes, Quirl B. Carnes, Grenade Donaldson Gilliland, John Eckford Gilliland, David Cornelius "Jack" Webb, David Franklin Webb, Grover Cleveland Webb, and Lake Thomas Webb; "West, Milton Horace," *HOT*.

33. AGSR: Oscar J. Rountree; *SAE*, Aug. 23, 24, 1910, May 23, 1911; *DMN*, Aug. 19, 1910; *Houston Post*, Dec. 14, 1911; *Corpus Christi Caller-Times*, Dec. 14, 15, 1911; *San Antonio Light*, Dec. 7, 1911; Harris, Harris, and Sadler, *Texas Ranger Biographies*, 329; Ivey, *Ranger Ideal, Volume 3*, 20; FAG: Oscar J. Rountree.
34. *SAE*, May 23, 24, 25, Dec. 8, 14, 1911; *Yoakum Weekly Times*, May 27, 1911; *San Antonio Light*, Dec. 7, 1911; *Galveston Daily News*, Dec. 14, 1911; *Houston Post*, Dec. 14, 1911; *Austin Daily Statesman*, Dec. 14, 1911; FAG: Dennis Bangs Chapin; Anne W. Hooker, "Bee, Carlos," *HOT*; Hubert J. Miller, "Edinburg, TX," *HOT*.
35. Wright, "Memoir," 135, 145–146 [third quote]; Genealogy Notes, Emanuel A. Wright to Pete Tumlinson, Dec. 9, 1953 [second quote], Emanuel A. Wright to C. L. Sonnichsen, Oct. 31, 1962, Charlie Brown to Emanuel A. Wright, Sept. 17, 1971, Wright Papers; AGSR: C. B. Brown; Thirteenth Census, 1910, Wilson County, TX; William B. Wright, *Career Hunting: Texas Ranger vs. Standard Oiler* (El Cajon, CA: Privately printed, 1983), 2, 4 [first quote], 13 [second quote]; *SAE*, July 18, 1916; *FCJ*, July 14, 21, 28, 1916, Dec. 15, 1966; Gilliland, *Wilson County Rangers*, 33–34; FAG: Charles Buckner Brown, Sanford Brown. Information concerning the son that the Wrights lost in infancy is hard to find, but the *Floresville Chronicle Journal* in an obituary of William L. Wright on March 13, 1942, mentioned that he died on Dec. 27, 1907. A genealogy website says his name was Clifford, and he died in 1903. See *FCJ*, Sept. 16, 1960, Dec. 15, 1966, "Mary Ann Brown," accessed Mar. 18, 2020, https://ancestors.familysearch.org/en/26WM-LCD/mary-ann-brown-1871-1958.

36. Emanuel A. Wright to Shriber, Oct. 17, 1966, Wright Papers; Wright, "Memoir," 83; *Austin American*, Jan. 29, 1909; *SAE*, Dec. 16, 1909, Apr. 28, 1910; *Houston Post*, Mar. 16, 1909. William L. Wright's engraved Colt .45 revolver is on display in the Texas Ranger Hall of Fame and Museum in Waco, Texas. A note in the Wright Family Papers at the Texas Rangers Heritage Center in Fredericksburg, says the engraving was done by Cuno Helfricht, the master engraver for the Colt factory during this period. A certification letter from the Colt Manufacturing Company confirms that the pistol was manufactured in January 1910 and was engraved at the factory. See Kathleen J. Hoyt "To Whom It May Concern," Nov. 6, 2006, Wright Family Papers, TRHC.

Notes for Chapter 4

1. Emanuel A. Wright, "Memoir" (Typescript, n.d., E. A. "Dogie" Wright Papers, DBCAH), 81–82, 84–86, 90, 119; AGSR: Deonicio Acosta; US Bureau of the Census, Twelfth Census, 1900, Population, Wilson County, TX, and Thirteenth Census, 1910, Population, Wilson and Karnes County, TX; Allison Mayfield, *Biennial Report of the Secretary of State of the State of Texas, 1896* (Austin, TX: Ben C. Jones & Company, 1897), 229; D. H. Hardy, *Biennial Report of the Secretary of State of the State of Texas, 1900* (Austin, TX: Von Boeckmann, Schutze, and Company, 1900), 255; W. R. Davie, *Supplemental Biennial Report of the Secretary of State, 1908* (Austin, TX: Von Boeckmann-Jones Company, 1908), 211; F. C. Weinert, *Biennial Report of the Secretary of State of the State of Texas, 1914* (Austin, TX: Von Boeckmann-Jones Company, 1914), 343; *Galveston Daily News*, Aug. 1, 1911; *SAE*, Mar. 28, 1914, Aug. 27, 1915; *FCJ*, Feb. 5, Sept. 3, 17, 1915, Feb. 14, 1916; Charles H. Harris III, Francis E. Harris, and Louis R. Sadler, *Texas Ranger Biographies: Those Who Served 1910–1921* (Albuquerque: University of New Mexico Press, 2009), 1–2; Maude T. Gilliland, *Horsebackers of the Brush Country: A Story of the Texas Rangers and Mexican Liquor Smugglers* (Brownsville: Springman-King Company, 1968), 83, 126; FAG: Dionicio J. Acosta, Paul Casares, Adolfo G. Flores, Alex Klaus. Pablo "Paul" Casares went with William L. Wright on at least one hunting trip near Cotulla. See *FCJ*, Dec. 8, 1916.
2. Wright, "Memoir," 84–85, 94–96, 101, 135, 152, 191; William L. Wright to James A. Harley, Dec. 26, 1917, AGC; AGSR: Thomas Connolly, John J. Edds, R. W. Lorenz; TRHFM: John J. Edds; Texas

Comptroller, Confederate Pension Applications: Gertrude C. Edds, TSLA; Texas Legislature, "Proceedings of the Joint Committee of the Senate and the House in the Investigation of the Texas State Ranger Force," 8 vols. (Typescript, n.d. [1919], DBCAH), 8: 1,424, 1,518; U.S. Department of War, Compiled Service Records of Confederate Soldiers Who Served in Organizations from Texas (Record Group 109, National Archives, Washington, DC), Second Texas Cavalry: Jesse Edds; Weinert, *Biennial Report of the Texas Secretary of State, 1914*, p. 343; C. J. Bartlett, *Supplemental Biennial Report of the Secretary of State, 1916* (Austin, TX: A. C. Baldwin & Sons, 1917), 248; *SAE*, Jan. 9, 1911, Sept. 18, 1915 [quote], Jan. 20, 1918, Apr. 5, 1948; *FCJ*, Sept. 24, 1915, Oct. 5, 1917, Feb. 14, 1930, Aug. 19, 2004; Harris, Harris, and Sadler, *Texas Ranger Biographies*, 68, 100, 229; Darren L. Ivey, *The Ranger Ideal, Volume 3: Texas Rangers in the Hall of Fame, 1898–1987* (Denton: University of North Texas Press, 2021), 26, 30; Thad Sitton, *The Texas Sheriff: Lord of the County Line* (Norman: University of Oklahoma Press, 2000),79; Maude T. Gilliland, *Wilson County Texas Rangers, 1837 to 1977* (Privately printed, 1977), 126; FAG: Jess W. Edds, John Joseph Edds, Royal Wade Lorenz; Shirley Grammar, "Concrete Cemetery," accessed Feb. 5, 2020, http://www.cemeteries-of-tx.com/etx/guadalupe/cemetery/ concrete.htm.

3. Wright, "Memoir," 87–88; Sitton, *Texas Sheriff*, 79; FAG: Collie Dykes; U.S. Department of War, World War I Draft Registration Cards: Halford Pace (Record Group 163, National Archives, East Point, GA); U.S. Office of the Quartermaster General, WWI Transportation Service, Passenger Lists: Halford Pace (Record Group 92, National Archives, College Park, MD); U.S. Office of the Quartermaster General, Headstone Applications for Military Veterans, 1925–1963: Halford Pace (Record Group 92, National Archives, Washington, DC).
4. Wright, "Memoir," 97–99; Texas Department of Criminal Justice, Convict Record Ledgers, 1849–1954: David Gee (#3671), TSLA; *SAE*, Nov. 18, 19, 1910, Aug. 7, Dec. 27, 1911, Jan. 1, July 8, 1912; *Galveston Daily News*, Dec. 27, 1911 [quote]; *Houston Post*, Jan. 5, 1912; Sitton, *Texas Sheriff*, 79; Charles G. Downing, "Rodriguez, Jose Policarpo," *HOT*.
5. Wright, "Memoir," 99–101; *Corpus Christi Caller*, Oct. 13, 1915; *SAE*, Oct. 25, 28, 1915, Jan. 1, 1916; *Houston Post*, Oct. 27, 1915; *Austin American*, Oct. 27, 1915; *FCJ*, Oct. 29, 1915; Sammy Tise, *Texas County Sheriffs* (Albuquerque: Oakwood Press, 1989), 395.

6. Wright, "Memoir," 102; *SAE*, Jan. 10, 12, 1916; *FCJ*, Jan. 14, 21, 1916, May 18, 1917, Apr. 10, 1925. The Mexican who escaped with A. Emiliano Sopra has not been identified, but the African American was probably Felix Robinson, an eighteen-year-old farmer who had been sentenced on Jan. 1, 1916, to two years in the state penitentiary for burglary. Received at Huntsville on Jan. 23, 1916, he was discharged on Oct. 28, 1917. See Texas Convict Record Ledgers: Felix Robinson (#38787).
7. Wright, "Memoir," 59, 81; Interview with Zora Belle Wright Fore, Dec. 7, 1973, South Texas Oral History & Folklore Collection, South Texas Archives, James C. Jernigan Library, Texas A&M University at Kingsville; Texas Convict Record Ledgers: Enrique Mata (#39753); *FCJ*, Nov. 19, Dec. 3, 1915, Jan. 21, Nov. 24, 1916; *Laredo Weekly Times*, Dec. 5, 1915, Jan. 16, May 7, 21, 1916; [San Antonio] *La Prensa*, May 23, 25, 1916; Sitton, *Texas Sheriff*, 79; FAG: Susana Gaitan. Sheriff Wright's daughter, Zora Belle Wright Fore, recalled that the gaited horse's name was Mack.
8. Wright, "Memoir," 119; Rudolph Kleberg, comp., *The Texas Criminal Reports: Cases Argued and Adjudged in the Court of Criminal Appeals of the State of Texas, Volume 72* (Austin, TX: Von Boeckmann-Jones Company, 1915), 100–103; Texas Convict Record Ledger: Lazaro Arranda (#33399); *Galveston Daily News*, Aug. 1, 1911 [quotes]; *SAE*, July 30, Aug. 1, 1911; *Austin Daily Statesman*, Aug. 2, 1911; FAG: Joe Ludwig, Rudolph J. Woellert.
9. Texas Convict Record Ledger: Nemencio de la Zerda (#33358) [relationship to Wright's former deputy unknown], Bartolo Garcia (#37882), Antonio Castro (#41976); *Fort Worth Star-Telegram*, Mar. 25, 1910, *SAE*, Dec. 17, 1910, May 23, Oct. 16, 1911, Feb. 23, 1915, Apr. 13, 1916 [quote]; *FCJ*, Sept. 17, Oct. 1, 1915, Mar. 31, Apr. 7, 1916, Nov. 9, 16, 1917; *Victoria Daily Advocate*, Mar. 29, 1916; [San Antonio] *La Prensa*, Mar. 29, 1916; FAG: Alonso S. Coy. There is no record of Malecio Gilan being sent to the state prison system, but Antonio Escobeda, a twenty-three-year-old Mexican boiler maker, was sentenced to seven years for second-degree murder in January 1912 and sent from Wilson County to Huntsville the next month. He escaped in November 1914. See Texas Convict Record Ledger: Antonio Escobeda (#32672).
10. Wright, "Memoir," 90; Texas Convict Record Ledger: John Britton (#39758); *FCJ*, May 18, 26 [quote], 1917; *SAE*, June 9, 1916; FAG: Edna "Lena" *Mills* Tejada.

11. *SAE*, Jan. 10, 1913; *Houston Post*, Jan. 10, 1913; FAG: Theodor Erdmann, James Frank Henson, Henry Jasper Price. Erdmann is buried at Hobson in Karnes County, Texas; his wife, Emilie, lived until 1936 and is buried with him.
12. *SAE*, Oct. 17, Nov. 28, 1914; *Houston Post*, Oct. 21, 1914; *FCJ*, Feb. 5, 1915; Ivey, *Ranger Ideal, Volume 3*, 25–26; FAG: Norman D. Cone, Dave S. Coy, Chris Fred House, Lonnie Leon Parks, Lucibe Gertrude Passmore Parks, George Washington Parks, Phillip Hines Tom.
13. Texas Convict Record Ledgers: Herbert Dodd (#40265), Lewis Dodd (#40477); *Houston Post*, Oct. 28, 1915, July 22, 1916; *Austin Daily Statesman*, Oct. 31, 1915; *SAE*, Oct. 31, Nov. 1, 1915, Apr. 25, July 20 [quote], Oct. 26, 28, 1916; "Marble Falls Bank Robbed," *Texas Bankers Record* 5 (Nov. 1915), 45; Tise, *Texas County Sheriffs*, 43, 124, 250, 319, 364, 454, 494–495; FAG: Robert Hamilton "Robbie" Heinatz II, Hugh Miller Jr., Horace Faulkner Pirtle, Nathaniel Thomas Stubbs, James Cannon Wall.
14. Texas Convict Record Ledger: Felix Tudyk (#39,591); *Victoria Daily Advocate*, Nov. 20, 1915; FAG: Lucy Ciomperlik Szcech, Felix Joseph Tudyk.
15. Wright, "Memoir," 67–68; Notes (Handwritten [probably by Emanuel A. "Dogie" Wright], n.d.), Wright Papers. This event occurred in 1910 or earlier if Dogie Wright is riding a stick horse. There are a lot of Cales in the Thirteenth Census, 1910, Population, Wilson County, TX, but no Kales, and none fit the description given by Dogie. There is also no record of a Cale, or Kale, from Wilson County about that time in the Texas Convict Record Ledger.
16. Wright, "Memoir," 86–87; *FCJ*, Oct. 6, 13, 1916; *Houston Post*, Oct. 8, 1916; *SAE*, Nov. 20, 1916; *FSJ*, Nov. 24, 1916.
17. Wright, "Memoir," 91–94, 103; *Palestine Daily Herald*, Mar. 6, 1917; *SAE*, Mar. 7, 20, May 22, 28, June 8, 1917; *FCJ*, Mar. 23, May 18, 1917; *Shiner Gazette*, June 9, 1949; Harris, Harris, and Sadler, *Texas Ranger Biographies*, 400; FAG: Anton Bohuslav, Benjamin Watt Fly, William Thomas "Willie" Matlock Sr.; "West, Milton Horace," *HOT*.
18. Wright, "Memoir," 138, 139; Obituary for William L. Wright, n.d., in Scrapbook, Wright Papers; Rudolph Kleberg, comp., *The Texas Criminal Reports: Cases Argued and Adjudged in the Court of Criminal Appeals of the State of Texas, Volume 75* (Austin, TX: Von Boeckmann-Jones Company, 1916), 63–66; *Houston Post*, Feb. 17, 1912; *Galveston Daily News*, Feb. 17, 1912; *Bryan Daily Eagle and Pilot*,

Aug. 14, 1914; *SAE*, Aug, 15, 1914, Feb. 27, 1915; *Corpus Christi Caller-Times*, Mar. 8, 1942; Tise, *Texas County Sheriffs*, 118, 221, 296; West C. Gilbreath, *Death on the Gallows: The Encyclopedia of Legal Hangings in Texas* (Fort Worth, TX: Wild Horse Press, 2017), 3, 159, 160; Clifford R. Caldwell and Ron DeLord, *Eternity at the End of a Rope: Executions, Lynchings, and Vigilante Justice in Texas, 1819–1923* (Santa Fe: Sunstone Press, 2016), 521.

19. Wright, "Memoir," 139; Obituary for William L. Wright, n.d., in Scrapbook, Wright Papers; *Corpus Christi Caller-Times*, Mar. 8, 1942 [quote]; *Houston Post*, June 28, 1908; *SAE*, Aug. 1, 1908, Mar. 8, 1942; *Marshall News Messenger*, Mar. 8, 1942; *Pampa Daily News*, Mar. 8, 1942; *Abilene Reporter-News*, Mar. 8, 1942; Gilbreath, *Death on the Gallows*, 391–394. For the obituary for William L. Wright written by Robert B. "Bob" McCracken, see *Corpus Christi Caller Times*, Mar. 8, 1942.
20. Texas Legislature, "Proceedings," 8: 1,522–1,523; *SAE*, Aug. 19, 1912, May 19, 1915; *FCJ*, Feb. 26, 1915.
21. Wright, "Memoir," 137; *Galveston Daily News*, Nov. 21, 1911; *SAE*, Nov. 20, 21, 22, 1911, Jan. 6, 1912; Ivey, *Ranger Ideal, Volume 3*, 23-24 ; FAG: David Twing Wheeler Jr.
22. *FCJ*, Dec. 17, 1915, May 11, 1917 [quote]; Richard B. McCaslin, *Sutherland Springs, Texas; Saratoga on the Cibolo* (University of North Texas Press, 2017), 175, 181.
23. Wright, "Memoir," 139–140; Texas Convict Record Ledger: J. M. Farmer (#41308), Charles Francis (#41309); *SAE*, May 12, 1916, Feb. 7, May 23 [quote], 1917; *FCJ*, Dec. 15, 1916, Jan. 19, Feb. 9, 23, Mar. 9, 23, May 18, 1917; FAG: Lee Mayes McDaniel.
24. *FCJ*, Feb. 2, Mar. 2, 1917; [San Antonio] *La Prensa*, Mar. 8, 1917; *SAE*, Nov. 1, 1917; *Southwestern Reporter, Volume 198: December 5, 1917 to January 9, 1918* (St. Paul, MN: West Publishing Company, 1918), 946–948.
25. Wright, "Memoir," 77. The birth names for the three Wright sons, in order, are Charley H. ("Pat"), Maurice H. ("Jack"), and Emanuel A. ("Dogie") Wright.
26. Wright, "Memoir," 85; E. A. Wright to Mrs. Joe Shriber, Oct. 17, 1966, Wright Papers; *SAE*, Jan. 1, Mar. 16, July 12, 1915; *FCJ*, Jan. 1, 1915 [quotes], Jan. 4, 1918, Mar. 13, 1942; *Houston Post*, March 23, 1916; FAG: Charles Buckner Brown, Frederick Hayes "Fred" Brown, Robert Sanford Brown.

27. Wright, "Memoir," 141; *Austin American*, Jan. 29, 1909 [first and second quotes], Feb. 28, 1911, Aug. 2, 1914; *El Paso Morning Times*, Aug. 10, 1910; *Houston Post*, Apr. 23, July 9, 1911, July 11, 1913; *Galveston Daily News*, July 2, 1911; *El Paso Herald*, July 10, 1913; *SAE*, July 11, 1913, Aug. 8, 14, 1914, July 13, 1915; *FCJ*, May 14, 1914, July 16, 1915 [third, fourth and fifth quotes].
28. Wright, "Memoir," 116; *SAE*, Aug. 5, 1913, July 8, 18, 1914; *FCJ*, May 25, 1917; Sitton, *Texas Sheriff*, 79; Gary Price, "Ball, Thomas Henry [1859–1944]," *HOT*.
29. *SAE*, Aug. 16, 27, 1915; *FCJ*, Aug. 20, 1915; Tise, *Texas County Sheriffs*, 288; FAG: William Henry Edds, Robert A. Wiseman; Don M. Coerver, "Plan of San Diego," *HOT*. The best study of the Plan de San Diego and its impact is Charles H. Harris III and Louis R. Sadler, *The Plan de San Diego: Tejano Rebellion, Mexican Intrigue* (Lincoln: University of Nebraska Press, 2013).
30. Wright, "Memoir," 78–80; *San Antonio Light*, May 11, 1916; *Austin American*, May 12, 23, 1916; *FCJ*, May 19, 1916; Benjamin H. Johnson, *Revolution in Texas; How a Forgotten Revolution and Its Bloody Suppression Turned Mexicans into Americans* (New Haven, CT: Yale University Press, 2003), 147, 155; Harris and Sadler, *Plan De San Diego*,140–155; Caldwell and DeLord, *Eternity at the End of a Rope*, 544; John Boessenecker, *Texas Ranger: The Epic Life of Frank Hamer, The Man Who Killed Bonnie and Clyde* (New York: Thomas Dunne Books, 2016), 187; Charles H. Harris III and Louis R. Sadler, *The Texas Rangers in the Mexican Revolution: The Bloodiest Decade, 1910–1920* (Norman: University of Oklahoma Press, 2004), 140, 304–308; James A. Sandos, *Rebellion in the Borderlands: Anarchism and the Plan de San Diego, 1904–1923* (Norman: University of Oklahoma Press, 1992), 160–162; Ivey, *Ranger Ideal, Volume 3*, 28–29; Agnes G. Grimm, "Velazquez, Eulalio," *HOT*.
31. Wright, "Memoir," 79 [quote]; John L. Wortham, *Supplemental Biennial Report of the Secretary of State, 1912* (Austin, TX: Von Boeckmann-Jones Company, 1913), 247; *SAE*, July 6, 1916 [second quote]; *Austin American Statesman*, July 13, 1916; FAG: Salvador T. Rodriguez. William L. Wright's call for peaceful cooperation contrasted sharply with the actions of Texas Ranger Captain John J. Sanders, who commanded the company in which Wright's oldest son, Charles H. "Pat" Wright, served. Sanders, when he learned that Texas Circuit Court Judge T. Wesley Hook had forwarded a protest about the killings of José M. Morín and Victoriano

Ponce to President Woodrow Wilson, pistol-whipped Hook in the hall outside his courtroom. Harris and Sadler, *Plan de San* Diego, 155; Sandos, *Rebellion in the Borderlands*, 161–162.

32. Wright, "Memoir," 24, 150, 151; AGSR: Charles H. Wright; TRHFM: Charles H. Wright; William B. Wright, *Career Hunting: Texas Ranger vs. Standard Oiler* (El Cajon, CA: Privately printed, 1983), 4; *FCJ*, May 12, 1916, Oct. 25, 1918, Oct. 26, 1923; *SAE*, May 13, 1916, Oct. 27, 1918, June 24, 1919; *Corpus Christi Caller-Times*, June 29, 30, 1938; Gilliland, *Horsebackers*, 114; Harris, Harris, and Sadler, *Texas Ranger Biographies*, 415, 416, 427. Among the first men arrested in Wilson County for refusing to register for the draft were three with Hispanic surnames: Hemeregildo Garcia, Jesus Juanto, and Manuel Montoya. See *FCJ*, June 22, 1917.

33. C. C. McDonald to Henry Hutchings, Dec. 12, 1916, AGC [quotes]; William L. Wright to Roy W. Aldrich, Feb. 28, 1920, Roy W. Aldrich Papers, Archives of the Big Bend, Bryan Wildenthal Memorial Library, Sul Ross State University, Alpine, TX; Emanuel A. Wright to Shriber, Oct. 17, 1966, "Dogie" [Emanuel A. Wright] to "Maude" [Maude T. Gilliland], Oct. 4, 1976, Genealogy Notes, Wright Papers; Wright, *Career Hunting*, 4, 5; James A. Harley, *Biennial Report of the Adjutant General of Texas, from January 1, 1917, to December 31, 1918* (Austin, TX: Von Boeckmann-Jones, 1919), 56; *FCJ*, Jan. 15, Feb. 19, 1915; July 14, 21, 28, 1916; *SAE*, Feb. 14, Aug. 22, 1915, July 18, 1916; *Brenham Daily Banner-Press*, Feb. 18, 1915; FAG: Sanford Brown, Hugh Simpson Tom; Elizabeth Newman Tumlinson; "Our Family History: The Genealogy of Robert and Christina Barritt," accessed Jan. 20, 2020, http://tree.barrittfamily.net/getperson.php?personID=I473&tree=dyal_speckels. Hugh Simpson Tom was an uncle of Emanuel Tom, the tracker, and he may have been related to Sanford N. Brown's mother, whose maiden name was Tom. He had a huge funeral in Floresville with lots of honorary pallbearers, including Brown. William L. Wright served as an active pallbearer for his friend. Wright's mother also spent much time in Victoria at the home of her daughter, Cornelia Elizabeth Wright Cline, Wright's older sister, which indicates that the two siblings cooperated in caring for their mother. See *FCJ*, Sept. 22, 1916. William L. Wright's youngest son's name was given as "Simp Tom Wright" in an illustrated brief report of his participation, along with Clarice Myers, in a Red Cross parade at Floresville in December 1918. See *FCJ*, Jan. 4, 1918.

Notes for Chapter 5

1. AGSR: George A. Monkhouse; James A. Harley, *Annual Report of the Adjutant General of Texas for the Year Ending December 31, 1918* (Austin, TX: Von Boeckmann-Jones Company, 1919), 3, 4, 7, 11, 12; *Fort Worth Star-Telegram*, Nov. 28, 1917; *DMN*, Nov. 29, 1917; *McAllen Monitor*, Mar. 8, 1942; *Harlingen Valley Morning Star*, Mar. 8, 1942; Charles H. Harris III and Louis R. Sadler, *The Texas Rangers in the Mexican Revolution: The Bloodiest Decade, 1910–1920* (Norman: University of Oklahoma Press, 2004), 328–329; Robert M. Utley, *Lone Star Lawmen: The Second Century of the Texas Rangers* (New York: Oxford University Press, 2007), 55–57; James R. Ward, "The Texas Rangers, 1919–1935: A Study in Law Enforcement" (Ph.D. Diss., Texas Christian University, 1972), 8; Herbert H. Lang, "Harley, James A.," *HOT*.
2. J. J. Sanders to Walter F. Woodul, Nov. 21, 1917 [quotes], AGC; William L. Wright to James A. Harley, Oct. 4, Nov. 14, 1917 [telegram and letter], Harley to William L. Wright, Nov. 24, 1917, RFC; AGSR: Charles F. Stevens, W. L. Wright; *FCJ*, Nov. 16, 30, 1917; *SAE*, Nov. 25 [first quote], 30, 1917; *Seguin Enterprise*, Nov. 23, 1917 [last quote]; *Fort Worth Star-Telegram*, Nov. 28, 1917; *DMN*, Nov. 29, 1917; Harris and Sadler, *Bloodiest Decade*, 329; Charles H. Harris III, Francis E. Harris, and Louis R. Sadler, *Texas Ranger Biographies: Those Who Served 1910–1921* (Albuquerque: University of New Mexico Press, 2009), 361–362; Sammy Tise, *Texas County Sheriffs* (Albuquerque: Oakwood Press, 1989), 43.
3. Emanuel A. Wright, "Memoir" (Typescript, n.d., E. A. "Dogie" Wright Papers, DBCAH), 3; William L. Wright to Harley, Nov. 30, 1917 [second quote], RFC; Harley, *Annual Report of the Adjutant General, 1918*, pp. 7, 11; *Flatonia Argus*, Dec. 20, 1917; *Palacios Beacon*, Dec. 21, 1917 [first quote]; *Taft Tribune*, July 11, 1946.
4. Wright, "Memoir," 84–86, 96, 101, 128–129, 135, 154; William L. Wright to Roy W. Aldrich, Feb. 28, 1920, Roy W. Aldrich Papers, Archives of the Big Bend, Bryan Wildenthal Memorial Library, Sul Ross State University, Alpine, TX; AGSR: Dionicio J. Acosta, Thomas Connolly, John J. Edds, Sidney S. Hutchison, Royal W. Lorenz, Grover C. Oliphant, James P. Perkins, William S. Peterson, Thomas N. Pullin; William S. Peterson to Henry Hutchings, Apr. 16, 1916, AGC; TRHFM: Sidney S. Hutchison, James P. Perkins; *SAE*, Sept. 18, 1915, Dec. 14, 31, 1917, Jan. 20, 1918; *FCJ*, June 21, 1918, Harris,

Harris, and Sadler, *Texas Ranger Biographies*, 1–2, 68, 100, 196, 229, 273–274, 305, 306, 311; FAG: Sidney Sills Hutchison, Royal Wade Lorenz, Grover Cleveland "Cleve" Oliphant, Thomas Nolan Pullin; Shirley Grammar, "Concrete Cemetery," accessed Feb. 5, 2020, http://www.cemeteries-of-tx.com/etx/guadalupe/cemetery/concrete. htm. Thomas N. Pullin is a great-great-grandfather of Hall of Fame pitcher Nolan Ryan, according to Charles L. Olmsted, *The Good, The Bad, The Butlers: Story of a Texas Pioneer Family* (Bloomington, IN: iUniverse, 2015), 195–196.

5. Wright, "Memoir," 84, 152, 157; William L. Wright to Aldrich, Feb. 28, 1920, Aldrich Papers; AGSR: Marvin N. Butler, William B. Butler, Monroe M. Wells, Wright C. Wells; TRHFM: Monroe Wells; *SAE*, Dec. 14, 1917, *Taft Tribune*, July 11, 1946; Harris, Harris, and Sadler, *Texas Ranger Biographies*, 49, 398, 399; FAG: Sykes C. Butler, William Bryan Butler; Elizabeth Newman Tumlinson, Monroe Madison Wells; "Our Family History: The Genealogy of Robert and Christina Barritt," accessed Jan. 20, 2020, http://tree.barrittfamily.net/getperson.php?personID=I473&tree=dyal_speckels.
6. AGSR: Ferrell E. Holloman, Harold W. Adams; Harley to William L. Wright, Dec. 19, 1917, RFC; TRHFM: H. W. Adams; *SAE*, Jan. 23, Feb. 17, 1918; Harris, Harris, and Sadler, *Texas Ranger Biographies*, 2, 185.
7. Wright, "Memoir," 126–129; William L. Wright to Lon L. Willis, July 18, 1918 [quotes], Wright Papers; Jesse Perez, "Reminiscences, 1870–1927" (Typescript, n.d. [1927], DBCAH), 2–4, 6–7, 12–19, 25–26, 30–40, 44, 60, 64; AGSR: Marvin N. Butler, Ferrell E. Holloman, Desiderio Perez, Jesse Perez, James P. Perkins, Thomas N. Pullin, Robert Bell Sutton, Emanuel A. Wright; Harris, Harris, and Sadler, *Texas Ranger Biographies*, 49, 185, 305, 311, 416; Darren L. Ivey, *The Texas Rangers: A Registry and History* (West Jefferson, NC: McFarland & Company, 2010), 189; FAG: Desiderio "Jessie" Perez. Emanuel A. "Dogie" Wright was well enough to accompany his father back to Laredo in August 1918, after William L. Wright traveled to Floresville to cast his ballot for William P. Hobby as governor, but the official records do not contain a date for his resignation. See *FCJ*, Aug. 2, 1918.
8. William L. Wright to Harley, Dec. 6 [third quote], 19, 1917, AGC; John A. Valls to William L. Wright, Nov. 16 [second quote], 30, 1917, William L. Wright to Harley, Nov. 18, Dec. 2, 11 [fourth and fifth quotes],

21, 1917, RFC; *Laredo Weekly Times*, Aug. 30, Sept. 5, 1915; [San Antonio] *La Prensa*, Jan. 5, 1918; William W. Sterling, *Trails and Trials of a Texas Ranger* (Privately printed, 1959), 168–170; FAG: John Anthony Valls [first quote].

9. William L. Wright to Harley, Dec. 6, 11, 1917, RFC; T. C. Mitchell to Harley, Nov. 30, 1917 [first quote], H. B. Holmes to Harley, Nov. 30, 1917 [second quote], W. W. Bogel to Harley, Dec. 22, 1917, Harley to Bogel, Dec. 29, 1917, Hanson to Harley, Feb. 1, 8 [final quote], 1918, AGC; Texas Legislature, "Proceedings of the Joint Committee of the Senate and the House in the Investigation of the Texas State Ranger Force," 8 vols. (Typescript, n.d. [1919], DBCAH), 1: 211; AGSR: William Martin Hanson; Harley, *Annual Report of the Adjutant General, 1918*, pp. 59–60; Utley, *Lone Star Lawmen*, 58–64; Harris, Harris, and Sadler, *Texas Ranger Biographies*, 114; FAG: William Martin Hanson; Monica Muñoz Martínez, "Porvenir Massacre," *HOT*. Martínez provides much detail concerning the Porvenir Massacre in the third chapter of *The Injustice Never Leaves You: Anti-Mexican Violence in Texas* (Cambridge: Harvard University Press, 2018). See also Miguel A. Levario, *Militarizing the Border: When Mexicans Became the Enemy* (College Station: Texas A&M University Press, 2012), 29–34.

10. William L. Wright to Harley, Dec. 17, 21 [first quote], 1917, RFC; *Laredo Weekly Times*, Dec. 23, 1917 [second, third, fourth quotes]; *SAE*, Jan. 1, 1918 [fifth quote]; Harris and Sadler, *Bloodiest Decade*, 329.

11. William L. Wright to Harley, Nov. 14, 1917, RFC; Wright, "Memoir," 1, 2, 6; *SAE*, Dec. 27 [quote], Jan. 2, 1918; *FCJ*, Nov. 16, 1917 [second and third quotes], Jan. 4, 11, 1918; Tise, *Texas County Sheriffs*, 546–547; Robert M. Denhardt, *The King Ranch Quarter Horses* (Norman: University of Oklahoma Press, 1995), 66–67. At least two cases that remained open when William L. Wright stepped down as sheriff were later resolved. Alberto Saenz committed a felony in Wilson County then fled to Tennessee and Mexico. Three members of Wright's Ranger company—John J. Edds, Sidney S. Hutchison, and Juan C. Gonzales—arrested Saenz in Rio Grande City in February 1920, and Sheriff Alfred B. Carnes of Wilson County came and got him. See FCJ, Feb. 13, 1920. Anderson J. Peeler Oliver allegedly killed a man in Floresville, then fled to Oklahoma with most of his family. He was shot and killed in a San Antonio hotel in 1924 while serving as a deputy sheriff for the town of Sentinel, where he had settled. See *Houston*

Post-Dispatch, Dec. 26, 27, 28, 1924; *Galveston Daily News*, Dec. 26, 27, 1924; *Austin American*, Dec. 26, 28, 1924; FAG: Anderson J. Peeler Oliver.

12. William L. Wright to Harley, Dec. 17, 26 [first and second quotes], 28, 29, 1917, RFC; Wright, "Memoir," 3; *SAE*, Dec. 31, 1917; *FCJ*, Jan. 4, 1918 [third quote]; *Harlingen Valley Morning Star*, Mar. 8, 1942; *McAllen Monitor*, Mar. 8, 1942; *Taft Tribune*, July 11, 1946; Darren L. Ivey, *The Ranger Ideal, Volume 3: Texas Rangers in the Hall of Fame, 1898–1987* (Denton: University of North Texas Press, 2021), 12.
13. Hanson to Harley, Feb. 20, 1918, John J. Edds to Aldrich, Feb. 4, 1921, AGC; Sterling, *Trails and Trials*, 411–412; Harris and Sadler, *Bloodiest Decade*, 368–369; Charles H. Harris III and Louis R. Sadler, *The Texas Rangers in Transition: From Gunfighters to Criminal Investigators* (Norman: University of Oklahoma Press, 2019), 12. For a great analysis of the changes along the Rio Grande in this period, see David Montejano, *Anglos and Mexicans in the Making of Texas, 1836–1986* (Austin: University of Texas Press, 1987), especially chapters 5 and 6.
14. *Houston Post*, Mar. 9, 1918; *SAE*, Mar. 9, 1918; *Austin American*, Mar. 10, 1918; *Fort Worth Star-Telegram*, Mar. 14, 1918; *McAllen Monitor*, Mar. 8, 1942; *Harlingen Valley Morning Star*, Mar. 8, 1942; Texas Legislature, "Proceedings," 6: 1,169–1,175, 1,187, 1,191–1,192; Harris and Sadler, *Bloodiest Decade*, 369, 371; Tise, *Texas County Sheriffs*, 288; Harris, Harris, and Sadler, *Texas Ranger Biographies*, 362–363; Tony Bill, "J. T. Canales and the 1919 Texas Ranger Investigation," *South Texas History I* (June 25, 2013), 8, 16; FAG: William Preston Franklin, William Cody Franklin, Dudley Victor "Duncan" Stilwell; "The Historic San Antonio Viejo," accessed Feb. 13, 2020, http://www.eastfoundation.net/our-story/the-historic-san-antonio-viejo/; Henry Chappell, "Horses to Ride, Cattle to Cut: The San Antonio Viejo Ranch of Texas," accessed Feb. 13, 2020, https://www.landreport.com/ 2017/06/horses-to-ride-cattle-to-cut/.
15. Hanson to Harley, Mar. 28, 1918, AGC; Texas Legislature, "Proceedings,"6 : 1,172–1,175; *Houston Post*, Mar. 9, 1918; *SAE*, Mar. 9, 12, 1918; *Fort Worth Star-Telegram*, Mar. 14, 1918; Harris and Sadler, *Bloodiest Decade*, 371; Bill, "Canales and the 1919 Texas Ranger Investigation," 8, 11.
16. William L. Wright, Report on the Bandit Raid on the East Ranch, Mar. 7, 1918, AGC [also Walter P. Webb Collection, Volume 20, DBCAH]; AGSR: John C. Draper, William H. Edds, S. L. Franklin,

D. V. Stillwell, Oscar Thompson; Texas Legislature, "Proceedings," 6: 1,136–1,137, 1,177, 1,190, 1,191; U.S. Bureau of the Census, Thirteenth Census, 1910, Population, Frio County, TX, and Fourteenth Census, 1920, Population, LaSalle County, TX (Record Group 29, National Archives, Washington, DC); *SAE*, Mar. 9, 1918; *FCJ*, Mar. 15, 1918; Sadler and Harris, *Bloodiest Decade*, 369, 524, 527, 550, 564; Harris, Harris, and Sadler, *Texas Ranger Biographies*, 74, 92, 101, 115, 262, 377; Tise, *Texas County Sheriffs*, 288; Walter P. Webb, *The Texas Rangers: A Century of Frontier Defense* (Boston: Houghton Mifflin, 1935), 509, 510; Bill, "Canales and the 1919 Texas Ranger Investigation," 11; FAG: William Henry Edds.

17. William L. Wright, Report on the Bandit Raid, Tom East to Woodul, Mar. 11, 1918, Hanson to Harley, Mar. 28, 1918, AGC; Texas Legislature, "Proceedings," 6: 1,191–1,192, 1,530; *SAE*, Mar. 9, 10, 11, 12 [quote], 1918; *Houston Post*, Mar. 9, 1918; *Austin American*, Mar. 10, 1918; *New York* [NY] *Times*, March 11, 1918; *Fort Worth Star-Telegram*, Mar. 14, 1918; *Taft Tribune*, July 11, 1946; Ivey, *Registry*, 223; Harris and Sadler, *Bloodiest Decade*, 369–370; Webb, *Texas Rangers*, 509, 510; Ivey, *Ranger Ideal, Volume 3*, 32–33; Bill, "Canales and the 1919 Texas Ranger Investigation," 11; "Historic San Antonio Viejo." Interestingly, Dudley V. Stilwell, known as "Duncan" and "Bud," who was a specific target of the raiders' ire, was removed as a Special Ranger in the late spring of 1918 for being "rough" and bossy. Tom T. East managed to have Stilwell reinstated but transferred him to the King Ranch operations at Kingsville, where he died of emphysema at the age of twenty-three in October 1918. See Woodul to East, June 3, 18, 1918, East to Woodul, June 14, 1918, AGC; FAG: Dudley Victor "Duncan" Stilwell. A writer for the *Floresville Chronicle Journal* declared that the reports of Mexicans killed during William L. Wright's pursuit were "so badly confused and different" that he would not provide a total. See *FCJ*, Mar. 15, 1918.
18. William L. Wright to Willis, July 18, 1918 [first, second, third quotes], Wright Papers; James Callan to Harley, Sept. 2, 1918, Harley to Callan, Sept. 6, 1918, Adolph Lorenz to N. H. Browne, July 9, 1918 [fourth quote], Harley to A. D. Rogers, Sept. 19, 1918, AGC; Texas Legislature, "Proceedings," 6: 1,137–1,139; James C. Fifield, *The American Bar: Contemporary Lawyers of the United States and Canada* (Minneapolis, MN: Privately published, 1918), 652. The Cattle Raisers Association of Texas became the Texas and Southwestern Cattle Raisers Association in 1921.

19. H. W. Adams to William L. Wright, Jan. 20, 1919, AGC; Wright, "Memoir," 96; Texas Legislature, "Proceedings," 3: 481, 507, 509, 4: 697–698, 771, 8: 1,530; Fourteenth Census, 1920, Population, Cameron County, TX; *SAE*, Aug. 9, 1918 [quote]; *Laredo Weekly Times*, Aug. 11, 1918; *San Antonio Evening News*, Feb. 14, 1919; Ivey, *Ranger Ideal, Volume 3*, 30, 34; Evan Anders, *Boss Rule in South Texas: The Progressive Era* (Austin: University of Texas Press, 1982), 10–11, 37–38; FAG: George Druschel.
20. Texas Legislature, "Proceedings," 1: 69–71, 74–78; *Mercedes Tribune*, Oct. 4, 18, 1918; *Houston Post*, Feb. 8, 1919; *Galveston Daily News*, Feb. 14, 1919; Anders, *Boss Rule*, 177–179, 183–186, 255–266; Ivey, *Ranger Ideal, Volume 3*, 35–36; Anthony R. Carrozza, *The Dukes of Duval County* (Norman: University of Oklahoma Press, 2017), 6–26; Evan Anders, "Parr, Archer," *HOT*; Martin Donell Kohout, "Duval County," *HOT*.
21. John J. Edds to Roy W. Aldrich, Dec. 15, 1918 [second quote], Roy W. Aldrich Papers, DBCAH; William L. Wright to Wesley D. Cope, Nov. 3, 1920 [third quote], dictation on Tape 8.1 in James R. Ward Collection, West Texas Collection, Angelo State University, San Angelo, TX; Ivan A. White to Thomas H. Barton, Apr. 1, July 3, 1924, Aldrich to White, July 14, 1924, William S. Peterson to Aldrich, June 22, July 30, 1924, Aldrich to Peterson, June 24, July 31, 1924, Mrs. Henry O. [Gertrude Ramsland] Schaleben to Barton, July 18, 1924, Aldrich to Schaleben, July 24, 1924, AGC; Texas Legislature, *In the Senate of Texas, D. W. Glasscock Contestant vs. A. Parr Contestee, Supplement to the Senate Journal; Regular Session of the 36th Legislature 1919* (Austin, TX: A. C. Baldwin & Sons, 1919), 382–389 [first quote], 390–442, 446–476, 479, 481–482, 483–488, 495, 514–535; Harris and Harris, *Texas Rangers in Transition*, 170–173; FAG: Henry Oliver Schaleben. The political activists in Hidalgo County in 1924 almost convinced William S. Peterson to quit Wright's company and campaign for sheriff against the incumbent, Anderson Y. Baker, a former Ranger who cooperated with the established Democrats. Instead, Peterson remained a Ranger until he was discharged, along with many comrades, in early 1925 after Miriam A. "Ma" Ferguson took office as governor.
22. William L. Wright to Harley, December 6, 11, 1917, May 12, 1918 [quote], General Order No. 5, Headquarters, Texas Ranger Force, June 4, 1918, AGC; Harley, *Annual Report of the Adjutant General, 1918*, 7, 11; AGSR: Boon Oliphant; Harris, Harris, and Sadler, *Texas*

Ranger Biographies, 274; Harris and Sadler, *Bloodiest Decade*, 329; Mike Cox, *Time of the Rangers: Texas Rangers from 1900 to the Present* (New York: Forge Books, 2009), 91; FAG: James Monroe Fox, James Boone Oliphant; Martinez, “Porvenir Massacre.”

23. J. T. Canales to Woodul, July 22, 1918, Woodul to Canales, July 24, 1918, AGC; AGSR: A. T. Canales; *FCJ*, Jan. 10, 1919; *Austin American*, Feb. 11, 1919; Utley, *Lone Star Lawmen*, 68–69, 71–72, 76–77; Webb, *Texas Rangers*, 513–515; Cox, *Time of the Rangers*, 86–90; John Boessenecker, *Texas Ranger: The Epic Life of Frank Hamer, The Man Who Killed Bonnie and Clyde* (New York: Thomas Dunne Books, 2016), 184–188, 190; Ward, “Texas Rangers,” 11–14. Martínez, in *The Injustice Never Leaves You*, has a thorough discussion of the investigation initiated by José T. Canales in Chapter Four.
24. W. T. Vann to Walter W. Hollingsworth, Jan. 14, 1919, J. T. Canales to Vann, Jan. 17, 1919, AGC; Texas Legislature, “Proceedings,” 1: 6a [sixth quote], 17 [second quote], 69–71, 74–78, 81, 84, 5: 857 [first quote], 3: 579–580, 582 [third quote] 4: 616, 681 [fourth quote], 696 [fifth quote]; AGSR: W. L. Wright; Special Order No. 6, Headquarters, Texas Ranger Force, Jan. 30, 1919, in TRHFM: William L. Wright; *Houston Post*, Feb. 1, 6, 1919; *Austin American*, Feb. 11, 1919; *San Antonio Evening News*, Feb. 12, 1919; Harris and Sadler, *Bloodiest Decade*, 175, 449; Cox, *Time of the Rangers*, 91; Tise, *Texas County Sheriffs*, 86; Anders, *Boss Rule*, 268, 270; Robert Wooster, “Heywood, Alba,” *HOT*; “Alba Heywood, 1859–1921,” accessed Feb. 15, 2020, https:// www.wikitree.com/wiki/Heywood-369. This was not the first time that Virginia Yeager had falsely accused Rangers of invading her home. See Harris and Sadler, *Bloodiest Decade*, 175.
25. Texas Legislature, “Proceedings,” 1: 3–4 [quotes], 16, 17, 3: 482; *FSJ*, Feb. 14, 1919; Anders, *Boss Rule*, 266–267; Utley, *Lone Star Lawmen*, 72; Harris and Sadler, *Bloodiest Decade*, 421–422; Cox, *Time of the Rangers*, 88; Boessenecker, *Texas Ranger*, 188; Charles H. Harris III and Louis R. Sadler, “Texas Rangers and the Mexican Revolution,” *Tracking the Texas Rangers: Twentieth Century*, ed. Bruce A. Glasrud and Harold J. Weiss Jr. (Denton: University of North Texas Press, 2013), 77. Historian Benjamin H. Johnson includes a brief recounting of the three incidents that involved John J. Edds in *Revolution in Texas; How a Forgotten Revolution and Its Bloody Suppression Turned Mexicans into Americans* (New Haven, CT: Yale University Press, 2003), 163–164.

26. John J. Edds to "To Whom It May Concern," n.d. [ca. Sept. 9, 1918], AGC [transcribed as "Edds to Paul Perkins or Oscar Thompson, n.d.," in Webb Collection, Volume 20]; "Proceedings," 3: 482, 485, 500–503, 4: 738–741, 761, 763–766, 768, 770; AGSR: Eduardo Izaguirre; Webb, *Texas Rangers*, 510–511; Harris and Sadler, *Bloodiest Decade*, 421–422; FAG: Eduardo Yzaguirre.
27. Texas Legislature, "Proceedings," 4: 761–762, 765–767, 769, 761–762, 6: 1,306, 1,309–1,312, 8: 1,521; William L. Wright to Harley, Sept. 7, 1918, Hanson to Harley, Sept. 16, 1918 [quotes], Webb Collection, Volume 20.
28. Texas Legislature, "Proceedings," 4: 765, 770; 5: 912–914 [quote], 6: 1,298–1,3052; Martínez, *The Injustice Never Leaves You*, 198–202.
29. Texas Legislature, "Proceedings," 1: 3–4, 135–136, 3: 482, 493–494, 496–497, 499, 507, 7: 1,342–1,349, 1,353–1,354, 1,363.
30. Texas Legislature, "Proceedings," 3: 467–469, 471–473, 475 [quote].
31. Texas Legislature, "Proceedings," 3: 493–494, 496–497, 499–500, 503, 507, 7: 1,345–1,347, 1,349, 1,350, 1,351–1,355, 1,357, 1,351–1362; George F. Howard, *Supplemental Biennial Report of the Secretary of State of the State of Texas, 1918* (Austin, TX: A. C. Baldwin & Sons, 1916), 232; Tise, *Texas County Sheriffs*, 473; FAG: Emilo Naranjo; Cynthia E. Orozco, "Guerra, Gustavo A.," *HOT*.
32. Royal Collins to Aldrich, Feb. 22, 1922, AGC; Texas Legislature, "Proceedings," 3: 468–469, 473–474, 476–477, 507, 7: 1,342, 1,349; *San Antonio Evening News*, Feb. 7, 1919; FAG: Sgt. Norman Lee Dickens.
33. Robert Oosterveen to William P. Hobby, Oct. 18, 1918, AGC [also in Webb Collection, Volume 20, together with undated statements from M. Monroe Wells, Zaragosa Sánchez, and Jesus Sánchez]; Texas Legislature, "Proceedings," 1: 3–4, 135–136, 3: 483–484, 487–490, 493, 4: 782–786; *San Antonio Evening News*, Feb. 7, 1919; Webb, *Texas Rangers*; 511–513; Harris and Sadler, *Bloodiest Decade*, 422–423.
34. Oosterveen to Hobby, Oct. 18, 1918, AGC [also in Webb Collection, Volume 20, along with undated statements from Monroe Wells, Zaragosa Sanchez, and Jesus Sanchez]; William L. Wright to D. W. Low, October 9, 1918, Webb Collection, Volume 20;Texas Legislature, "Proceedings," 1: 3–4, 126, 135–136, 3: 490–491, 4: 783–786, 806, 5: 914 [quotes], 8: 1,519–1,520, 1,526–1,529; John G. McKay, *Biennial Report of the Secretary of State of the State of Texas, 1916* (Austin, TX: A. C. Baldwin & Sons, 1916), 232; *San Antonio*

Evening News, Feb. 7, 1919; Harris and Sadler, *Bloodiest Decade*, 422–423; Utley, *Lone Star Lawmen*, 72, 79–80; Cynthia E. Orozco, "Garza, Higinio, Jr.," *HOT*.

35. James B. Wells to Hanson, Nov. 2, 1918, AGC; Texas Legislature, "Proceedings," 3: 482, 491, 510, 4: 781, 5: 888 [second quote]; *SAE*, Feb. 4, 1919; *San Antonio Evening News*, Feb. 7, 1919; *FCJ*, Jan. 30, Feb. 6, 1920 [first quote]; Utley, *Lone Star Lawmen*, 82; Martínez, *The Injustice Never Leaves You*, 201–205.
36. Texas Legislature, "Proceedings," 3: 481, 8: 1,424 [second quote], 1,425, 1,518, 1,522–1,523; AGSR: J. J. Edds; TRHFM: John J. Edds; *FCJ*, Sept. 15, 1916; *SAE*, Sept. 16, 1916 [third and fourth quotes]; *San Antonio Evening News*, Feb. 14, 1919 [first quote]; Sadler and Harris, *Bloodiest Decade*, 154, 256–260; Anders, *Boss Rule*, 200–213. Henry L. Ransom is the principal focus of the second chapter in Martínez, *The Injustice Never Leaves You*, while she discusses John J. Edds on pp. 198–205. Zapata, the county seat of Zapata County, is on the Rio Grande fifty miles south of Laredo.
37. H. H. Dunn to Hanson, Oct. 21, 1918, AGC [fourth quote]; Texas Legislature, "Proceedings," 4: 616–617, 696–697 [first, second, third quotes], 781; Anders, *Boss Rule*, 227–228; Utley, *Lone Star Lawmen*, 72, 79 [fifth, sixth quotes]; Paul N. Spellman, *Capt. John H. Rogers, Texas Ranger* (Denton: University of North Texas Press, 2003), 194–196. John H. Rogers also declared during the legislative investigation that there was "no better officer" on the Ranger Force than William L. Wright. See *FCJ*, Feb. 14, 1919.
38. Texas Legislature, "Proceedings," 1: 125–126, 5: 942–943 [quote], 8: 1,523–1,525; Ward, "Texas Rangers," 16–17.
39. William L. Wright to Aldrich, Feb. 28, 1920, Aldrich Papers, Archives of the Big Bend; AGSR: Dionicio J. Acosta, William B. Butler, Thomas Connolly, Sterling O. Durst, H. L. Hamer, Austin T. Hamilton, Royal W. Lorenz, Grover C. Oliphant, Madison Monroe Wells, W. L. Wright; TRHFM: William Bryan Butler, Austin T. Hamilton, Royal W. Lorenz, G. C. Oliphant, Madison Monroe Wells; Harley, *Annual Report of the Adjutant General, 1918*, 60–62, 80; Harris, Harris, and Sadler, *Texas Ranger Biographies*, 1–2, 49, 68, 96, 161–163, 229, 273, 306, 415, 427; Boessenecker, *Texas Ranger*, 17, 143–144, 146–149, 153–161, 183, 200; Cox, *Time of the Rangers*, 91, 94; FAG: Sterling Orlando "Sod" Durst, Harrison Lester Hamer. In the summer of 1918, William L. Wright was told to post a detachment of his company

near Brownsville to support Company F, commanded by his cousin, William W. Taylor. Subsequently, four privates from Company F were listed as being under Wright's command, and when Taylor left the Rangers at the end of 1918, Sterling O. Durst, Harrison L. Hamer, and Austin T. Hamilton, who must have been three of those four, officially transferred to Company K. See Harris and Sadler, *Bloodiest Decade*, 420.

40. F. A. Hamer to Harley, Mar. 23, 1919, Harley to "Sergeant Frank Hamer," Mar. 26, 1919, Charles H. Flato Jr. and Caesar Kleberg to Harley, Mar. 28, 1919, Ben T. Tumlinson Jr. to Aldrich, Apr. 20, 1919, Earl R. Wright to Aldrich, June 28, 1919, AGC; Earl. R. Wright to William L. Wright, Apr. 21, 1919, Wright Family Papers, TRHC [quote]; Special Order No. 21, Headquarters, Texas Ranger Force, Mar. 10, 1919, in TRHFM: James P. Perkins, Benjamin T. Tumlinson Jr., and E. R. Wright; Special Order No. 27, Headquarters, Texas Ranger Force, Mar. 19, 1919, in TRHFM: State Rangers, Company K; AGSR: Samuel P. Chesshire, H. L. Hamer, John E. Hensley, Ben T. Tumlinson Jr., Earl Ray Wright; Utley, *Lone Star Lawmen*, 81–82; Harris and Sadler, *Bloodiest Decade*, 534; Boessenecker, *Texas Ranger*, 201; Harris, Harris, and Sadler, *Texas Ranger Biographies*, 59–60, 74–75, 383, 415–416; Dan E. Kilgore, *A Ranger Legacy: 150 Years of Service to Texas* (Austin, TX: Madrona Press, 1973), 63; FAG: John Edward Hensley.
41. Wright, "Memoir," 150, 151; William L. Wright to Willis, July 18, 1918, Emanuel A. Wright to Mrs. Joe Shriber, Oct. 17, 1966, Wright Papers; Edds to Harley, April 30, 1919, AGC; AGSR: Charlie Hays Wright, Emanuel A. Wright; TRHFM: Charles H. Wright; William B. Wright, *Career Hunting: Texas Ranger vs. Standard Oiler* (El Cajon, CA: Privately printed, 1983), 4, 5; *FCJ*, May 12, 1916, Jan. 10, 1919; *SAE*, May 13, 1916; Harris, Harris, and Sadler, *Texas Ranger Biographies*, 415, 416, 427; Maude T. Gilliland, *Horsebackers of the Brush Country: A Story of the Texas Rangers and Mexican Liquor Smugglers* (Brownsville: Springman-King Company, 1968), 114; FAG: Cornelia Elizabeth Wright Cline, Fredrich Alois "Fritz" Skarke; "Our Family History."
42. Hobby to Harley, May 19, 1919, AGC [also in Webb Collection, Volume 21]; Utley, *Lone Star Lawmen*, 78 [first quote], 86; Cox, *Time of the Rangers*, 95–96 [second quote], 97; Webb, *Texas Rangers*, 516; Harris and Sadler, *Rangers in Transition*, 29–30; Ward, "Texas Rangers," 21–23.

Notes for Chapter 6

1. J. T. Canales to James A. Harley, Aug. 31, 1918, W. Henry Edds to William P. Hobby, May 12, 1919, W. Henry Edds to Harley, May 12, 1919, Hobby to Harley, May 19, 1919, Harley to W. Henry Edds, May 20, 1919, Roy W. Aldrich to L. B. Carter, Nov. 16, 1921 [quote], AGC [correspondence between W. Henry Edds and Harley also in TRHFM: William L. Wright]; *DMN*, Feb. 11, 1921; *Fort Worth Star-Telegram*, Feb. 12, 1921; *McAllen Monitor*, Mar. 8, 1942; *Harlingen Valley Morning Star*, Mar. 8, 1942; James A. Harley, *Biennial Report of the Adjutant General of Texas for the Two Years Ending December Thirty-First, A.D. One Thousand, Nine Hundred, and Twenty* (Austin, TX: Von Boeckmann-Jones Company, 1921), 44; Robert M. Utley, *Lone Star Lawmen: The Second Century of the Texas Rangers* (New York: Oxford University Press, 2007), 70–71, 73, 88–97; Charles H. Harris III and Louis R. Sadler, *The Texas Rangers in the Mexican Revolution: The Bloodiest Decade, 1910–1920* (Norman: University of Oklahoma Press, 2004), 419–420; John Boessenecker, *Texas Ranger: The Epic Life of Frank Hamer, The Man Who Killed Bonnie and Clyde* (New York: Thomas Dunne Books, 2016), 172–177; Darren L. Ivey, *The Texas Rangers: A Registry and History* (West Jefferson, NC: McFarland & Company, 2010), 187; FAG: Charles Francis Stevens, Fred Tate, Sgt. Delbert Timberlake; "Inspector Fred Tate," accessed May 1, 2020, https://www.odmp.org/officer/13098-inspector-fred-tate; Jim Coffey, "Will Wright: Rangers and Prohibition," accessed Feb. 16, 2020, https://www.texasranger.org/wp-content/uploads/2017/07/BIO-Will-Wright.pdf.
2. Robert D. Brown to Harley, July 9, 1919, Roy W. Aldrich to Brown, July 15, 1919, John E. Hensley to Aldrich, July 16, 1919, Aldrich to Hensley, July 18, 1919, Juan C. Gonzalez to Aldrich, Aug. 1, 1919, Aldrich to Harrison L. Hamer, Oct. 16, Dec. 4, 1919, Hamer to Aldrich, Dec. 31, 1919, J. P. Cottingham et al. to Aldrich, Dec. 5, 1919, Aldrich to Cottingham, Dec. 5, 1919, Wright C. Wells to Cope, Jan. 15, 1920, W. T. Vann to Hobby, Dec. 13, 1919, Hobby to Vann, Dec. 16, 1919, David C. Webb to William L. Wright, Jan. 13, 1920, Aldrich to Webb, Jan. 24, 1920, Brown to Aldrich, Feb. 9, 1923, AGC; AGSR: Harold W. Adams, Robert D. Brown [second and third quotes], Sam P. Chesshire, John J. Edds, Juan C. Gonzalez, H. L. Hamer, Roy L. Hearn, John E. Hensley, Sidney S. Hutchison, Stanley Morton, Jesse Perez, William S. Peterson, Darwin E. Singleton, Robert Bell Sutton, Ben T. Tumlinson,

David C. Webb, and Wright C. Wells; Special Order No. 1, Headquarters, Texas Ranger Force, Jan. 14, 1920, and Wesley D. Cope to H. L. Hamer, Jan. 8, 1920, in TRHFM: Harrison L. Hamer; TRHFM: Robert D. Brown; Emanuel A. Wright, "Memoir" (Typescript, n.d., E. A. "Dogie" Wright Papers, DBCAH), 162–163, 175; William B. Wright, *Career Hunting: Texas Ranger vs. Standard Oiler* (El Cajon, CA: Privately printed, 1983), 16 [fourth quote], 20, 26, 27; John R. Peavey, *Echoes from the Rio Grande* (Privately printed, 1963), 187–191; *Houston Post*, Dec. 21, 1919 [first quote]; *Corpus Christi Caller-Times*, July 12, 1953; *FCJ*, Mar. 12, 1920, June 24, 1932; Charles H. Harris III and Louis R. Sadler, *The Texas Rangers in Transition: From Gunfighters to Criminal Investigators* (Norman: University of Oklahoma Press, 2019), 30; Sammy Tise, *Texas County Sheriffs* (Albuquerque: Oakwood Press, 1989), 473; Charles H. Harris III, Francis E. Harris, and Louis R. Sadler, *Texas Ranger Biographies: Those Who Served 1910–1921* (Albuquerque: University of New Mexico Press, 2009), 2, 45, 59–60, 100, 126, 161–162, 172, 174, 196, 261, 304–306, 349, 368, 383, 396, 399, ; Maude T. Gilliland, *Wilson County Texas Rangers, 1837 to 1977* (Privately published, 1977), 129; FAG: Robert Dueroc "Rob" Brown, Roy Lee Hearn, John Edward Hensley, Darwin Eldridge Singleton Sr., David C. "Jack" Webb.

3. Special Order No. 11, Headquarters, Texas Ranger Force, Mar. 24, 1920, Aldrich to Stanley M. Morton, May 11, 1921, Aldrich to Hubert P. Brady, Sept. 25, 1920, Brady to Aldrich, n.d., AGC; AGSR: Harold W. Adams, Hubert P. Brady [quote], Robert D. Brown, Sidney S. Hutchison, Desiderio Perez, Jesse Perez; *SAE*, Dec. 5, 1919, Sept. 25, 1920; *El Paso Herald-Post*, Sept. 27, 1920; *Palestine Daily Herald*, Oct. 2, 1920; *Abilene Daily Reporter*, Oct. 3, 1920; *Weatherford Daily Herald*, Oct. 5, 1920; *FCJ*, Sept. 20, 1957; TRHFM: H. W. Adams, Robert D. Brown, Sidney S. Hutchison, William Sanders Peterson; Harris, Harris, and Sadler, *Texas Ranger Biographies*, 40–41; Maude T. Gilliland, *Horsebackers of the Brush Country: A Story of the Texas Rangers and Mexican Liquor Smugglers* (Brownsville, TX: Springman-King Company, 1968), 102; FAG: Hubert Patrick Brady. "Red" is a nickname for Hubert P. Brady found in James R. Ward, "The Texas Rangers, 1919–1935: A Study in Law Enforcement" (Ph.D. Diss., Texas Christian University, 1972), 43, and it also is written on a photograph of him in the Walter P. Webb Collection, DBCAH.

4. John A. Valls to Thomas D. Barton, Feb. 27, 1921, AGC; Morton to Aldrich, Apr. 21, 1921, Aldrich to Morton, May 14, 1921, RFC; Hayes M. Wallis to Aldrich, Aug. 17, 1923, AGC; AGSR: Robert A. Boyd, Roy L. Hearn, W. L. Miller, William L. Miller, Stanley Morton, Desiderio Perez, Jesse Perez, Hayes M. Wallis, Peter B. Winn; *Galveston Daily News*, Feb. 11, 1921; Utley, *Lone Star Lawmen*, 86, 93; Harris and Sadler, *Rangers in Transition*, 32, 36, 38, 40, 48; Harris, Harris, and Sadler, *Texas Ranger Biographies*, 39, 165–166, 255, 392–393, 411; Ida Harbison Luttrell, *The Road to Randado* (Spring, TX: Panther Creek Press, 2004), 127–129. The other two captains who continued in Ranger service were Jerry Gray and Roy W. Aldrich. Wright's renewal prompted Mrs. J. E. King, the chair of the Board of Texas Penitentiaries, to write to Thomas D. Barton on Feb. 11, 1921 that "as a peace officer, Mr. Wright has no peer." (AGC) John A. Valls, District Attorney at Laredo, added his praise for Wright as well and renewed his efforts to have him stationed in his city. See Valls to Barton, Feb. 13, 1921, AGC.
5. Wright, "Memoir," 97 [quotes]; Barton to William L. Wright, Mar. 23, 1921, William L. Wright to Aldrich, Aug. 28, 1921 [quotes], dictation on Tape 8.1 in James R. Ward Collection, West Texas Collection, Angelo State University, San Angelo, TX; Valls to Barton, Feb. 27, 1921, Barton to Valls, Mar. 23, 1921, John J. Edds to Aldrich, Mar. 27, Apr. 11, June 19, July 21, Dec. 15, 1921, Jan. 15, Feb. 3, 1922, Aldrich to John J. Edds, Mar. 29, Apr. 29, Dec. 27, 1921, Jan. 13, 21, Feb. 17, 1922, William S. Peterson to Aldrich, July 30, 1921, Aldrich to Emanuel A. Wright, Sept. 9, 1921, Aldrich to Samuel P. Chessire, Sept. 13, 1921, AGC; AGSR: Samuel P. Chesshire, John J. Edds, Roy L. Hearn, David C. Webb, Peter B. Winn; *Beaumont Enterprise*, Sept. 1, 1921; Harris and Sadler, *Rangers in Transition*, 49–50, 55; Harris, Harris, and Sadler, *Texas Ranger Biographies*, 100; Gilliland, *Wilson County Texas Rangers*, 129; Ward, "Texas Rangers," 65. William S. Peterson and his colleagues at Mission also distinguished themselves earlier in 1921 with a series of arrests for alcohol and gambling violations that included Mayor James E. Haynes of Mercedes and three deputy sheriffs. See Peterson to Aldrich, Feb. 8, 1921, AGC. For more about Samuel P. Chesshire and the King Ranch, see Duane M. Leach, *Caesar Kleberg and the King Ranch* (College Station: Texas A&M University Press, 2017), 2–3, 170–172, 219, 250. The president of the First National Bank in Rio Grande City was among those who asked

that John J. Edds be returned after his transfer. See Lawrence R. Brooks to Barton, Mar. 24, 1921, AGC.

6. Barton to Light Townsend, Feb. 8, 1923, Aldrich to C. R. Park, Mar. 19, 1923, Aldrich to Townsend, Mar. 22, 1923, AGC; AGSR: Robert A. Boyd, G. D. Gilliland, Light Townsend, Hayes M. Wallis; TRHFM: Light Townsend; *FCJ*, June 2, 1922; William W. Sterling, *Trails and Trials of a Texas Ranger* (Privately printed, 1959), 376–377; Gilliland, *Horsebackers*, 90, 93, 102, 129; Harris and Sadler, *Rangers in Transition*, 415; Harris, Harris, and Sadler, *Texas Ranger Biographies*, 53–54; Paul N. Spellman, *Capt. John H. Rogers, Texas Ranger* (Denton: University of North Texas Press, 2003), 104–105; FAG: Grenade Donaldson Gilliland, Asa Light Townsend. Grenade D. "Don" Gilliland was married to Maude T. Gilliland. The meeting between John H. Rogers and Asa Light Townsend at Columbus may never have occurred. See Darren L. Ivey, *The Ranger Ideal, Volume 2: Texas Rangers in the Hall of Fame, 1874–1930* (Denton: University of North Texas Press, 2018),677–678.
7. Jesse Perez to Harley, June 6, 1919, Gonzalez to Aldrich, Jan. 31, Feb. 3, 17, 25, 1923, Perez to William L. Wright, Feb. 3, 1923, Perez to Aldrich, Feb. 3, 1923, Aldrich to Perez, Feb. 5, 1923, Robert D. Brown to Aldrich, Feb. 9, 1923, Aldrich to William E. Burford, Feb. 8, 1923, Gonzalez to William L. Wright, Feb. 10, 1923, Aldrich to Gonzalez, Feb. 14, 27, Mar. 13, 1923, Aldrich to H. N. Hall, Apr. 16, 1923, Aldrich to Owen Alexander, Apr. 24, 1923, Lake T. Webb to Barton, May 30, 1923, Aldrich to Chell M. Baker, June 16, 29, July 9, 1923, Baker to Aldrich, July 12, 1923, Aldrich to Lake T. Webb, Sept 7, 1923, William A. Dial to Aldrich, Dec. 12, 22, 1923, William B. Wright to Aldrich, Feb. 5, July 1, 31, 1924, Aldrich to William B. Wright, Feb. 12, Aug. 2, 1924, Union Securities Company to Barton, Mar. 4, 1924, Aldrich to Union Securities company, Mar. 6, 1924, Aldrich to William L. Wright, Mar. 6, 1924, AGC; Wright, "Memoir," 134, 135; Jesse Perez, "Reminiscences, 1870–1927" (Typescript, n.d. [1927], DBCAH), 65–74; AGSR: Chell M. Baker, Hubert P. Brady, W. E Burford [quote], Dan Coleman, William A. Dial, Juan C. Gonzalez, Howard N. Hall, Edgar B. Harrell, William L. Miller, Desiderio Perez, Jesse Perez, Ben T. Tumlinson, David C. Webb, Lake T. Webb; TRHFM: Chell M. Baker, Dan Coleman, Edgar B. Harrell, Eugene Tumlinson, W. B. "Bill" Wright; *Columbus Colorado County Citizen*, July 22, 1926; Wright, *Career Hunting*, 15–18, 24–26; Harris and

Sadler, *Rangers in Transition*, 46, 48, 182; Utley, *Lone Star Lawmen*, 6; Harris, Harris, and Sadler, *Texas Ranger Biographies*, 40–41, 45, 100, 126, 161–162, 172, 174, 304–305, 396; Tise, *Texas County Sheriffs*, 473; Boessenecker, *Texas Ranger*, 242; Mike Cox, *Time of the Rangers: Texas Rangers from 1900 to the Present* (New York: Forge Books, 2009), 117, 408; John H. Jenkins and H. Gordon Frost, *"I'm Frank Hamer:" The Life of a Texas Peace Officer* (Austin, TX: State House Press, 1993), 126; Dan E. Kilgore, *A Ranger Legacy: 150 Years of Service to Texas* (Austin, TX: Madrona Press, 1973), 63; FAG: Hubert Patrick Brady, Grenade Donaldson Gilliland, Howard Nathan "Happy" Hall Sr., Roy Lee Hearn, John Edward Hensley, Desiderio "Jessie" Perez, Ben T. Tumlinson Jr., Eugene H. Tumlinson; J. Will Falvella, "Captain Wright—A Gallant Texas Ranger," *Frontier Times* (Sept. 1924), 6–7; Coffey, "Wright: Rangers and Prohibition;" "William A. Dial," accessed Feb. 17, 2020, https://cemetery.tspb.texas.gov/ pub/ user_form.asp?step =1&pers_id= 2356; "Isaac Edgar Clark," Texas Legislators: Past & Present, accessed Feb. 17, 2020, https://lrl. texas gov/mobile/member Display.cfm? MemberID=2385. The members of Company D who became federal officers include Brady, Brown, Edds, Gilliland, Gonzalez, Hamer, Hensley, Hearn, Perez, Eugene Tumlinson, Jack Webb, and Lake Webb. William E. Burford is the nephew of William T. Burford, the sheriff with whom William L. Wright worked during the Reese-Townsend Feud in 1899. See FAG: William E. Burford, William T. Burford; "Colorado County Obituaries: Burford," accessed May 15, 2020, http://www.colorado countyhistory. org/obits/b/burford.htm. The *Western Weekly Magazine* in 1929 noted that William L. Wright had the dubious distinction of having mentored more men for the United States Border Patrol than any other lawman in Texas. See *FCJ*, Dec. 27, 1929.

8. Samuel C. Mayes to Aldrich, July 21, 1924, Asa Light Townsend to Aldrich, July 21, 1924, Aldrich to Townsend, July 28, 1924, AGC; Perez, "Reminiscences," 61; AGSR: Tom G. Brady, Edgar B. Harrell, Sam C. Mayes, John W. Sadler, James Warren Smith, Eugene H. Tumlinson; TRHFM: Edgar B. Harrell; Harris and Sadler, *Bloodiest Decade*, 410, 559; Harris, Harris, and Sadler, *Texas Ranger Biographies*, 334; FAG: Thomas Giles Brady; "Our Family History: The Genealogy of Robert and Christina Barritt," accessed Jan. 20, 2020, http:// tree.barrittfamily.net/getperson. php?personID=I473&tree=dyal_speckels.

9. AGSR: Charles F. Cochran; TRHFM: Charles F. Cochran; *Wichita Falls Daily Times*, Aug. 18, 1922; *Sherman Daily Democrat*, Aug. 18, 1922; *Houston Post*, Aug. 19, 1922; *Temple Daily Telegram*, Aug. 19, 1922; Mike Cox, *Texas Ranger Tales: Stories That Need Telling* (Lanham, MD: Taylor Trade Publications, 1997), 193–195; FAG: Oscar S. "Sonny" Warnke; Mike Cox, "The Three-Hour Texas Ranger," accessed Feb. 17, 2020, http://www. texasescapes.com/MikeCoxTexasTales/Three-hour-Texas-Ranger.htm.
10. Aldrich to Hamer, Dec. 4, 1919, Covey C. Thomas and Alfred B. Carnes to Hobby, Dec. 16, 1919, Thomas and Carnes to Hobby and Cope, Dec. 17, 1919, Aldrich to Thomas, Dec. 18, 1919, AGC; Texas Legislature, "Proceedings of the Joint Committee of the Senate and the House in the Investigation of the Texas State Ranger Force," 8 vols. (Typescript, n.d. [1919], DBCAH), 1: 80; *Galveston Daily News*, Nov. 4, 1919, *SAE*, Nov. 11, 19, 1919, Dec. 5, 8, 11, 31, 1919; *Zavala County Sentinel*, July 22, 1933; FAG: John Wesley Lowe, S. Calvin Tullos, William G. Tullos.
11. Emanuel A. Wright to Mrs. Joe Shriber, Oct. 17, 1966, Wright Papers; Interview with Zora Belle Wright Fore, Dec. 7, 1973, South Texas Oral History & Folklore Collection, South Texas Archives, James C. Jernigan Library, Texas A&M University at Kingsville; *SAE*, Nov. 23, 1919; *Fort Worth Star-Telegram*, Nov. 22, 1919; *Austin American*, Nov. 22, 1919; *Marshall News Messenger*, Nov. 22, 1919; *Weatherford Daily Herald*, Nov. 22, 1919; *Temple Daily Telegram*, Nov. 22, 1919; *DMN*, Nov. 23, 1919; *FCJ*, Nov. 28, 1919, Apr. 10, 1925; *Houston Post*, Dec. 21, 1919; *McAllen Monitor*, Mar. 8, 1942; *Harlingen Valley Morning Star*, Mar. 8, 1942 [second quote]; Sterling, *Trails and Trials*, 413 [first quote]; Darren L. Ivey, *The Ranger Ideal, Volume 3: Texas Rangers in the Hall of Fame, 1898–1987* (Denton: University of North Texas Press, 2021), 38. Wright told a reporter that his attacker's name was "Davilla," but he was identified in several accounts as Jose Corona. See *Corsicana Democrat and Truth*, April 9, 1925; *San Patricio County News*, April 30, 1925. There is a Jose Corona buried in the Old City Cemetery at Brownsville whose grave marker records his death date as Nov. 21, 1919. See FAG: Jose Corona [third quote].
12. Aldrich to Ben T. Tumlinson Jr., July 7, 1921 [quote]; Texas Legislature, "Proceedings," 4: 805; Harley, *Biennial Report of the Adjutant General ... One Thousand, Nine Hundred, and Twenty*, 13; James A. Harley, *Annual Report of the Adjutant General of Texas for the Year Ending December 31,*

1918 (Austin, TX: Von Boeckmann-Jones Company, 1919), 62; *FCJ*, Apr. 10, 1925; Sterling, *Trails and Trials*, 83–84, 86; Wright, *Career Hunting*, 20, 24; Peavey, *Echoes from the Rio Grande*, 206–207; Harris and Sadler, *Bloodiest Decade*, 420–421; Cox, *Time of the Rangers*, 107, 125, 133; Harris and Sadler, *Rangers in Transition*, 44–45; George T. Diaz, *Border Contraband: A History of Smuggling Across the Rio Grande* (Austin: University of Texas Press, 2015), 95–96; Homero S. Vera, "Los Tequileros," *El Mesteno* 3 (Feb. 2000): 4. During the first month of state prohibition, Ranger Benjamin T. Tumlinson Jr. complained that there was a lot of bootlegging at San Diego, but he could get little support from federal authorities because they found that local officials would not convict anyone they arrested. By late June 1919, he and federal officers were cooperating in chasing smugglers. See Aldrich to Ben T. Tumlinson Jr., May 28, 1919, Ben T. Tumlinson Jr. to Aldrich, May 31, June 30, July 8, 1919, and Aldrich to E. R. Gallagher, June 10, 1919, AGC. Historian George T. Diaz notes that tequila smuggling from Mexico never reached the magnitude of the flow from Canada or the coasts due to the proximity of cities elsewhere and public distaste for tequila, which did not change until the 1970s.

13. William L. Wright to Aldrich, Dec. 10, 1920, Roy W. Aldrich Papers, Archives of the Big Bend, Bryan Wildenthal Memorial Library, Sul Ross State University, Alpine, TX; William L. Wright to Aldrich, Jan. 23, Apr. 23 [first quote], 1921, Tape 8.1, Ward Collection; William L. Wright to Aldrich, Mar. 6, 1922, William L. Wright to Barton, Mar. 6, 1922, Tape 8.2, Ward Collection; Aldrich to H. M. Wallis, Feb. 17, 1922 [fourth quote], Tumlinson to Aldrich, Mar. 10, 1922, Aldrich to Light Townsend, Feb. 17, 1923, AGC; Aldrich to Hubert P. Brady, Feb. 24, 1922, RFC; Wright, *Career Hunting*, 16 [second and third quotes], 17; *Austin Daily Statesman*, Sept. 21, 1924; *Corsicana Daily Sun*, Sept. 23, 1924; Sterling, *Trails and Trials*, 76, 82, 83; Harris and Sadler, *Rangers in Transition*, 51; Bossenecker, *Texas Ranger*, 31; Cox, *Texas Ranger Tales*, 183–190; Gilliland, *Horsebackers*, 26; Walter P. Webb, "Veteran Ranger Protects Border," *State Trooper* 6 (September 1924): 13–14; Ward, "Texas Rangers," 57; Coffey, "Wright: Rangers and Prohibition."
14. "Buck" [Darwin E. Singleton] to Aldrich, Oct. 16, 26, Nov. 7, 1919, Aldrich to Singleton, Nov. 9, 1919, Tom Laymance to Aldrich, Feb. 15, Mar. 17, 1923, Aldrich to Laymance, Feb. 17, 1923 [quote], AGC; AGSR: Tom I. Laymance, Darwin E. Singleton; Harris and Sadler, *Rangers in Transition*, 12; FAG: John Edward Hensley, Johnnie

Phillips Hensley, Lyna Wright Hensley; "Women and the Rangers: Mothers, Wives, & Daughters," accessed Feb. 26, 2020, https://www.texasranger.org/wp-content/uploads/2017/10/History-Women-and-the-Rangers.pdf; FAG: Darwin Eldridge Singleton Sr. A survey of the Texas Adjutant General Service Records for Company D during the period of Wright's command, 1919 to 1925, reveals eleven married members: Boyd, Brown, Burford, Gonzalez, Hall, Hamer, Hensley, Perez, Sadler, Singleton, and Townsend. Lyna Wright may have joined John E. Hensley in the field before she married him; he wrote to Aldrich on Dec. 12, 1922 (AGC), that his "wife" was staying with him in the State Hotel at Corpus Christi. Howard N. Hall apparently never relocated his wife from Del Rio during the four months that he served with Company D at Mission. See Howard N. Hall to Aldrich, May 14, 1923, AGC.

15. G. W. Egerton to Harley, Mar. 5, 1919, O. A. McCracken to Harley, Mar. 31, Apr. 11, 1919, George D. Dewees to Harley, Apr. 1, 1919, A. C. Eschenburg to Harley, Apr. 1, 1919, Aldrich to McCracken, Apr. 1, 16, 1919, John H. Rogers to Harley, Apr. 14, 1919, Aldrich to Rogers, Apr. 16, 1919, Sam Fore Jr. to William P. Hobby Apr. 27, 1919, Charlie H. Wright to Hobby, Apr. 28, 1919, Charlie H. Wright to Harley, Apr. 28, 1919, T. O. Morris to Hobby, Apr. 28, 1919, S. V. Houston to Hobby, Apr. 28, 1919, Hobby to Houston, Apr. 30, 1919, Hobby to Morris, May 1, 1919, Hobby to Fore, May 1, 1919, John J. Edds to Harley, May 3, 1919 [quote], Aldrich to John J. Edds, May 15, Sept. 10, 1919, Feb. 17, 1921, Aldrich to Fore, May 15, 1919, Aldrich to Houston, May 15, 1919, Aldrich to Charles H. Wright, May 15, 1919, John J. Edds to Aldrich, Sept. 15, Oct. 12, Nov. 3, Dec. 1, 1919, Feb. 15, 1920, Feb. 14, Mar. 1, 4, 1921, AGC; *SAE*, June 24, 1919; *FCJ*, June 27, 1919; *Laredo Weekly Times*, Feb. 20, 1921; Harris and Sadler, *Rangers in Transition*, 47–48. John H. Rogers, in his recommendation for Charles H. "Pat" Wright, wrote, "if he is anything like his father he will make an excellent officer." See Rogers to Harley, Apr. 14, 1919, AGC. After Pat Wright became a Customs officer, he also became a roommate at Rio Grande City for John J. Edds, who took the opportunity to move out of a house where "centipedes, rats, fleas and snakes had gotten so numerous that it was really dangerous." See John J. Edds to Aldrich, Mar. 5, 1921, AGC. William L. Wright continued to have trouble with Sheriff Gustavo A. Guerra and his allies long after the departure of Edds. See E. E. Neal to Aldrich, Sept. 6, 1923, AGC.

16. William L. Wright to Cope, Jan. 20, 1920, Cope to William L. Wright, Sept. 21, 1920, Tape 8.1, Ward Collection; William L. Wright to Aldrich, Jan. 6, 1920 [first quote], Aldrich Papers, Archives of the Big Bend; Ben T. Tumlinson Jr. to Aldrich, May 20 [second quote], Aug. 11, 1920, Hobby to Cope, Sept. 21, 1920, T. A. Coleman to Hobby, Sept. 22, 1920, Pat Craighead to Cope, Sept. 23, 1920, Robert J. Kleberg to Cope, Sept. 23, 27, 1920, Cope to Coleman, Sept. 23, 1920, Cope to Craighead, Sept. 23, 1920, Cope to Kleberg, Sept. 27, 1920, AGC; AGSR: Marcus W. Hines; TRHFM: Marcus W. Hines; *SAE*, June 24, 1919, Sept. 24, Nov. 29, Dec. 5, 12 [fourth and fifth quotes], 19, 1920; *Flatonia Argus*, Jan. 8, 1920 [third quote]; *Galveston Daily News*, Dec. 2, 1920; *FCJ*, Dec. 3, 1920; *Falfurrias Facts*, July 1, 1938; Ivey, *Ranger Ideal, Volume 3*, 39–42.
17. William L. Wright to Cope, Dec. 17, 1920, Tape 8.1, Ward Collection; Sidney S. Hutchison to Aldrich, Apr. 7, 1921 [quote], Apr. 23, 1919 [correct date: 1921], undated [Nov. 1921], Sept. 15, 20, 1922, Aldrich to Hutchison, April 9, 14, Dec. 16, 1921, Jan. 26, Sept. 16, 1922, AGC; Harris and Sadler, *Rangers in Transition*, 12; Ward, "Texas Rangers," 85–86. Sidney S. Hutchison believed that William L. Wright was deliberately withholding money from him, while Wright insisted that he had been paid in full. Some funds were finally disbursed by Roy W. Aldrich in early 1922.
18. Aldrich to William S. Peterson, Feb. 10, 1921, AGC; *Laredo Weekly Times*, Feb. 20, 1921; Pat M. Neff, *The Battles of Peace* (Fort Worth, TX: Pioneer Publishing, 1925), 38 [quote], 71–76, 137–143; Harris and Sadler, *Rangers in Transition*, 27–32; Utley, *Lone Star Lawmen*, 86, 88; Cox, *Time of the Rangers*, 106; Norman D. Brown, *Hood, Bonnet, and Little Brown Jug: Texas Politics, 1921–1928* (College Station: Texas A&M University Press, 1984), 21–26, 36, 47, 130; Ward, "Texas Rangers," 49.
19. Valls to Adjutant General [Barton], Feb. 27, 1921, William L. Wright to Barton, Sept. 13, 1921 [also in Webb Collection, Volume 21, DBCAH], John J. Edds to Aldrich, Sept. 19, 1921 [first quote], Aldrich to John J. Edds, Sept. 22, 1921, AGC; Perez, "Reminiscences," 50, 77–80; Wright, "Memoir," 174; William L. Wright to Barton, Feb. 28, 1921, William L. Wright to Aldrich, May 31, Aug. 17, 1921, Tape 8.1, Ward Collection; *Fort Worth Star-Telegram*, Feb. 20, 1921; *Austin Statesman*, May 22, 1921; *Laredo Weekly Times*, July 31, Aug. 7, Sept. 18, 1921; *FCJ*, Aug. 21, Sept. 30 [second and third quotes], 1921; *Austin American*,

Sept. 16, 1921; *Corpus Christi Caller-Times*, Dec. 4, 1921; Sterling, *Trails and Trials*, 91; Wright, *Career Hunting*, 20; Harris and Sadler, *Rangers in Transition*, 49–50; Walter P. Webb, *The Texas Rangers: A Century of Frontier Defense* (Boston: Houghton Mifflin, 1935), 557; Diaz, *Border Contraband*, 99–100; Ivey, *Ranger Ideal, Volume 3*, 42–43; Homero S. Vera, "Los de Parás," *El Mesteno* 3 (Feb. 2000): 16; Ward, "Texas Rangers," 54–56; Coffey, "Rangers and Prohibition." Desiderio "Jesse" Perez and Robert S. "Bob" Rumsey had already been working together at Laredo; in the summer of 1921 they captured Tomas Salinas, who had been leading a small band in robbing people along the Rio Grande. See John J. Edds to Aldrich, Sept. 2, 1921, Aldrich to John J. Edds, Sept. 8, 1921, AGC. Roy W. Aldrich learned about the gun battle on September 12, 1921 when he received a letter the next day from Emanuel A. "Dogie" Wright, the Captain's son, who wrote that "Papa had a little fight in the lower country." See Emanuel A. Wright to Aldrich, Sept. 13, 1921, Aldrich to Emanuel A. Wright, Sept. 14, 1921, AGC.

20. William L. Wright to Barton, Nov. 19, 24 [quotes, also in Webb Collection], 1921, William L. Wright to Aldrich, Dec. 2, 1921, Tape 8.2, Ward Collection; Perez, "Reminiscences," 80–82; Wright, "Memoir," 231–232; U.S. Bureau of the Census, Fourteenth Census, 1920, La Salle County, TX, and Fifteenth Census, 1930, Starr County, TX (Record Group 29, National Archives, Washington, DC); AGSR: Roland A. Gouger; *FCJ*, Sept. 30, 1921; *Waco News-Tribune*, Nov. 19, 1921; *Austin American*, Nov. 19, 1921; *Laredo Weekly Times*, Nov. 20, 27, 1921; *Galveston Daily News*, Nov. 23, 1921; *Corpus Christi Caller-Times*, Dec. 4, 1921; *Austin Statesman*, July 14, 15, 1922; *Junction Eagle*, July 21, 1922; *Austin Statesman*, Feb. 21, 1941; Utley, *Lone Star Lawmen*, 97; *Cox, Time of the Rangers*, 107; Gilliland, *Horsebackers*, 25; Webb, "Veteran Ranger Protects Border," 13; Ward, "Texas Rangers," 56–57; Coffey, "Rangers and Prohibition;" FAG: William Paul Cotulla, Roland Andy Gouger; "Pedigree Resource File: John Albritton Gouger," accessed Feb. 29, 2020, https://www.familysearch.org/ark:/61903/2:2:SPF7-8QQ . Roy W. Aldrich had John J. Edds send him copies of the pictures of William L. Wright with his captured contraband so he could give them to Walter P. Webb, who was just beginning his work on the history of the Rangers. See Aldrich to John J. Edds, Jan. 21, 1922. Among the lawmen impressed with William L. Wright's achievements in 1921 was "Special Detective" Frequin D. Leydecker of

the Whitney Central Bank in New Orleans, who invited Wright to join him for Mardi Gras the following year. Wright declined. See Frequin Leydecker to William L. Wright, Feb. 8, 1922, William L. Wright to Leydecker, Feb. 10, 1922, AGC; FAG: Frequin D. Leydecker. Allegedly the three men captured on November 17, 1921, were lassoed from their horses by Frank Smith. See Ivey, *Ranger Ideal, Volume 3*, 43–44.

21. Henry B. Yelvington to Barton, Nov. 17, 1924, AGC; AGSR: Henry B. Yelvington; *San Antonio Light*, Apr. 15, 1927 [first quote]; *FCJ*, May 6, 1927; Harris and Sadler, *Bloodiest Decade*, 574; Walter P. Webb, "Rangers Reorganized," *The State Trooper* 8 (July 1927): 13 [second quote, which translates as "The Devil Captain rides again."]
22. William L. Wright to S. H. Woods, n.d., William L. Wright to Aldrich, May 31, 1921, Aldrich to T. M. West, n.d, William L. Wright to Barton, June 22, 1921, Tape 8.1, Ward Collection; *Austin Statesman*, Feb. 25, 1921; Ward, "Texas Rangers," 85; Coffey, "Rangers and Prohibition." The three detained by Edds were Frank E. Laborde, who was released to his wife, and two men reported only by their last names, Marks and Cortez. Laborde was the son of a prominent local businessman, and his mother's maiden name was Marks. See Lizeth Elizondo, "LaBorde, Francois," NHOT; FAG: Frank Laborde.
23. Ben T. Tumlinson Jr. to Aldrich, Apr. 8, 22, 29, 1921, Aldrich to William L. Wright, Sept. 15, 1921, Tape 8.1, Ward Collection; Aldrich to "Friend Ben," Sept. 10, 17, 22, 1921, Tumlinson to Aldrich, June 13, 17, Sept. 12 [quote], 21, Oct. 14, Nov. 27, 1921, Tumlinson to William L. Wright, Oct. 16, 1921, Horace McCord Jr. to Pat Neff, Nov. 7, 1921, Aldrich to Tumlinson, Nov. 23, 1921, Aldrich to R. N. Hall, Apr. 16, 1923, AGC; AGSR: Ben T. Tumlinson Jr.; Harris and Sadler, *Rangers in Transition*, 46–47; David Allen White, "Churches and Clergy in the Diocese of West Texas," accessed May 11, 2020, https://www.dwtx.org/download_ file/view/3250/; FAG: Rev. Jay S. Budlong, Benjamin Thomas Tumlinson Jr. In another interesting case, Tumlinson pursued a Mexican who robbed the Alice post office of $3,000, only to find his body in the brush after he committed suicide. See Ben T. Tumlinson Jr. to Aldrich, Oct. 1, 1921, AGC. Roy W. Aldrich heard that Tumlinson killed himself, but he wrote "that is hard for me to believe." See Aldrich to J. A. Gillon, June 18, 1923 (AGC).
24. Perez, "Reminiscences," 74–77; Wright, "Memoir," 175–181; "Antonio I. Villarreal," accessed Mar. 16, 2020, https://www.chihuahuamexico.com/index.php?option=com_content&task=view&id=2557&Itemid=40;

"Pablo González Garza," accessed Mar. 16, 2020, https://www.chihuahuamexico.com/index.php?option=com_content&task=view&id=1529&Itemid=30; [San Antonio] *La Prensa*, Jan. 13, 1921.

25. William L. Wright to Barton, May 9, 1921, Gonzalez to William M. Ryan, Oct. 16, 1921, Hayes M. Wallis to Ryan, Oct. 18, 1921, Tape 8.1, Ward Collection; William S. Peterson to Aldrich, Oct. 22, 1921, AGC; *Galveston Daily News*, Feb. 28, Mar. 12, Apr. 4, 1921; *El Paso Herald*, Mar. 1, 1921; *Austin Statesman*, Mar. 23, Apr. 28, 1921, Apr. 2, 1923; *Houston Post*, Apr. 29, 1921; *Waco News-Tribune*, Apr. 29, 1921, Apr. 2, 1923; Harris and Sadler, *Rangers in Transition*, 55; Nicholas Villanueva, *The Lynching of Mexicans in the Texas Borderlands* (Albuquerque: University of New Mexico Press, 2017), 171; F. Arturo Rosales, *Pobre Raza* (Austin: University of Texas Press, 1999), 102–103, 120; Ward, "Texas Rangers," 56.
26. William L. Wright to Aldrich, March 6, 1922, Tape 8.2, Ward Collection [third, fourth, and fifth quotes]; *Mercedes Tribune*, Jan. 18, 1922 [first and second quotes].
27. Peterson to Aldrich, June 2, July 30, 1922, AGC; Ivey, *Ranger Ideal, Volume 3*, 45.
28. Ben T. Tumlinson Jr. to Aldrich, July 28, 1922, RFC [quote]; Perez, "Reminiscences," 83–84; *San Antonio Evening News*, July 25, 1922; *Abilene Daily Reporter*, July 28, 1922; *Brownwood Bulletin*, July 28, 1922; *Houston Post*, July 29, 1922; *Temple Daily Telegram*, July 29, 1922; *Wichita Daily Times*, July 28, 1922; *Austin Statesman*, July 28, 29, 1922; *Marshall Messenger*, July 28, 1922; *Sherman Daily Democrat*, Aug. 16, 1922; *Bryan Weekly Eagle*, Aug. 17, 1922; *Meridian Tribune*, Aug. 18, 1922; Neff, *Battles of Peace*, 71–76, 140–141; Brown, *Hood, Bonnet, and Little Brown Jug*, 82–86; Cox, *Time of the Rangers*, 113–114; Harris and Sadler, *Rangers in Transition*, 94–108, 163; Utley, *Lone Star Lawmen*, 98–100; Ward, "Texas Rangers," 76–78, 80. Ben T. Tumlinson Jr. did go to Galveston in September 1920, the only one from Company D to do so. See Cope to Ben T. Tumlinson Jr., Sept. 21, 1920, Ben T. Tumlinson Jr. to Aldrich, Sept. 27, 1920, Special Order No. 50, Headquarters, Texas Ranger Force, Sept. 22, 1920, Aldrich to Charles W. Price, Feb. 17, 1921, Ben T. Tumlinson Jr. to Aldrich, Mar. 9, 1921, AGC. For a good discussion of the railroad strike at Denison, see Mark Stanley, "Portrait of a Southern Progressive: The Political Life and Times of Governor Pat M. Neff of Texas, 1871–1952" (Ph.D. Diss, University of North Texas, 2011).

29. Ben T. Tumlinson Jr. to Aldrich, July 28, 1922, RFC; Tom Cole to Aldrich, Aug. 4, 1922, Aldrich to Cole, Aug. 7, 1922, Aldrich to John E. Hensley, Aug. 28, 1922, Aldrich to Peterson, Aug. 28, Oct. 4 [quote], 1922, D. C. Webb to Aldrich, Sept. 9, 1922, Ben T. Tumlinson Jr. to Aldrich, Sept. 11, Oct. 10, 1922, William L. Miller to Aldrich, Sept. 28, 1922, Jesse McDowell to Aldrich, Oct. 9, 1922, Aldrich to McDowell, Oct. 13, 1922, AGC; *Jacksboro Daily Gazette*, Aug. 3, 1922; *Temple Daily Telegram*, Aug. 9, 18, 1922; *Sherman Daily Democrat*, Aug. 9, Oct. 1, 1922; *Austin Statesman*, Aug. 9, 1922; *Brownwood Bulletin*, Aug. 9, 1922; *Corsicana Daily Sun*, Aug. 9, 1922; *Wichita Daily Times*, Aug. 9, 1922; *Bryan Weekly Eagle*, Aug. 10, 1922; *Marshall Messenger*, Aug. 11, 1922; Sterling, *Trails and Trials*, 413–414; Utley, *Lone Star Lawmen*, 98–100; Harris and Sadler, *Rangers in Transition*, 102; Cox, *Time of the Rangers*, 115; Ward, "Texas Rangers," 79; Coffey, "Rangers and Prohibition."
30. Gonzalez to Aldrich, July 25, Sept. 22, Dec. 9, 1922, Aldrich to Gonzalez, Aug. 28, Sept. 8, 1922, Perez to Aldrich, Sept. 11, Oct. 14 [first to third quotes], 1922, Hensley to Aldrich, Aug. 1, 11, Sept. 6, 1922, Aldrich to Hensley, July 29, 31, Aug. 2, 5, 7, 9, 10, 11, Oct. 2, 30, 1922, Peterson to Aldrich, July 31, Aug. 3, 18, Oct. 3 [fourth quote], 1922, Aldrich to Peterson, Aug. 1, 1922, AGC.
31. *Brownwood Bulletin*, July 22, 1922; *Weatherford Daily Herald*, July 22, 1923; *Austin Statesman*, July 22, 1922; *Abilene Reporter*, July 23, 1922; *Galveston Daily News*, July 25, 1922; *Amarillo Globe*, Sept. 30, 1929; *Waxahachie Daily Light*, Sept. 30, 1929; *Shamrock Texan*, Oct. 9, 1929; *Hebbronville News*, Oct. 9, 1929; *Longview Daily News*, Oct. 11, 1929; Brown, *Hood, Bonnet, and Little Brown Jug*, 51–59; Harris and Sadler, *Rangers in Transition*, 198–208; Utley, *Lone Star Lawmen*, 88; Cox, *Time of the Rangers*, 100; Boessenecker, *Texas Ranger*, 271; Jenkins and Frost, "*I'm Frank Hamer*," 101; Tise, *Texas County Sheriffs*, 395; Gilliland, *Horsebackers*, 115–116; Ward, "Texas Rangers," 60–62 65–66; Frank Wagner, "Timon, Walter Francis," *HOT*. Historian Darren L. Ivey has noted that another point of contention between the political factions in Corpus Christi was that Walter J. Timon's followers were mostly Catholic while Samuel J. "Fred" Roberts relied primarily on Protestant support. See Ivey, *Ranger Ideal, Volume 3*, 47.
32. *Austin American*, Oct. 16, 1922; *Houston Post*, Jan. 7, 1923; *Corpus Christi Caller-Times*, Mar. 12, 2018; Harris and Sadler, *Rangers in Transition*, 163; Boessenecker, *Texas Ranger*, 272–275; Jenkins and

Frost, "*I'm Frank Hamer*," 121–122; Ward, "Texas Ranger," 84; FAG: Samuel Johnson "Fred" Roberts, Gustavus E. "Gus" Warren, Dove Warren. The classic study on the rise and fall of the second Ku Klux Klan in Texas remains Charles C. Alexander, *The Ku Klux Klan in the Southwest* (University of Kentucky Press, 1965), but it does not mention the shooting of Samuel J. "Fred" Roberts.

33. Perez, "Reminiscences," 85–88; *Austin American*, Oct. 16, 1922; *San Antonio Evening News*, Nov. 24, 1922; *Houston Post*, Jan. 7, 1923; *Fredericksburg Standard*, Feb. 13, 1923; Boessenecker, *Texas Ranger*, 273; Ivey, *Ranger Ideal, Volume 3*, 47–48, 50–51; Ward, "Texas Ranger," 84.
34. *Houston Post*, Oct. 4, 1915; *SAE*, Oct. 4, 1915; *Corpus Christi Caller*, Sept. 3, 11, 1915; *Houston Post*, Jan. 7, Oct. 9, 1923; *Fredericksburg Standard*, Jan. 13, Feb. 13, 1923; *Kingsville Record*, May 27, 1925; *Corpus Christi Caller-Times*, May 14, 1948, Mar. 12, 2018; Harris and Sadler, *Rangers in Transition*, 162–164; Boessenecker, *Texas Ranger*, 275; Anthony R. Corrozza, *Dukes of Duval County: The Parr Family and Texas Politics* (Norman: University of Oklahoma Press, 2017), 9–10; Evan M. Anders, *Boss Rule in South Texas: The Progressive Era* (Austin: University of Texas Press, 1982), 177–178; FAG: Joseph Arnold "Joe" Acebo, Tilford Lee Petzel.
35. Historical Notes (Manuscript, n.d., probably by Emanuel A. "Dogie" Wright), Wright Papers; Int. with Zora Belle Wright Fore, Dec. 7, 1973; *Austin American*, Oct. 16, 1922; *Corpus Christi Caller-Times*, Mar. 12, 2018; Boessenecker, *Texas Ranger*, 273, 275; Jenkins and Frost, "*I'm Frank Hamer*," 122–123 [quote]. For photographs of William L. Wright's gun from the "Citizens of Corpus Christi," see Doug Dukes, *Firearms of the Texas Rangers: From the Frontier Era to the Modern Age* (Denton: University of North Texas Press, 2020), 355–357.
36. Aldrich to Hubert P. Brady, Feb. 24, Apr. 8, 1922, RFC; William L. Wright to Barton, Aug. 30, 1922 [first, second, and third quotes], Aldrich to William L. Wright, n.d., William L. Wright to Aldrich, Oct. 2, 1922 [fifth quote], Tape 8.2, Ward Collection; Jack Webb to Aldrich, Aug. 19, Nov. 9, 1922, W. A. Dial to Aldrich, Nov. 1, 1922, Aldrich to Webb, Nov. 15, 1922, Dial to Aldrich, Sept. 2, 8, 1923, AGC; Perez, "Reminiscences," 1–2, 82, 89–91; *Brownwood Bulletin*, Nov. 9, 1922; *Austin American*, Nov. 10, 1922; *Houston Post*, Nov. 11, 1922; Sterling, *Trails and Trials*, 88–91; Utley, *Lone Star Lawmen*,

100; Harris and Sadler, *Rangers in Transition*, 51–53, 102, 106; Diaz, *Border Contraband*, 102; Ward, "Texas Rangers," 80, 82. Rather than the obvious historical reference to William L. Wright's ancestry, the "Tumlinson Carbine" label may simply have originated in David C. "Jack" Webb's request for two Winchesters "cut off 5 inches like Ben Tumlinson's" from Jacob H. Petmecky. See Webb to Aldrich, Mar. 19, Nov. 9, 1922, and invoice from Petmecky Company for "3 Tomlinson Carbines," Apr. 8, 1922, AGC. The three guns listed in the invoice were "Expressed to Capt. W. L. Wright, Laredo, Texas." Pictures of two of William L. Wright's shortened Winchesters, as well as comments on those and the Thompson submachine gun, can be found in Doug Dukes, *Firearms of the Texas Rangers*, 278, 289, 355–358.

37. Depositions of Augustin Villareal Zarate, Nov. 14 and 29, 1922, Depositions of Rafael Hernandez, Nov. 14 and 29, 1922, Deposition of Manuel Mora, Nov. 14, 1922, Deposition of Alberto Albarez, Nov. 14, 1922, Deposition of Francisco Perez, Nov. 28, 1922, Deposition of Savino Casares, Nov. 28, 1922, Deposition of Lino Cortez, Nov. 29, 1922, Deposition of S. L. Henson, Nov. 29, 1922, Deposition of Tol Humphries, Nov. 29, 1922, Deposition of T. J. Buckow, Nov. 29, 1922, Wright to Barton, Dec. 1, 1922, AGC [quotes]; *Moberly* [MO] *Monitor-Index*, Nov. 15, 1922; *Wellington* [KS] *Daily News*, Nov. 15, 1922; *Ottowa* [KS] *Herald*, Nov. 16, 1922; *Pittsburgh* [PA] *Post-Gazette*, Nov. 16, 1922; *Brownwood Bulletin*, Nov. 22, 24, 1922; *Wichita* [KS] *Daily Eagle*, Nov. 23, 1922; *Weatherford Daily Herald*, Nov. 24, 1922; *Longview News-Journal*, Nov. 24, 1922; *Corsicana Daily Sun*, Nov. 24, 1922; *FCJ*, Dec. 1, 1922; Harris & Sadler, *Rangers in Transition*, 168–170; Ivey, *Ranger Ideal, Volume 3*, 48–49; Martin G. Urbina, Joel E. Vela, and Juan O. Sanchéz, *Ethnic Realities of Mexican Americans* (Springfield, IL: Charles C. Thomas, 2014), 109–110. Historians William D. Carrigan and Clive Webb say that the investigations by Texas Rangers and federal authorities in the lynching of Elías Villareal Zarate and others in the 1920s led to an end to such cases involving Mexicans and Mexican Americans. See *Forgotten Dead: Mob Violence Against Mexicans in the United States, 1828–1948* (New York: Oxford University Press, 2013), 149–151.

38. Pelton B. Harbison to William L. Wright, Apr. 16, 1923, William L. Wright to Barton, April 27, 1923, Tape 8.2, Ward Collection; Perez, "Reminiscences," 91–92, 113–114; TRHFM: Jesse Perez Sr.; *Austin American*, Dec. 19, 20, 1922; *Laredo Weekly Times* Dec. 24, 1922; *FCJ*,

Apr. 10, 1925; Harris and Sadler, *Rangers in Transition*, 53–54 [quote]; Diaz, *Border Contraband*, 96–97, 100–103; Webb, *Texas Rangers*, 556; Ivey, *Ranger Ideal, Volume 3*, 49–52; Tise, *Texas County Sheriffs*, 288; Vera, "Los Tequileros," 18; Maude T. Gilliland, "The Remarkable Texas Rangers," *Quarterly of the National Association and Center for Outlaw and Lawman History* 5 (Jan. 1980): 18–21; Ward, "Texas Rangers," 83; Coffey, "Rangers and Prohibition." William B. Wright recalled that the November 1922 scouting party included him, his father, Brady, Dial, Gonzalez, Hensley, Sadler, J. Warren Smith, Frank Smith, and Jack Webb. See Wright, *Career Hunting*, 20. Rumors of plots to kill William L. Wright persisted into the fall of 1923, when William M. Hanson wrote to him that a failed ambush reported that month was probably meant for him. See Peavey, *Echoes from the Rio Grande*, 226. Wright used the Las Animas fight as an example when he told a reporter that smugglers always "fight and shoot to kill," then run, rather than surrender. See *FCJ*, Apr. 10, 1925. In a much later article in the *Houston Chronicle Magazine*, Frank Smith is quoted as saying that he killed Silvano Gracia during the fight at Las Animas, believing him to be the man he saw shoot Robert S. Rumsey execution-style. An undated clipping of this article is in the James Warren Smith Jr. Papers, Texas Collection, Baylor University, Waco, TX.

39. AGSR: W. A. Taylor; 1920 Census, Population, Zapata County; *Coleman Democrat-Voice*, Mar. 24, 1922; *FCJ*, July 8, 1938; *Austin Statesman*, Feb. 21, 1941; FAG: Walter W. Musgrave, William Alonzo Taylor. Henry B. Yelvington wrote that the Juan Pena fight occurred in May 1926, but William L. Wright was not serving as a Texas Ranger at that time.
40. William L. Wright to Aldrich, Apr. 27, 1923, Wallis to Aldrich, Nov. 25, 1923, Tape 8.2, Ward Collection; Dial to Aldrich, Oct. 14, Nov. 8, Dec. 2, 1923, AGC [with monthly scouting reports enclosed]; Perez, "Reminiscences," 93; *SAE*, Dec. 29, 1922; *Austin Statesman*, Dec. 29, 1922; *San Patricio County News*, Aug. 30, 1923; *FCJ*, Sept. 7, 1923 (first quote); *Brownsville Herald*, Nov. 23, 1923 (second quote); Tise, *Texas County Sheriffs*, 39; Harris and Sadler, *Rangers in Transition*, 48–49, 55, 109; Ivey, *Ranger Ideal, Volume 3*, 50–52; Ward, "Texas Rangers," 91; Coffey, "Rangers and Prohibition." The men who were arrested in Brownsville were Jesus Marroquin, Guadalupe Garcia, Florentino Barrientos, and 13-year-old Manuel Saldivar. Ironically, Robert D. Brown was nominated to be a Ranger captain just

one month before he was arrested at Weslaco. See Humes B. Galbraith to Aldrich, Feb. 9, 1923, Joseph C. Hutcheson Jr. to Barton, Feb. 16, 1923, J. C. George to Barton, Feb. 17, 1923, Aldrich to George, Mar. 6, 1923, AGC.

41. William M. Hanson to Neff, May 28, 1923, Aldrich to Hanson, June 16, 1923, Hanson to Aldrich, June 20, 1923, Valls to Barton, June 22, 1923 [first and second quotes], Aldrich to Valls, June 25, 1923 [third quote], AGC.

42. Barton to William L. Wright, Jan. 16, 1924, Tape 8.2, Ward Collection [quote]; Kevin Dunne to Barton, May 6, 1923, Jesse Wright to Frank Hamer, May 7, 1923, R. R. Bledsoe to Barton, May 7, 1923, J. B. Wheatley to Barton, May 7, 1923, H. L. Hilliard to Hamer, May 8, 1923, Hilliard to Aldrich, May 8, 1923, Aldrich to Hilliard, May 9, 1923, Aldrich to Dunne, May 14, 1923, Thomas Bell to Aldrich, July 17, 1923, Aldrich to Bell, July 21, 1923, Barton to Duncan S. Wright, Jan. 16, 1924, Aldrich to Duncan S. Wright, Feb. 18, 1924, AGC; AGSR: Duncan S. Wright, R. R. Bledsoe; *Victoria Advocate*, Jan. 10, 1924; *Houston Post*, Jan. 16, 1924; *Marshall News Messenger*, Jan. 16, 1924; *Austin American*, Jan. 17, 1924; *FCJ*, Jan. 18, 1924; *Corpus Christi Caller-Times*, Oct. 21, 1956; Harris and Sadler, *Rangers in Transition*, 61, 165–166. No family connection between Duncan S. Wright and William L. Wright has been found.

43. Mark Philips to Barton, Mar. 7, 1924, Light Townsend Affidavit, Mar. 25, 1924, Tape 8.2, Ward Collection; Dial to Aldrich, Dec. 7, 1924, Aldrich Papers, Archives of the Big Bend; Harris and Sadler, *Rangers in Transition*, 180.

44. Wright to Aldrich, May 16 [first quote], Sept. 2, 14 [third quote], 18, Oct. 24, Nov. 17 [fourth quote], 1924, Tape 8.2, Ward Collection; Townsend to Aldrich, Aug. 21, 1924, AGC [second quote]; *FCJ*, Apr. 25, Oct. 3, 1924, Apr. 10, 1925; Harris and Sadler, *Rangers in Transition*, 62; Ward, "Texas Rangers," 113.

45. Wright, *Career Hunting*, 27–28; Webb, *Texas Rangers*, 551–553 [first quote], 553–556 [second quote].

46. Townsend to Aldrich, Sept. 11, 1924 [quote], Aldrich to Peterson, Sept. 2, 1924, Peterson to Aldrich, Aug. 29, Sept. 14, 1924, AGC; *Brenham Daily Banner-Press*, Aug. 29, 1924; *Houston Post-Dispatch*, Aug. 29, 30, Sept. 4, 1924; *Mercedes Tribune*, Sept. 4, 1924; *Raymondville Willacy County News*, Sept. 4, 1924; Peavey, *Echoes from the Rio Grande*, 277–280; FAG: William C. Peterson. Gerardo Zamora had

been an election judge for the primaries in July and August 1924. See *Mercedes Tribune*, Sept. 4, 1924.

47. Aldrich to Dial, Sept. 21, 1923, Dial to Aldrich, Sept. 27, 1923, AGC; *Brownwood Bulletin*, Jan. 16, 1925; *Paducah Post*, Jan. 22, 1925; Neff, *Battles of Peace*, 139; Brown, *Hood, Bonnet, and Little Brown Jug*, 158; Harris and Sadler, *Rangers in Transition*, 184–197, 213–215; Cox, *Time of the Rangers*, 115–123; Utley, *Lone Star Lawmen*, 105–107, 110–111; Ivey, *Ranger Ideal, Volume 3*, 54–55; Tise, *Texas County Sheriffs*, 43; Julian Samora, Joe Bernal, and Albert Peña, *Gunpowder Justice: A Reassessment of the Texas Rangers* (Notre Dame, IN: University of Notre Dame Press, 1979), 67–76; Walter P. Webb, "Texas Rangers in Eclipse," *The State Trooper* 7 (Jan. 1925): 13–14; Ward, "Texas Rangers," 98–103, 121; Zelime Vance Gillespie, "Tobin, John Wallace," *HOT*.
48. William L. Wright to W. Mark McGee, Jan. 28, 30, 1925, Tape 8.2, Ward Collection; *Cameron Herald*, June 14, 1923; *Austin Statesman*, July 23, 1924; *Jacksboro Gazette*, July 31, 1924; *Seminole Sentinel*, July 31, 1924; *Flatonia Argus*, July 31, 1924; *Orange Daily Leader*, Jan. 30, 1925; *Taylor Daily Press*, Jan. 30, 1925; *Cooper Review*, Feb. 6, 1925; *Austin American*, Jan. 30, 1925; *Waco News-Tribune*, Jan. 30, 1925; *Hallettsville Herald*, Feb. 3, 1925; *Lampasas Daily Leader*, Feb. 6, 1925; Utley, *Lone State Lawmen*, 111; Cox, *Time of the Rangers*, 123–124; Walter P. Webb and M. F. Kennedy, "With the Texas Rangers," *The State Trooper* 7 (Oct. 1925): 11–12; Webb, "Texas Rangers in Eclipse," 13–14; Webb, "Veteran Ranger Protects Border," 13–14; Ward, "Texas Rangers," 115–117, 123–125; FAG: William Mark McGee.
49. Brown, *Hood, Bonnet, and Little Brown Jug*, 26–27, 258, 270–274; Harris and Sadler, *Rangers in Transition*, 215–217, 262; Utley, *Lone Star Lawmen*, 111; Cox, *Time of the Rangers*, 124–127; Carol O. Wilson, *In the Governor's Shadow: The True Story of Ma and Pa Ferguson* (Denton: University of North Texas Press, 2014), 161, 164, 173, 177; Webb and Kennedy, "With the Texas Rangers," 11–12; Webb, "Texas Rangers in Eclipse," 13–14; Ward, "Texas Rangers," 124–125. About forty percent of the pardons issued by Governor Miriam A. Ferguson came after she lost the 1927 election to her attorney general, Daniel J. "Dan" Moody. See Ken Anderson, *Dan Moody: Crusader for Justice* (Georgetown, TX: Georgetown Press, 2008), 110–112.

50. William L. Wright to Aldrich, June 5, 1921, Tape 8.1, Ward Collection; AGSR: William M. Ryan; Wright, *Career Hunting*, 29; Sterling, *Trails and Trials*, 115 [third quote], 414; *Lampasas Daily Leader*, Feb. 20, 1925; *Corsicana Democrat and Truth*, Apr. 9, 1925; *FCJ*, Apr. 10, 1925; *San Patricio County News*, Apr. 30, 1925 [first quote]; Harris and Sadler, *Rangers in Transition*, 220–221; Utley, *Lone Star Lawmen*, 112 [second quote]; Cox, *Time of the Rangers*, 127; Ward, "Texas Rangers," 126.
51. Sam C. Mayes to Aldrich, Jan. 7, 1925, Aldrich Papers, Museum of the Big Bend; AGSR: William E. Burford, Dan Coleman, Grenade D. Gilliland, Juan C. Gonzalez, John E. Hensley, Sam C. Mayes, William S. Peterson, John W. Sadler, J. Warren Smith, Asa Light Townsend, Eugene H. Tumlinson, W. L. Wright; TRHFM: William Sanders Peterson, William L. Wright; *Austin Statesman*, Mar. 30, 1925; *Colorado County Citizen*, July 22, 1926; Harris and Sadler, *Rangers in Transition*, 217; Harris, Harris, and Sadler, *Texas Ranger Biographies*, 306; FAG: William Edward Burford, John E. Hensley, William Sanders Peterson.
52. William L. Wright to Aldrich, June 14, 1925, Aldrich Papers, DBCAH [seventh quote]; *FCJ*, Apr. 3 [first and second quotes], 10 [third, fourth, fifth, and sixth quotes], 1925; *Corsicana Democrat and Truth*, Apr. 9, 1925; *San Patricio County News*, Apr. 30, 1925; Harris and Sadler, *Rangers in Transition*, 12–13, 218.
53. Wright, *Career Hunting*, 23; *Corpus Christi Caller*, Mar. 30, 1925 [sixth and seventh quotes]; *Hebbronville News*, Apr. 1, 1925 [second and third quotes]; *San Patricio County News*, Apr. 30, 1925 [fourth and fifth quotes]; Webb, "Veteran Ranger Protects Border," 14; Falvella, "Captain Wright" [first quote].
54. Wright Family Bible Record, Wright Papers; Wright, "Memoir," 5, 10–11, 148; AGSR: Grover C. Webb, Charlie Hays Wright, Emanuel A. Wright; TRHFM: Grover C. Webb; Wright, *Career Hunting*, 4, 29, 30; *FCJ*, Mar. 11, 1921, Oct. 26, 1923, Jan. 2, 1925; Harris, Harris, and Sadler, *Texas Ranger Biographies*, 416; Falvella, "Captain Wright;" FAG: Blake D. Fore. Among the pallbearers for William L. Wright's mother were two of his former deputies, Thad J. Rees and Alfred B. Carnes, who was the sheriff of Wilson County at the time. See *FCJ*, Oct. 26, 1923. Kelly Lytle Hernandez devotes much attention to Emanuel A. "Dogie" Wright in Chapter One of *Migra! A History of the U.S. Border Patrol* (Berkeley: University of California Press, 2010).

55. James W. Galbreath to Harley, Dec. 17, 1917, William L. Wright to Harley, Dec. 17, 1917, AGC [first quote]; *FCJ*, Nov. 20, 27 [second and third quotes], 1925; Feb. 19, May 28, July 30, 1926; *Yoakum Daily Herald*, Nov. 28, 1925; *Lampasas Daily Leader*, Nov. 27, 1925; *Hallettsville Herald*, Aug. 10, 1926; *Hebbronville News*, Aug. 31, 1927; Harris and Sadler, *Rangers in Transition*, 218; Ivey, *Ranger Ideal, Volume 3*, 57–58; Tise, *Texas County Sheriffs*, 395.

Notes for Chapter 7

1. J. D. Hall to William L. Wright, May 3, 1927, TGC; William L. Wright to J. Warren Smith, Nov. 2, 1934 [quote], James Warren Smith Sr. Papers, Texas Collection, Baylor University; AGSR: William L. Wright; *Austin Statesman*, Aug. 6, 1926; *Waco News-Tribune*, Aug. 6, 1926; *Cuero Daily Record*, April 29, 1927; *Jim Hogg County Enterprise*, May 13, 1937; William W. Sterling, *Trails and Trials of a Texas Ranger* (Privately printed, 1959), 415; Norman D. Brown, *Hood, Bonnet, and Little Brown Jug: Texas Politics, 1921–1928* (College Station: Texas A&M University Press, 1984), 302; Robert M. Utley, *Lone Star Lawmen: The Second Century of the Texas Rangers* (New York: Oxford University Press, 2007), 117–118; Charles H. Harris III and Louis R. Sadler, *The Texas Rangers in Transition: From Gunfighters to Criminal Investigators* (Norman: University of Oklahoma Press, 2019), 208, 266–267, 292–293.
2. Special Order No. 7, Headquarters, Texas Ranger Force, Apr. 30, 1927, in TRHFM: W. W. Taylor; Special Order No. 8, Headquarters, Texas Ranger Force, May 14, 1927, in TRHFM: William L. Wright; *Panola Watchman*, May 4, 1927; *FCJ*, May 6, 13, 20, 1927; *DMN*, Mar. 23, 1930; Sterling, *Trails and Trials*, 414–415; Harris and Sadler, *Rangers in Transition*, 298; Utley, *Lone Star Lawmen*, 119–120; Charles H. Harris III, Francis E. Harris, and Louis R. Sadler, *Texas Ranger Biographies: Those Who Served 1910–1921* (Albuquerque: University of New Mexico Press, 2009), 4, 114, 160–161, 176–177, 332–333, 361; Walter P. Webb, "Rangers Reorganized," *The State Trooper* 8 (July 1927): 13; James R. Ward, "The Texas Rangers, 1919–1935: A Study in Law Enforcement" (Ph.D. Diss., Texas Christian University, 1972), 145–146, 151, 163. In comparison, Texas Ranger salaries in 1919 were $150 for captains, $100 for sergeants, and $90 for privates.

3. J. F. Andrews et al. to Daniel J. Moody, Apr. 30, 1927, William L. Wright to Moody, May 4, 1927, John A. Valls to Moody, May 6, 1927, Moody to Valls, May 10, 1927, TGC [fifth and sixth quotes]; *FCJ*, July 22, 1927, Jan. 13, 1928; *San Patricio County News*, July 21, 1927; *Austin Statesman*, Aug. 6, 1926 [third quote]; *Hebbronville News*, Aug. 31, 1927 [fourth quote], Oct. 12, 1927 [seventh quote], Nov. 2, 1927 [eighth quote]; Utley, *Lone Star Lawmen*, 119; John Boessenecker, *Texas Ranger: The Epic Life of Frank Hamer, The Man Who Killed Bonnie and Clyde* (New York: Thomas Dunne Books, 2016), 303 [first quote]; Darren L. Ivey, *The Ranger Ideal, Volume 3: Texas Rangers in the Hall of Fame, 1898–1987* (Denton: University of North Texas Press, 2021), 58. For the "El Capitan Diablo" quote, see *San Antonio Light*, Apr. 15, 1927; *FCJ*, May 6, 1927; Walter P. Webb, "Rangers Reorganized," *The State Trooper* 8 (July 1927): 13.
4. AGSR: W. W. Taylor; *Hebbronville News*, Mar. 7, 1928; Harris, Harris, and Sadler, *Texas Ranger Biographies*, 375–376; Harris and Sadler, *Rangers in Transition*, 354; Charles H. Harris III and Louis R. Sadler, *The Texas Rangers in the Mexican Revolution: The Bloodiest Decade, 1910–1920* (Norman: University of Oklahoma Press, 2004), 428; Sammy Tise, *Texas County Sheriffs* (Albuquerque: Oakwood Press, 1989), 307; FAG: William W. Taylor, William P. "Buck" Taylor.
5. Jack T. Laughlin to Roy W. Aldrich, Nov. 1, 1923, AGC; Laughlin to Moody, Nov. 14, 1929, TGC; Emanuel A. Wright, "Memoir" (Typescript, n.d., E. A. "Dogie" Wright Papers, DBCAH), 14 [quote]; AGSR: P. F. Dyches, C. M. Ezell, J. T. Laughlin, Samuel Cloud Mayes, James Warren Smith, Robert W. Sumrall; Special Order No. 25, Headquarters, Texas Ranger Force, Dec. 31, 1927, in TRHFM: William L. Wright; Special Order No. 4, Headquarters, Texas Ranger Force, Feb. 1, 1928, in TRHFM: Sam C. Mayes; TRHFM: James W. Smith; *Coleman Democrat-Voice*, Sept. 3, 10, 1931; Harris, Harris, and Sadler, *Texas Ranger Biographies*, 96, 221, 367, 422; FAG: Pinkney F. "Pink" Dyches, Clarence Marvin Ezell, Samuel Cloud "Sam" Mayes, William E. Young.
6. N. D. Buie to Moody, Aug. 11, 1927, TGC; AGSR: Fred E. Griffin [second quote], J. C. Parker, R. E. Poole, Harold Slack, Thad Tarver, C. C. Wren; Special Order No. 7, Headquarters, Texas Ranger Force, Apr. 30, 1927, in TRHFM: William E. Young; F. C. Weinert, *Biennial Report of the Secretary of State of the State of Texas, 1914* (Austin, TX: Von Boeckmann-Jones Company, 1914), 257; *Hebbronville News*, Mar. 7,

1928; *Fort Worth Star-Telegram*, Jan. 3, 1929 [first quote]; *DMN*, Jan. 22, 1929; Tise, *Texas County Sheriffs*, 319; FAG: Thad Tarver, C. C. Wren, Robert E. Poole.

7. Wright, "Memoir," 14; William L. Wright to Roy W. Aldrich, Sept. 5, 1927, William L. Wright to Taylor Nichols, Oct. 2, 13, 24, 1927, dictation on Tape 3.1 in James R. Ward Collection, West Texas Collection, Angelo State University, San Angelo, TX; *Hebbronville News*, Nov. 2, 1927 [quote]; *DMN*, Dec. 4, 1927; Utley, *Lone Star Lawmen*, 123–124; Harris and Sadler, *Rangers in Transition*, 246, 248–253, 303–320, 356–358; Diana D. Hinton and Roger M. Olien, *Oil in Texas: The Gusher Age, 1895–1945* (Austin: University of Texas Press, 2002), 146–147; Roger M. Olien and Diana D. Olien, *Oil Booms: Social Change in Five Texas Towns* (Lincoln: University of Nebraska Press, 1982), 7, 8, 15–16, 37–38, 176; George T. Diaz, *Border Contraband: A History of Smuggling Across the Rio Grande* (Austin: University of Texas Press, 2015), 104–105; Ward, "Texas Rangers," 152, 160. During this time, as William L. Wright relocated his headquarters from town to town, his wife Mary Ann Brown Wright, or Mollie, moved their home as well, with their youngest son Houston Tom "Simp Tom" Wright in tow. See *FCJ*, May 20, 1927, Aug. 31, 1928.
8. Aldrich to William L. Wright, Nov. 30, 1927, William L. Wright to Aldrich, Dec. 1, 1927, William L. Wright to Robert L. Robertson, Nov. 28, Dec. 8, 23, 1927, Jan. 17, Feb. 15, 1928, Robertson to William L. Wright, Dec. 16, 1927, Tape 3.1, Ward Collection; Lee J. Marks to Moody, Dec. 12, 1927, TGC [quote]; AGSR: Henry D. Glasscock; *San Antonio Gazette*, Jan. 27, 1906; Tise, *Texas County Sheriffs*, 310. Henry D. Glasscock was a veteran of the Ranger operations in Borger. See Harris and Sadler, *Rangers in Transition*, 251–253, 358.
9. William L. Wright to Robertson, Jan. 17, 31, Feb. 5, 15, 1928, and n.d., Tape 3.1, Ward Collection; William L. Wright, Report of Company A, Feb. 24, 1928, and Report Concerning Feb. 24, 1928, Raid at Wink, Tape 11.1, Ward Collection; AGSR: J. T. Laughlin, Henry D. Glasscock; Special Order No. 25, Headquarters, Texas Ranger Force, Dec. 31, 1927, in TRHFM: James W. Smith; *Lampasas Daily Leader*, Jan. 13, Mar. 2, 1928; *FCJ*, Jan. 27, Mar. 2, 1928; *Hebbronville News*, Mar. 7, 1928 [first quote]; *New York* [NY] *World*, Mar. 25, 1929; *El Paso Herald*, Sept. 20, 1929 [second quote]; Harris and Sadler, *Rangers in Transition*, 356–359; Utley, *Lone Star Lawmen*, 124; Tise, *Texas County Sheriffs*, 310; Olien and Olien, *Oil Boom Towns*, 14–15, 37–38, 133–136,

139–140, 176; Ward, "Texas Rangers," 160–161. Governor Daniel J. Moody's investigation led to the removal of three Special Rangers. See W. M. Davis to Moody, Jan. 18, 22, 1927, May 5, 11, 1927, June 8, 1927, Nov. 4, 1927, Jan. 24, 1928, Moody to Davis, Jan. 20, 1927, May 14, 27, 1927, Nov. 10, 1927, William H. Kirby to Moody, May 22, 1927, Deposition of Elgin Dodge, July 14, 1927, Deposition of J. W. Hillman, July 14, 1927, Moody to Harry T. Odneal, July 16, 1927, Odneal to Moody, July 19, 1927, Henry E. Webb to Moody, July 19, 20, 1927, Atticus Webb to Moody, July 26, 1927, Jack Allen to Moody Oct. 29, Nov. 5, 1927, Moody to Jack Allen, Nov. 1, 8, 1927, Ben F. Allen to Moody, Oct. 29, 1927, Moody to Ben F. Allen, Nov. 2, 1927, Moody to S. R. Moore, Nov. 1, 1927, Moody to Roy Kight, Nov. 1, 11, 1927, Kight to Moody, Nov. 10, 1927, Moody to Sam Haynes, Nov. 1, 1927, Moody to C. R. Sutton, Nov. 1, 1927, C. R. Sutton to Moody, Nov. 7, 1927, W. E. Martin to Moody, Nov. 3, 1927, J. F. Sutton to Kight, Nov. 3, 1927, J. F. Sutton to Moody, Nov. 9, 1927, Moody to J. F. Sutton, Nov. 12, 1927, W. P. Rutledge to Moody, Nov. 8, 1927, Moody to Rutledge, Nov. 10, 1927, E. C. Stearns to Moody, Nov. 8, 1927, C. A. Jones to Moody, Nov. 15, 1927, Marks to Moody, Dec. 6, 12, 19, 1927, Moody to Lee J. Marks, Dec. 7, 15, 1927, Montague to Moody, Jan. 18, 1928, Moody to Montague, Jan. 20, 1928, TGC; AGSR: Jack T. DeGraftenreid, Roy Kight, Harry T. Odneal; Harris and Sadler, *Rangers in Transition*, 356–357. When local leaders in Marfa protested Wright's relocation to McCamey, Moody explained that the failure of the Special Rangers necessitated the change. See J. C. Fuller to Moody, Jan. 20, 1928, M. D. Bownds to Moody, Jan. 20, 1928, Hunter Metcalfe to Moody, Jan. 20, 1928, Moody to Metcalfe, Jan. 20, 1928, L. C. Brite to Moody, Jan. 20, 1928, Moody to Brite, Jan. 20, 1928, J. D. Burton to Moody, Jan. 20, 1928, Moody to Burton, Jan. 20, 1928, TGC.

10. William L. Wright to Robertson, Jan. 31, 1927, Feb. 5, 25, Mar. 11, 24, 1928, and n.d., Tape 3.1, Ward Collection; Sam C. Mayes to William L. Wright, Feb. 1, 2, 1928, William L. Wright, Report of Company A, Feb. 24, 1928, William L. Wright, Report Concerning Feb. 24, 1928, Raid at Wink, Tape 11.1, Ward Collection; *Austin Statesman*, Jan. 19, 1928; *Abilene Morning Reporter-News*, Feb. 5, 1928; *FCJ*, Mar. 2, Apr. 27, 1928; *Hebbronville News*, Mar. 7, 1928 [quote]; *Des Moines* [IA] *Tribune*, Mar. 22, 1928; *Lubbock Avalanche-Journal*, Apr. 1, 1928; Harris and Sadler, *Rangers in Transition*, 359; Ward, "Texas Rangers,"

161; FAG: Clarence Lee "Heavy" Brecheen. While newspaper accounts refer to the shooting victim in McCamey as R. F. McCay, R. F. McKay, or Red Mackay, Murl Burzette was admitted to the local hospital with a gunshot wound in his left arm on Feb. 3, 1928 and died the next day, and his father, B. F. Burzette, traveled from Iowa to Texas to settle his estate after Will Brake and his wife confessed. See "Murl Burzette," Texas Death Certificates, 1890–1976, accessed Mar. 5, 2020, https://www.fold3.com/image/90346596.

11. Montague to Moody, Feb. 12, 21, 1928, TGC; AGSR: Robert W. Sumrall; TRHFM: Robert W. Sumrall; *Coleman Democrat-Voice*, Sept. 10, 1931; Utley, *Lone Star Lawmen*, 125–129; Harris and Sadler, *Rangers in Transition*, 373–377; Boessenecker, *Texas Ranger*, 323–337; Walter P. Webb, *The Texas Rangers: A Century of Frontier Defense* (Boston, MA: Houghton Mifflin, 1935), 533–538; Mike Cox, *Time of the Rangers: Texas Rangers from 1900 to the Present* (New York: Forge Books, 2009), 136–137; "Upton County, Texas, Crime News," accessed Mar. 5, 2020, http://genealogytrails.com/tex/bigbend/upton/news_crime.html.
12. Rufus C. Van Zandt to Thomas D. Barton, Dec. 28, 1922, RFC; AGSR: R. C. Van Zandt; William L. Wright to Aldrich, April 28, 1939, Aldrich Papers, DBCAH; Wright, "Memoir," 15; *Abilene Morning Reporter-News*, Mar. 18, 1928; *El Paso Herald*, Mar. 28, 1928; *FCJ*, Mar. 30, Apr. 27, 1928; *SAE*, Oct. 2, 1928; Sterling, *Trails and Trials*, 97–99; Harris and Sadler, *Rangers in Transition*, 249–250, 305, 359–360; Utley, *Lone Star Lawmen*, 116; Ivey, *Ranger Ideal, Volume 3*, 60; Boessenecker, *Texas Ranger*, 307; Tise, *Texas County Sheriffs*, 436; Brownson Malsch, *"Lone Wolf" Gonzaullas, Texas Ranger* (Norman: University of Oklahoma Press, 1998), 63–64; Ward, "Texas Rangers," 161; FAG: Edgar B. Kiser; Brian Norwood, "Two Gun Dick Herwig," accessed Mar. 6, 2020, https:// newmexicohistoryblog.wordpress.com/2018/02/13/two-gun-dick-herwig/. Rufus C. Van Zandt had not distinguished himself as a Railroad Ranger and was discharged early, and he clashed with Sheriff Jack Allen at Crane, but William L. Wright apparently found him to be a useful ally. See Allen to Moody, Nov. 5, 1927, TGC; Harris and Sadler, *Rangers in Transition*, 107–108.
13. William L. Wright to Robertson, Mar. 6, 11, 1928, Tape 3.1, Ward Collection; *FCJ*, Apr. 27, 1928; *Corsicana Daily Sun*, May 28, 1928; *Borger Daily Herald*, Aug. 30, 1928; *El Paso Herald*, Oct. 15, 1928; *El Paso Evening Post*, Oct. 17, 1928; *FCJ*, Apr. 27, 1928; Harris and

Sadler, *Rangers in Transition*, 357; Olien and Olien, *Oil Boom Towns*, 67, 136–137; FAG: Julian R. Ostrom.

14. *FCJ*, July 20, 1928 [quote]; *Marshall News Messenger*, July 21, 1928; *Austin American*, July 21, 1928; *Lubbock Morning Avalanche*, Aug. 8, 1928; *Lubbock Avalanche-Journal*, Aug. 19, 1928; *Waxahachie Daily Light*, Aug. 21, 1928; Tise, *Texas County Sheriffs*, 548; Ward, "Texas Rangers," 162; FAG: David J. Pickle. The names of the Special Rangers who accompanied Wright are not known. It should be noted that David J. Pickle was the judge who was involved in the 1919 beating of John R. Shillady, executive secretary of the NAACP, in Austin. See Monica Muñoz Martínez, *The Injustice Never Leaves You: Anti-Mexican Violence in Texas* (Cambridge, MA: Harvard University Press, 2018), 219–221.
15. *Lampasas Daily Leader*, Sept. 18 [first quote], Oct. 19, 1928; *Breckenridge American*, Sept. 19, 1928; *Brownwood Bulletin*, Sept. 19, Oct. 11, 1928; *El Paso Herald*, Oct. 15, 1928; *El Paso Evening Post*, Oct. 17, 1928 [second quote]; Harris and Sadler, *Rangers in Transition*, 364; Olien and Olien, *Oil Boom Towns*, 67, 137.
16. J. J. Johnson to Daniel J. Moody, Aug. 27, 1928, C. A. Davis to Moody, Sept. 14, 15, 1928; Moody to Davis, Sept. 18, 1928, TGC; William L. Wright to Robertson, Sept. 9, 1928, Tape 3.1, Ward Collection [last quote]; Harris and Sadler, *Rangers in Transition*, 360–361.
17. *El Paso Evening Post*, Dec. 19, 20, 1928; *Lincoln* [NE] *Star*, Dec. 19, 1928; [Lincoln] *Nebraska State Journal*, Dec. 19, 1928; *Waco News-Tribune*, Dec. 19, 1928; Harris and Sadler, *Rangers in Transition*, 362; Ivey, *Ranger Ideal, Volume 3*, 61–62; Ward, "Texas Rangers," 162; FAG: Paul C. Burcham.
18. *Austin Statesman*, Dec. 20, 1928; *Austin American*, Dec. 24, 1928; *Waco News-Tribune*, Dec. 24, 1928; *El Paso Evening Post*, Dec. 25, 1928; *FCJ*, Jan. 4, 1929 [quotes]; Harris and Sadler, *Rangers in Transition*, 318; Olien and Olien, *Oil Boom Towns*, 138; FAG: John Harrison "Toughie" Northcutt.
19. William L. Wright to Robertson, Feb. 14, 1929, Tapes 11.2, Ward Collection [first quote]; AGSR: R. Y. Secrest; Wright, "Memoir," 14, 16; *El Paso Herald*, Oct. 15, 1928; *El Paso Evening Post*, Oct. 17, 1928, July 12, 1929 [second quote]; *Coleman Democrat-Voice*, Aug. 29, 1929 [third quote]; Harris and Sadler, *Rangers in Transition*, 363–364; Olien and Olien, *Oil Boom Towns*, 67, 139; Paul N. Spellman, *Capt. John H. Rogers, Texas Ranger* (Denton: University of North Texas Press,

2003), 221; Ward, "Texas Rangers," 165; FAG: Julian R. Ostrom; Julia Cauble Smith, "Wink, TX, " *HOT*. An alumnus of Southern Methodist University, Smythe H. Lindsay later became an Episcopal minister and published a prominent Episcopalian newsletter, *The Anglican Press*. See "Smythe Lindsay is dead," *The Living Church* 154 (Jan. 22, 1967), 9.

20. William L. Wright to Robertson, Aug. 27, 1929, Tape 11.2, Ward Collection [quotes]; James Warren Smith Sr., Diary (Manuscript, n.d.), entries for June 3 and 7, 1929, Texas Collection, Baylor University, Waco, TX; *Abilene Reporter-News*, July 14, 1929; Harris and Sadler, *Rangers in Transition*, 363; Olien and Olien, *Oil Boom Towns*, 138; A. R. and R. B. Buckelew, "The Discovery of Oil in South Arkansas, 1920–1924," *Arkansas Historical Quarterly* 33 (Autumn 1974): 233, 234; "Chief of Police Rufus Nicholson Gilbreath," *Officer Down Memorial Page*, accessed Mar. 9, 2020, https://www.odmp.org/officer/18634-chief-of-police-rufus-nicholson-gilbreath; Steven Teske, "Norphlet (Union County)," *Encyclopedia of Arkansas*, accessed Mar. 9, 2020, http://www.encyclopediaofarkansas.net/encyclopedia/entry-detail.aspx?entryID=6156.

21. *SAE*, Oct. 2, 1928 [first quote]; *Corpus Christi Times*, Nov. 24, 1929 [second and third quotes]; *Pampa Daily News*, May 27, 1931; *Corsicana Daily Sun*, May 27, 1931; *Abilene Morning News*, May 28, 1931; *Paducah Post*, May 28, 1931; *Odessa News-Times*, May 29, 1931; Harris and Sadler, *Rangers in Transition*, 363, 412; Ivey, *Ranger Ideal, Volume 3*, 65; Tise, *Texas County Sheriffs*, 269.

22. William L. Wright to Robertson, Nov. 4, Dec. 1, 1928, Tape 3.1, Ward Collection; *Waco News-Tribune*, Nov. 4, Dec. 1, 2, 12, 9, 21, 1928; *Lubbock Morning Avalanche*, Nov. 4, Dec. 1, 2, 6, 7, 21, 1928; *Corsicana Daily Sun*, Nov. 29 [quote], 30, Dec. 18, 20, 1928; *Bryan Eagle*, Nov. 30, 1928; *DMN*, Dec. 5, 6, 8, 20, 1928; *Fort Worth Star-Telegram*, Dec. 6, 7, 1928; *Bonham Daily Favorite*, Dec. 7, 1928; *Austin Statesman*, Dec. 21, 1928; *Breckenridge American*, Dec. 21, 1928; Harris and Sadler, *Rangers in Transition*, 365; Ward, "Texas Ranger," 162–163. After James W. Luman's appeal was denied in June 1929, he served two years in prison, then relocated to Borger, where he later worked for almost four decades as an inspector for the Texas and Southwestern Cattle Raisers Association with a commission as a Special Ranger, which he first obtained from Governor Miriam A. "Ma" Ferguson in 1933. See Ivey, *Ranger Ideal, Volume 3*, 61–62; FAG: James William "Dutch" Luman, Ola Fay Finchum Luman. Van Leach Finchum,

described as a forty-two-year-old former convict, was sentenced to five years in prison for burglary in 1950. See *Pampa Daily News*, July 9, 1950. Van Leach Finchum and Ola Faye Finchum Luman were siblings. See "Ola Faye Finchum," *Family Search*, accessed Mar. 5, 2020, https://ancestors.familysearch.org/en/LDMN-7CS/ola-faye-finchum-1911-1978.

23. William L. Wright to Robertson, Aug. 27, 1929 [quotes], J. Warren Smith to Robertson, Jan. 29, 1929, Tape 11.2, Ward Collection; Moody to William L. Wright, Sept. 18, 1929, Moody to E. G. Tarlton, Sept. 18, 1929, Moody to Francis A. Hamer, Sept. 18, 1929, AGC; Spellman, *Captain Rogers*, 221; Harris and Sadler, *Rangers in Transition*, 363–365; Ivey, *Ranger Ideal, Volume 3*, 62–63; Ward, "Texas Rangers," 164–165; FAG: James Carroll Bates, Jewel Pearl Tyra Hogan, Jackie Mae Whiteside.
24. *FCJ*, Oct. 28, 1932; *Odessa American*, May 19, 1933; *El Paso Herald-Post*, June 24, 1933; *Waco Tribune-Herald*, June 25, 1933; Tise, *Texas County Sheriffs*, 167; Harris and Sadler, *Rangers in Transition*, 365–366.
25. *Odessa American*, May 19, 1933; Harris and Sadler, *Rangers in Transition*, 365–366.
26. Mrs. W. S. Pate to J. Warren Smith, Mar. 19, 1934, James Warren Smith Sr. Papers, Texas Collection, Baylor University; *Waco News-Tribune*, Mar. 26, 1925; *FCJ*, Oct. 28, 1932; *Pecos Enterprise*, May 19, 1933; *El Paso Herald-Post*, June 24, 1933; *Waco Tribune-Herald*, June 25, 1933; Rudolph Kleberg, comp., *The Texas Criminal Reports: Cases Argued and Adjudged in the Court of Criminal Appeals of the State of Texas,, Volume 88* (Columbia, MO: E. W. Stephens Publishing Company, 1921), 248–253; Ivey, *Ranger Ideal, Volume 3*, 63–65.
27. William L. Wright, Report of Company A, June 23, 1930, Tape 9.1, Ward Collection; *Big Spring Daily Herald*, May 25, June 27, 1930; *Big Lake Wildcat*, July 18, 1930 [quotes]; *El Paso Evening Post*, Dec. 1, 1930; *Abilene Morning Reporter-News*, June 22, Dec. 14, 1930; *Lubbock Avalanche-Journal*, May 5, 2013; Harris and Sadler, *Rangers in Transition*, 365, 412–414; Gordon L. Hooper, *Pioneer History of Crane County Before 1925* (Bloomington, IN: iUniverse, 2012), 181–182; Ward, "Texas Rangers," 174; FAG: Thomas Carwin Barnsley Sr., Ira McKee; John Leffler, "Crane County," *HOT*; FAG: William Rex Billingsley; "List of People Executed in Texas, 1930–1939,"

accessed Mar. 16, 2020, https:// en.wikipedia.org/wiki/List_of_people executed_ in_Texas,_1930%E2%80%9339.

28. *Lampasas Daily Leader*, Jan. 23, 31, Feb. 6, 1931; *Austin American*, Jan. 27, 1931; *FCJ*, Feb. 6, 1931; *Fredericksburg Standard*, Feb. 6, 1931; *Longview Daily News*, Nov. 1, 1931; Sterling, *Trails and Trials*, 183 [quote], 199, 205; Ross S. Sterling and Ed Kilman, *Ross Sterling, Texan: A Memoir by the Founder of Humble Oil and Refining Company*, ed, Don E. Carleton (Austin: University of Texas Press, 2007), 131–132; Harris and Sadler, *Rangers in Transition*, 386–388, 390; Utley, *Lone Star Lawmen*, 143; Boessenecker, *Texas Ranger*, 379; Darren L. Ivey, *The Texas Rangers: A Registry and History* (West Jefferson, NC: McFarland & Company, 2010), 185–187; Ward, "Texas Rangers," 181–184; "Sterling, Ross Shaw," *HOT*; "Sterling, William Warren," *HOT*. The governor and adjutant general were not related.
29. William L. Wright to William W. Sterling, May 5, 1932 [first, second, third quotes], Hamer to Wright, May 6, 1932 [fourth quote], Tape 10.1, Ward Collection; *Lampasas Daily Leader*, Aug. 1, 1932 [fifth quote]; AGSR: James G. Rooney, W. W. Taylor; Harris and Sadler, *Rangers in Transition*, 412–413; Utley, *Lone Star Lawmen*, 145–149; Tise, *Texas County Sheriffs*, 502; Ward, "Texas Rangers," 185.
30. *FCJ*, Sept. 25, 1931; *Lampasas Daily Leader*, June 15, 17, 1932; *Lubbock Morning Avalanche*, June 15, 1932; *Marshall Morning News*, June 16, 1932; *Seminole Sentinel*, June 16, 1932; *Odessa News-Times*, June 17, 1932; *Weimar Mercury*, June 24, 1932; AGSR: Edgar T. Neal; Tise, *Texas County Sheriffs*, 200, 454; Robert W. Stephens, *Texas Ranger Sketches* (Privately printed, 1972), 102–103; FAG: Edgar Thomas Neal.
31. *Abilene Reporter-News*, May 28, June 16, 23, 1932; *Lubbock Morning Avalanche*, May 28, June 15, 23, 1932; *Lampasas Daily Leader*, June 15, 17, 1932; *Seminole Sentinel*, June 16, Dec. 22, 1932; *Marshall Morning News*, June 16, 1932; *Odessa News-Times*, June 17, 1932; *Weimar Mercury*, June 24, 1932.
32. *Abilene Reporter-News*, May 28, June 16, 23, 1932; *Lubbock Morning Avalanche*, May 28, June 15, 23, 1932, Feb. 3, 1933; *Marshall Morning News*, June 16, 1932; *Seminole Sentinel*, June 16, Dec. 22, 1932.
33. *Abilene Reporter-News*, Jan. 31, Feb. 4, 1933; *Lubbock Avalanche-Journal*, Jan. 31, Feb. 2, 5, May 28, 1933; *Corsicana Daily Sun*, Feb. 1, 1933; *Lubbock Morning Avalanche*, Feb. 4, 5, 1933; Texas Department of Criminal Justice, Convict Record Ledgers, 1849–1954:

Jodie Edwards (#72531), O. M. Herring (#72532), Elmer Slaughter (#72535).

34. William L. Wright to Smith, May 3, 1933, Smith Papers, Texas Collection, Baylor University; *Nolan County News*, Sept. 15, 1932; *FCJ*, Nov. 25, Dec. 23, 1932, Jan. 27, 1933; *SAE*, Jan. 22, 1933; *Brownsville Herald*, July 6, 1934, Feb. 17, 1935; *Corpus Christi Caller Times*, Mar. 7, 1942; Sterling, *Trails and Trials*, 264–269; Sterling and Kilman, *Ross Sterling*, 202, 207–208, 210–212; Harris and Sadler, *Rangers in Transition*, 392–393, 429–432, 435; Utley, *Lone Star Lawmen*, 150–153; Cox, *Time of the Rangers*, 134, 156–157; Tise, *Texas County Sheriffs*, 395; Carol O. Wilson, *In the Governor's Shadow: The True Story of Ma and Pa Ferguson* (Denton: University of North Texas Press, 2014), 192–193; Ward, "Texas Rangers," 205–210; FAG: James W. Galbreath, Paul Elventon Cox.

35. Ivey, *Ranger Ideal, Volume 3*, 67–68.

36. *FCJ*, Jan. 26, 1934; Paul N. Spellman, *Captain Rogers*, 111–113; Darren L. Ivey, *The Ranger Ideal, Volume 2: Texas Rangers in the Hall of Fame, 1874–1930* (Denton: University of North Texas Press, 2018), 479–481; Américo Paredes, *With His Pistol in His Hand: A Border Ballad and Its Hero* (Austin: University of Texas Press, 1958), 59–64; FAG: Daniel Boone Choate.

37. *Brownsville Herald*, Feb. 17, 1935 [quotes]; *FCJ*, Feb. 22, 1935; Harris and Sadler, *Rangers in Transition*, 487–488, 491–492, 495; Cox, *Time of the Rangers*, 166; Utley, *Lone Star Lawmen*, 167–168; Ward, "Texas Rangers," 214–224, 226–229. William L. O'Daniel would be the eighth governor for whom William L. Wright worked as a Texas Ranger.

38. *Brownsville Herald*, Feb. 17, May 15, 1935; *Lampasas Daily Leader*, May 15, 1935; *Uvalde Crier*, June 1, 1980 [third quote]; AGSR: William W. McMurrey; TRHFM: William (Bill) McMurrey; Sterling, *Trails and Trials*, 121, 416 [first quote]; Utley, *Lone Star Lawmen*, 168; Ivey, *Registry*, 187, 206; Maude T. Gilliland, *Horsebackers of the Brush Country: A Story of the Texas Rangers and Mexican Liquor Smugglers* (Brownsville, TX: Springman-King Company, 1968), 111; Ward, "Texas Rangers," 229 [second quote].

39. *Brownsville Herald*, Aug. 24, 25, 1896; AGSR: A. W. Allee, A. Y. Allee, Edgar T. Neal; Carl Nesbitt, *Report of Adjutant General of the State of Texas, January 15, 1935, to December 31, 1936* (Austin, TX: Lone Star Printing Company, 1937), 36; Harris, Harris, and Sadler, *Texas Ranger Biographies*, 5; David Johnson, *The Cornett-Whitley Gang: Violence*

Unleashed in Texas (Denton: University of North Texas Press, 2019), 194–195; Beatriz de la Garza, *A Law for the Lion: A Tale of Crime and Injustice in the Borderlands* (Austin: University of Texas, 2003), 121–125; Norman Youngblood, "Allee, Alfred Young," *HOT*; "Texas Ranger Alfred Young Allee," accessed Mar. 16, 2020, http://sherrysharp.com/genealogy/getperson.php?personID=I32502&tree=Roots. Three years after killing Alfred Y. Allee, City Marshal A. Joseph Barthelow of Laredo was with William L. Wright in his first gunfight during the smallpox riot at that town in 1899.

40. Nesbitt, *Report of Adjutant General*, 36; *Brownsville Herald*, Feb. 17, 1935; *Lampasas Daily Leader*, May 15, 1935; *SAE*, Sept. 7, 1969; AGSR: Leo H. Bishop, Leo Henderson Bishop, Fred D. Holland, Martin E. Trejo; K. S. Foster, "Early Members of the Fort Worth Police Department," 36, 38, 40, 48, accessed Mar. 16, 2020, https://www.freewebs.com/hinzd/Rosters/FWPD%20ROSTERS.pdf. For an excellent discussion of Leo Bishop's role at San Augustine, see Jody E. Ginn, *East Texas Troubles: The Allred Rangers' Cleanup of San Augustine* (Norman: University of Oklahoma Press, 2019).
41. Powers R. Fenner to Roy W. Aldrich, Aug. 11, 1922, AGC; Nesbitt, *Report of Adjutant General*, 36; AGSR: Levi Duncan, Power R. Fenner, Powers Fenner; TRHFM: Power R. Fenner; *Laredo Weekly Times*, Sept. 18, 1921; *Madera Tribune*, July 15, 1937; *Harlingen Valley Morning Star*, July 18, 1937; Joe H. Bridge Jr., *Joe H. Bridge: Texas Ranger, 1936–1956* (Privately printed, 1998), 4–18; Mona D. Sizer, *Texas Justice: Bought and Paid for* (Plano: Republic of Texas Press, 2001), 55; "Joseph Henry Marion Bridge (1891–1956)," accessed Mar. 16, 2020, https://www.wikitree.com/wiki/ Bridge-1325. Powers R. Fenner also "pulled a little rough stuff" while he was serving as a Railroad Ranger, and Captain Roy W. Aldrich told William L. Miller of William L. Wright's Company D to make him return a gun he had confiscated. See Aldrich to William L. Miller, Aug. 28, 1923, AGC.
42. *McAllen Monitor*, Mar. 18, 1935, *Corsicana Daily Sun*, Mar. 18, 1935; *Waco News-Tribune*, Mar. 19, 1935; *Corsicana Semi-Weekly Light*, Mar. 19, 1935; *Austin American*, Mar. 19, 1935; *Lubbock Morning Avalanche*, Mar. 19, 1935; *Corpus Christi Caller-Times*, Mar. 19, 1935; Harris and Sadler, *Rangers in Transition*, 494–496; Utley, *Lone Star Lawmen*, 170–171; Wilson, *In the Governor's Shadow*, 197.
43. Nesbitt, *Report of Adjutant General*, 36; AGSR: William Shely, Albert R. Mace; TRHFM: Maro Woodley Williamson; *Austin Statesman*,

Apr. 2, 3, 1935; *Pampa Daily News*, Apr. 2, 1935; *Paris News*, Apr. 2, 1935; *Longview News-Journal*, Apr. 2, 1935 [quote]; *DMN*, Oct. 19, 1938; *Corpus Christi Caller-Times*, Jan. 6, 1939; *Eagle Lake Headlight*, Nov. 15, 2017; Harris and Sadler, *Rangers in Transition*, 499–500; Tise, *Texas County Sheriffs*, 395, 319; FAG: Albert Ramon Mace Sr., Maro Woodley Williamson, Zeno A. Smith.

44. *Brownsville Herald*, Feb. 17, May 9, 15, 1935; *Lampasas Daily Leader*, May 15, 1935; *McAllen Daily Press*, Nov. 24, 25, 1935; *Harlingen Valley Morning Star*, Nov. 24, 1935; *McAllen Daily Monitor*, Nov. 25, 26, 1935; FAG: Lewis R. Hammerly; "Rogers C. Kelley," accessed Mar. 16, 2020, https://grandlodgeoftexas.org/ grand-master/rogers-c-kelly/.
45. Henry Hutchings, *Report of the Adjutant General of the State of Texas, January 18, 1933, to December 31, 1934* (Austin, TX: Knape Printing Company, 1935), 46; TRHFM: Maro Woodley Williamson; Utley, *Lone Star Lawmen*, 158–160, 167, 171–173, 176, 179–188, 190–191, 195–196; Harris and Sadler, *Rangers in Transition*, 491, 505–508; Cox, *Time of the Rangers*, 156–157, 167–170, 174–177; Ward, "Texas Rangers," 211–213, 227–233, 235, 237; Bill Carter, "Garrison, Homer, Jr.," *HOT*.
46. Nesbitt, *Report of Adjutant General*, 36; AGSR: E. M. Davenport, J. B. Wheatley; TRHFM: E. M. Davenport; *Longview News-Journal*, Nov. 5, 1935; *El Paso Times*, Nov. 5, 1935; *Corpus Christi Caller-Times*, Nov. 8, 1935; *Mexia Weekly Times*, Nov. 8, 1935; Gilbert Mers, *Working the Waterfront: The Ups and Downs of a Rebel Longshoreman* (Austin: University of Texas Press, 1988), 88–92, 94–97, 106–107; Harris and Sadler, *Rangers in Transition*, 502–503, 510–511; Tise, *Texas County Sheriffs*, 280, 418; Kemp Dixon, *Chasing Thugs, Nazis, and Reds: Texas Ranger Norman K. Dixon* (College Station: Texas A&M University Press, 2015), 53–54; Rebecca Anne Montes, "Working for American Rights: Black, White, and Mexican American Dock Workers in Texas During the Great Depression" (Ph.D. Diss., University of Texas at Austin, 2005), 27–28, 38–39, 51–54, 69–74, 94; FAG: Everard Meade Davenport Jr., Jerome B. Wheatley; "Corpus Christi Longshoremen Strike Against Poor Working Conditions and Benefits, 1935," accessed Mar. 16, 2020, https://nvdatabase.swarthmore.edu/content/corpus-christi-longshoremen-strike-against-poor-working-conditions-and-benefits-1935.
47. Mers, *Working the Waterfront*, 91, 93, 95–100, 105–113; Harris and Sadler, *Rangers in Transition*, 510–512; Montes, "Working for American

Rights," 83–86, 89–90, 113–114. The only African American longshoreman that submitted a statement claimed he was beaten and humiliated by "Ranger Monroe," but there was no Texas Ranger by that name at Corpus Christi in the fall of 1935. See Montes, "Working for American Rights," 86–87. Mers produced his final draft of his memoirs in 1987, so his focus on Alfred Y. Allee II may have been influenced by Allee's prominent role in later civil rights' disputes.

48. *Harlingen Valley Morning Star*, Sept. 29, 1936; *Corpus Christi Caller-Times*, Oct. 14, 1936; *McAllen Daily Monitor*, Nov. 4, 1936.
49. William L. Wright to Smith, July 30, 1936 [quote], Smith Papers, Texas Collection, Baylor University; *Borger Daily Herald*, Feb. 10, 1929; *Corsicana Daily Sun*, June 15, 1929, Sept. 3, 1941; *Austin American*, Feb. 8, 10, 1929, Nov. 4, 1936; *Austin American Statesman*, June 16, 1929; *Fort Worth Star-Telegram*, June 17, 1929, Apr. 7, May 7, July 15, Sept. 24, Nov. 4, 1936, Sept. 3, 1941; *Mexia Weekly Herald*, Apr. 10, 1936; *El Paso Herald-Post*, Apr. 11, 1936; *El Paso Times*, May 7, Oct. 6, 1936.
50. *McAllen Daily Press*, Nov. 22, 1936; Sizer, *Texas Justice*, 1–62; Cox, *Time of the Rangers*, 180, 425; Ivey, *Ranger Ideal, Volume 3*, 70–73.
51. *Brownsville Herald*, Jan. 24, 1937; Tise, *Texas County Sheriffs*, 86.
52. *Brownsville Herald*, Jan. 27, 1937 [quotes].
53. *Harlingen Valley Morning Star*, May 6, 1937; *Corpus Christi Caller-Times*, Aug. 30 [quote], Oct. 18, Dec. 2, 1937; *Goose Creek Daily Sun*, Oct. 20, 1937; *Weimar Mercury*, Aug. 12, 1938; *Falfurrias Facts*, July 24, 2014; Ivey, *Ranger Ideal, Volume 3*, 74–75; FAG: Fremont L. McCollum, Serapio L. Sendejo. The familial relationship between William L. Wright and Halsey Wright, if any, has not been determined.
54. "Just Elementary" (Typescript, n.d.) in TRHFM: William L. Wright; *McAllen Daily Monitor*, May 11, 1936; FAG: Hugh Perry Clark.
55. TRHFM: Quincy J. Lowman, Hugh Jack Phares, W. E. "Ebb" Riggs; *Corpus Christi Caller-Times*, Jan. 18, Apr. 19, 22, May 5, June 13, 17 [quote], July 15, 1938. Anthony Bellitt, age 23, lived in Denver, Colorado, in 1940 with his wife and a one-year-old daughter, who was born in Corpus Christi. See U.S. Bureau of the Census, Sixteenth Census, 1940, Population, Denver, CO (Record Group 29, National Archives, Washington, DC).
56. AGSR: W. E. Riggs; TRHFM: W. E. "Ebb" Riggs; *Fort Stockton Pioneer*, July 24, 1931; *Corpus Christi Caller-Times*, Aug. 25, 30,

1938; Tise, *Texas County Sheriffs*, 290, 561; Gilliland, *Horsebackers*, 145; FAG: William Wiley Ainsworth, George Bell Clegg.

57. Newspaper clipping, n.d., in Wright Papers, also in TRHFM: William L. Wright [second and third quotes]; *Abilene Reporter-News*, Sept. 14, 1938; *Harlingen Valley Morning Star*, Sept. 15, 1938; *Taft Tribune*, Sept. 22 [fourth quote], Oct. 20 [first quote], 1938, Mar. 2, 1939; *San Patricio County News*, Oct. 20, 27 [fifth quote], Nov. 3, 1938; *Aransas Pass Progress*, Feb. 23, Apr. 27, 1939; FAG: James Thomas Cole.
58. *FCJ*, July 21, 1939 [second and third quotes]; *McAllen Monitor*, Mar. 8, 1942; *Harlingen Valley Morning Star*, Mar. 8, 1942 [first quote]; *Waco Tribune-Herald*, Oct. 2, 1977; Tise, *Texas County Sheriffs*, 395.
59. *Harlingen Valley Morning Times*, Aug. 27, 28, 1936; *Breckenridge American*, Aug. 30, 1936 [first and second quotes]; *Timpson Daily Times*, Sept. 1, 1936; *Timpson Weekly Times*, Sept. 4, 1936; *DMN*, Apr. 14, 1938; *FCJ*, Apr. 22, 1938 [other quotes].
60. TRHFM: Milam H. Wright; *FCJ*, Jan. 8, 1932, Feb. 18, May 13, July 1, 7, 1938; *Harlingen Valley Morning Star*, Mar. 7, 1937 [quote], July 1, 1938; *Corpus Christi Caller-Times*, June 28, 29, 30, 1938; *Brownsville Herald*, June 29, 1938; *Jim Hogg County Enterprise*, June 30, 1938; *Falfurrias Facts*, July 1, 1938; William B. Wright, *Career Hunting: Texas Ranger vs. Standard Oiler* (El Cajon, CA: Privately printed, 1983), 4; Gilliland, *Horsebackers*, 114; FAG: Charley Hayes Wright, Milam Harper Wright; "Our Family History: The Genealogy of Robert and Christina Barritt," http://tree.barrittfamily.net/getperson.php?personID=I473&tree=dyal_speckels, accessed Jan. 20, 2020. For a good brief biography of Charles H. "Pat" Wright, see Ivey, *Ranger Ideal, Volume 3*, 74–75.
61. *Corpus Christi Caller-Times*, Aug. 15, 1939; *Harlingen Valley Morning Star*, Aug. 24, 1939; Cox, *Time of the Rangers*, 184; Utley, *Lone Star Lawmen*, 199.

Notes for Epilogue

1. "W. L. 'Will' Wright, 1868–1942," accessed Mar. 18, 2020, https://www.texasranger.org/texas-ranger-museum/hall-of-fame/william-lee-wright/ [quotes].
2. *Harlingen Valley Morning Star*, Aug. 24, 1939 [first quote]; *FCJ*, Aug. 25, 1939 [second to fifth quotes].

3. *Corpus Christi Caller-Times*, Aug. 30, 1939 [first to fifth quotes]; William W. Sterling, *Trails and Trials of a Texas Ranger* (Privately printed, 1959), 416 [sixth and seventh quotes].
4. Ferdinand V. "F.V."Arnim to O'Daniel, Aug. 20, 1939, Mrs. Charles A. Mangham [Rosa Bell Tobey Mangham] to William L. O'Daniel, Aug. 21, 1939; J. W. Sylvester, E. L. Ferguson, and Forrest R. Waldrop to O'Daniel, Aug. 21, 1939, Reuben Williams to Mangham, Aug. 25, 1939 [quote], TGC; Fred Gantt, *The Chief Executive in Texas: A Study in Gubernatorial Leadership* (Austin: University of Texas Press, 1964), 134; FAG: Ferdinand Victor Armin, Rosa Bell Tobey Mangham.
5. Emanuel A. Wright to Mrs. Joe Shriber, Oct. 17, 1966, Special Ranger Commission for William L. Wright, Jan. 30, 1941, in Scrapbook, E. A. "Dogie" Wright Papers, DBCAH; *El Paso Herald*, Oct. 24, 1928 [quotes]; *Corpus Christi Caller-Times*, Oct. 22, 1939, Mar. 7, 1942; *FCJ*, July 7, Oct. 27, Nov. 10, 1939, Mar. 1, Apr. 19, 26, 1940, Apr. 1, 1949, Sept. 16, 1960; *SAE*, Mar. 8, 1942; TRHFM: William L. Wright; FAG: Blake Davidson Fore, Zora Belle Wright Fore; "Our Family History: The Genealogy of Robert and Christina Barritt," accessed Jan. 20, 2020, http://tree.barrittfamily.net/getperson.php?personID=I473&tree=dyal_speckels. In September 1939, $200 had the same buying power as $3,642 in September 2019. See the online Consumer Price Indicator Inflation Calculator.
6. Emanuel A. Wright, "Memoir," 22–25, 28–31, Wright Papers, DBCAH; *Corpus Christi Caller-Times*, Mar. 7, 8, 1942; *McAllen Monitor*, Mar. 8, 1942; *Harlingen Valley Morning Star*, Mar. 8, 1942; *FCJ*, Mar. 13, 20, 1942, Sept. 24, 1943, Jan. 26, Sept. 7, Oct. 5, 26, 1945; *Abilene Reporter-News*, Sept. 3, 1945; *Austin Statesman*, Sept. 18, 1945; FAG: Jerry William Oxford; Texas Death Certificates, 1890–1976: William Lee Wright, accessed Jan. 20, 2020, https://www.fold3.com/image/90346596. For more on Houston Tom "Simp Tom" Wright's experiences during World War II, see Robert S. LaForte and Ronald E. Marcello, *Building the Death Railway: The Ordeal of American POWs in Burma, 1942–1945* (Lanham, MD: Rowman & Littlefield, Publishers, 1993), and Kelley E. Crager, *Hell Under the Rising Sun: Texan POWs and the Building of the Burma-Thailand Death Railway* (College Station: Texas A&M University Press, 2008). Both works reference the interview with Wright (OH 0466) found in the Oral History Collection of the University of North Texas, Denton, TX.

7. *FCJ*, Oct. 26, 1923, July 1, 1938, Mar. 13, 1942, Sept. 16, 1960, Dec. 15, 1966; *Corpus Christi Caller-Times*, Mar. 9, 1942; FAG: Capt. Robert Lee Bobbitt Sr., Sam Lane Fore Jr., William Owen Murray Jr., Joseph Thomas Sheehy; Irene Van Winkle, "Cowboy Camp Meeting Founder was Lawman and Preacher," accessed Mar. 17, 2020, http://wkcurrent.com/cowboy-camp-meeting-founder-was-lawman-and-preacher-p1219-71.htm. When William W. Sterling became the Texas adjutant general in 1931, he appointed Dr. Pierre B. Hill as a Ranger captain. See Charles H. Harris III and Louis R. Sadler, *The Texas Rangers in Transition: From Gunfighters to Criminal Investigators* (Norman: University of Oklahoma Press, 2019), 385.
8. Historical Notes (Typescript, n.d.) in Wright Papers; Interview with Zora Belle Wright Fore, Dec. 7, 1973, South Texas Oral History & Folklore Collection, South Texas Archives, James C. Jernigan Library, Texas A&M University at Kingsville; *Corpus Christi Caller-Times*, Mar. 8, 1942 [first quote]; *McAllen Monitor*, Mar. 8, 1942; *Harlingen Valley Morning Star*, Mar. 8, 1942 [second to fourth quotes]; *SAE*, Mar. 8, 1942; FAG: Robert Burrow "Bob" McCracken. The *Floresville Chronicle Journal* reported that Wright died "while seated in his chair." See *FCJ*, March 13, 1942.
9. Frankie S. Crabtree to Emanuel A. Wright, Mar. 16, 1965, Historical Notes, Wright Papers; U.S. Bureau of the Census, Sixteenth Census, 1940, Population, El Paso County, TX (Record Group 29, National Archives, Washington, DC); *FCJ*, June 5, 1942, July 4, 1947, Apr. 25, 1958, Sept. 16, 1960, Dec. 15, 1966; *San Antonio Express-News*, June 18, 1967 [first quote]; *San Diego Evening Tribune*, June 27, 1967; FAG: Mary Ann Brown Wright, Maurice Humphry Wright, James Lloyd Whitfield; Richard Bailey, "Starr County Strike," *HOT*; FAG: William Leonidas "Rattlesnake Willie" Wright [second quote]. Zora Belle Wright Whitfield was the daughter of Dogie and Mabel B. "Tiny" Love, who married in July 1928 at her Sierra Blanca ranching family's home. See *FCJ*, July 27, 1928, May 18, 1951; FAG: Emanuel Avant Wright, Mabel Beulah Wright. A monument in the shape of a giant peanut stands near William L. Wright's memorial on the grounds of the courthouse in Floresville. It honors Joseph T. Sheehy, the husband of Wright's niece Inez E. Warren Sheehy, for his leading role in growing the popular legumes in Wilson County. See FAG: Joseph Thomas Sheehy.

10. *FCJ*, Dec. 10, 1943, July 7, 1983 [second quote]; Robert W. Stephens, *Texas Ranger Sketches* (Dallas, TX: Privately printed, 1972), iii; FAG: William Leonidas "Rattlesnake Willie" Wright [first quote].
11. Mike Cox, *Gunfights and Sites in Texas Ranger History* (Charleston, SC: Arcadia Publishing, 2015), 85; Charles H. Harris III and Louis R. Sadler, *The Texas Rangers in the Mexican Revolution: The Bloodiest Decade, 1910–1920* (Norman: University of Oklahoma Press, 2004), 500; *Waco Tribune-Herald*, Oct. 2, 1977; *San Antonio Light*, Apr. 24, 1983; Richard O. Cook, "The Making of the FTRA Frontier Battalion Ranger Sculpture," accessed Mar. 18, 2020, https://www.facebook.com/formertexasrangers/photos/pcb.734759756650048/734759133316777/?type=3&theater; "Texas Ranger Hall of Fame," accessed Mar. 18, 2020, https://www.texasranger.org/texas-ranger-museum/hall-of-fame/.
12. Emanuel A. Wright to Shriber, Oct. 17, 1966, Wright Papers; Harry Moore to William L. Wright, Dec. 6, 1917, AGC; *FCJ*, June 1, 1934, Jan. 20, 1939, Nov. 1, 1946, July 4, 1947, May 18, 1951, Mar. 7, 1952, Dec. 15, 1966; William B. Wright, *Career Hunting: Texas Ranger vs. Standard Oiler* (El Cajon, CA; Privately printed, 1983), 4–5; Harris and Sadler, *Bloodiest Decade*, 586n; LaForte and Marcello, *Building the Death Railway*, 185, 202; Maude T. Gilliland, *Horsebackers of the Brush Country: A Story of the Texas Rangers and Mexican Liquor Smugglers* (Brownsville, TX: Springman-King Company, 1968), 115–116; Sammy Tise, *Texas County Sheriffs* (Albuquerque: Oakwood Press, 1989), 270. Maurice H. "Jack" Wright wed Helen M. W. Gorden in 1919 and William B. "Bill" Wright married Mildred P. Edgar in 1928, while Houston Tom "Simp Tom" Wright married twice: Gertrude V. Grunert in 1947 and, after Gertrude died in 1961, Louise B. V. Purcell in 1963. See *FCJ*, June 27, 1919, Sept. 19, 1947; FAG: Houston Tom Wright, Maurice Humphry Wright; "Our Family History." Good brief biographies of all of Wright's sons, as well as his daughter, can be found in Ivey, *Ranger Ideal, Volume 3*, 77–79.

Bibliography

Primary Sources

Manuscripts

Unpublished

Aldrich, Roy W. Papers. Archives of the Big Bend, Bryan Wildenthal Memorial Library, Sul Ross State University, Alpine, TX.

———. Papers. Dolph Briscoe Center for American History, University of Texas at Austin.

Fore, Zora Belle Wright. Interview, Dec. 7, 1973. South Texas Oral History & Folklore Collection, South Texas Archives, James C. Jernigan Library, Texas A&M University at Kingsville.

Perez, Jesse. "Reminiscences, 1870–1927." Typescript, n.d. [1927], Dolph Briscoe Center for American History, University of Texas at Austin.

Smith, James Warren, Sr. Papers. Texas Collection, Baylor University, Waco, TX.

Vertical Files. Texas Ranger Research Center, Texas Ranger Hall of Fame & Museum, Waco.

Webb, Walter P. Collection. Dolph Briscoe Center for American History, University of Texas at Austin.

Ward, James R. Collection. West Texas Collection, Angelo State University, San Angelo, TX.

Wright, E. A. "Dogie." Papers. Dolph Briscoe Center for American History, University of Texas at Austin.

Wright, Houston Tom. Interview. Oral History Collection, University of North Texas, Denton.

Wright Family. Papers. Texas Rangers Heritage Center, Fredericksburg.

Published

Bridge, Joe H., Jr. *Joe H. Bridge: Texas Ranger, 1936–1956*. Privately printed, 1998.

Busch, Carl G. "The Incredible Mr. Busch," *Cinquapin* 2, No. 5 (1980), 50.

"Editor Killing in Texas," *The Fourth Estate*, April 21, 1898.

Fifield, James C. *The American Bar: Contemporary Lawyers of the United States and Canada*. Minneapolis, MN: Privately published, 1918.

"January Bank Elections," *Texas Bankers Record* 4 (Sept. 1914), 61.

"Marble Falls Bank Robbed," *Texas Bankers Record* 5 (Nov. 1915), 45.

McCaslin, Richard B., ed., *A Soldier's Letters to Charming Nellie: The Correspondence of Joseph B. Polley, Hood's Texas Brigade*. Knoxville: University of Tennessee Press, 2008.

Mers, Gilbert. *Working the Waterfront: The Ups and Downs of a Rebel Longshoreman*. Austin: University of Texas Press, 1988.

N. W. Ayer & Son's American Newspaper Annual. Philadelphia: N. W. Ayer & Son, 1902.

N. W. Ayer & Son's American Newspaper Annual. Philadelphia: N. W. Ayer & Son, 1906.

N. W. Ayer & Son's American Newspaper Annual. Philadelphia: N. W. Ayer & Son, 1908.

"New Corporations," *Industrial Development and Manufacturers Record* 51 (Feb. 7, 1907), 118.

Peavey, John R. *Echoes from the Rio Grande*. Privately printed, 1963.

Pettingill's Newspaper Directory and Gazetteer. New York: Pettingill & Co., 1903.

Rowell's American Newspaper Directory. New York: Printer's Ink Newspaper Company, 1907.

Rowell's American Newspaper Directory, Volume 32. New York: Printer's Ink Publishing Company, 1900.

Smithwick, Noah. *The Evolution of a State*. Austin, TX: Gammel Book Company, 1900.

"Smythe Lindsay is dead," *The Living Church* 154 (Jan. 22, 1967), 9.

Sterling, Ross S., and Ed Kilman. *Ross Sterling, Texan: A Memoir by the Founder of Humble Oil and Refining Company*, ed, Don E. Carleton. Austin: University of Texas Press, 2007.

Sterling, William W. *Trails and Trials of a Texas Ranger*. Privately printed, 1959.

Stringfield, Thomas. *Captured by the Apaches*. Hamilton, TX: Herald Print, 1911.

Wright, William B. *Career Hunting: Texas Ranger vs. Standard Oiler*. El Cajon, CA: Privately printed, 1983.

Government Documents

Unpublished

Texas Adjutant General. Departmental Correspondence, 1846–1943, Texas State Library and Archives, Austin.

Texas Adjutant General. Service Records. Texas State Library and Archives, Austin.

———. Frontier Battalion Correspondence. Texas State Library and Archives, Austin.

———. Frontier Battalion Records. Texas State Library and Archives, Austin.

———. Muster Roll Index Cards, 1838–1900. Texas State Library and Archives, Austin.

———. Ranger Force Correspondence. Texas State Library and Archives, Austin.

———. Ranger Force Records. Texas State Library and Archives, Austin.

Texas Comptroller. Confederate Pension Applications. Texas State Library and Archives, Austin.

———. Republic of Texas Claims. Texas State Library and Archives, Austin.

———. Tax Rolls. Texas State Library and Archives, Austin.

Texas Department of Criminal Justice. Conduct Registers, 1855–1945. Texas State Library and Archives, Austin.

———. Convict Record Ledgers, 1849–1954. Texas State Library and Archives, Austin.

———. Governor. Correspondence. Texas State Library and Archives, Austin.

———. Legislature. "Proceedings of the Joint Committee of the Senate and the House in the Investigation of the Texas State Ranger Force," 8 volumes. Typescript, n.d. [1919]. Dolph Briscoe Center for American History, University of Texas at Austin.

United States. Bureau of the Census. Eighth Census, 1860. Record Group 29. National Archives, Washington, DC.

———. Ninth Census, 1870. Record Group 29, National Archives, Washington, DC.

———. Twelfth Census, 1900. Record Group 29. National Archives, Washington, DC.

———. Thirteenth Census, 1910. Record Group 29. National Archives, Washington, DC.

———. Fourteenth Census, 1920. Record Group 29. National Archives, Washington, DC.

———. Fifteenth Census, 1930. Record Group 29. National Archives, Washington, DC.

———. Sixteenth Census, 1940. Record Group 29. National Archives, Washington, DC.

United States. Department of War. Compiled Service Records of Confederate Soldiers Who Served in Organizations from Texas. Record Group 109, National Archives, Washington, DC.

———. World War I Draft Registration Cards. Record Group 163, National Archives, East Point, GA.

———. Office of the Quartermaster General. WWI Transportation Service, Passenger Lists. Record Group 92, National Archives, College Park, MD.

———. Headstone Applications for Military Veterans, 1925–1963. Record Group 92, National Archives, Washington, DC.

Published

Bartlett, C. J. *Supplemental Biennial Report of the Secretary of State, 1916*. Austin, TX: A. C. Baldwin & Sons, 1917.

Curl, J. R. *Biennial Report of the Secretary of State of the State of Texas, 1904*, Austin, TX: Gammel-Statesman Publishing Company, 1904.

Davie, W. R. *Supplemental Biennial Report of the Secretary of State, 1908*. Austin, TX: Von Boeckmann-Jones Company, 1908.

Hardy, D. H. *Biennial Report of the Secretary of State of the State of Texas, 1900*. Austin, TX: Von Boeckmann, Schutze, and Company, 1900.

Harley, James A. *Annual Report of the Adjutant General of Texas for the Year Ending December 31, 1918*. Austin, TX: Von Boeckmann-Jones Company, 1919.

———. *Biennial Report of the Adjutant General of Texas, from January 1, 1917, to December 31, 1918*. Austin, TX: Von Boeckmann-Jones, 1919.

———. *Biennial Report of the Adjutant General of Texas for the Two Years Ending December Thirty-First, A.D. One Thousand, Nine Hundred, and Twenty*. Austin, TX: Von Boeckmann-Jones Company, 1921.

Howard, George F. *Supplemental Biennial Report of the Secretary of State of the State of Texas, 1918*. Austin, TX: A. C. Baldwin & Sons, 1916.

Hutchings, Henry. *Report of the Adjutant General of the State of Texas, January 18, 1933, to December 31, 1934*. Austin, TX: Knape Printing Company, 1935.

Kleberg, Rudolph, comp. *The Texas Criminal Reports: Cases Argued and Adjudged in the Court of Criminal Appeals of the State of Texas, Volume 55*. Chicago: T. H. Flood & Company, 1909.

———, comp. *The Texas Criminal Reports: Cases Argued and Adjudged in the Court of Criminal Appeals of the State of Texas, Volume 72*. Austin, TX: Von Boeckmann-Jones Company, 1915.

Kleberg, Rudolph, comp. The *Texas Criminal Reports: Cases Argued and Adjudged in the Court of Criminal Appeals of the State of Texas, Volume 75*. Austin, TX: Von Boeckmann-Jones Company, 1916.

———, comp. *The Texas Criminal Reports: Cases Argued and Adjudged in the Court of Criminal Appeals of the State of Texas, Volume 88*. Columbia, MO: E. W. Stephens Publishing Company, 1921.

Mayfield, Allison. *Biennial Report of the Secretary of State of the State of Texas, 1896*. Austin, TX: Ben C. Jones & Company, 1897.

McKay, John G. *Biennial Report of the Secretary of State of the State of Texas, 1916*. Austin, TX: A. C. Baldwin & Sons, 1916.

Monkhouse, George A. *Annual Report of the Adjutant General of Texas for the Year Ending December 31, 1918*. Austin, TX: Von Boeckmann-Jones Company, 1919.

Nesbitt, Carl. *Report of Adjutant General of the State of Texas, January 15, 1935, to December 31, 1936*. Austin, TX: Lone Star Printing Company, 1937.

Official Register of the United States, 1907. 2 volumes. Washington: Government Printing Office, 1907.

Scurry, Thomas. *Biennial Report of the Adjutant General of Texas for 1899–1900*. Austin, TX: Ben C. Jones & Company, 1900.

Shannon, Ogden K. *Biennial Report of the Secretary of State of the State of Texas, 1906*. Austin, TX: Von Boeckmann-Jones, 1907.

Southwestern Reporter, Volume 45: April 18 to June 20, 1898. St. Paul, MN: West Publishing Company, 1898.

Southwestern Reporter, Volume 198: December 5, 1917 to January 9, 1918. St. Paul, MN: West Publishing Company, 1918.

Texas Legislature. *In the Senate of Texas, D. W. Glasscock Contestant vs. A. Parr Contestee, Supplement to the Senate Journal; Regular Session of the 36th Legislature 1919*. Austin, TX: A. C. Baldwin & Sons, 1919.

Tod, John G. *Biennial Report of the Secretary of State of the State of Texas, 1902*. Austin, TX: Von Boeckmann-Jones, 1902.

Townsend, W. B. *Supplemental Biennial Report of the Secretary of State, 1910*. Austin, TX: Austin Printing Company, 1911.

United States Senate. *Investigation of Mexican Affairs*. Senate Document 285, Volume 1. 66th Congress, 2nd Session (Serial Set 7,665).

Weinert, F. C. *Biennial Report of the Secretary of State of the State of Texas, 1914*. Austin, TX: Von Boeckmann-Jones Company, 1914.

White, John P., comp. *Texas Criminal Reports, Volume 39*. Austin, TX: Ben C. Jones & Company, 1898.

Wortham, John L. *Supplemental Biennial Report of the Secretary of State, 1912*. Austin, TX: Von Boeckmann-Jones Company, 1913.

***Newspapers** (published in Texas unless otherwise indicated)*

Abilene Daily Reporter
Abilene Morning News
Abilene Morning Reporter-News
Abilene Reporter-News
Albany News
Alice Echo
Alpine Avalanche
Aransas Pass Progress
Austin American
Austin American Statesman
Austin Daily Statesman
Austin Weekly Statesman
Beaumont Enterprise
Big Lake Wildcat
Big Spring Daily Herald
Bonham Daily Favorite
Borger Daily Herald
Breckenridge American
Brenham Daily Banner
Brenham Daily Banner-Press
Brooklyn [NY] *Daily Eagle*
Brownsville Daily Herald
Brownsville Herald
Brownwood Bulletin
Bryan Daily Eagle and Pilot
Bryan Eagle
Bryan Morning Eagle
Coleman Democrat-Voice
Columbus Colorado County Citizen
Corpus Christi Caller
Corpus Christi Caller-Times
Corpus Christi Times
Corsicana Daily Sun
Corsicana Democrat and Truth
Corsicana Semi-Weekly Light
Cuero Daily Record

Dallas Morning News
Des Moines [IA] *Tribune*
Eagle Lake Headlight
El Paso Evening Post
El Paso Herald
El Paso Herald-Post
El Paso Morning Times
El Paso Times
Flatonia Argus
Floresville Chronicle Journal
Fort Stockton Pioneer
Fort Worth Gazette
Fort Worth Morning Register
Fort Worth Star
Fort Worth Star-Telegram
Fredericksburg Standard
Galveston Daily News
Goose Creek Daily Sun
Hallettsville New Era
Harlingen Valley Morning Star
Hebbronville News
Houston Daily Post
Houston Post
Houston Post-Dispatch
Jim Hogg County Enterprise
Junction Eagle
Kerrville Mountain Sun
LaGrange Journal
Lampasas Daily Leader
Lampasas Leader
Laredo Times
Laredo Weekly Times
Liberty Vindicator
[Lincoln] *Nebraska State Journal*
Longview Daily News
Longview News-Journal
Lubbock Avalanche-Journal
Lubbock Morning Avalanche
Madera Tribune

Marshall Morning News
Marshall News Messenger
McAllen Daily Monitor
McAllen Daily Press
McAllen Monitor
Mercedes Tribune
Mexia Weekly Herald
Mexia Weekly Times
New Orleans [LA] *Picayune*
New York [NY] *Times*
New York [NY] *World*
Nolan County News
Odessa American
Odessa News-Times
Palacios Beacon
Palestine Daily Herald
Palo Pinto County Star
Pampa Daily News
Panola Watchman
Paris News
Pecos Enterprise
San Antonio Evening News
San Antonio Express
San Antonio Express-News
San Antonio Gazette
[San Antonio] *La Prensa*
San Antonio Light
San Francisco [CA] *Call*
San Patricio County News
Schulenburg Sticker
Seminole Sentinel
Sherman Daily Democrat
Shiner Gazette
Stephenville Empire
Taft Tribune
Temple Daily Telegram
Texas Bankers Record
Timpson Daily Times

Timpson Weekly Times
Uvalde Crier
Uvalde Leader News
Victoria Daily Advocate
Waco News-Tribune
Waco Tribune-Herald
Waxahachie Daily Light
Weatherford Daily Herald
Weimar Mercury
Wichita Falls Daily Times
Yoakum Weekly Times
Zavala County Sentinel

Secondary Sources

Articles and Chapters

Bill, Tony. "J. T. Canales and the 1919 Texas Ranger Investigation," *South Texas History* I (June 25, 2013).

Buckelew, A. R. and R. B. "The Discovery of Oil in South Arkansas, 1920–1924," *Arkansas Historical Quarterly* 33 (Autumn 1974).

Casto, Stanley D. "Texas Sportsmen and the Conservation of Bird Life, 1890–1915," *East Texas Historical Journal* 44 (March 2006).

Falvella, J. Will. "Captain Wright, A Gallant Texas Ranger," *Frontier Times* (September 1924).

Charles H. Harris III and Louis R. Sadler, "The 1911 Reyes Conspiracy: The Texas Side," *Southwestern Historical Quarterly* 83 (Apr. 1980).

Kilgore, Dan E. "Two Six Shooters and a Sunbonnet: The Story of Sally Skull," *Legendary Ladies of Texas*, ed. Francis E. Abernethy. Dallas, 1981; reprint, Denton: University of North Texas Press, 1994.

Swanson, Doug J. "The Horrible Truth of Love Field's Texas Ranger Statue," *D Magazine*, https://www.dmagazine.com/publications/d-magazine/2020/june/texas-rangers-love-field-statue-jay-banks-frank-hamer/.

Vera, Homero S. "Los Tequileros," *El Mesteno* 3 (Feb. 2000).

Webb, Walter P. "Rangers Reorganized," *The State Trooper* 8 (July 1927).

———. "Veteran Ranger Protects Border," *State Trooper* 6 (September 1924).

Weiss, Harold J., Jr. "The Texas Rangers Revisited: Old Themes and New Viewpoints," *Southwestern Historical Quarterly* 97 (April 1994).

Books

Alexander, Bob. *Riding Lucifer's Line: Ranger Deaths Along the Texas-Mexico Border*. Denton: University of North Texas Press, 2013.

———. *Whiskey River Ranger: The Old West Life of Baz Outlaw*. Denton: University of North Texas Press, 2016.

———. *Winchester Warriors: Texas Rangers of Company D*. Denton: University of North Texas Press, 2009.

——— and Donaly E. Brice. *Texas Rangers: Lives, Legend, and Legacy*. Denton: University of North Texas Press, 2017.

Anders, Evan. *Boss Rule in South Texas: The Progressive Era*. Austin: University of Texas Press, 1982.

Ariens, Michael. *Lone Star Law: A Legal History of Texas*. Lubbock: Texas Tech Press, 2011.

Baillo, F. B. *A History of the Texas Press Association*. Dallas, TX: Southwestern Printing Company, 1916.

Banks, Herbert C. *Daughters of the Republic of Texas Patriot Ancestry Album*. Paducah, KY: Turner Publishing Company, 1995.

Boessenecker, John. *Texas Ranger: The Epic Life of Frank Hamer, The Man Who Killed Bonnie and Clyde*. New York: Thomas Dunne Books, 2016.

Brice, Donaly E. *The Great Comanche Raid: Boldest Attack of the Texas Republic*. Austin, TX: Eakin Press, 1987.

Brown, John H. *Indian Wars and Pioneers of Texas*. Austin, TX: L. E. Daniell, 1896.

Brown, Norman D. *Hood, Bonnet, and Little Brown Jug: Texas Politics, 1921–1928*. College Station: Texas A&M University Press, 1984.

Caldwell, Clifton R., and Ron DeLord. *Eternity at the End of a Rope: Executions, Lynchings, and Vigilante Justice in Texas, 1819–1923*. Santa Fe: Sunstone Press, 2016.

———. *Texas Lawmen, 1900–1940: More of the Good and the Bad*. Charleston, SC: Arcadia Press, 2012.

Carrozza, Anthony R. *The Dukes of Duval County*. Norman: University of Oklahoma Press, 2017.

Cox, Mike. *Gunfights and Sites in Texas Ranger History*. Charleston, SC: Arcadia Publishing, 2015.

———. *Texas Ranger Tales: Stories That Need Telling*. Lanham, MD: Taylor Trade Publications, 1997.

———. *The Texas Rangers: Wearing the Cinco Peso, 1821–1900*. New York: Forge Books, 2008.

Cox, Mike. *Time of the Rangers: Texas Rangers from 1900 to the Present*. New York: Forge Books, 2009.

Crager, Kelley E. *Hell Under the Rising Sun: Texan POWs and the Building of the Burma-Thailand Death Railway*. College Station: Texas A&M University Press, 2008.

Crouch, Barry A., and Donaly E. Brice. *The Governor's Hounds: The Texas State Police, 1870–1873*. Austin: University of Texas Press, 2011.

De la Garza, Beatriz. *A Law for the Lion: A Tale of Crime and Injustice in the Borderlands*. Austin: University of Texas Press, 2003.

Denhardt, Robert M. *The King Ranch Quarter Horses*. Norman: University of Oklahoma Press, 1995.

Diaz, George T. *Border Contraband: A History of Smuggling Across the Rio Grande*. Austin: University of Texas Press, 2015.

Dixon, Kemp. *Chasing Thugs, Nazis, and Reds: Texas Ranger Norman K. Dixon*. College Station: TexasA&M University Press, 2015.

Dobie, J. Frank. *Coronado's Children: Tales of Lost Mines and Buried Treasure of the Southwest*. Dallas, TX: Southwest Press, 1930.

DuCoin, Candice. *Lawmen on the Texas Frontier*. Round Rock, TX: Riata Books, 2007.

Dukes, Doug. *Firearms of the Texas Rangers: From the Frontier Era to the Modern Age*. Denton: University of North Texas Press, 2020.

Gantt, Fred. *The Chief Executive in Texas: A Study in Gubernatorial Leadership*. Austin: University of Texas Press, 1964.

Gilbreath, West C. *Death on the Gallows: The Encyclopedia of Legal Hangings in Texas*. Fort Worth: Wild Horse Press, 2017.

Gilliland, Maude T. *Horsebackers of the Brush Country: A Story of the Texas Rangers and Mexican Liquor Smugglers*. Brownsville: Springman-King Company, 1968.

———. *Wilson County Texas Rangers, 1837 to 1977*. Privately printed, 1977.

Ginn, Jody E. *East Texas Troubles: The Allred Rangers' Cleanup of San Augustine*. Norman: University of Oklahoma Press, 2019.

Glasrud, Bruce A., and Harold J. Weiss Jr., eds. *Tracking the Texas Rangers: Twentieth Century*. Denton: University of North Texas Press, 2013.

Harris, Charles H., III, and Louis R. Sadler. *The Plan de San Diego: Tejano Rebellion, Mexican Intrigue*. Lincoln: University of Nebraska Press, 2013.

———. *The Texas Rangers in the Mexican Revolution: The Bloodiest Decade, 1910–1920*. Norman: University of Oklahoma Press, 2004.

———. *The Texas Rangers in Transition: From Gunfighters to Criminal Investigators*. Norman: University of Oklahoma Press, 2019.

Harris, Charles H., III, and Louis R. Sadler, III, Francis E. Harris, and Louis R. Sadler. *Texas Ranger Biographies: Those Who Served 1910–1921*. Albuquerque: University of New Mexico Press, 2009.

Hernandez, Kelly Lytle. *Migra! A History of the U.S. Border Patrol*. Berkeley: University of California Press, 2010.

Hinton, Diana D., and Roger M. Olien. *Oil in Texas: The Gusher Age, 1895–1945*. Austin: University of Texas Press, 2002.

Hooper, Gordon L. *Pioneer History of Crane County Before 1925*. Bloomington, IN: iUniverse, 2012.

Hughes, William J. *Rebellious Ranger: Rip Ford and the Old Southwest*. Norman: University of Oklahoma Press, 1964.

Hunter, Marvin. *Pioneer History of Bandera County*. Bandera, TX: Privately printed, 1922.

Ivey, Darren L. *The Ranger Ideal, Volume 2: Texas Rangers in the Hall of Fame, 1874–1930*. Denton: University of North Texas Press, 2018.

———. *The Ranger Ideal, Volume 3: Texas Rangers in the Hall of Fame, 1898–1987*. Denton: University of North Texas Press, 2021.

———. *The Texas Rangers: A Registry and History*. West Jefferson, NC: McFarland & Company, 2010.

Jenkins, John H., and J. Gordon Frost. *"I'm Frank Hamer:" The Life of a Texas Police Officer*. Austin, TX: Pemberton Press, 1968.

Johnson, Benjamin H. *Revolution in Texas; How a Forgotten Revolution and Its Bloody Suppression Turned Mexicans into Americans*. New Haven, CT: Yale University Press, 2003.

Johnson, David. *The Cornett-Whitley Gang: Violence Unleashed in Texas*. Denton: University of North Texas Press, 2019.

Kearney, James C., Bill Stein, and James Smallwood. *No Hope for Heaven, No Fear of Hell: The Stafford-Townsend Feud of Colorado County, Texas, 1871–1911*. Denton: University of North Texas Press, 2016.

Kilgore, Dan E. *A Ranger Legacy: 150 Years of Service to Texas*. Austin, TX: Madrona Press, 1973.

Knowles, Thomas W. *They Rode for the Lone Star: The Saga of the Texas Rangers*. Dallas, TX: Taylor Publishing Company, 1999.

LaForte, Robert S., and Ronald E. Marcello, *Building the Death Railway: The Ordeal of American POWs in Burma, 1942–1945*. Lanham, MD: Rowman & Littlefield, Publishers, 1993.

Leach, Duane M. *Caesar Kleberg and the King Ranch*. College Station: Texas A&M University Press, 2017.

Levario, Miguel A. *Militarizing the Border: When Mexicans Became the Enemy*. College Station: Texas A&M University Press, 2012.

Luttrell, Ida Harbison. *The Road to Randado*. Spring, TX: Panther Creek Press, 2004.

Malsch, Brownson. *"Lone Wolf" Gonzaullas, Texas Ranger*. Norman: University of Oklahoma Press, 1998.

Martinez, Monica Muñoz. *The Injustice Never Leaves You: Anti-Mexican Violence in Texas*. Cambridge: Harvard University Press, 2018.

McCaslin, Richard B. *Sutherland Springs, Texas; Saratoga on the Cibolo*. Denton: University of North Texas Press, 2017.

McKiernan-González, John. *Fevered Measures: Public Health and Race at the Texas-Mexico Border, 1848–1942*. Durham: Duke University Press, 2012.

Miler, Thomas L. *The Public Lands of Texas, 1519–1970*. Norman: University of Oklahoma Press, 1972.

Montejano, David. *Anglos and Mexicans in the Making of Texas, 1836–1986*. Austin: University of Texas Press, 1987.

Moore, Stephen L. *Eighteen Minutes: The Battle of San Jacinto and the Texas Independence Campaign*. Dallas, TX: Taylor Publishing Company, 2003.

———. *Savage Frontier: Rangers, Rifles, and Indian Wars in Texas*. 4 volumes. Denton: University of North Texas Press, 2007–2010.

Murphree, Nellie. *A History of DeWitt County*, ed. Robert W. Shook. Privately printed, 1962.

Olien, Roger M. and Diana D. Olien. *Oil Booms: Social Change in Five Texas Towns*. Lincoln, OR: University of Nebraska Press, 1982.

Olmsted, Charles L. *The Good, The Bad, The Butlers: Story of a Texas Pioneer Family*. Bloomington, IN: iUniverse, 2015.

Paine, Albert B. *Captain Bill McDonald, Texas Ranger: A Story of Frontier Reform*. New York: J. J. Little & Ives Company, 1909.

Paredes, Américo. *With His Pistol in His Hand: A Border Ballad and Its Hero*. Austin: University of Texas Press, 1958.

Parsons, Chuck. *The Sutton-Taylor Feud: The Deadliest Blood Feud in Texas*. Denton: University of North Texas Press, 2009.

———. *Captain John R. Hughes, Lone Star Ranger*. Denton: University of North Texas Press, 2011.

———. *Texas Ranger Lee Hall: From the Red River to the Rio Grande*. Denton: University of North Texas Press, 2020.

———, and Marianne E. Hall Little. *Captain L. H. McNelly, Texas Ranger: The Life and Times of a Fighting Man*. Austin, TX: State House Press, 2001.

Procter, Ben H. *Just One Riot: Episodes of Texas Rangers in the 20th Century*. Austin, TX: Eakin Press, 1991.

Samora, Julian, Joe Bernal, and Albert Peña. *Gunpowder Justice: A Reassessment of the Texas Rangers*. Notre Dame: University of Notre Dame Press, 1979.

Sandos, James A. *Rebellion in the Borderlands: Anarchism and the Plan de San Diego, 1904–1923*. Norman: University of Oklahoma Press, 1992.

Sitton, Thad. *The Texas Sheriff: Lord of the County Line*. Norman: University of Oklahoma Press, 2000.

Sizer, Mona D. *Texas Justice: Bought and Paid for*. Plano: Republic of Texas Press, 2001.

Smith, Howard E. *History of Public Health in Texas*. Austin: Texas State Department of Health, 1974.

Sonnichsen, C. L. *I'll Die Before I Run: The Story of the Great Feuds of Texas*. New York: Devin-Adair Company, 1962.

The Sons of the Republic of Texas. Nashville, TN: Turner Publishing Company, 2001.

Sowell, Andrew J. *Early Settlers and Indian Fighters of Southwest Texas*. Austin, TX: Ben C. Jones & Company, 1900.

Spellman, Paul N. *Capt. J. A. Brooks, Texas Ranger*. Denton: University of North Texas Press, 2007.

———. *Capt. John H. Rogers, Texas Ranger*. Denton: University of North Texas Press, 2003.

Stephens, Robert W. *Texas Ranger Sketches*. Dallas, TX: Privately printed, 1972.

Swanson, Doug J. *Cult of Glory: The Bold and Brutal History of the Texas Rangers*. New York: Viking Press, 2020.

Tise, Sammy. *Texas County Sheriffs*. Albuquerque: Oakwood Press, 1989.

Utley, Robert M. *Lone Star Justice: The First Century of the Texas Rangers*. New York: Oxford University Press, 2002.

———. *Lone Star Lawmen: The Second Century of the Texas Rangers*. New York: Oxford University Press, 2007.

Villanueva, Nicholas. *The Lynching of Mexicans in the Texas Borderlands*. Albuquerque: University of New Mexico Press, 2017.

Webb, Walter P. *The Texas Rangers: A Century of Frontier Defense*. Boston, MA: Houghton Mifflin, 1935.

Weiss, Harold J., Jr. *Yours to Command: The Life and Legend of Texas Ranger Captain Bill McDonald*. Denton: University of North Texas Press, 2009.

Wilbarger, Josiah W. *Indian Depredations in Texas*. Austin, TX: Hutchings Printing House, 1889.

Wilkins, Frederick. *Defending the Borders: The Texas Rangers, 1848–1861*. Austin, TX: State House Press, 2001.

———. *The Legend Begins: The Texas Rangers, 1823–1845*. Austin, TX: State House Press, 1996.

Wilson, Carol O. *In the Governor's Shadow: The True Story of Ma and Pa Ferguson*. Denton: University of North Texas Press, 2014.

Dissertations

Montes, Rebecca Anne. "Working for American Rights: Black, White, and Mexican American Dock Workers in Texas During the Great Depression." Ph.D. Diss., University of Texas at Austin, 2005.

Stanley, Mark. "Portrait of a Southern Progressive: The Political Life and Times of Governor Pat M. Neff of Texas, 1871–1952." Ph.D. Diss, University of North Texas, 2011.

Ward, James R. "The Texas Rangers, 1919–1935: A Study in Law Enforcement." Ph.D. Diss., Texas Christian University, 1972.

Websites

"Alba Heywood, 1859–1921," https://www.wikitree.com/wiki/Heywood-369

"Burwell, William M.," http://genealogytrails.com/tex/gulfcoast/jackson/jackson_biographies.html

Cardenas, Alfredo E. "Indian Raid Prompts Request for Soldiers," http://www.soydeduval.com/2015/04/indian-raid-prompts-request-for-soldiers/

"Cattle Trails from Wyoming Tails and Trails," http://www.wyomingtalesandtrails.com/cattletextrail2.html

Chappell, Henry. "Horses to Ride, Cattle to Cut: The San Antonio Viejo Ranch of Texas," https://www.landreport.com/2017/06/horses-to-ride-cattle-to-cut/

"Chief of Police Rufus Nicholson Gilbreath," *Officer Down Memorial Page*, https://www.odmp.org/officer/18634-chief-of-police-rufus-nicholson-gilbreath

Coffey, Jim. "Will Wright: Rangers and Prohibition," https://www.texasranger.org/wp-content/uploads/2017/07/BIO-Will-Wright.pdf

"Colorado County Obituaries: Burford," http://www.colorado countyhistory.org/obits/b/burford.htm

Cook, Richard O. "The Making of the FTRA Frontier Battalion Ranger Sculpture," https://www.facebook.com/formertexasrangers/photos/pcb.734759756650048/734759133316777/?type=3&theater

"Corpus Christi Longshoremen Strike Against Poor Working Conditions and Benefits, 1935," https://nvdatabase.swarthmore.edu/content/corpus-christi-longshoremen-strike-against-poor-working-conditions-and-benefits-1935

Cox, Mike. "The Three-Hour Texas Ranger," http://www. texasescapes.com/MikeCoxTexasTales/Three-hour-Texas-Ranger.htm

———. "Two Braids," http://www.texasescapes.com/MikeCoxTexasTales/141TwoBraids.htm

Elliott, Bobbie, and Bill Stein, "Colorado County District Court Records, Criminal Cause File Index, 1837–1930," http://library.columbustexas.net/history/Criminal%20Causes. htm

Find a Grave, https://www.findagrave.com/

"The First Legal Execution in Wilson County," *Wilson County, TXGen Web*, http://hometownchronicles.com/tx/wilson/martinezm.htm

Foster, K. S. "Early Members of the Fort Worth Police Department," https://www.freewebs.com/hinzd/Rosters/FWPD%20ROSTERS.pdf

Grammar, Shirley. "Concrete Cemetery," http://www.cemeteries-of-tx.com/etx/guadalupe/cemetery/concrete.htm

Handbook of Texas, https://tshaonline.org/handbook/online/browse

"The Historic San Antonio Viejo," http://www.eastfoundation.net/our-story/the-historic-san-antonio-viejo/

"Inspector Fred Tate," https://www.odmp.org/officer/13098-inspector-fred-tate

"Isaac Edgar Clark," Texas Legislators: Past & Present https://lrl.texas gov/mobile/memberDisplay.cfm?MemberID=2385

"John Edgar Trainer," http://losttexasroads.com/people/64-trainer-john-edgar

"John T. Littleton," Texas Legislators: Past & Present, https://lrl.texas.gov/legeleaders/members/memberdisplay.cfm?memberID=4549

"Joseph Eli Newman," https://www.wikitree.com/wiki/Newman-6224

"Joseph Henry Marion Bridge (1891–1956)," https://www.wikitree.com/wiki/Bridge-1325

"La Vernia Postmasters," http://losttexasroads.com/people/46-la-vernia-postmasters

"Legend of the Stone Maps," http://www.treasurenet.com/forums/superstition-mountain-legends/461199-legend-stone-maps-68.html

Linne, Henry A. "Henry Scott Sisk," https://www.geni.com/people/Henry-Sisk/6000000028147293357

"List of People Executed in Texas, 1930–1939," https://en.wikipedia.org/wiki/List_of_people_executed_in_Texas,_1930%E2%80%9339

"Mary Ann Brown," https://ancestors.familysearch.org/en/26WM-LCD/mary-ann-brown-1871-1958

Norwood, Brian. "Two Gun Dick Herwig," https://newmexicohistoryblog.wordpress.com/2018/02/13/two-gun-dick-herwig/

"Ola Faye Finchum," *Family Search*, *https://ancestors.familysearch.org/en/LDMN-7CS/ola-faye-finchum-1911-1978*

"Our Family History: The Genealogy of Robert and Christina Barritt," http://tree.barrittfamily.net/getperson.php?personID=I473&tree=dyal_speckels

"Raid of 1878," https://historicdistrict.com/Genealogy/ lasalle/raid.asp

"Rogers C. Kelley," https://grandlodgeoftexas.org/grand-master/rogers-c-kelly/

Texas Death Certificates, 1890–1976, https://www.fold3.com/image/90346596

"Texas Ranger Hall of Fame," https://www.texasranger.org/texas-ranger-museum/hall-of-fame/

"Texas Rangers." Bullock Museum, Austin, TX, https://www.thestoryoftexas.com/discover/campfire-stories/texas-ranger

Teske, Steven. "Norphlet (Union County)," *Encyclopedia of Arkansas*, http://www.encyclopediaofarkansas.net/encyclopedia/entry-detail.aspx?entryID=6156

"Texas State Cemetery: Lamartine Pemberton Sieker," https://cemetery. tspb.texas.gov/pub/user form.asp?step=1&pers_id= 934

"Thad J. Rees: Farmer, Rancher Freighter, Trail Driver and Lawman," http://wilsoncounty history.org/Moments/Thad%20J. %20Rees.pdf

"Thomas Wesley Stringfield," http://heathcock.org/genealogy/ps06/ps06_188.html

"The Tumlinson Family of the DeWitt Colony," http://www.sonsof dewitt colony.org/tumlinsonfam.htm

"Tumlinson Saga," https://www.desertusa.com/mb3/viewtopic.php?t=3339&start=40

"Upton County, Texas, Crime News," http://genealogytrails.com/tex/ bigbend/upton/news_crime.html

Van Winkle, Irene. "Cowboy Camp Meeting Founder was Lawman and Preacher," http://wkcurrent.com/cowboy-camp-meeting-founder-was-lawman-and-preacher-p1219-71.htm

"W. L. 'Will' Wright, 1868–1942," https://www.texasranger.org/texas-ranger-museum/hall-of-fame/william-lee-wright/

Westbrook, Barbara M. "Rossville Brothers Served as Texas Rangers," http://atascosacounty.blogspot.com/2008/04/rossville-brothers-served-as-texas.html

"William A. Dial," https://cemetery.tspb.texas.gov/ pub/user_form.asp?step=1&pers_id= 2356

"William Old," https://arizonagravestones.org/view.php?id=86496

Youngblood, Norman. "Allee, Alfred Young," *HOT*; "Texas Ranger Alfred Young Allee," http://sherrysharp.com/genealogy/getperson.php?personID=I32502&tree=Roots

Index

A

B

C

D

H

K

L

O

P

S

T

U

V

W